D1566403

The Young
RICHELIEU

An early seventeenth-century engraving of Richelieu. Reproduced by permission of the Bibliothèque Nationale, Paris.

The Young
RICHELIEU

A Psychoanalytic Approach
to Leadership

Elizabeth Wirth Marvick

The University of Chicago Press
Chicago and London

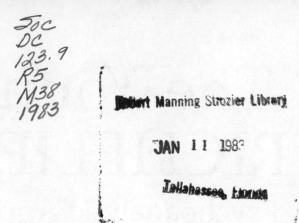
Elizabeth Wirth Marvick holds her doctorate in political science from Columbia University and has taught at the City University of New York, the California Institute of Technology, the Claremont Graduate School, and the University of California, Los Angeles. She has been a Fulbright lecturer at the University of Bordeaux. Mrs. Marvick is the editor, with A. J. Reiss, of *Community Life and Social Policy: Selected Papers of Louis Wirth* (1956), and of *Psychopolitical Analysis: Selected Writings of Nathan Leites* (1977).

The University of Chicago Press, Chicago 60637
The University of Chicago Press, Ltd., London
© 1980, 1983 by The University of Chicago
All rights reserved. First published 1983
Printed in the United States of America
90 89 88 87 86 85 84 83   5 4 3 2 1

Library of Congress Cataloging in Publication Data

Marvick, Elizabeth Wirth.
  The young Richelieu.

  Bibliography: p.
  Includes index.
  1. Richelieu, Armand-Jean du Plessis, duc de, 1585–
1642—Personality.   2. Statesmen—France—Biography.
3. France—History—Louis XIII, 1610–1643.   I. Title.
DC123.9.R5M38   1983   944'.032'0924 [B]   82-24754
ISBN 0-226-50904-4
    0-226-50905-2 (paperback)

To Dwaine Marvick
My Foundation

I shall not take it upon myself to tell the story of his life; another than he cannot be capable of that. What men have seen of it is nothing compared with what they do not know; for each great deed he has made a thousand fine calculations. Posterity would care little to know what success met his enterprises if it could learn the secret ways he has for conducting affairs and the many kinds of considerations that he raises in deliberating upon them. Bare description of what he carries out will be less useful than an account of his counsels, and of all the thoughts that come to him before deciding. Art and cause surpass by far works and effects. . . . Truly, it is this unfailing method of undertaking, arranging, and perfecting that would be better to know than his life story. . . .

But to that treasure there is no key but his.

Hay Du Chastelet, 1635

Contents

Preface

It was an early decision in this work to render all texts into English. In the translation, exactness was given priority over felicity although I allowed myself considerable license with punctuation, partly because of the uncertainty of early modern indications.

I am indebted to many institutions and persons for help. My work was advanced in 1975-1976 by a grant to lecture at the University of Bordeaux under the Fulbright-Hays Act. The University Research Library of the University of California, Los Angeles, made much of the needed research possible. The Regenstein Library of the University of Chicago and the Newberry Library were also facilitating. Dr. Margaret Nickson was especially helpful in the search for manuscripts at the British Library.

Like many others I have an incalculable debt to the people and government of France for their liberal sharing of the treasures of their archives and libraries. In my case, in addition to the great Bibliothèque Nationale and the national archives of Paris and the provinces, I am very grateful to the University of Paris, Sorbonne, for access to the Archive de la Famille Richelieu, and to the staff of the Bibliothèque Victor Cousin where it is held.

For their kindness in reading all or part of a manuscript version and for helpful suggestions I thank Donald Bailey, Michel de Certeau, Jean-Louis Flandrin, Peter Gay, Micheline Guiton, Peter Loewenberg, Lucian Pye, Orest Ranum and Louise Strouse. All translations, unless otherwise noted, are mine. I am indebted, however, to Louis Marvick and Andrew Marvick who helped improve some of them. I owe much, too, to the Office of Academic Computing at UCLA, and especially to Joan Slottow, who generously made available her programming inventiveness, as well as her remarkable grasp of editorial problems, to help immeasurably in production of a book.

I am grateful also to Andrew Lossky, whose profound knowledge of early modern Europe enabled me to correct many errors. I was helped to avoid mistakes and redundancies by the unsurpassed critical powers and

ix

analytical insight of Nathan Leites. As always he was generous with his time beyond the claims of friendship. The advice and support of Dwaine Marvick were indispensable in every way, at all stages.

For all the defects that remain, despite this expert help, I am, of course, entirely responsible.

Part 1 PERSPECTIVES

1 Introduction: Richelieu and the Analysis of Leadership

The great political leader of every kind and time is a type, yet
not a thing unique, but only the apex of a pyramid from which
there is a continuous variation down to the average and from it
to the sub-normal values. And yet not only is "leading" a special
function, but the leader also something special, distinguishable—
wherefore there is no sense . . . in asking: "Where does that
type begin, then?" and then to exclaim: "This is no type at all!"[1]

1. Richelieu in Political Context

Greatness has been ascribed to few political figures as often as to Armand-
Jean Du Plessis de Richelieu. As a French historical personality he has been
universally judged distinctive. "Few men," writes an editor of his papers,
"have been greater in themselves."[2] Even standing, as he did, between the
genial figure of Henri Le Grand and the lustrous one of the Sun King,
Louis XIII's Cardinal-Duke-Prime Minister seems larger than life—in Sainte-
Beuve's words, a "colossus" among Pygmies.[3]

There is also virtual consensus on the direction of Richelieu's influence.
Thierry represents the general view of his attempt at "innovation": he
strove to accomplish a "revolutionary task" on behalf of French kings,
aimed against an internal feudal hierarchy and rival foreign powers:

> He undertook to accelerate so strongly the movement toward
> unity and civil equality, and to carry it so far that, thenceforward,
> it would be impossible to retrogress. . . . He raised royalty above
> the ties of family and . . . precedents; he isolated it in its sphere
> as the living idea of public salvation and national interest.[4]

Few would disagree: Richelieu was an apostle of French national autonomy
and royal absolutism.

1

Yet it is more difficult to determine whether or how his role was original.

Seemingly, Richelieu was not distinctive in his political thought. Religious wars in the last half of the sixteenth century evoked a strong nationalist, royalist reaction in France. "The schism of the Reformation," explains Aulard, "hastens formation of national consciousness."[5] The suffering caused by civil conflict was blamed on centrifugal forces exerted by great nobles and religious factions within the realm, and by foreign states—including the Holy See—outside it. It seemed to many that only a national force emanating from the center—from the king—could bring surcease to these ills. Under the resourceful, authoritative leadership of Henri IV, who succeeded to the throne in 1589, the popularity of the monarchy revived. The divine healing powers of French kings were once again proclaimed, with the purpose, as Bloch suggests, of reinforcing an image of the king as sole source of authority capable of restoring well-being to the nation.[6]

Richelieu, born in 1585, was to become but one of many who, yearning for a powerful France, asserted that kingly authority was unlimited by any earthly power. The year that saw his birth also marked the opening of the last and bloodiest revolt of the Catholic League against the crown. By the time that he arrived in Paris, as a young boy, to begin school, the royalist, nationalist reaction against these disorders was well advanced there. As the century closed, political theories that emphasized constitutional restraints on the temporal powers of kings were going out of fashion in France. Before Henri IV's reign came to an end, André Du Chesne, a royal historiographer, elaborated the sacerdotal character of the French monarchy. No longer was it held that the king was first among equals; instead he was unrivalled sovereign within his realm.[7] Others asserted the French king's supremacy over a Gallican church independent of any temporal authority.[8]

In taking up the cause of royal absolutism, affirming that the monarch held his powers directly from the Almighty, Richelieu was therefore not original; he was conforming with an important tendency in political thought. Thus, as he neared adulthood, his political views were representative of his time: absolutist theories were "in the air."[9]

It was not, then, the originality of his thinking that distinguished Richelieu. Rather, it was as an actor that he made his mark on the history of France. As Louis XIII's prime minister he shaped state policy from 1624 until nearly the end of the reign in 1643. What constitutional theorists articulated as principles, Armand de Richelieu attempted to put into practice. It is this performance that won him his reputation for greatness.

Yet it has been argued that Richelieu's actual achievement was no more successful or enduring than that either of his predecessors or of his successors. His economic policies were largely failures.[10] His cherished aim to make France a great maritime power was not to be implemented through his efforts.[11] Most of the changes he wrought in French political institutions were small; few were lasting.[12] His death at the end of 1642 left the monarch in a weak position. Louis was to rule for less than a year over a France at war, virtually bankrupt, and a people in misery. Nor were Richelieu's plans for reconciling Protestants and Catholics to bear fruit: even his strategy for sustaining political unity in the presence of religious division did not survive the reign of Louis XIV. He failed, moreover, in his basic aim to bring stability to French royal government: the turbulence and uncertainty of the regency that followed Louis XIII's death in 1643 recapitulated the turmoil that had followed the reign of his father, Henri IV.

Nor can it be convincingly claimed that Richelieu's policies were innovative. Major steps of his regime tending towards centralization of the government had been anticipated by others.[13] His mercantilist schemes, also, dated from earlier regimes.[14] Most of his fiscal reforms lacked originality. As a statesman his judgment was fallible, his foresight restricted, his insight often flawed.

Despite these limitations, many even of the cardinal's critical contemporaries regarded his performance with admiring wonder. James Howell, advisor to the future Charles II, was well aware of the failures of Richelieu's regime and the impermanence of its successes. Yet he could not refrain from holding it up to his young pupil as an object of emulation:

> All those years this great minister sate at the helm may be term'd a time of miracles, by that prodigious course of constant successes matters had abroad and at home, as if he had struck a nail in Fortunes wheele, that shee should not turne all the while.[15]

So profuse an appreciation—and there are many like it—from so shrewd an observer raises the question: If it was not primarily the success and originality of Richelieu's policies that inspired this admiration, to what, instead, is owed his extraordinary reputation?

The superlatives of historians provide a clue: most often they refer not to Richelieu's actions but to the qualities of mind and heart that accompanied those actions. Their appraisals suggest that it was the *spirit* that animated his performance rather than the performance itself that made him appear different from those who preceded him, those who collaborated with him, and those who were to follow him.

What was this spirit that seemed to set Richelieu apart from most other leaders of his time?

2.   Richelieu as Innovator

Among the outstanding personal qualities often observed in Louis XIII's prime minister is an unremitting drive towards active manipulation of the political environment. His motivation for achievement is seen as constant

3

and pressing. A biographer has praised his "dauntless" resolution. His activity was "tireless," his animosities "remorseless."[16] As chief administrator he was "intrepid," "indefatigable."[17]

In his passionate aspiration for great achievement, for mastering his own fate and that of others, Richelieu's attitude stood at the point farthest distant from one of timidity and resignation.[18] Richelieu's intense concentration on planning and achieving goals doubtless contributes to Mignet's often-quoted judgment: "All the things that he did, he intended."[19]

One of the cardinal's contemporaries, Charles de Montchal, was also his avowed enemy. Nevertheless, he too gave Richelieu credit for exceptional capacity—a "superior mind (*esprit sublime*)," and a nature that was "active, vigilant and adroit, and highly capable of all kinds of affairs." In summing up, Montchal uses a suggestive word. The prime minister was, he tells us, "bold in enterprise (*hardi à entreprendre*)."[20] Indeed, the spirit Richelieu brought to statecraft was like that attributed since to a certain kind of "capitalist"—an entrepreneurial daring.

Schumpeter has defined entrepreneurship as innovation in *combining* factors leading to output: "The function of entrepreneurs is to reform or revolutionize the pattern of production." One who performs this function does old or new things in new ways.[21]

The "entrepreneurial type," in Schumpeter's meaning of this term, is not an inventor, but one who has the "personality and will power" to "act with confidence beyond the range of familiar beacons and to overcome . . . resistance."

Richelieu undertook and pursued the political calling with the zest of an entrepreneur. His outstanding qualities were like those of the pilot of a new industry: his leadership was effective "by virtue of personal force and personal responsibility for success."[22]

A modern student of the cardinal's administration sees his outstanding qualities in this light. "Richelieu's great power," writes Orest Ranum, "rested not so much on a mastery of details, or even upon his administrative genius, but rather on the force of his personality."[23] In Schumpeter's view of entrepreneurship, too, neither originality of conception nor technical proficiency is the predominant quality. Its function, he writes, does not "essentially consist in either inventing anything or otherwise creating the conditions which the enterprise exploits." Instead, he suggests, "it consists in getting things done."[24] And, as Ranum again observes, Richelieu exhibited prominently an "eagerness to get things done."[25] His own descriptions of his projects continually reveal him to be the quintessential man of action, bent on accomplishment—on deeds, not words.

As in economic ventures, political entrepreneurship calls for managerial ability, consisting of foresight, the capacity for ruling others, and confidence. One who undertakes enterprises on uncharted ground is apt to minimize danger, confronting uncertainty with boldness. Thus he may become a guarantor towards those whom he enlists in his projects.[26]

Introduction

The record of Richelieu's life demonstrates these characteristics: a strong drive toward great accomplishment, a high confidence in the success of his own daring, a willingness to bear risks for others. Perhaps nowhere, however, is the combination more clearly apparent than in an address he delivered to the king before an assembly of notables not long after he had assumed the high office he was to fill until he died. This conference was organized by the cardinal himself to gather support for programs he planned to undertake on Louis's behalf. It was primarily a question of raising money.

Richelieu's speech begins with an exaggerated appreciation of the great strides that have been made in the first full year of his ministry—accomplishments which he credits, necessarily, to the king:

> There is no need, in my opinion, Sire, to represent to this distinguished company the great actions Your Majesty has taken in the past year . . . since . . . there is no one who fails to see that God wished to make use of . . . Your Majesty to accomplish in a short time . . . what many thought to be impossible in the course of centuries.

But the last thing in Richelieu's mind is to rest on these laurels. He must drive forward:

> Matters are now, thank God, in good enough condition, but one could not dare promise oneself they will remain so forever, and one would have to lack judgment entirely not to recognize that they must be pushed farther ahead.

The choice of a future course involves an enormous risk. The only options are extreme danger or complete security:

> It is necessary, inevitably, either to leave this realm exposed to the enterprises and evil designs of those who daily meditate its downfall and ruin, or to find sure expedients to insure it against them (*en garantir.*)

But, if the risk is great, the returns from success are high. In fact, its prospect is millenarian:

> Finally, all things will be in the state in which, for long, people of good will have desired them to be, in which they will be able to remain for whole centuries, and in which the blessings of heaven will be perpetual companions of the power and deeds of kings, who will have no other aim but the glory of God, the greatness of their realm, and the happiness of their subjects.

Confronted with these drastic alternatives of perdition or utopia, most people might find their resolution faltering: "One might well think," he continues, "and perhaps I might think it myself, that it is easy to propose such fine designs; that it is agreeable to speak of them, but that their execution is difficult." Richelieu reassures the faint-hearted: If his plans are followed, a "necessity"—renovating the state—which yet "seems impossible," will, on the contrary be not only achievable but even "very easy for His Majesty." The cardinal himself stands as guarantor for its accomplishment. Notwithstanding many obstacles, understandably so intimidating to others, he assures his hearers that the schemes he has devised are eminently feasible. He is ready to get the job done. He boldly promises success, not only ultimately, but quite soon, and according to a definite timetable: "After having thought well about it I dare to say, in the presence of the king, that expedients may be found by which, in six years, one will see the end and perfection of this work." All that is needed is the quick compliance of his audience with his designs. "This assembly must be short as to its duration;" it will be long as to its effects. "Few words and many results will show the good intentions of those who compose it."

If those present fall in with his plans for them, they will find that the king will surpass himself in his efforts on behalf of the state. Louis will reap the honor of the glorious results: "The glory of causing it [the state] to be reborn again (le faire renaistre de nouveau) is reserved to the virtue of so great a prince." Richelieu's reward will be the pride in achievement of his own great aims. The cardinal takes up the pen himself to make this final avowal: "I should feel myself most particularly indebted to God, on that occasion, if He took me two hours after the accomplishment of so high, so glorious, and so holy a design."[27] The satisfaction of having created a chef d'oeuvre so sanctified is well worth dying for.

The object of Richelieu's ambitions was, of course, political. His masterpiece was to be a state transformed. The term "state-building"—for which no French equivalent comes to mind—has been used by William F. Church to describe the cardinal's aims:

> In internal affairs, the Cardinal's many undertakings were consistently directed toward one major, comprehensive end: state-building. Indeed, all his acts on many fronts may be subsumed under this single head.[28]

State-building—the erection of a political edifice that did not exist before—calls forth the entrepreneurial spirit. The innovativeness of Richelieu's performance lay not in his possession of this spirit (nor in his possession by it), but in the fact that he applied it—at the highest level—to a political aim.

3.   The Cultural Context of Richelieu's Innovation

Armand de Richelieu came of age at a time when the spirit of enterprise had not yet widely penetrated French economic life.[29] It was, however, a time favorable to religious entrepreneurship.

The sixteenth century had seen the wildfire spread of Calvinism in France. The first decades of the century that followed were marked by the rise of

Introduction

Catholic reforms: "During the first half of the seventeenth century a work of Catholic restoration was accomplished," writes Chalumeau. It was, he assays, "a veritable transformation."[30]

The Society of Jesus was in the vanguard of reforming Catholicism, applying the zeal of its members to producing a new educational system for French children.[31] Among Richelieu's contemporaries his intimate associate Père Joseph, as well as Pierre de Bérulle, Saint Vincent de Paul, and Saint François de Sales, together with the female colleagues respectively so important for each one of them, brought the renovating spirit to bear on existing religious organizations and to the founding and organizing of a host of new ones. Within a space of three decades after the start of the seventeenth century, the Calvarians, Jesuits, Oratorians, Lazarists, Visitandines, Ursulines and others had staked claims for a part in advancing the cause of Catholic reform.[32]

The leaders of these movements exemplified the spirit which animated the Puritans: God was to be glorified in an earthly calling. Through mundane endeavor sacred aims would be advanced.

The Puritan spirit, as described by Max Weber, called for glorifying God by earthly, methodical achievements. With its spread, from the fifteenth century onward, secular affairs came to be invested with emotions that had formerly been confined to the cloister. "The religious life of the saints," he observes, was "no longer lived outside the world in monastic communities, but within the world and its institutions."[33] By the end of the sixteenth century French religious life showed, among Protestant and Catholic clergies alike, the influence of these ideals.[34]

In Catholic France near the beginning of the seventeenth century, the worldly orders were imbued with a more intense spirituality and a more demanding asceticism than many of the older contemplative confraternities. Thus "Monsieur Vincent" warns a follower against excessive penitence: ample opportunity exists for virtue in everyday life.[35] The innovation of Saint François, too, consisted in his practicality: he gave lessons that were "concrete" and "imitable."[36] In those years Jesuit and Capuchin leaders, bent on creating an "apostolic work," made their words of practical advice on how to work out salvation in daily activities circulate more widely than did the inspirational messages of more mystic communities.[37]

Yet even so contemplative an order as the Carmelites, when transplanted to French soil, took on the worldly zeal of the new spirit. Although works of Saint Theresa continued to be much published in France, Spanish mysticism seems to have undergone a transformation in the hands of the reformed French Carmel. Its organizer, Barbe Acarie, despite a reputation for being "purely mystical" was nevertheless "actively enterprising at the same time," notes Prunel, spurring devotion to venture out from the cloister in order to "reach, little by little, the best French society."[38]

Nevertheless, for most of these early religious reformers, permissible worldliness stopped short of participation in politics. The practical organizing skill which Saint François de Sales and Saint Jeanne de Chantal together brought to the foundation and administration of the new Order of the Visitation contrasted with the unworldly disinterestedness of their aims.[39]

Like all movements that seek to revive primitive Christianity, the strivings of this reforming generation had radical aspects: "The Christian ideal means . . . renunciation of the material social ideal of all political and economic values," writes Troeltsch. Necessarily it connotes, he contends, "an entire transformation" of values.[40] Like the Calvinists, the vanguard of the Catholic counter-reformation had an anti-contemporary impact. Even the French Carmelites were conscious of challenging existing value systems. In organizing a complex apparatus to save the souls of women they gladly risked the public's incomprehension, taking pleasure in noting that the ordinary Frenchman is "astonished to see us seek so eagerly for something the world recks little of."[41]

Richelieu's entrepreneurial zeal for state-building paralleled these efforts of that new "generation of saints."[42] His drive towards political accomplishment bore marks of a spirit similar to theirs in its combination of passion and calculation. What distinguished his ambition for achievement was that it aimed to transform the world through politics.

An attitude incompatible with earlier Christian fatalism made Richelieu, like his missionary counterparts, ready to take responsibility for shaping the future. With him, as with them, conduct that before had lacked moral value—conscientious, systematic, persistent effort—now became ideals of everyday behavior. In this he resembled not only the new saints of the religious sector, but also the capitalist achievers portrayed by Max Weber:

> A man's life in his calling is an exercise in ascetic virtue, a proof of his state of grace through his conscientiousness, which is expressed in the care and method with which he pursues his calling. What God demands is rational labor in a calling. . . . The emphasis is always placed on this methodical character of worldly asceticism, not . . . on the acceptance of the lot which God has irretrievably assigned to man.[43]

Richelieu made of the political vocation a "calling" like that of the Puritan zealots who sought to glorify God in earthly, methodical achievement. His novelty lay in the arena he chose for passionate, yet disciplined, action.

The innovative nature of Richelieu's role is suggested by a comparison of his performance with that of Henri IV. Henri's leadership qualities have often been seen as foreshadowing the cardinal's spirit. In his energy and courage the ex-Calvinist ruler showed, possibly, influence of the reforming spirit that was reanimating religious life.

Henri, however, was careful to validate his administration by appeals to tradition; his aims were rationalized always in the conservative terms of continuity. In "boldness," writes Thierry, Richelieu "surpassed by far the great king who preceded him."[44] Indeed, on such a radical policy as an attempt to bypass the provincial governments, which Major has perceived as a precursor of Richelieu's supposed absolutist designs,[45] later writers in the cardinal's camp faulted the former monarch for a deficiency in this very quality. Henri, they wrote, "did not dare to undertake" the job of suppressing the Languedocian Estates.[46] The cardinal's greater daring was something in which his entourage took pride.

No sooner did the young Richelieu make his début on the national stage than he revealed his intent to transform his world. On that occasion in 1615 the novelty of his utopian aspirations seems clear in passages in which he dwells upon the future in store for Louis XIII under his guidance. Nothing will satisfy him and his colleagues, he tells the king, except that the monarch's reforms are actually put into practice, "not for a day, but for always." And if this is done, what a prospect is in store!

> Everything will be done with just weight and measure, the reign of reason will be powerfully established, justice will regain its due integrity . . . merit will be rewarded . . . letters and arts will flourish; religion will blossom anew. . . . The church will regain its luster . . . virtue alone will rule in it. . . . The people will be delivered from oppressions. . . . In a word, all France will be restored to the best condition that our prayers could wish for it.[47]

This utopia is not a mere renaissance. It is to be a state of affairs far better than any that preceded it. Implicitly rejecting earlier views that had seen history as cyclically repetitive,[48] or tending towards degeneration from an earlier, better time, Richelieu envisages a golden age on earth "that marks" as J. B. Bury notes in another context, "a stage in the growth of intellectual optimism which we can trace from the sixteenth century."[49]

Once Richelieu reached a secure position at the helm of the state he revealed his ambition: With himself to chart the course, Louis will be enabled to steer the ship of state to a perfect future in safe harbor:[50] "The king's intention is to rule it in such a fashion that his reign equals and *surpasses* the best one of those past, and serves as example and rule to those of the future."[51] By applying intelligence and effort to the machinery of state a giant stride will be taken towards perfection.

In this, once more, Richelieu's renovating vision had its counterpart in the aspirations of religious reformers. Thus even the members of such an ancient monastery as Fontevrault felt the pressure of its reforming abbess exhorting them to strive to excel the past. She presents to her religious the rules of their order, "for whose entire perfection and conservation your holy profession obliges you to work with all your power." Making every word and deed conform to the demanding regulations so that each one may be "the example for all the others who successively *must augment* and immortalize, *from century to century,* the practice and good odor of our blessed forerunners."[52] Like this community of Fontevrault, France, with Louis at its head and Richelieu as navigator, was to voyage toward perfection.

Christian elite corps relied on methodical approaches to salvation. In this spirit Jeanne de Bourbon exhorts her community to study to adjust "all your words and actions to the level of this holy regulation, that each one of you make it, by the rectitude of his or her life, a living rule."[53] In a like spirit Saint François de Sales celebrated the anniversary of his ordination as the day he was "enrolled in the militia of Jesus Christ."[54] Method and discipline were the watchwords for the march of Christ's reforming army toward perfection.

For Richelieu, too, method was the key to achieving the ideal world that he meant to fashion of the state of France. The polity was to be continually guaranteed for the centuries by the system he meant to build into it. He was concerned that royal authority be self-sustaining, that state boundaries should become self-protecting, that trade and commerce would be self-replenishing. It detracts little from the significance of this dynamic perspective on the state "machine" that the actual expedients he adopted were often unoriginal, inefficient, archaic in inspiration, based on ignorance or misapprehension of essential facts. His conception was nevertheless in contrast with traditional views of the state in which political tactics were not chosen according to their utility for implementing a vision of the future, but instead sought and found in precedent.

Richelieu's systematic approach was seen in the methodical way he mapped every political strategy, conducted every campaign. Here again his innovation seems to have lain in bringing to political life perspectives that were penetrating other areas of thought. In this case it was not only in religious life, but also in scientific inquiry that the introduction of method and system was producing revolutionary effects. More than one writer has seen a parallel between Richelieu's style of thought and that of a French architect of mathematical innovation. Many of Descartes' pages, writes Léon Noël, "would not surprise over the signature of Richelieu."[55] He continues: "Without knowing it, Richelieu is a Cartesian; by instinct he applies, on his own count, the four rules set by Descartes."[56]

In Richelieu's theological works, too, a new methodicalness is perceptible to students of trends in religious thought. Noting his intention, in his *Perfection du chrestien,* to be "clear and concise," Cognet writes:

> He develops the quasi-geometrical plan of his work. . . . His systematic application of Thomism to mysticism certainly constitutes, in that epoch, originality.[57]

Of all the strategies devised by Richelieu to direct the state in accordance with his aims for it, none more clearly shows new, systematic arrangements than his lifelong efforts to organize and control communications.

Introduction

Possibly no statesman before Richelieu had striven as deliberately, nor as persistently, to assure himself of the maximum influx of reports on latest developments. Once in power, he innovated in the systematic collection of demographic and economic data.[58] But from his earliest days he was assiduous in the collection of news. The concept of information as "news" was, as Thomas points out, in itself a novelty arising from a new concept of history as "linear"—progressive rather than repetitive.[59] The demand for news and the expression of an obligation felt to give it are frequent features of Richelieu's youthful correspondence. Even in the early years at Luçon a far-flung network of correspondents regularly addressed political reports to him like officers to a commanding general although he was a bishop with no political post whatever. Thus he received a report, probably solicited, on reactions to Henri IV's death in Arles and Marseilles. Later, a colleague jokingly wrote in a newsy letter from Paris, "Don't think that I write this Gazette for no payment," and, *after* Richelieu's entry into the ministry in 1616, a regular informant in Rome wrote, promising to "continue in the same way" to write the bishop all the news.[60]

Striking as Richelieu's concern for the inflow of information appears, his activity as a producer of news and other forms of communication seemed to his contemporaries more distinctive still. Richelieu's constant planning and striving for effective tactical use of printed words is, perhaps, the most conspicuous of his innovations.

Only recently had the press acquired practical possibilities as a major instrument of state control. The cardinal was virtually the first to attempt fully to exploit these possibilities. Assignments of political polemics were rationalized under his aegis; the pamphleteers "systematically gathered around him." By such rational division of labor and methodical supervision of output Richelieu organized his propaganda machine: "Thus is the attitude of 'The Powers' systematized."[61] Richelieu's strategy of systematic response could have served as a model for Lasswell's notion of an "instant reply plan,"[62] so well did it exemplify the "very decided intention of the cardinal to grant no respite to his adversaries." None was allowed by him to "catch his breath" before an appropriate rejoinder to the slightest criticism issued from the efficient assembly line of Richelieu's propaganda factory.[63]

As in controlling opinion, so also in controlling other forms of behavior, Richelieu's innovative efforts were designed to install political machinery that would *automatically* influence the state in the direction he desired.

Long before he acquired political power Richelieu adopted, as Bishop of Luçon, tactics to deal with those under his control that he hoped would produce the self-sustaining mechanism he desired. Thus, at the beginning of his career, he was concerned to acquire a new seminary for his diocese that would give his flock the "means to extricate *itself* from ignorance,"[64] revealing a favorable view of self-help that was by no means shared by all of his clerical colleagues. Soon after this he produced an explication of the catechism which he labelled an instruction book for Christians. Written in the vernacular to insure maximum comprehension and dissemination, it is a "do-it-yourself" guide to proper conduct. In introducing it he expresses the hope that its availability will reduce the need for continual vigilance and intervention by the clergy. The faithful will be enabled by its use to take their own measures to improve their standing in the sight of God.[65]

The novelty of Richelieu's perspective on governmental policy becomes apparent with his début on a national platform in 1615. His aim is to install mechanisms that will make the state self-regulating. Thus, in his major address to the Estates General he reveals criteria for evaluating political strategy that are instrumentally moral rather than ends in themselves. He advocates ending the sale of government offices not because it is virtuous, in principle, to reward merit, but because the king will acquire power, by this means, to defend his influence through patronage. At the assembly of notables in 1626 he suggests that the value of punishing criminals lies not in the services rendered to justice by execution of the wicked, but in the deterrent power of the example thus provided.[66]

To reach the high goals that Richelieu held out before the latter assembly he promised that new rules and regulations were largely unnecessary. Economy of means was a prime desideratum: not many and continual, but few and exceptional expedients need be adopted to make the state machine run efficiently of itself.[67] "In order to reestablish this state in its original splendor," he proclaims, in a passage prepared in his own hand, "a lot of ordinances are not needed, but instead real executions." For him it is an axiom that "one kills the sick by overloading them with remedies, as well as by withholding them entirely."[68]

Thus the job of the statesman is to devise the pulleys, levers and springs that will make the laws self-administering, producing a clockwork of perpetual motion. He advises: "This assembly should be short as to its duration, but perpetual as to the fruit that it bears."[69] In striving for once-and-forever arrangements that will resolve all problems, Richelieu once again reveals his millenarian vision.

In Richelieu's aspirations there is nothing of the utopian philosopher of ancient times. Indeed, in an early work of which he was probably the principal author, Plato's utopia is deprecated as having consisted only of idle dreams rather than practical schemes. At the time this pamphlet appeared, Richelieu had recently entered the royal council as chief minister of the adolescent Louis XIII. Addressing the king, a passage forecasts:

> You will make of this realm not a Republic of Plato, where all consisted of nothing but ideas, but an animated body which will act by its own springs (*ses ressors*) and where all things will be seen infallibly to occur as it will have been resolved that they should under your authority.[70]

Towards the end of the reign the prediction is pronounced a reality. The cardinal is the one who "by the springs of his mind causes the whole machine of the realm to move."[71]

In this metaphor of a self-animating contrivance that will run like clockwork the king is, no doubt, the "mainspring," but the machine that is set in motion is of Richelieu's design and creation.

2 Private and Public Faces: The Quest for the Leader's Personality

Such grandeur in his designs; such boldness in executing them![1]

Whether a set of demands and expectations is highly idiosyncratic or shared with many others, there lie behind it wishes, fantasies, and beliefs in a combination that is unique for each individual. To identify some features of Richelieu's perspectives that were representative of his cultural milieu is only one step towards understanding distinctive patterns in the thoughts and feelings that supported them.

1.   Behind the Vision: Dreams

While the statesman's methods, in Richelieu's conception, had much in common with the methodical aspirations of the missionary reformer or the Puritan entrepreneur of his day, his vision of ultimate aims was distinguished from that of either of those in being neither otherworldly nor prosaic. An affective quality was associated with his ambition for achievement and his methodical tactics that distinguished his outlook both from the zeal of the missionary saints and from the systematic matter-of-factness of Max Weber's capitalist, Puritan achiever. Patriotic feeling animated his drive for accomplishment.

More than one writer has compared Richelieu, in the intensity of this feeling, to a hero of Corneille.[2] Another is inclined to forgive his obdurate qualities in consideration of his "profoundly patriotic heart."[3] An intimate servitor of the cardinal himself attested, "His heart was altogether French."[4] Almost all who have considered the emotional tone of Richelieu's ambition have seen his austerity and self-discipline colored by a vision of France.

Students of the growth of patriotic sentiment in France have tended to see, under the old regime, a fusion of the concept of the *patrie* with that

14

of the crown or the person of the king.[5] At the beginning of the seventeenth century, as has already been noted, one form taken by nationalistic reaction against recent civil disturbance was a movement to enhance the institution of kingship. During Richelieu's youth the popularity of Henri IV contributed further to fusing loyalties to crown and country. Under the much admired Vert Galant, writes Aulard, "the growth of crown-centered patriotism . . . reached its climax."[6] In later years the cardinal would take the lead, on Louis XIII's behalf, in merging the symbols of fatherland with those of the king. But examination of Richelieu's early attitudes shows his patriotism to be a sentiment easily distinguishable from his royalism. In his youthful writings and speeches it is signalled not by allusions to the *patrie*, but by fervent evocation of *La France*.

"*Patrie*," cultural historians have concluded, is a word of scholarly origin—"neither spontaneous nor popular."[7] First found in the sixteenth century, during the years when Richelieu was growing up, it saw increasing use, especially by the *noblesse de robe*.[8] Nevertheless, although the future prime minister had close kinship connections with this magisterial class, the word *patrie* was not favored by him.[9]

"France," on the other hand was a romantic and popular conception. "At least as old as the French language itself," it appears in the earliest poetic works.[10] Though it was often invoked by poets at tne time when Richelieu was beginning his career, it seems to have been infrequently used in contemporary political literature. In preference to it the king, his ministers, and the clergy referred to the "realm," the "state," the "crown" and its "subjects," to the "French" or even to the "people."[11] Richelieu's frequent use of "France" seems distinctive among political men of his time.

In his earliest published correspondence *France* frequently figures as an entity quite independently of references to the crown, the king, or the queen. In a letter to a woman friend he uses the word in comparing his country bishopric unfavorably with all others in the nation. A year or two later, this early impression given of his consciousness of national personality is reinforced by his seeming awareness of a national *opinion*. Thus he compliments a correspondent by writing that he knows his great merit "by the acclaim (*bruit*) of all France." In another early letter of politeness to a high royal officer he excuses himself for the "crime" of importuning one who "bears one of the heaviest responsibilities in France."[12] In that same year his patriotism approaches jingoism: a letter refers to government policy "heaping glory upon us at the expense of the enemies of France."[13] As he comes nearer the seat of power, in 1613, "La France" figures in a condolence message to the secretary of state. Here the term appears, in a strongly patriotic context, three times.[14]

At last, in 1615, Richelieu had the opportunity to address "France" in person when, at the concluding session of the Estates General assembly in Paris, he represented the clergy in a presentation before the king. Here he pictures himself as appearing before "all France"—a term that appears twice more in his speech. "France,"—on one occasion "our France"—is mentioned no fewer than thirteen times in this speech, almost as often as that *église* whose appointed spokesman he was. References to the "realm" and to the "state" are far outnumbered by this designation of the nation— France—which he personifies as a living being—suffering, reviving, relapsing, hoping, and, of course, listening to his own words.[15]

It is noteworthy that the exceptional form of Richelieu's sentiment has been little remarked.[16] While there has been a general sense that he innovated in French politics, the originality of his role has most often been sought in his programs and strategies for achieving central policy objectives. His vision of nationhood, however, seems as innovative as any particular aim or method of his statecraft. With him, seemingly, a secular patriotism stood in place of the proselytizing zeal of his clerical colleagues or the more traditional, dynastic aims of his rulers. His conception of "France" bears more relationship to that of a recent day than it did to his own.

This innovative word-use may have, on account of its resemblance to much later usage, escaped the notice of those seeking to identify characteristics that gave Richelieu his singularity. Nevertheless, it seems to have made an unconscious impression upon some who have studied his writings. Thus Antoine Adam refers incidentally to "the new energetic France Richelieu wanted to create."[17] Indeed, Richelieu's enterprising mission of state-building was not confined to the apparatus of government; his aspiration was not merely to glorify the monarchy and establish unchallenged royal rule. In words and deeds it was France itself that he strove to "create."

2. A "New Man"

"Innovations," writes Schumpeter, "are always associated with the rise to leadership of New Men."[18] One sense in which men are "new" is in representing a group new to the leadership arena. Did Richelieu belong to such a group?

Certain of Richelieu's words in his address to the closing session of the Estates General assembly in 1615 accentuate, by showing his distinctive views on the nation he conceived himself to be addressing, the contrast between his perspectives and those of the groups that were then most politically influential in France.

He opens his speech by comparing the present conference with a practice followed in the pagan Roman empire, according to which citizens were annually invited to air their grievances to their ruler in a public ceremony. In Richelieu's imagination, it appears here, France is a new empire; Paris its metropolis: "Your Majesty having assembled all his subjects in the capital city of his realm, Rome of France, regular seat of its kings, it seems that his intention may be to introduce a similar holiday in his state."[19] Considering this fantasy along with those of his allusions to France already cited, we gain a picture of a unified kingdom, unrivalled in strength, dominating a wide territory, itself dominated by a culture radiating from the center, personified by an enlightened monarch. This poetic conception had an ancient tradition.[20] No doubt it had also some power over the popular imagination. In early seventeenth century politics, however, it had but limited application.

This sense of France as a unified territorial entity, centered on its capital city, was weak among those with the most influence on the country's destiny—the ruling family and the high nobility. At the very time that Richelieu delivered his address, leading great lords with little patriotism were challenging the authority of Louis XIII's head of government, Marie de Medici, whose sense of allegiance to her adopted country was scarcely stronger than the affinity she felt with the king of Spain and with her Italian family. As in the case of many a French ruler before her, this Florentine regent's interests in France were dynastic rather than nationalistic. Her kin had interests and holdings outside the bounds of France; her son's jurisdiction was not surely established over every part within it. As Richelieu spoke she was in the process of cementing a double alliance of marriage with France's great rival and potential enemy, Hapsburg Spain.

Even the naming of Paris as the habitual royal seat, though also validated by tradition, was to an extent a romantic conception. Coming from Richelieu in 1615 it may have been intended as a challenge to centrifugal forces that were at that time predominant in national councils. In the light even of that tradition, the Louvre was only one of the French renaissance monarch's many strongholds, and by no means the favorite nor the one most frequently sojourned in.[21] The king of France was often a veritable itinerant. Some, such as François I, had been "beset by truly pathological agitation," causing them to wander from one headquarters to another. None was wedded to his residence in the capital city. Lestocquoy remarks, "The king must be crowned at Rheims; as for Paris, it is not obligatory for him to live there." For Louis XIII, as for his father and many other ancestors, the ideal royal seat was a country château, "surrounded by a forest alive with game."[22] Indeed, Louis's first fleeting encounter with Paris, when he was almost three, was acutely distasteful to him.[23]

The young king's feeling of being linked to a unified country and located at its center, however, was far stronger not only than that of his foreign mother but also than that of his brother or sisters who had had less contact with Paris and less occasion for travel about the realm than he. All were to marry into foreign princely houses. Gaston, whose marriage to a princess of Lorraine would be contracted against his brother's and Richelieu's wishes, regularly conspired with foreign potentates to advance his own designs of later years, frequently settling abroad with this aim.

Still less than the royal family did many of the great nobles feel an allegiance to that France which Richelieu evoked so eloquently. For the most part they regarded the king as merely first among equals; several did not acknowledge even that priority. They saw the interests of the royal house as a family affair, rather than a national concern. This nobility, Tapié summarizes, "French though it might be, felt a certain solidarity with foreign nobles, and found it natural, when it had an insult to avenge, to ask help from or offer services to another king, even were he the enemy of the king of France."[24]

The doubtful patriotism of the high warrior class prevailed equally amongst most of the high ecclesiastics then so influential in Marie de Medici's councils. Among them were several Italian grandees whose allegiances were shared by such ambitious French princes of the church as Cardinals Du Perron and La Rochefoucauld. Still another was the Archbishop of Rheims whose great family of Guise had been historic rivals of reigning dynasties.

Thus, while the quality of patriotic feeling that Richelieu showed in his first important address may have struck a chord of favorable response in some who heard him, it was scarcely a note that could be expected to evoke enthusiasm from those high-ranking personages then most influential in state affairs.

Yet Richelieu was himself already a prelate high in the ecclesiastical hierarchy and, as such, of a noble rank which enabled him to pretend to equal footing with the military as well as the clerical elite. How had he acquired a romantic, patriotic picture of France in 1615, and of its center, Paris, that was so atypical of the ruling group in which he found himself?

As Mousnier has remarked, "French society of the seventeenth century remains profoundly military."[25] Nominally, the clerical estate ranked highest in French society; in practice the nobility of the sword came first. Missionary leaders of the Counter-Reformation, much as they might strive to change the moral order, were as yet far short of reversing priorities of the temporal world.

In that world, the concern of each noble family was to concentrate its resources in support of the capacity of its eldest son to take his place among the military elite and to effect an advantageous marriage. "An abbey or bishopric," on the other hand, "was a resource of the last-born." It was not for beneficiaries of such posts either to bring glory to the family name or to perpetuate the family tree. "Even though the clergy was the first order of the state, there was between the cuirass and the cassock the same distance as that between the eldest and his brothers."[26]

And Richelieu was the youngest of three sons born to the noble family of François de Richelieu. While his eldest brother was early placed as a royal page, to tread in the footsteps of their warrior-trained father, following a military career in all-male groups in camp and court, Armand remained in the remote country manor, in a household dominated by women, his rearing fashioned to equip him to make the best of what residual opportunities the family might later be able to claim on his behalf. His early education, supervised by his widowed mother, was in the hands of an obscure provincial cleric.

One who is excluded from the scene of significant action, constrained to watch from the periphery, may form notions of the whole that are poetically idealized. Yearning to participate in great affairs, a young boy, confined to the provinces by family necessity may, in his imagination, endow those affairs with romantic allure.

No direct report exists of Richelieu's views of his country and its center in these early years. But certain of his later scattered comments give clues to the perspective he may have formed during a boyhood that was felt as distant from the main events of his time.

When Richelieu had reached the height of power in the state he recalled, in a rare personal reminiscence, sensations he had once had, as a young bishop, in a poor, rustic diocese. He tells of the dreams he then entertained, in a community even more isolated than his native one, of momentous undertakings in the great world:

> More than thirty years ago, being attached to the duties of the episcopacy in the diocese of Luçon near La Rochelle, I often thought, in the midst of a profound peace, of the means of bringing that place around to obedience to the king. Those thoughts then passed in my mind like dreams or vain imaginings. . . . They seemed formerly mere chimeras.[27]

Richelieu's words seem to reflect thoughts a young boy might have had, confined to a quiet country manor far from the capital, learning by hearsay of the exploits and opportunities of father, uncles, and oldest brother, whose exciting careers were unfolding at the center of action, while he entertained fantasies of great exploits of his own.

Richelieu had, later, another occasion to entertain this reverie he reports himself as having had as a young cleric, stranded near La Rochelle. The opportunity to deliver the harangue for the clergy at the Estates General assembly in 1615 was a heady one. Afterwards, however, nothing seemed immediately to have changed. Within a few months the bishop found himself back in his poor, distant Luçon, writing ruefully to a sponsor at court: "The sterility of this country, which produces nothing, prevents me from sending you news."[28] The "profound peace" of this period, which he later recalled, could also be a condition of sterility, in which idle imagination, rather than significant action held sway. The prototype for this regret at being excluded from the metropolis may lie in his boyhood experience.

Richelieu's preparation for life as the younger son in a female-centered country house contrasted with that of his oldest brother, early located amongst male companions and mentors, to be prepared for a military career. The contrast was one replicated throughout France in countless noble households. Also often replicated, however, was the reversal of family fortunes and personal fates which determined, in Richelieu's case, that it should be he, rather than the eldest of his line, who would make the family name famous and dominate the political life of his generation. In this sense Richelieu's leadership represented a "new" group in early modern French politics, that of the traditionally subordinated younger sons.

Eventually, Richelieu himself was sent to Paris to continue his schooling. At the time he arrived, about 1595, there was already reason to expect that the opportunities for displacement of the older sons, reared according to the dominant military pattern, by younger ones, exponents of a culture in which feminine influence was more important, would increase.

In the last quarter of the sixteenth century, not only the *grands* but the young warrior group in general had experienced an attrition of their numbers. To the hazards to which the *noblesse d'épée* was habitually exposed— duels and casual violence—had been added the heightened incidence of death from assassination or battle due to the intense religious struggles.[29] Demographic patterns, had they been visible to those who formed them, could well have given encouragement to new groups—such as the clergy or magistracy—aspiring to political leadership.[30]

The conduct of new men bears the mark of their distinctive cultures: They exhibit new manners as well as substantively innovative behavior.

Richelieu's conduct had such distinguishing marks. Certain features of it impressed his contemporaries as atypical for one in his position. Especially was he credited with a self-control extraordinary for one so highly placed.

"There has perhaps never been a minister of state as equal to himself as he is," wrote an apologist for the prime minister, "nor one whose impulses are so much under his control." On this point, apparently, the reporter was confident that he would not be contradicted; Richelieu's self-restraint was something that "one and all recognize in him."[31]

Another who had had an opportunity to observe Richelieu at close hand and who, writing in England, had no reason not to disclose the truth, likewise fixed upon this self-control as the cardinal's most conspicuous quality: "He had so great a command over his passions," writes Du Grès, "that even in the most extreme adversity they were at his beck and call."[32] And the Englishman, James Howell, similarly beyond the reach of French influence, also reports that the strict rein Richelieu kept on himself was his most distinctive characteristic. Howell writes that the prime minister "seldom . . . gave way to impetuous motions," nor did he show "furious sallies of passions."[33]

Part of the significance of these observations lies in the fact that, by modern criteria, Richelieu's self-control does not seem as striking as it did to his contemporaries. The strong impression apparently made on them by his personal behavior may, therefore, be accounted for by its contrast with then prevailing standards of conduct.

Indeed, it seems that Richelieu's customary dissembling or control of his emotions was exceptional when compared with the behavior of many of those who were most influential politically. Warriors brought to the highest circles of French society an impetuous self-indulgence in rage and lust alike. Passionate outbreaks were commonplace at the highest level.

The royal family itself set an example to other courtiers in giving way to impulses and testifying to feelings with physical signs. Henri IV's appetite for gambling, food, drink, women, and violent sport was unbridled. Furthermore, he wore his feelings on his sleeve. Nor were his wife, Marie de Medici, and his son, Louis XIII, accustomed to inhibit demonstration of their loves and hates. Teeth-gnashing, trembling, biting of lip or finger, and complexion color changes were frequently noted as evidence of the sentiments of these and other great personages. Writing of Henri IV's cousin, the prince de Condé, Aumale comments: "In those times temperance was not a very common virtue [and]. . . . the profusion with which the chronicles of the time attributed shameful vices to so many people diminished the effect of these accusations."[34] From the monarch on down, in the court of Richelieu's youth, anger was likely to be followed by assault, lust by rape.[35]

In this setting it is easier to appreciate the impression made by Richelieu's self control. Sometimes described as sinuous and supple, sometimes depicted, as in the memorable portraits by Philippe de Champaigne, as calm and austere, his manner was in almost all cases free of those "impetuous motions" and "furious sallies" seen in those around him.

In Richelieu's wake many were to follow who demonstrated a like self-controlled temperament in the conduct of public affairs; some sponsored by him or modeling themselves on his example. But at the time he first appeared on the political scene such characteristics among highly placed secular persons seem to have been sufficiently unusual to attract notice. Indeed, self-control of any appetites often was regarded by courtiers as unusual and admirable.[36]

In another circle, however, self-restraint and austerity had become the norm.[37] Among the newly important group of moral reformers those characteristics that have here been linked to the experience of children raised in a feminine setting were conspicuous virtues.[38] Some of these pioneering religious leaders passed across the political stage from time to time, exciting admiration more often than emulation among those highly placed at court. The link of such missionaries with feminine rearing was often simple: some of these "new men" *were* women. The partnerships in spiritual enterprise formed by such as Père Joseph, Cardinal de Bérulle, Saint Vincent de Paul and Saint François de Sales with outstanding women reformers bore fruit in the later success of the Catholic renovation among leading noble-women.[39]

Less obvious, but probably important as demonstrating the connection between family experience and innovating social role was the felt affinity with female values variously expressed or shown by the leading male missionaries of the reform. Thus François de Sales describes to Saint Chantal his sensation of unity with her.[40] Père Joseph, in whose religious work collaboration with women was equally central, came from a family closely comparable with Richelieu's. Though the elder of two sons, he early assumed the austere habit of a Capuchin monk, leaving to his cadet the worldly responsibility for the family fortune and posterity. His relationship with his mother, particularly close and enduring, is revealed in his religious writing.[41]

Richelieu himself, though a cleric, was primarily, of course, a political man, while for the most part the saintly pioneers of reform did not enter the field of political decision making. Even Père Joseph's eventual deep involvement in day-to-day politics was achieved as the agent of Richelieu's designs.

Yet the prime minister's personal history had elements in common with those spiritual leaders whose careers paralleled his on a separate plane. Certain patterns of rearing seem to have left on the behavior of many of them, as on his, an indelible feminine stamp.

Nevertheless, demographic, social and cultural influences can go only so far towards explaining an individual performance. While many a younger son of mixed noble ancestry may have been predisposed to become a publicist for nationalism, a Gallican priest, a royalist magistrate, or a missionary reformer, few besides Richelieu initiated measures to advance French autonomy and royal absolutism. And none more ardently, steadily, and spectacularly took the lead in all he attempted. To explain such a highly individuated career one must descend from general conditions that supported it to personal history.

3. A Note on Methods

The accumulation of nearly four centuries of research is bound to daunt one who proposes to say something new about Richelieu's character. Even the presentation of previously unpublished personal documents on his early history is insufficient to justify the effort: what has not already been consulted may have been neglected for good reasons.

It is the availability of the hypotheses of psychoanalysis, so far largely unapplied to Richelieu's record, that promises additional insight. Psychoanalytic theory, through refocussing attention on childhood experience, offers new understanding of adult character. In its light, not only previously unpublished matter acquires new meaning; much material by and about the Richelieus that has been cited before also acquires new importance if it has never been "listened to" with an ear that is attentive to latent meanings in imagery and emphasis, in oversight and inconsistency, in repetition and denial.

Some have supposed that if an inquiry attempts psychological understanding of an historical figure, it must do so at the expense of attention to documentary evidence. Thus Pierre Blet has complained of the "disservice to history" done by those who have claimed "to sound the kidneys and hearts" of their subjects. Richelieu, he believes, has been falsely represented by those who have "substituted a simplistic (*élémentaire*) psychology for the analysis of ancient (*antiques*) documents."[42]

Such substitution has no part in the approach used here. On the contrary, the wearying study of minute details of ancient documents is central to psychoanalytic method. Authenticating sources is especially important for such an inquiry. It is essential to identify what is actually the work of the subject of the study.

Determining authorship, however, is a reciprocal process. As understanding of the subject's character deepens through review of his experiences and his behavior patterns (including words indubitably originating with him), the ability grows to authenticate or discredit other words as his. This kind of analysis is not circular; it could better be described as spiralling: progressively, the protagonist emerges in the round. If the procedure is successful, the historian comes to recognize his subject's work as he would that of a personal acquaintance. As with gossip that is inconsistent with the picture of an intimate, so with information inconsistent with the achieved characterization of an historical figure; the burden of proof is on the new, jarring evidence. If documents inconsistent with the developing portrayal of Richelieu are finally incontestably ascribed to him, it becomes the task either to consider altered pictures of the dynamics of his character or to deepen understanding of it by identifying special features of the context in which the surprising behavior took place.

The point has been elaborated concerning the attribution to Richelieu of the *Testament politique*, since its first publication in 1688, in Holland, the object of dispute. While not arguing against the historical interest of this work, Richard Lodge considers "entirely untenable" a French colleague's claim that it reflects Richelieu's "powerful personality." Quite to the contrary, he concludes, "if its authenticity could be conclusively proved, the current estimates of Richelieu would have to be not merely added to, but profoundly modified."[43]

For those concerned only with establishing details of the *official* record, ascertainment of personal authorship is often not central. This, for example, is the perspective of the learned compiler of the comprehensive new edition of Richelieu state papers.[44] On the other hand, if a document cannot be traced to the hand or mind of the cardinal himself, it is not an exponent of his *personal* history. As Voltaire remarks, "If he neither wrote it nor dictated it, then it is not by him."[45]

The significance of attribution for personality inquiry may be illustrated with an example from the so-called *Testament politique.* The main text of this work, as recent scholarship has revealed, follows the pattern of the putative *Mémoires de Richelieu:* it is primarily a compilation of various documents emanating from published and unpublished sources, including Richelieu's own collection.[46] The originals selected for inclusion in the version of 1688, insofar as they have been identified, were for the most part highly edited and much revised by an unknown hand or hands. Here again, much of the text has value for the official history of the regime. At the same time, it may be valueless or misleading for an understanding of Richelieu's personality.

Thus, in Richelieu's papers is found a heavily reworked passage, entirely in his own handwriting,[47] apparently prepared at about the time the British navy was frustrated by French defenses at La Rochelle in 1628. The finished memorandum displays vivid and distinctive imagery. It describes the significance of sea power and the manner of acquiring it:

> Of all inheritances the sea is the one over which all sovereigns claim the most sway, and yet it is the one over which each one's rights are the least clarified. Empire over this element has never been well assured to anyone; it has been subject to various changes according to the inconstancy of its nature, so jealous and so full of vanity that she [*sic*] abandons herself always to him who flatters her most and who has so much love for her that he keeps himself in a state to possess her by violence against all those who could dispute his right to her by reason. In a word, the true titles to this empire are might and not right. It is necessary to be powerful to pretend to this inheritance.[48]

In French, of course, awareness of the connection between the sea and the mother is enhanced by their homonymy: *la mer* and *la mère*.[49] As Richelieu reworks the passage, the sea-mother becomes infinitely desirable, but capricious, subject to flattery, and, finally, conquerable only by force rather than by reason.[50] The changes will be seen to have significance for insight into his development and character.

As the reader can determine first-hand,[51] Richelieu's first version of this memorandum lacks much that is suggestive in the imagery of his finished piece. In the former it is not the feminine sea itself that is inconstant, jealous and vain; it is the masculine "this element." And in the revision, the sea's conqueror becomes one who "has so much love for her" rather than one who would simply "prevent it" from being claimed by another.

Yet the version that appears in the *Testament politique* removes much of the color from Richelieu's final text. It also significantly changes the meaning, deprecating rather than condoning the use of force to gain control of the sea. The compilers revert to masculine nouns and pronouns and substitute new phrases for some of the author's. Their Richelieu becomes one "whose power is so unlimited" rather than one who is enamored of the sea, and who contends not with him who would claim "his right to her" but with those who would dispute "domination" of "this element." Perhaps the cardinal's metaphorical flights were too headily suggestive for the editors of his purported testament. For present purposes, however, close study of original texts, and their alterations, is essential.

An additional example of the process of spiral analysis is presented by another prolonged controversy over an alleged Richelieu text. Towards the end of the last century, an archivist "discovered" a manuscript entitled, "Instructions for Conducting Myself on First Appearing at Court."[52] Because the document seemed, in many ways, to describe the way in which the young courtier Richelieu actually *did* conduct himself when he arrived in Paris in 1610, the discoverer triumphantly attributed the authorship to Richelieu. Somewhat later Gabriel Hanotaux, after first hesitating, finally unqualifiedly accepted the "find."[53] In the mind of Jules Lair, however, first confrontation with the document raised doubts. Some of the behavior recommended by the supposed Richelieu was manifestly inconsistent with that of the man whom Lair "knew." Some of the phrases seemed incongruent with Richelieu's style. Lair looked for, and found, through handwriting and ancillary evidence, proof that the work was not by Richelieu but by Pierre Matthieu, historiographer of Henri IV.[54]

Accepting Lair's refutation of Baschet's attribution leads to further insights into Richelieu's character: The document could not have been his work because it reveals a self-consciousness of conflict between public seemliness and private desires which was alien to Richelieu; because its mere survival is inconsistent with Richelieu's policy of secrecy; because there are in it avowals of aims that Richelieu did not have. Through Lair's documentary research the "real" cardinal comes one step more out of the shadows.

The potential of such research for producing additional insights into Richelieu's character has been, since Lair's day, greatly augmented by psychoanalysis, a system which permits understanding of personality in genetic and developmental terms. It will be for the reader to judge whether, with the help of this system, the present inquiry succeeds in bringing the cardinal's nature farther into the light.

4. Following the Leader

While the importance of personal characteristics in explaining the performance of an innovative political leader can scarcely be overestimated, these must be considered in relation to the behavior of those others on whose support the success of his enterprise depends.

The economist, indeed, is apt to conceive of personal characteristics needed for leadership in interpersonal terms. To Frank Knight, for example, courage in the face of danger and willingness to take risks give the entrepreneur the "capacity for ruling others." He who leads the way along uncharted paths needs the courage to take responsibility for others; he stands as their guarantor.[55] For him to be successful he must communicate his personal vision to others and evoke from them the needed response:

> Even leadership which influences merely by example, as artistic or scientific leadership, does not consist simply in finding or creating the new thing but in so impressing a social group with it as to draw it on in its wake.[56]

The leader must possess the ability to overcome that opposition that necessarily arises from the difference between himself and others:

> To act with confidence beyond the range of familiar beacons and to overcome . . . resistance requires aptitudes that are present in only a small fraction of the population and that define the entrepreneurial type as well as the entrepreneurial function.[57]

Evidently, the entrepreneur's success is a function not only of his own personality but also of the characteristics of those whom he seeks to lead. Thus Knight sees the power of personal confidence in a leader depending partly on the extent to which there is in society at large "a scarcity of self-confidence."[58]

Recent scholars have maintained there existed, at the time Richelieu began his career, a wide distribution of certain popular attitudes that could be considered, in the present perspective, favorable to acceptance of his schemes. Receptivity to confident leadership might be inferred, for example, from a rise in the level of public anxiety that some have perceived at that time, apparently inspired by the destruction and uncertainty accompanying the religious wars of the last half of the sixteenth century. Robert Mandrou has discerned such a wave of popular anxiety towards the end of that century, shown in preoccupation with Satanical manifestations, that "may have extended to the humblest populations, the broadest social strata."[59] Similar intimations of heightened anxiety are suggested by Robert Muchembled's study of the correspondence of Artesian noblemen in that same "epoch of instability and turmoil."[60] The religious schism itself, by raising problems for many, may have created a climate more disposed to accept resolution from a centralized political authority. Isolated examples from literature of the time could be cited to indicate that the presence of Protestant dissenters accentuated, especially among the military elite, an intolerance of ambiguity.[61]

More directly relevant to the popular state of mind as it might have borne on receptivity to Richelieu's centralizing aims is Mousnier's appraisal of a disposition among the lower orders to see, at that time of universal insecurity of peasant and townsman, a promise of protection of their interests in aggrandizement of royal power:

> The rights of the strong were well enough protected by the nature of things. The rights of others could only be protected by the power of the king. . . . Under such social conditions the true guarantee of rights was royal sovereignty.[62]

Yet, while many may willingly fall in with the leader's designs, it is characteristic of public response to an innovator that few share his vision, others only partially perceive it, and most misunderstand, reject, or fail to apprehend it. Certainly Richelieu's vision, strategy and tactics were misinterpreted by his contemporaries at all levels. Few of them, Lodge thinks, "were able to estimate his greatness or to appreciate his aims." He finds it ironical that "the statesman who has been hailed by the almost unanimous opinion of later generations as the grandest figure among those who have contributed most to the greatness of France" in his own time failed to attract the enthusiasm of his countrymen and in fact, apparently, "in his later years . . . was detested by the populace."[63]

Any such generalization about public opinion in a traditional society must rest on weak foundations. Local particularism limits the weight that can be given even to systematic attempts to assay mass opinion in the premodern age. Lodge's conclusion that Richelieu was popularly detested is apparently based on such signs as bonfires kindled in many provinces to celebrate news of his death. It is counterbalanced by the testimony of witnesses who perceived popular anxiety and sensed a general feeling of deprivation among Parisians when they learned of the same event.

Less difficult to judge is the extent to which the style and objectives of Richelieu's leadership resonated with tacit or expressed demands of those members of higher orders who were his potential collaborators. Among these, of course, his enemies were legion. It is no problem to identify some of them as representing interests and cultures that were threatened by Richelieu's innovation. He had little appeal for those noblemen typical of earlier regimes whose provincial and tribal loyalties took precedence over their allegiance to king and country: most of the great lords of the realm failed to respond favorably to the new leader. Within other groups, such as the lay and clerical intelligentsia, there was less consensus: receptivity to the new leader's designs varied among factions and an individual could respond differently to different aspects of his schemes.[64] Thus one contemporary appreciated Richelieu's zeal, his strategical ingenuity, his administrative methods, but failed to understand the central part in animating his behavior that was played by his nationalism. "Had he been as active for the universal good of Christendom," writes Howell, "as he was for the interests and safety of his own country," his example would have seemed wholly emulable for this Englishman's own pupil, the future Charles II.[65] In a different frame, a highly placed French cleric whose response to Richelieu's ambitions was strongly hostile interpreted all of his behavior as an aspect of a single motive—the desire to dominate. Thus the cardinal's rationalization of administrative functions and allocation of responsibility for collecting information were seen by Montchal as mere *ad hoc* tactics to limit the ken of his collaborators in order to sequester all power for himself.[66]

Many of those who became Richelieu's constant and effective supporters had or acquired kinship with him. Their family histories very often resembled his own in many respects, even to origins concentrating in that region in and around Poitou in which he had been reared. These histories also included, as in the cases of the La Porte-Meillerayes, Bouthilliers, and L'Aubespines, important prior government service.[67] Thus, while many became the "creatures" of Richelieu and the instruments of his designs, their careers might have followed comparable paths had the cardinal never become their master, even though the historic significance of their activity would have been less without the integration he gave it.

The rearing of Richelieu's age-mate, André Du Chesne, for example, paralleled, in province and capital, the prime minister's own. Born in Ile Bouchard, not far from Richelieu, partially schooled in nearby Loudun, Du Chesne was the son of a doctor of Henri IV. He became a nationalistic historian and a propagandist for royal absolutism before Richelieu acquired power. Called "my good neighbor" by the cardinal, he became one of his leading apologists.[68] Yet his official career might not have been greatly different had Richelieu never appeared on the scene.

Nevertheless, Richelieu certainly had the power to inspire an ardor among many of such close collaborators beyond what can be explained by the claims of kinship, career interest, or shared beliefs. This was one mark of his success as an entrepreneur. The zeal he enlisted even sometimes exceeded his desires: "overkill" is a characteristic effect of the outstanding political leader.[69]

Examination of the personal bases of Richelieu's early support is one object of the present study. Such analysis is preliminary to an understanding of his later record as prime minister and moving spirit of a new French regime. Yet, for France, Richelieu's personal history and character, the motives of his close supporters, and the social and psychological bases for his popular following would have counted for nothing except for the fact that, eventually, he was able to enlist the collaboration of one whose authority counted for almost everything—the king.

The aim of the present volume is to discover, through an analysis of Richelieu's early history, how far that enlistment can be explained as a function of his personal characteristics. The work is, therefore, a portrayal of Richelieu before Louis XIII. Its method follows, as far as possible, an experimental design: illustrations of Richelieu's conduct are taken from situations in which he acts alone. Evidence on his perspectives is preferably chosen from documents originating before he became a major state figure. In all cases his personal stamp—whether in early writings or in later state papers—must be distinguished from that of others.

This study is thus a prelude to the main act: it sets the stage for considering the earliest phase of Richelieu's ministration to Louis XIII. It ends at the beginning of a collaboration.

The bishop of Luçon who is portrayed here would become the stand-in—the alter ego—of the king; in Thierry's terms, "less a minister in the exact sense of the word than a proxy for royalty's universal power." If the ultimate aim of my study is to understand the dynamics of the collaboration, a second portrayal will be needed after this beginning—that of Louis XIII. For as Thierry concludes, "By a strange concurrence of circumstances, it was found that that prince . . . had in his character . . . everything that could respond to the conditions of such a role."[70]

Thenceforward the history of the regime must take account of that character and those conditions. It is another story.

Part 2 PRECEDENTS

3 The Richelieu Heritage: Armand's Father

The greatest honor, most worthy of all
That shall to the ages give your name most renown,
Is e'er having kept faith with the Princes Royal.[1]

The career of Armand de Richelieu's father compassed the strife-ridden history of France in the last half of the sixteenth century. François Du Plessis de Richelieu was about eleven years old in 1559 when King Henri II died an accidental death, unleashing civil war. The religious struggles during the next thirty-five years were especially destructive in Poitou, the region of the Richelieu family estate.[2] They gave to that province a reputation for violence which was to be important many years later for the future statesman's prospects.

François de Richelieu's fortunes were linked to those who ruled France between 1559 and 1590. He was a page at court when the reign of François II began in the earlier year. With the death of that young king, in 1560, the ten-year-old Charles IX succeeded to the throne, bringing regent power to his mother, Catherine de Medici, whose uncertain leadership contributed to the wars of religion. François was a young soldier in the forces of the crown when the massacre of Protestant leaders on Saint Bartholomew's Day triggered renewed civil war in August, 1572. By 1574, when the death of Charles IX brought back the twenty-three-year old duc d'Anjou from Poland to become Henri III of France, François was in the service of this new king. He remained attached to Henri as the latter's concessions to the Protestants gave rise, in 1576, to the Catholic League, a coalition against the monarchy led by the Angevin family of Guise. In 1588 François was in Henri III's service as the latter escaped from Paris after the Day of Barricades on which the League took control of the capital city. François assisted Henri when he arranged for the assassination of all but one of the

Guise leaders in 1588. He continued to serve this king, last of the Valois line, when Henri designated his brother-in-law, the Protestant Henri de Navarre, as his heir. When, in 1589, Henri III was in turn assassinated, François de Richelieu immediately gave his allegiance to the successor, now Henri IV. But François died in 1590, during the continuing civil war, before the new king was able, by abjuring his Protestant faith in 1593, to inaugurate a period of stability and recovery.

When illness carried off François de Richelieu, now a captain in the guards of Henri IV, he left to his sons a mixed heritage. He bequeathed them a somewhat alloyed aristocratic status, together with an economic position close to ruin. His public life was an example of faithful service to the crown. His private life was dominated by violence, infidelity and profligacy.

1.   The Milieu

The maternal and paternal families of Armand-Jean Du Plessis de Richelieu shared a social status. Their cultural histories, too, overlapped. Both sides were noble. Both were mostly Poitevin in origin; both families possessed landed estates in Poitou. Armand's two grandfathers were both loyal servants of the crown. While there was an occasional Protestant among the Du Plessis-Richelieus and the La Porte-Meillerayes, there were not, so far as is known, any politically rebellious Huguenots nor any Leaguers nor excessively zealous Catholics. Members of both families seem to have been content to allow the crown to mediate between contesting faiths. In each group religious belief was not mystical. Among this *petite noblesse* of Poitou, as among the Artesian nobility described by Muchembled, God the Father's position in the heavenly realm seemed to parallel that of the monarch in the temporal domain. In each place a single figure—God or the king—dominated the imagination of the faithful.[3]

It is probable that most notables of the region had some degree of contact with one another. As in rural England of that time, the countryside was only sparsely flecked with *seigneurs*. Goubert has described the poverty of the social landscape around Beauvais for a somewhat later, "normal" time of periodic famine and constant stringency.[4] During the wars of religion the proneness of aristocrats to kill one another contributed to their scarcity. Thus it is likely that members of Armand de Richelieu's father's and mother's families had been mutually acquainted for some years before they became allied by marriage. Supporting this supposition is the fact that when Armand's father was taken as a child to be a page at court, he was introduced there by François Pidoux, physician to Catherine de Medici. The Pidoux were Poitevin doctors, lawyers and officials who were also allied with the La Porte-Meilleraye family of Armand's mother.[5]

Thus the social disparity between the two families should not be exaggerated. Nevertheless, their histories diverged in important ways. The Richelieus were of the warrior class: day by day concern with commercial or professional matters was considered demeaning; their men bore arms in the service of their masters, and their relations with kings were personal and informal. Richelieu's mother's clan, on the other hand, formed part of the nobility of the robe: they were lawyers, judges and officials. In their recent history were tradesmen and artisans. Their services to the crown were rendered in professional, formal capacities; there is no sign that they ever took up arms in defense of their leaders.[6]

2.   The Tradition of the Richelieus

The Du Plessis had been *seigneurs* of the territory of Richelieu only since the end of the fifteenth century.[7] It may be, however, that they had long entertained a claim for more ancient noble lineage. When, in power, the cardinal assigned a renowned historian to retrace the family tree, the latter provided a Du Plessis-Richelieu genealogy distinguished by unalloyed gentility reaching back into the dark ages and connecting the Du Plessis with the royal house.[8]

The matter of Richelieu's origins was not settled by Du Chesne's efforts, however. The brilliant genealogy was disbelieved by the cardinal's enemies:

> He had published throughout the realm books on his genealogy,
> falsified in many parts . . . where . . . they made him not only
> of high and noble extraction, equal to the most noble families of
> the kingdom, but even descended from royal forebears.[9]

At least one authority was alleged to be among these contemporary detractors. A manuscript of the time attributes to the leading genealogist, Jean Du Bouchet, an account claiming that the cardinal's father's family was separated by only four generations from a bourgeois ancestor. According to this story, the title of Du Plessis and the signory of Richelieu had come into the family thanks to favors granted by an apothecary's daughter to a bishop of Poitiers in the late fifteenth century. The mid-seventeenth century document containing these statements also contains details corroborated by contemporary testimony.[10]

The truth of the Du Plessis-Richelieu claim to antique noble status is immaterial to present concerns, though the cardinal's interest in establishing such a claim is significant. By the end of the sixteenth century, ancient title to land had lost the importance it had possessed of mutual obligation based on territorial allegiance. For the bond between suzerain and vassal had been substituted a master-supporter (*maître-fidèle*) relationship in which the link was supposed to be sentiment. This was a survival of the feudal norm of love-motivated reciprocal service between knight and warrior-overlord.[11] Masters were not, of course, chosen for sentimental reasons. In order for a young nobleman to rise, he needed to make a good bargain for his services. His choice of a patron was determined by opportunity, chiefly consisting in his family connections.

In the mid-sixteenth century, the Du Plessis-Richelieu prospects of improving their modest family status depended on their success in allying themselves with others higher on the social ladder through forming such master-supporter relationships. One important means for this was marriage. Du Chesne, Armand de Richelieu's favored genealogist claimed—on rather doubtful grounds—a royal ascendance for his patron's paternal ancestors.[12] It is certain, however, that this grandfather married, in 1542, Françoise de Rochechouart, a member of one of the first families of France, several of whose near antecedents were distinguished for military service to the Valois kings. The attainability of such a well-connected alliance by this family of minor nobility must have been due to her lack of money or property. Apparently Françoise was an old maid, dependent on the patronage of rich noblewomen, when she married Louis de Richelieu.[13] By many accounts her social pretensions made her "proud" and "haughty," and the standards she brought to her descendants reflected her high aristocratic heritage.

The behavior of Richelieu's paternal forebears throws light on one element in this heritage. Many Richelieu men had been ready to defend family honor by violent means. Accounts of conduct demonstrating this trait could well have figured as stories told to the Richelieu children during the cardinal's boyhood, perhaps while his grandmother was still living with them in the family home.[14]

Indifference to physical danger was displayed conspicuously by Richelieu's paternal precursors. Among these were several warriors with a reputation for brutality. Most notorious in this respect was the cardinal's great uncle, Captain Antoine Du Plessis, described as an "ill-famed man, noted for his thieveries, looting, and blasphemy, a great ruffian and bully of all the bordellos." Antoine was killed in a Paris brawl in 1576, "by ruffians like himself whom, being with some whores in a neighboring house . . . he had gone to berate and throw out of the place, being displeased that they had undertaken to brawl and whore so near his own dwelling."[15] Armand de Richelieu's own father was the heir of this man who, close to his nephew, sponsored the terms of his marriage contract and served as his commander in the regiments of the duc de Montpensier.[16]

The record left by Richelieu's father was to resemble that of his uncle Antoine: it early presented examples of the use of force. François Du Plessis, IV, Sieur de Richelieu, was the younger of two brothers. Their father died when the children were small. The elder brother died violently, victim of a neighboring *seigneur* with whom there was a family feud. Honor was invoked, it is reported, through the "vanity" of Françoise de Rochechouart,

François's widowed mother, who recalled her younger son from his ecclesiastical studies to require him to avenge his brother's murder. François fulfilled the assignment: from an ambush in a nearby ditch he watched his neighbor leave his keep; then he emerged, with some retainers, to slay him.[17] This murder has been placed in 1565 or 1566. In the latter year a more important event in the future of the Richelieu family took place. François Du Plessis, now eighteen years old, was married to Suzanne de La Porte, a fifteen-year old girl of nearby Parthenay.[18] By this alliance François acquired an increment in fortune which gave him new opportunities for advancement.

3. François's Career

At the time his marriage contract was signed in 1566, François de Richelieu was an ensign (*guidon*) in the military service of the son of the duc de Montpensier. He had replaced his dead brother in this capacity. The princely Montpensier family was enlisted on the side of the crown against challenges from Protestant separatists on the one side and the extremist anti-Protestantism of the Catholic League on the other. François's uncle, the terrible Antoine "The Monk," was a captain in the same army. François's military service to the Montpensiers continued, perhaps into 1575, when Henri III returned from Poland to succeed Charles IX as King of France. That he had previously accompanied Henri, then Duc d'Anjou, to Poland in 1573, has never been proved. Such an absence, however, would explain the apparent fact that his marriage to Suzanne produced no children until 1578, although the two were first registered as co-domiciled in Paris in 1569.[19]

By 1575 François was acting as *Prévôt de l'Hôtel du Roi*, an office in the king's household. In this capacity he was charged with keeping order in the royal suite and provisioning it, as well as mediating the relationships between crown and town during the peregrinations of the court. When he assumed this post its functions were mostly under control of the powerful duc de Guise, *Grand Maître de France*. In 1577 we find the provost acting as a liaison officer and messenger for the king. In the following year Henri III established François as *Grand Prévôt de France*, combining the provostship of the *Hôtel* with the higher office.[20] In making this appointment the king charged his provost not only with the duties of making advance arrangements for court travels and cleaning up after departures, but also made him chief of police for affairs concerning the king's personal following. "The said grand provost will diligently see to it that justice in his majesty's retinue and court shall be well and faithfully administered," said the ordinance describing the duties of the office.[21] In this capacity François was responsible for enforcement of the king's commands to those in his personal service. His own staff included judges, armed men (archers) and executioners.[22] Richelieu's father continued in this post, first until the death of Henri III in 1589, and afterward, under Henri IV, until the end of his own life in 1590.

As Grand Provost, François de Richelieu bound himself to the service of a king who sometimes felt himself dangerously persecuted, and who was known to be quite often inclined to cruelty. As a personal police agent for Henri, this Richelieu's duties were varied and frequently strenuously taxing. Sometimes they were also unmentionable: In his records of expenditures between 1575 and 1589 there are disbursements for "certain matters concerning his service which the king does not wish to be declared or mentioned."[23]

Of the duties falling to the grand provost that did not have to be concealed, most involved some degree of violence. So zealous was François's service in furthering, and even anticipating, the violent aims of Henri III that a regulation of the *Conseil d'Etat*, the supreme royal administrative board, attempted to limit his discretion by introducing new procedures to be followed in carrying out the king's justice.[24] Manifestly, however, the regulations availed little to restrain this Richelieu, whose performance as the king's policeman earned for him the court nickname of "Tristan the Hermit"—after the fearsome marshall of the sadistic Louis XI.[25]

As an example of these duties, consider a job carried out by François in 1586. Officers of the League had challenged Henri's authority at Montargis and were captured. The grand provost had them put to death on the wheel, then beheaded, and their severed heads exhibited in front of the Louvre, for "Henri III took pleasure in seeing hangings [and] rackings, and always tried to witness executions from some window."[26]

Many of his contemporaries believed that François de Richelieu was one of those who, on orders of Henri III, participated in fatally stabbing the duc de Guise and, later, in killing his brother the cardinal at the château de Blois in 1588. While other accounts indicate that this was not the case, it is certain that he was an accomplice in the plot, facilitated the murders, and helped prevent disturbances after the event.[27] Hearsay information, purporting to have originated with the confessed assassin of Cardinal de Guise, holds that François de Richelieu was among those who refused, when asked by the king, to do that murder.[28] What is known about the grand provost, however, rather suggests that, had he been asked, he would willingly have complied. It is more plausible that this was considered a job for military rather than household officers.

If this Richelieu did not commit the actual murders, he is known to have performed one service connected with them that was, if less daring, more consistent with his usual duties. After the event the duke's dead body lay on the floor, covered by a cloak, for "a good two hours," according to a contemporary. It was then "lifted by the sieur de Richelieu, Grand Provost of France who, by command of the king, had it burned in . . . a downstairs room . . . and the ashes thrown into the river." The same service was later performed for the remains of the duke's brother.[29] It seems that, in this instance, François was not the killer; instead, he was the undertaker.

The day after the murder of the duc de Guise Richelieu was called upon by the king to perform a different kind of deed. With unsheathed sword in hand, followed by a crowd of armed men, he burst into the general assembly of the Estates General, then meeting at Blois, and arrested five leading deputies.[30] It was an act of terror, designed, together with the assassinations, to put opponents of the king in fear of their lives.

François de Richelieu served his master well. The relationship of *maître-fidèle* was supposed to be reciprocal. During those years, however, the king was not always in a position to show appreciation by gifts of money. At the time of the coup against the Guises, in particular, Paris and other important places were held by enemies of the crown. Henri III was attempting, from Touraine, together with his chosen successor, Henri de Navarre, to reconquer his realm. The favors the king had at his disposal were restricted by the emptiness of the royal exchequer. Although Richelieu's salary was raised again and again, he could not always collect it.

It was easier for Henri III to confer less tangible honors. Such, for example, was the upgrading of the title of the office of *Prévôt de l'Hôtel* to *Grand Prévôt de France* in 1578. In 1583 the Richelieu family acquired from the king the rights to the bishopric of Luçon—another mixed benefit. The diocese was one of the smallest and poorest in France. It was, moreover, in a region dominated by a Protestant majority. François's uncle, Jacques Du Plessis, was assigned to act as bishop and as custodian for the family of the doubtful perquisites attached to this office. Again, in 1585, François de Richelieu was made a member, by the king's authority, of the *Ordre du Saint Esprit*, an honorary fraternity created by Henri III himself, limited to a hundred of his most loyal servitors.

The coup against the Guises in the autumn of 1588 was a turning point in the fortunes of the crown party. By eliminating the two most important League leaders, the king disorganized the forces opposed to him. But Henri III was not allowed the time to profit from this opportunity. He too died at an assassin's hands, in the summer of the following year.

The Huguenot Henri de Navarre contrasted with his predecessor in personality as well as religion. The last of the Valois was suspicious, vengeful, and sexually perverse; the first of the Bourbons trusting, forgiving, and womanizing. Despite this contrast, François was one of the very first to take an oath of fidelity to the new king.

At first it seemed that Henri IV would not differ from Henri III in appreciating François de Richelieu's services. He continued him in the duties of Grand Provost. By 1590, however, the new king was seemingly attempting to restrict Richelieu's well-known predilection for severity.[31] In that same year also Henri made a grant to the provost of 20,000 *écus* and appointed him to a captaincy in the royal guards. The large size of this bonus—four or five times the official salary of the provostship—makes it plausible that this was the price for Richelieu's relinquishing his office, even though he apparently continued to perform the function of provost for a time after he was appointed captain. Richelieu's reputation for fierceness may well have led Henri, with his conciliatory strategy, to "kick him upstairs."[32]

Although François died on the battlefield of Gonesse in July of that same year, his death was due to illness. It seems also that the illness had been rather a long one: on May 6, 1590, Henri IV assured his captain in writing "that he will give his widow and his heirs all the gifts he has conferred on him"—a promise that may have been prompted by Richelieu's apprehension that death was approaching.[33]

While François de Richelieu's appointment as guards captain may have represented a decline in power and in the king's confidence, it was a promotion on the social ladder. The position of provost was among the less esteemed of principal offices in the king's personal establishment. As Prévôt de l'Hôtel Richelieu had ranked below such other gentlemen servants of the king as the Maître de l'Hôtel and the Premier Ecuyer, first gentleman of the king's chamber. While Henri III appears to have intended to upgrade Richelieu's status by creating the office of Grand Prévôt de France, the post still ranked last on its higher level, below the chief officers of the king's bedroom, stable, hunt, and table.[34] This anxious king may have hoped, by bestowing an increment in dignity on Richelieu, to increase the provost's capacity to protect him. But then, as now, the non-military enforcer of law and order commanded little respect. Policemen have generally been less honored than officer-soldiers. Executioners receive even less esteem. François de Richelieu's office combined both these functions. Nor did the predilections of Henri III do anything to improve the regard in which they were held. The provost himself was depicted by political enemies as the lowest of the king's retainers, "dragging along the chamber pot."[35]

What the office of Grand Provost lacked in honor, however, it could make up for in material rewards. While it may have been years before salaries or gratuities could be collected, the post itself was considered a richly rewarding one because it offered many opportunities for taking side-payments. The provost had the power, for example, to grant exemptions from sumptuary laws—exemptions for which many courtiers and bourgeois were willing to pay substantial sums. The office included also the right to license and regulate suppliers of bread, wine, meat and fodder to the royal household and to grant the sought-after certificates of maîtrise to tailors and other artisans that allowed them to practice their crafts in Paris. Each of these privileges could be granted in exchange for some consideration. Self-enrichment by such means was the norm.[36]

Traces remain that show Richelieu using these powers of granting and withholding favors. A Guise supporter, for example, reports being warned by the grand provost of his impending arrest by Henri III's "Forty-five," a private body guard.[37] Such opportune information was surely worth some favor in return. The probability that Richelieu trafficked also in commercial favors is suggested by the fact that despite his chronic insolvency he was always able to find money to borrow and third parties to stand as security for loans. Many of these lenders and bondsmen seem to have been persons who stood to benefit from favors he could give.[38] In this manner an officer of the crown acquired a clientele.

A glimpse of this process is given by a letter—one of the few to survive that was written by François de Richelieu himself. In it he responds to an affluent patron—one Antoine de Buisson, Sieur de Bournazel—who has asked for information on his status at court and requested the provost's sponsorship there. Should the petitioner pay out 2,000 *écus* to some unnamed solicitor in order to make sure of favorable consideration? The date is October 28, 1588, during the meeting of the Estates General at Blois, whence comes François's reply:

> Sir: I received the letter which you were pleased to send me by Monsieur de Comblat in response to which I shall add nothing in the way of an account of what is new in this court, relying for that on his ability, having told him everything I thought you should know, and assuring you further that having well considered the present situation, neither he nor I have dared to speak of your affairs, being aware that the climate (*saison*) is not right for it. It seems to me one must wait and see what comes of all these meetings. I advise you also to hold on to those two thousand *écus*. My opinion is that you should by no means be charged with that and that you have given enough service elsewhere. The king and everyone attached to the court are well satisfied with you, as you have always behaved admirably. I say this being certain that, if we carry on patiently, time will give us the means to show our gratitude (*reconnoistre*) to people like you.

The last paragraph shows the relationship between the writer and his correspondent:

> I thank you humbly for the horses that you send me. My means are not, at the moment, sufficient for their purchase. Grant, if you will, consideration of me and those who depend on me, begging you further to believe that you will never in this world command anyone who is readier to render you service than
> François Du Plessis[39]

Apparently the grand provost, conscious of his debt to this rich client, is by no means unwilling to advance the latter's cause at a proper occasion. In the meantime he accepts a loan of horses, perhaps for his personal use, certainly on account. Indeed, in the *maître-fidèle* relationship, once the favor was accepted, a payment of the kind desired by its giver was owed.

4. François's Personality

A. "Tristan the Hermit"

A grand provost ought to be discreet, loyal, ruthless, and inured to violence. François de Richelieu was the right man for such a job; only overzealousness with respect to the last two characteristics ever threatened to lose him the gratitude of the kings who employed him. The few letters he left, together with contemporary testimony, throw slight additional light on his character. The intelligence reflected by his letters is overlaid by an abrupt style expressing taciturnity and severity. An example of his "brusque frankness," in Deloche's term, is the following complaint to the duc de Guise declining to comply with his request for a favor. Guise wished restrictions placed on the garrisoning of royal troops in certain cities. Richelieu rejects the request as contrary to his orders and prejudicial to the king's interest:

> I should be sorry, Monseigneur, if anyone in this realm had a greater desire to obey your commands than I, but . . . I would be too remiss if I exceeded the instructions I have in a matter that would affect the good of His Majesty's service and your own charge. Besides this, you yourself participated in the decision you are now asking me to revise. . . . In any case I shall not fail to execute diligently the assignment that has been given me and if, thereafter, there should arise from this any problems, no one will be able to blame me for them.[40]

Richelieu's interest in remaining loyal to the king rather than obliging the duke is certainly understandable. His letter, however, lacks terms of grace or charm that would temper an impression of harsh rigidity—an impression consistent with the nickname that suggests one who is sombre and unyielding. The impression is further strengthened by another scrap of contemporary evidence: François figures in a satirical list of fictitious characterizations as "translator from the Latin" of a work on innocence designed to console martyrs.[41] This seems to accuse the grand provost not only of inhumanity, and, possibly, corruption, in carrying out the persecutions of Henri III, but also of a lack of high culture.

At the same time, the letter bespeaks a man of action—and of few words. His duties called for action to a high degree, and it was as a man of action that he acquired a distinctive—if not very savory—reputation. In later years, when the cardinal would deprecate "mere words" and praise, instead, "results," he was, in effect, extolling the virtues of a paternal model.

B.   Monumental Improvidence

Of all those who have written on François de Richelieu, not one has failed to notice the financial distress which chronically beset him. This conspicuous insolvency presents a puzzle. We have seen the grand provost willing to take advantage of the exceptional opportunities for pecuniary gain that his office offered. Yet none of his many efforts at self-enrichment ever seems to have succeeded in improving his position. Indeed, despite several financial advantages—his patrimony and a rich wife, as well as his lucrative post—the scale of his ruin became notorious in his lifetime. Both kings who employed him showed themselves aware of his money problems: Henri III recognized that "his grand provost Richelieu has insufficient wages for his support."[42] Henri IV took note of François's anxiety for his family's future after his death.[43]

It is true that sixteenth-century norms encouraged a certain amount of financial incompetence in gentlemen. The notion that business acumen was alien to nobility was in part a survival of the belief that the duties of the warrior are incompatible with "money-grubbing." In part also disdain for such concerns was encouraged by the Catholic renovation.[44] Yet many was the aristocrat of the time who managed to augment an acquired fortune by prudent management. Certainly not every *seigneur* conducted his affairs in such a way as to bring ruin to his family.

At the time of François's betrothal his prospect for winning fortune as well as glory seemed favorable. He was not only the sole surviving son of his father but also the prospective heir of his two uncles.[45] Suzanne de La Porte brought to the marriage more than the promise of a share in the property of her illustrious, successful father. She already possessed, as her mother's heiress, a substantial fortune in her own name. It is probable, moreover, that François de La Porte's largesse toward his only daughter was not confined to the terms of the marriage settlement. One report maintains that he made himself entirely responsible for the support of the young couple for the first three years of their marriage.[46] It seems certain that he produced the money necessary to buy the *Prévôté de l'Hôtel* to which Richelieu was appointed some time around 1574. The marquis de Montglat writes that with the "great sum of money" given him by La Porte, Richelieu "paid his debts and acceded to the post of Grand Provost."[47] Despite these bright initial prospects, and despite a marriage contract designed to protect the integrity of Suzanne's property, her rich holdings were alienated early in the marriage.[48] After dissipating his wife's fortune, Richelieu went on to mortgage most of his own patrimony.

Not all responsibility for these losses can be laid at the grand provost's door. At the time of his betrothal, the Richelieu estate was considerably encumbered. One provision in the marriage contract called for immediate payment of a part of the dowry to Françoise de Rochechouart, the bridegroom's mother. This has been attributed to her urgent need. Indeed, it has been assumed by most biographers that only dire financial necessity would have induced the "haughty" dowager to accept the downward step on the social ladder that an alliance with the La Portes represented.[49] In addition to prior charges against his estate, there would be important costs attached to the posts François was to fill in the royal establishment. Even with the initial purchase price of the provostship paid by his father-in-law, the cost of elevation to the post of *Grand Prévôt de France* may account for the disappearance of some of the family fortune. Further, high officers in the king's personal following were required to supply themselves with splendid attire—an exceptional financial burden. Beyond this, however, Richelieu threw himself into the life of the court in another way which was probably costly: he had a mistress there.[50]

None of these expenses, however, could plausibly have been so great as to be ruinous. The lucrative nature of the provostship alone should have more than offset such occupational costs; Deloche found that François's second in command, one Lugolly, succeeded in making a fortune from his post.[51] Yet, in spite of his readiness to serve ruthlessly and to seize opportunities, and in spite of the expressed gratitude of the two kings he served, Richelieu left his affairs "furiously embroiled."[52] So indebted did he become that a contemporary credited him with nearly extinguishing the family title. He died "so poor for his station in life . . . that he would have been the last sieur de Richelieu if Suzanne de La Porte had not restored his house by the good management she provided for the disorder in which he left his affairs."[53] He left creditors and liabilities so numerous that they would be a constant threat throughout the lifetime of his widow and of his eldest son, Henri. Thereafter they continued to press the surviving sister and brothers until, through political influence, Armand de Richelieu was finally able to bring an end to the pressure.[54] The grand provost's self-impoverishment was on so grand a scale that it calls for further explanation.

It seems not to have been considered important before that François de Richelieu was a constant speculator. Many documents show that he bought and sold IOUs of third parties. The unflattering account attributed to Jean Du Bouchet clearly implies that François was addicted to gambling. His new appointment as Grand Provost, it reports,

> caused him to throw himself into shares (*partis*). . . . The House of Richelieu was ruined by the speculations in which he engaged and all his property was sold by degrees.[55]

Sometimes Suzanne, his wife, was co-signer in these transactions. Her connections probably helped fend off multiplying financial difficulties. Sometimes the provost was involved in several loans in a single day. Investments of which records survive suggest his passion for high risks in hope of great gain. Perceiving this, Deloche comments on purchases of shares in future ship's booty:

> The most tempting of all [games] was that in which the ante was small compared with the enormous gain promised by fairy-tale descriptions of gold fields. . . . [It was] a game which catered to all passions and the most demanding imagination.[56]

Various pieces of evidence suggest that the "game" which appealed to Richelieu's "passions" was not only chronic involvement in get-rich-quick schemes, but actual gambling games. A speculative purchase of title to a ship and its quick resale to the king was one of a long train of transactions, any of which could have been arrived at in the course of settling up after an evening of cards. Indeed, on the eve of Henri III's fatal stabbing (which took place on August 1, 1589), Richelieu is reported to have begun a card game in princely company that continued until four the following morning.[57] Tending further to confirm a weakness for betting games is the fact that few of Richelieu's complicated financial transactions were for outright purchase or sale of real property, nor have records been found showing his purchase of the right to any office.[58] Investment in such assets could be very profitable, but their transfer, hedged by legal restrictions or requiring royal approval, could not be effected at the gaming table.

Court *mores* invited gambling. The new king Henri IV was an avid patron of gambling games. Accounts abound of fortunes won and lost during a single evening. "At the time," writes Deloche, "gambling was in everyone's bones."[59] Nevertheless, most managed to keep the temptation within bounds.

The constant travel required of the grand provost, coupled with the backroom atmosphere in which he usually found himself while obliged to wait in attendance on the king's comings and goings, would appear especially dangerous for one inclined to gambling. It is claimed that François de Richelieu's trip to England in the royal service netted him a gain of 4,000 francs—presumably from lucky wagers.[60] But most of Richelieu's ventures failed.

One undocumented story relates that after François de Richelieu's death the straitened circumstances of his family forced them to sell the emblem of one of his highest honors, the distinctive gold necklace and the cross of the *Ordre du Saint Esprit*.[61] This tale strains credulity: selling or pawning the insignia of such a sign of royal favor would be too public an act and too unseemly for a widow to risk. If indeed the decoration disappeared, it is more likely that Richelieu himself had earlier ventured it as collateral—and lost.

In any case, virtually all the properties which comprised his children's inheritance were alienated or encumbered over the years in order to pay

François's debts. Without additional testimony, the guess that this resulted from gambling by the elder Richelieu remains unconfirmed. Should evidence eventually corroborate that guess, however, it would add to the grand provost's well-documented history of monumental improvidence a weakness which was a cause for family shame.

Under "Forbidden Games" a moral arbiter of Cardinal Richelieu's epoch discusses the iniquity of gambling:

> Dice games and card games and those like them in which winning depends chiefly on chance are not only dangerous recreations . . . but . . . by nature wicked. . . . That is why they are forbidden by civil as well as ecclesiastical law. . . . Gain which ought to be the reward of industry is made the prize of fate. . . . These games . . . are . . . violent occupations . . . holding the mind in thrall. . . . Is there any sadder, more depressing and melancholy attention than that of gamblers?[62]

While carelessness and ignorance with respect to money matters could be appreciated in nobles, and condoned by them, an addiction to gambling was a vice. And what was a vicious, but pardonable, habit in a great prince or lord could bring disgrace on a family of poor nobility with a tenuous hold on aristocratic status.

4 Richelieu's Mother and Her Family

Petite bourgeoise that she was, she must have found herself much troubled in that House of Richelieu, filled even more by pretensions than by titles and offices.[1]

A growing disposition to acknowledge the importance of mothers for their sons' development has not led, so far as biographers of Armand de Richelieu are concerned, either to much attention to the influence exerted on him from Madame de Richelieu's side of the family nor to careful analysis of the character of Suzanne herself. It is puzzling that the important achievements of the La Porte-Meillerayes have not attracted more attention to the qualities of mind they possessed. It is also hard to explain why the evidence on Suzanne as an individual has not been connected with the cultural tradition of her father's house.

Biographers have, on the other hand, frequently stressed the tension between the recent bourgeois origins of the La Porte-Meillerayes and the Richelieus' claim to noble descent from warrior-gentlemen. It is no doubt on account of that "profoundly military" cast of seventeenth-century society noted by Mousnier that a historian of the Richelieus speculates on how much the "misalliance" of her son with "the *robe*"—that is, with a family of lawyers—must have "tortured" the status-proud mother of François de Richelieu.[2]

Inattention to Suzanne de La Porte herself is still more remarkable. We have already noted the tribute paid her by a contemporary for recouping the family fortunes by her good management. Her son's favorite genealogist even went so far as to give her credit for being "one of the wisest and most virtuous ladies of the age."[3] Yet the most judicious of Richelieu's biographers chooses to accept a description of her as "simple and sweet like a dove."[4] Aside from her "prudence" and taste for "order," her char-

45

acter has remained virtually untouched, even by one who had access to most of her surviving letters.[5] Here it will be the aim to appraise the distinctive cultural heritage, the outlook, and the personality of the woman with whom Richelieu spent his earliest years—his mother. For this, the first approach is through appraisal of her antecedents, especially of her father and his family.

1.   The La Porte-Meillerayes: A Family of the Robe

When François Du Plessis, Sieur de Richelieu, was committed, as a boy of eighteen, to marry the fifteen-year-old Suzanne de La Porte he could look forward to significantly improved life-prospects. Not only could he expect important monetary gains from the alliance; he could also anticipate, from his father-in-law's influence in high places, new opportunities to advance his career. For, according to a fellow Poitevin, François de La Porte was not merely a successful advocate in the Parlement de Paris, but "one of the most illustrious lawyers of the sixteenth century."[6] While local patriotism may have inspired this judgment, there was much in La Porte's career to support the evaluation.

Armand de Richelieu's maternal grandfather came from a long-established Poitevin family. If there were apothecaries and even lesser artisans among his near antecedents, such connections would not have been considered stigmata by many in the rural Poitou of the time.[7] In the civil turmoil of the last half of the sixteenth century, success in trade could lead to rapid social advancement. Crown commissions were bought and sold without need to show credentials of ancient noble standing. Raoul de La Porte, father of François, had been a tax collector for a local prince.[8] Jehan de La Porte, reputedly a brother of François, was a mere Poitevin *notaire* who acted on behalf of a Poitiers crown offical to levy quotas on surrounding parishes. The year 1575 found him, as Tallemant reports he learned at first hand, dealing in grain and pigeons.[9]

In no more than two generations it was possible for commercial success to be translated into upper class notability. This was the case, for example, with the Pidoux, a family that had a social history similar to that of the La Portes and friendship connections with them. A Pierre Pidoux died *Trésorier de France* at Poitiers in 1581. He too was originally a merchant and, succeeding in business, became mayor of the provincial capital. To obtain the post of local treasurer of the crown he was said to have paid 50,000 *livres*. He was doubtless a relation of the François Pidoux who was contemporaneously royal physician and who had provided François de Richelieu with his first court assignment. The son of this doctor was Jean Pidoux who succeeded his father as court physician. His service, like that of François de La Porte and his sons, extended into the reign of Henri IV. It is said that this king employed Jean "in the capacity of negotiator in his most important affairs."[10] By 1615 another Monsieur Pidoux had become, as Sieur de Malaguet, an honored Poitevin leader and hero, halting by his "zeal" the depredations of Condé's army, rampaging in the neighborhood.[11]

The step from commerce to noble status was made easier still by following the path to the position of *avocat*.[12] François de La Porte acquired his legal learning at the University of Poitiers. Like so many promising young men, he made an advantageous marriage. His first wife, Claude Bochard, Suzanne de La Porte's mother, brought a considerable dowry which included territories in Picardy. Among her maternal ancestors were some of higher status than any among the La Porte antecedents: in the female line she could point to progenitors equal in antique nobility to those claimed by the Du Plessis-Richelieus.[13]

François de La Porte's promise was amply justified by the event: he became one of France's most influential lawyers—legal advisor to the king and arbiter of professional training. "He shone in Paris," it is reported, "with all the talents that make a great man." While his compatriot's further claim that "he was the Oracle whom all France consulted"[14] may be somewhat exaggerated, La Porte's abilities do, in fact, seem to have won him high consideration at court. He became one of the chief consultants on legislation aimed at strengthening the control of the crown over French administration and the transfer of private property. He helped to draft the *Ordonnance d'Orléans* of 1560 which restricted venality in appointments to judicial office and curtailed freedom of testamentary disposition. It also limited the powers of the clergy over the temporal domain.[15] Curiously, and perhaps significantly, it included a provision requiring a bishop who did not reside in his diocese to forfeit its temporal revenues. Nearly fifty years later this requirement would oblige Armand de Richelieu, as the new bishop, to take up residency in the diocese of Luçon.

La Porte is said also to have had a part in drawing up the *Ordonnance de Moulins* (1566), a broad administrative reform that had the effect of centralizing authority and further concentrating it in the monarchy. Additionally, he is given credit for helping to compile the Code of Henri III, of which Barnabé Brisson, his friend and fellow Poitevin, is the attributed author.[16] A contemporary account credits Brisson with having co-sponsored, with François de La Porte, the early career of young François de Richelieu.[17]

Like most occupational skills of early modern times, legal specialization was a family affair. At least two of François de La Porte's brothers were lawyers. When François had two sons from his second marriage—Amador and Charles—they also were trained in the law. Suzanne's maternal grandfather, too, was a lawyer.[18]

The family's worldly status was further improved when one of the La Porte uncles came into possession of the estate and name of La Meilleraye, and by making Charles de La Porte his heir, introduced into the family the title of Marquis de La Meilleraye. Henri III showed his gratitude to the La Porte-Meillerayes by bestowing upon them the highest honors within his discretion. François de La Porte, counsel to the Order of Malta, was made a councillor of the king. His son, Charles de La Meilleraye, was a member of the Order of the Holy Spirit before François de Richelieu received that reward.[19] Thus the more nobly-born young officer followed his in-laws in distinctions, rather than preceding these social inferiors.

Amador de La Porte, the other son of François, became a chevalier of the Order of Malta. The "Commander," as such officers of this naval fraternity were called, was also a lawyer and, like his father, close to the king. We find Henri IV making a familiar reference to this La Porte at a time when the latter was conducting a legal appeal on behalf of Henri de Richelieu, Armand's oldest brother.[20] This uncle stood, after François de Richelieu's death, *in loco parentis* to his half-sister's brood, and he alone, of the relatives in his generation, outlived his famous nephew.

As important for Richelieu's future as the rapid rise in authority and status of the La Porte-Meillerayes was the effect on his character of their personal attributes. First of these, of course, were the intellectual qualities that contributed to their success. These will be examined later as they were shown by the two La Portes who most closely affected Armand—Suzanne and Amador. Here, however, one unusual feature of intellect may be noted as it appeared in their father, about whom less is known: François de La Porte was renowned as a teacher. His reputation on this score, apparently, made his "office . . . a veritable School of Jurisprudence." Many lawyers, it is reported, sat at the feet of this grandfather of the cardinal because of a "talent for teaching" he was seen to possess. This talent seems to have been owed in part to an exceptionally ingratiating quality: the "kindness and courtesy"[21] attributed to him in his professional relations are not characteristics commonly identified with effective law teachers in any age.

2. Suzanne de La Porte: A Woman of the "Noblesse Moyenne"

Only one document is known to survive in which Richelieu himself gives a view of his mother to a third person. Although this is a copied, truncated version of a letter written to his brother Alphonse, informing him of their mother's death, it is nevertheless interesting that he perceives her as victim:

> My dear brother, I greatly regret that you must learn from this letter the common loss we have had of our poor mother, although I am sure that . . . [in the other world] God has allotted her as many favors, consolations and pleasures as she had received in this one of frustrations, afflictions, and bitternesses.[22]

In the course of her married life Suzanne de La Porte had encountered many setbacks that could have been the cause of those "frustrations, afflictions, and bitternesses" to which her son refers. But of these, financial distress was the most obviously burdensome and persistent. The particular kind of "wisdom" which Du Chesne and others attributed to her was preeminently visible in her capacity, widowed as she was before the age of forty with five dependent children, to cope with the crushing burden of indebtedness which Captain Richelieu had bequeathed to his family.

There remains also only one known letter written by Armand to his mother. It too is concerned with her financial plight. He replies to her thanks for his offer of support and shelter, an offer tendered after the last income that allowed her to remain at Richelieu had been cut off. He does so, he says, "entirely voluntarily," expressing his appreciation of her success in rescuing his personal fortune:

> I offer myself cheerfully for the solace of your old age, relieving you from the high cost of the house in which you live. I offer myself both out of duty and out of inclination; out of duty as having received from you both life and property (*biens*).[23]

The credit Richelieu here gives his mother for good financial management is not inconsistent with her aristocratic status, although she may well have owed her ability to a bourgeois upbringing. The norm that made it slightly disreputable for noblemen to show much skill in advancing their pecuniary interests applied with less force to noblewomen. These could, quite honorably, have a head for affairs which their male counterparts were supposed to lack. Saint Vincent de Paul, for example, credited his well-born assistant, Louise de Marillac, with a gift for administration and finance that most men of her status did not possess. To give a male cleric control over the treasury of her religious order would, he thought, be a misstep: "Experience shows us," he wrote, "that it is absolutely necessary that women not be subordinate to men in such matters, especially for the treasury."[24]

Suzanne herself shared the view of her contemporaries that upper class women were better able than men to deal with money matters. She wrote to her daughter-in-law, a lady of fortune, high breeding, and princely connections, to thank her for disposing of a piece of property which had been a headache in the Richelieu family. "My dear daughter," she begins:

> I have seen what you sent me showing what you did about Le Caragnan. I am very happy that it is sold. If the matter had fallen into your hands earlier, my business would have been much better conducted, because there is nothing like women for taking good care of matters like that. If my son had only dropped one word in writing at the beginning, it would have been sold. Never mind—since it's over and done with I thank you for the trouble you have taken.[25]

As head of the family Henri's authority must be deferred to, but for actually conducting business there's nothing like a woman.

Armand was not the only Richelieu man to agree with Suzanne that women had special aptitude for financial management. His brother Henri shared the opinion. After Henri's loss of the wife whom Suzanne congratulated on her business sense, he answers a friend's letter of condolence in words that show that he, too, appreciated this characteristic. He writes not only of the "true affection we bore one another," but also of the additional merit his wife gave the relationship by the "infinity of affairs which she managed with such order and prudence."[26] Before his marriage he had written at least once to his brother Armand of the need he felt to bring "order" to these "affairs."[27]

Confidence in the ability of women to administer financial matters was later to be shown by Armand de Richelieu in his professional concerns. In a series of letters he wrote from his diocese of Luçon he gave a certain Madame de Bourges the power of factotum in purchasing objects for his establishment (and advancing the money for them), for representing his interests in a legal matter, and for selecting, leasing and furnishing a dwelling for him in Paris.[28] Later he was to use Madame Bouthillier, wife of his close friend and assistant, for the same purpose.

Richelieu's confidence in feminine skill in financial management could well have originated in his observation of his mother's role in extricating the family's affairs from the desperate condition in which they were left by her husband. When François de Richelieu died in August 1590 the family inherited a mass of debts so enormous and so confused that it would plague his widow all her life. Of the nearly two dozen letters of Suzanne which are known to have been preserved, several are concerned with her strategy in coping with this legacy. It is in this context that her culture and character emerge most clearly.

One of the earliest of these letters, written twelve years after her husband's death, is illustrative not only of Suzanne's perspectives and personality, but also of her relationship with her seventeen-year old son Armand. She writes to one of her creditors—like many others, a family acquaintance—summarizing the bleak prospect before her:

> I beg you to believe that I have as much regret and distress as you can have had inconvenience at the long patience you have been obliged to have in waiting for what is owed to Monsieur your father by the late Monsieur de Richelieu. But my creditors, having had all my children's property seized and rented out, have deprived me of the means to extricate myself from this affair as promptly as I had resolved to do in order to pay everyone something on account.
>
> I do not want to prevent you from bringing whatever prosecution or lawsuit you please, but only to tell you that the leasing of my children's property being already a fact, you could not do so

without difficulties which would serve nothing but to cause you loss and inconvenience.

We are in the process of getting advice on means to sell the royal domains and other income property left by the late M. de Richelieu, in order to pay creditors. I will do what is within my power so that you may be paid in good order, and I shall use all the diligence of which I am capable on your behalf, desiring to show you, and also Monsieur your father, that I am your very devoted and desirous to serve,

Suzanne de La Porte

The young Armand de Richelieu, then in Paris preparing, as the marquis Du Chillou, for a military career, was brought by his mother into this picture of stringency as the proposer of a propitiatory gesture—the only kind it was in the family's power to make. Suzanne's postscript relates:

My son Du Chillou writes to his brother that you would like to have some greyhounds. If you will send your lackey ahead when you come I will present you with a pair.[29]

No doubt this participation of Armand in the common problem of finances was not the first time he had helped his mother to ward off threats to the family by using reason and propitiation to conciliate those who were beleaguering them. It certainly was not the last.

In seeking, in those of her letters that remain, indications of Suzanne de La Porte's personal qualities, one may determine those expressions individual to her only by first identifying those typical of her milieu. These last are dominated by the theme of protecting and advancing Richelieu family interest. The survival of her immediate family is her persistent concern. This survival depends, in the first instance, on continuity of the lineage and, secondly, on the solidarity of family members in the face of adversity. In her concern with these two aims there is no reason to suppose that she was not striving for objectives that most women of her time, place and station would have pursued.

Suzanne's preoccupation with the continuity of her family focuses on the continuity of the lineage, in the first instance, and, secondly, on the solidarity of family members in the face of adversity.

The desire that the family line be uninterrupted was one cause of her concern for her eldest son's safety and his wife's fertility. Henri, by 1608 the only Richelieu brother not in holy orders, married late to a childless widow, Marguerite de Charmeaux.[30] The fervent wish that the marriage would produce an heir is a prominent theme of Suzanne's letters to her daughter-in-law, "who, with the help of God, will restore this House." She hopes for "your health which I desire you conserve in order to give me a handsome son when mine returns which I hope will be soon." She prays

God "with all my heart that He . . . gives me the grace of seeing you pregnant with a handsome son,"[31] and "I await His goodness to you in giving you a little son to be my cane in old age."[32] On hearing that Marguerite, after spending time with her husband, has been indisposed, Suzanne was "hopeful that you may have begun, because I am told that when you are pregnant you experience some discomfort." She adds what must already have been evident to the younger woman, "If it were that I would greatly rejoice."[33]

Children in the female line are by no means as important, even if they are as dearly loved. In a grief-stricken letter to Marguerite Suzanne reports the death of Françoise, her elder daughter, but she makes no reference to the plight of the two children of Françoise's marriage. Instead she voices increased concern for the safety of her eldest son, the soldier. Nicole, Suzanne's youngest child, was living with her mother during the whole period bridged by the letters, yet they contain not a single reference to her.

Equally characteristic of family perspectives common to the social class to which Suzanne belonged was the interchangeability of persons in performing roles which remained fixed. As a widow, Suzanne writes to her daughter-in-law how grateful she is to God for preserving her son "because he is the husband of both of us," just as Marguerite is "another myself."[34]

The religious culture reflected by Suzanne's letters seems also to have been unexceptional for her status and locale. Her religious perspectives have a starkness that perhaps shows the influence of Calvinism. In fact, though church records show she was a practicing Catholic, there were Protestants in her immediate family.[35] An average noblewoman, she gave no sign, in religious outlook, of the mystical zeal of the *dévotes* of her time, those female Catholic reformers so important in that age. On the other hand, her faith was devoid of the archaisms characteristic of belief among classes lower down in the social order.

As in the beliefs of the Catholic minor aristocracy of the Artesian region during the same period, Suzanne's devotion focussed on a single, father-like deity.[36] Jesus is never mentioned in her letters, any more than is the third component of the Holy Trinity. *"Notre Dame"* appears only once, because Marguerite has been to her shrine at Ardillers (presumably to pray for a son). As with the Artesian noblemen, too, "folkloricization" is absent. Her religious beliefs are simple: God is an all powerful force for justice who punishes the wicked and rewards the virtuous.

But Suzanne stresses God's power more than his benevolence. Thus she begins, "He is good; He will pity us," but continues by emphasizing his omnipotence: "He is the God of battles; He gives the victory to whom he pleases."[37] And, while she trusts that "because He is just," God will not long delay punishing the soldiers of the prince de Condé's army who, thinking themselves godlike, behave like devils, yet "I don't think He has reached that point yet."[38] Indeed, God renders justice in his own time; at the moment the enemy is gaining: "They have just come to tell me that Monsieur le Prince is at La Rochelle."[39]

Thus, while God's chastisements are terrible and immediate, reward comes to the virtuous chiefly in heaven. Here on earth our main hope must be to ward off disaster. When her beloved daughter dies it is because "it has pleased God to call her to Himself and withdraw her from the miseries of this world in order to make her blessed." She adds, "I believe her so because, since she is dead, I may tell you that she was very good and virtuous." Silence on the subject of Françoise's virtues did not avail to protect her while she lived. The blow of her death is perhaps a punishment of Suzanne herself inflicted by an angry God. One can only attempt to propitiate Him. As she hoped the gift of greyhounds might appease the vengeance of her creditor, so she hopes God will be satisfied by the sacrifice of Françoise: "I pray the good Lord that he may be content with this chastisement and that he will preserve what remains to us which is my dear son."[40]

Although free and omnipotent, God may choose to be moved by prayer. "I pray constantly for my son," she writes, and assures herself that Marguerite is not stinting either on prayers for Henri, because "I believe they will be more readily listened to than mine because you are much better than I." When she learns she is to be allowed to meet her daughter-in-law before she dies she notes, "God is, then, willing to give me this grace, as I have always begged him."[41]

Unlike Muchembled's Artesian nobility (who were, however, all men), Suzanne mentions neither the king nor the monarchy, nor indeed any political figures except as their behavior impinges on the safety of members of her family or their dependents. Yet it is possible that the likening of God's rule in heaven to the king's on earth, so typical of her culture, was also an analogy present in her mind.

Dependents play an important part in Suzanne's letters. The nuclear family of the early modern *noblesse* was surrounded by a circle of supporters to whom protection was owed in return for service. The interests of this entourage were solidary with those of the family. As a result, communications often seem less personal than collective. François de Richelieu, for example, asks in a letter considered earlier, for "consideration of me and all those who depend upon me."[42] In Suzanne's correspondence, too, this intertwining of family interests with those of dependents is frequently evident. To Marguerite she writes:

> I'm so put out that I don't know what I am about, as they have just killed my poor needleman whom I was sending to my son Luçon. . . . It afflicts me greatly to be the cause of his death.[43]

Of a similiar victimization of some of Marguerite's dependents during the invasion by Condé's troops, Suzanne fears that he may "treat us as badly as you tell me he has treated your subjects:"

> It makes me feel great pity and great sorrow that you have had the pain of seeing them afflicted in that fashion. Truly, a thing like that greatly affects the people to whom they belong.[44]

Responsibility lies heavily on the shoulders of one who has promised protection to a large group.

Except for her expressions of moral deference to her daughter-in-law, there is little in Suzanne de Richelieu's personal correspondence to support the attribution which has sometimes been made to her of a modesty arising from consciousness of her inferior social status. Those aspects of Suzanne's culture which have been considered here do not hint at a sense of social incapacity or inadequacy. Her concern for her dependents—tenants, children, servants—bespeaks a country *châtelaine* accustomed to authority and to the organization of a considerable landed establishment. Her allusions to great noblemen (Monsieur le Prince and the duc de Guise and his wife) disclose no sign that she regarded them with exceptional respectfulness. In the early years of her marriage Suzanne had become familiar with the ways of the royal court as a lady in waiting to Queen Louise, wife of Henri III.[45] This was an appointment she could as well have owed to her father's credit with the king as to her husband's family connections. If underneath there was a *bourgeoise* with a consciousness of deference due her "social betters," there is nothing in her letters to indicate this. On the contrary, they point to a person reared in a proud and confident tradition whose apprehensions have mainly to do with real, substantial threats to her family's welfare, coming from the world outside.

On the other hand, if the cultural perspective of Suzanne's letters is unremarkable for the *noblesse moyenne* to which her family belonged, there is also much in them that is not typical of the correspondence of like-situated women of her day. Her descriptions of her own emotions and of her performance suggest an unusual personality for a woman of her station.

3. Suzanne's Personality: Affects, Skills, Expectations

Spontaneous expressions of sympathy—in contrast with formal expressions of solicitude and condolence—are uncommon in early seventeenth century correspondence, especially in feminine correspondence. Women were, perhaps, as likely as men to express compassionate thoughts, but these were likely to be phrased in stilted, stereotyped forms. Women were generally less competent at self-expression: their letters reveal their inferior education, and Suzanne de La Porte is no exception in this. Nevertheless, as in the description of her afflictions in the letters just cited, her style has spontaneity that gives her outbursts unusual force. In another letter she tells the daughter-in-law she has not yet met not to fear, just because she has not received a letter, that she may have given some cause for annoyance. "You never have done so," she writes: "Furthermore, I love and honor you too much for you to think you could ever vex me—given that your disposition is not of that kind."[46] Suzanne begs her to "believe that I bear your troubles and anxieties," and "pray the good Lord soon to bring you out of them." Of the damage to Marguerite's tenants, "I share your feelings at their loss, because you could never have pain in which I do not participate, for I don't love my friends by halves." After her daughter-in-law's first visit has finally taken place Suzanne expresses, in a postscript, a sociable sentiment so warm that it is scarcely again to be met with before Madame de Sévigné: "I find so much to talk about in your company that I cannot readjust to my solitude."[47]

Nor is her solicitude confined to her household. The warmth of Suzanne's feelings for others is expressed not only for herself and her dependents but also for friends whose plight touches her. She awaits news of her neighbor, M. de Germigny, who is engaged in a lawsuit which "worries me to death." Of another acquaintance who is suffering from heavy charges: "They are devouring that man whose wife has been ill for four months." She hopes for a marriage advantageous to another young neighbor:

> He has gone to Coulombiers where he is doing everything he
> can to find out the decision, because his father doesn't want him
> to embark on anything in full view of everyone if he is to be
> dismissed in the end. Because I love him, I hope it will come
> about.[48]

Suzanne's wide acquaintance and the equally wide range of her curiosity and sympathy are expressively evoked in her correspondence. One long letter to a son—probably Henri—is filled with gossip about the local gentry:

> They say that there is an old Mme. de Cremille, grandmother of
> La Morynieres, whom they're talking of marrying to Aubespin
> from Chinon. If that were true it would be no child's play! But I
> can't believe it—the world is mad. There was also a rumor that
> old La Roche Du Mayne wanted to pay court to Madame de
> Goulaine.[49]

Most striking about Suzanne's character, as revealed in her letters, is her unflagging activity in attempting to influence the course of events as they affect her family and its possessions. A fatalistic resignation characteristic of much early seventeenth century feminine correspondence is lacking in her repertoire. Only when she is sure she has left no stone unturned to advance the interests she has espoused does she relax her efforts. Usually she is continually planning strategy and tactics to improve the family position.

Much of the practical bent shown by Madame de Richelieu's letters is directed toward implementing legal processes. Arguments used in the law are clearly familiar and come naturally to her. A long, complicated dispute with a neighbor over Henri's property rights is the subject of several letters. In one of these, legal reasoning animates the account that she is "glad" at last "to have the leisure to write" to her son. Henri's tenant has built a wall on the common boundary and the neighboring owners have knocked it down and threatened to go to court to prevent its being rebuilt. These have, however, reconsidered, as Suzanne informs her son, and both "father and son have pulled in their horns." She analyzes systematically the weakness of each of the complainants' arguments:

> After they heard what people were saying they thought that if it were to end in a law suit, all things considered, they would lose, because the right would be found on your side. It could not be otherwise, as Maître Gil assured your brother, because the wall can only be placed were it is; otherwise there could have been no way for a wagon to pass. As to what their memorandum says—that formerly the tenants had none—this is not prejudicial because . . . those others had not the means and didn't concern themselves so much with the security of their farm. . . . As for the complaint they make that their own wall was knocked down—he admits it was only dry stones, thrown up to obstruct the animals. They are simply seeking some kind of justification for what they destroyed. All this amounts to nothing now, and they are brought round to reason.[50]

Suzanne's strategy in the legal contests in which she and her family are frequently involved is to secure or reinforce the good will of those in a position to help her side. In her letters to her sons the means she devises for enlisting such support are sometimes quite complex. One person able to influence a case in which the Richelieus were involved had traded his horse to one of their dependents in return for a mare whose poor condition was concealed. The mare died even before it could be used. Madame de Richelieu has planned a way to make amends so that there will be no adverse consequences for her family:

> I asked Larefrere . . . to tell him, as though on his initiative, that he had learned that she [the mare] was dead and that he was giving him back his horse . . . preferring that the loss fall upon himself rather than on [the other]. . . . He told me this would be done tomorrow. It would have made a bad odor to have cheated him like that. The others would have been delighted at it.[51]

In planning strategy to bolster one's side, thoroughness is the key. The son of the victim of the bad mare bargain is being courted by the other side in order to induce him to take an action contrary to Richelieu interests. It is Suzanne's opinion that a representative of their family should be sent to see him to prevent it, especially because the rights of the one would be at the expense of the other.[52] She learns, however, that her son has not advised dispatching such an emissary: "If it were my affair, I would have sent him, because once having started a good business, if it fails to succeed only for lack of that, the loss of the money aside, it is worth while to venture fifteen or twenty *écus* to be relieved of this anxiety."[53]

A sense of equity is to be seen in her conception of legal justice. She is quick in judicial matters to identify the *quid pro quo* concept of fairness. The neighbor who destroyed Henri's tenant's fence will have to restore it. Not prudence only but justice requires restitution for the dead mare: "It would have seemed bad to him and he would have been right."[54] Essential to Suzanne's planning of tactics and strategy is the care she takes to be informed and to inform others. Her letters show a drive to speed up communication and a preoccupation with proper timing. "My son," she writes, "I greatly regret that that stupid nag wasn't speedier, in order that before the plaintiffs acknowledged their mistake I could have had the news from you so that all the rest could have been brought out without delay." Again, "I had the idea of sending Cry to Sieur Du Pont to speak to him about it, but I thought I would first have an answer to my letter, which I certainly would have if that rascal had hurried up as he said he would." And, "it will hold me up a good deal to wait for assurance" on a certain matter "until Le Boiseau returns."[55]

Suzanne's straining to give and receive needed information is inspired by caution. Much of her strategy is formed after consultation; a good many of the messages she sends and receives are transmitted with the aim of taking advice. Moreover, despite her impatience, she is careful to guard against acting without the fullest possible information. Dissimulation may be necessary to gain such information. Thus she instructs a son not to reveal what he has learned from her: "No one in the world knows I have written you about this point"; hence he is in a position to learn more by deception. She warns him, "You mustn't let on that you know anything about all that, because in that way you will see better who are really your loyal servants." She even supplies a cover to give her son credibility when he tells others that he has not been informed by her. She suggests that, since someone else is known to have transmitted a piece of news that she has also written him, he can without risk deny having been informed by her in order that no one suspects that his mother has told him other crucial facts of the case as well.

In the midst of planning measures to control future events, Suzanne continually expresses anxiety. While one such plan is in progress she writes her son, "My great fear at the moment is that he who must see you in

Paris . . . may leave too early." During the course of a lawsuit affecting the family's future she writes, "I await your news," and adds, "I am worried to death."[56]

At the time when it seems her destitution is imminent her worries intensify. As the probability grows that she will be forced from her home by creditors, she compares herself to a man then a prisoner in the Conciergerie:

> I find Vatan very well off. I should like to be as well lodged as he for the rest of my days. I should have no further worries if it weren't for these days of mine which make so much commotion and bear so little fruit.

Yet, though anxious, she is not fatalistic but instead still hopeful:

> I wish this affair would end . . . happily. I am greatly troubled by it. May God be willing . . . to remedy it and counsel me.[57]

But the anxiety continues. When deliberating what to do about her son Armand's proposal to shelter and support her, she writes him that she cannot express the "worry and irresolution in which I find myself." In a phrase that he also would often use, she writes that "anxiety is killing me."[58]

The approach of "this miserable war" intensifies her apprehension: "I swear that its alarms add, it seems to me, ten years to my old age . . . on account of the fears it brings." And, with the approach of the armies, these "alarms" are so "prodigious" that they "gave us eight consecutive days in which I stayed awake the entire time."[59]

Towards the end of her life her anxiety-proneness increases. On hearing from her daughter-in-law after the young Richelieu couple had finally made the desired visit and returned home she expresses her relief:

> I must confess that I was in extreme distress fearing that you were ill from having endured so many jars from the roads. . . . I am so apprehensive that having this stupid fantasy (*songe*) got me into such a state of fear that I didn't know what to think.[60]

Accustomed as she was to making an active response—taking the initiative to cope with threats—it is probable that in these months of turmoil the necessity to wait on decisions which she could not influence increased her tendency to feel anxious.

It is not certain which of Suzanne de Richelieu's many "frustrations, afflictions and bitternesses" her son Armand particularly had in mind when he wrote to inform his brother Alphonse of her death. Perhaps, as historians have surmised, she was victimized by the arrogance of her mother-in-law. It seems likely too that her husband's behavior brought not only ruin, but also humiliation upon herself and her family. Destitute in her old age, she was forced to accept the charity of her son Armand, and felt herself an undue burden on his shoulders: "The pain I have in causing you such trouble," she writes him, is such that "I see that I shall never have any joy until, knowing you all to be happy, I am in paradise."[61]

In her last year of life Suzanne had two new afflictions. There was, first, the terror and havoc wrought by an invading army; second, her anguish from the premature death of her beloved daughter.

Of all her trials, war was not the least. As the *châtelaine* of Richelieu, she saw her domain suffer ravages from soldiers under the leadership of an exceptionally brutal prince, Condé. His reputation preceded him as he descended on Poitou, for his marauders inflicted damage on the estate of Marguerite before he reached Suzanne's:

> They hold out hope for peace here, but I don't see much prospect of it, seeing that they tell us that Monsieur le Prince's army will be at L'Ile Bouchard on the twelfth to cross the water there. That's only three hours from here. If he treats us as badly as you tell me he treated your subjects we won't have great obligations to him.[62]

When the prince's army did overrun her domain with its three regiments of fierce *Lorrains*—those whom Suzanne compares to devils—her worst fears were realized:

> I have lived 49 years in this house where I have seen all the armies come through, but I have never heard talk of people such as this nor of such destruction as they bring. In truth I find it very rough because never before have any been lodged in what belongs to me. If they had only lived honestly, one would scarcely have complained of them, but each one ransoms his host, and they want to take women by force. They took one in my parish who was an old maid of nearly fifty years. Thank God that all the others kept away from here.[63]

As would be expected of Suzanne, she is not inclined to contemplate such conduct without trying to influence the course of events. "I would have sent a message to Monsieur le Prince to try to save our villages," she writes, but with her usual caution she sent a message to Henri, who was an officer in the nearby royal army, asking whether she might properly do this. She explains, "I didn't dare for fear that he would disapprove." She could well have jeopardized his status by communicating with his opponents. "He sent word [that it was all right] but then it was too late because they arrived the following day."[64] Clearly Henri, experiencing disgust and frustration at an order not to give Condé battle to prevent the Loire crossing, approved active intervention to protect his mother's parish.[65] The second great cause of Suzanne's grief is, exceptionally for the time, freely and fluently expressed in her letter to Marguerite near the beginning of the following year. "My dear daughter," she writes:

I write with tears in my eyes to tell you the sad news I received this morning of the death of my poor daughter Du Pont . . . which makes me have such regret that I cannot describe to you my grief and affliction. . . . Excuse me, for I can tell you no more. Grief overwhelms me. I pray God to give you his blessing and all that you desire.

A postscript adds, "She died from a pleurisy which lasted seventeen days."[66]

Despite the growing anxiety and the distress that Suzanne de Richelieu's letters often express, they belie the character given her by Hanotaux as "melancholy" and "modest."[67] On the score of melancholy, it is noteworthy that until almost the last, her optimism rarely fails to appear, even in the face of adversity against which her energy could not prevail. This optimism is shown too in one of her earliest letters, in which she reports to a friend of the family on the state of her children. Beginning with Armand, who is ill, she writes:

I believe if you were here the honor of your company would have more power to cure my invalid than any medicine. . . . He is continually tormented by his fever, from which I hope nevertheless a happy deliverance for him.

Given the uncertainty of survival in those days of medical helplessness, her tone seems cheerful enough. She looks again on the bright side where Henri is concerned, although his news is scarcely more reassuring:

My eldest also had a little sample of ill fortune, because a horse having collapsed on him, he had a dislocated shoulder. But it commences to get back in place, thank God, according to what they tell me.[68]

Receiving good news of this son during the war she comments that it is as though God has conducted him "by the hand" on this occasion, "as He has done all of his life." And at last when, towards the end of her life, she receives news that she is finally to be visited at Richelieu by her daughter-in-law, she expresses her intention to put past disappointments out of her mind. The visit will "make me forget all the suffering that the war has brought me; the troubles which I have had from it will no longer remain in my memory, peace being affirmed for me by your presence."[69]

After Suzanne's death her eldest son wrote the orphaned Nicole a letter of consolation. In it he paid his mother a tribute which, if it is partly conventional, also conveys an appreciation of her individual character. He stressed her affectionate qualities: "as, during your life, she was able well and truly to cherish and love you . . . you will never find again anywhere else what you have lost in her, since nothing can approach the love of mothers towards their children, and especially that which she bore hers."[70]

If there is formality in this commendation it may be due to the fact that, of Suzanne's three sons, Henri was the one who had lived least at home. It was characteristic of family relations of the time that formal kinship ties were not expected necessarily to coincide with affective kinship relationships.[71] Henri's eulogy of his mother's affective capacity may reflect as much a sense of filial duty as it does sentiment.

This was certainly not the case, however, with Armand de Richelieu, Suzanne's youngest son. In his only known letter to his mother he stresses the distinction between duty and sentiment in the obligations of children to their parents. But in offering to make himself responsible for her support in her old age he explains how, for him, formal obligation coincides with feelings:

> You are right . . . to conclude that I offer myself wholeheartedly (*du bon coeur*) as the solace of your old age. . . . I offer myself both from duty and from inclination. From . . . inclination, assuring you that that which I bear myself will never equal that which I have and shall have towards you unto the tomb.

He has given her a choice either of retiring to his priory at Coussaye or accepting a pension and remaining at Richelieu. He concludes, "If as a result of these offers made entirely voluntarily (*avec toutes franchises*) you are able to resolve on changing your residence, since I would thus have the greatest honor that could ever befall me I would consider that I had received over and over again (*quant et quant*) an exceptional blessing from God."[72]

In her condolence letter to Nicole, Marguerite, Henri's wife, drew attention to Suzanne's moral character and to her ability: "Would that it pleased God that in succeeding to her name I might also inherit her virtues and merits." Being sure however, (as she writes) that she will never be "able to attain to that point," she aspires only to replace, for her sister-in-law, some of the protective functions that Suzanne had performed.[73]

If Suzanne's behavior was typical in some respects of her culture, her affective capacity, her perspectives and her skills made her an unusual woman for her milieu. Some of her personal attributes were exceptional in ways that had also distinguished her celebrated father. Her keen sense of justice may have taken form under his influence. In her gift for systematic analysis, her habit of taking active measures to cope with problems, and the ease with which she reasoned in legal terms she further resembled François de La Porte. That outstanding lawyer's reputation for amiability, too, seems to have its sequel in Suzanne's warm personality. Her frank expression of affection for her children is particularly notable in its spontaneity. She extends these sympathetic sentiments beyond the nucleus of her family to dependents and other members of her rural circle.

These qualities of Suzanne persisted despite the severe suffering she experienced. While her sensibility no doubt contributed to her apprehension of dire possibilities, heightening an already high level of anxiety, it was an anxiety that usually inspired, rather than inhibited, inventiveness and action. In the face of adversity her resourcefulness, judgment, and resilient energy seem remarkable for a woman of her epoch and situation.

5 Family History and Richelieu's Career Perspectives

> Inherited schemata . . . are concerned with the business of
> "placing" the impressions derived from actual experience. . . .
> Wherever experiences fail to fit in with the hereditary schema,
> they become remodelled in the imagination.[1]

The legacy of one generation to the next is multifaceted: inheritors choose—consciously or unconsciously—from among salient options in their family history. There is much in Armand de Richelieu that resembles his Richelieu forebears, on the one hand, and those of the family of Suzanne de La Porte on the other. He shared with his brothers and sisters the same genetic "pool" as well as the same traditions. These traditions were variously exemplified by visible models that living relatives presented.

The choices each individual makes from among traditions and examples of conduct are influenced, of course, by a unique experience and constitution. But before seeking, in this individuality, an explanation for distinctive behavior, the givens of family environment must be described. After that, personal choices can be more clearly identified. What role did Richelieu play in his family? What was the relationship of other family members' performances to his own? Once these questions are answered, attention may turn to aspects of his character that were atypical, not only for his social position and cultural milieu, but also in his own family circle. Only then will it be possible to determine how his personal experiences had to be remodelled in his imagination to fit in with the "hereditary schema."

1.   One for All—All for One

The typical seventeenth-century French noble family was a solidary group. Members' solidarity, however, did not necessarily imply a commingling of means. On the contrary, division of labor was the rule. Team play—allocation of diverse roles among family members and their allies—is a closer description of that unity of aim and strategy, coupled with plurality of roles and techniques, that characterized family action. This norm of diversity within unity was one which, as will be seen, Armand de Richelieu accepted in a broader context, implicitly and explicitly, all his life. Conversely, unity of purpose prescribed that, should one family member die or fall by the way, not only was it necessary to close ranks, but also to assign the role of the one lost to another relation. Richelieu seems to have subscribed unreservedly to the principle that individual aims should be subordinated to the group demands. Thus it is not surprising that available evidence indicates he was always compliant with the career decisions that were determined for him in the name of family necessity.

In 1602 Richelieu had completed his academic training at the Collège de Navarre in Paris and was perfecting his horsemanship at the Academy, preparing to follow, in the footsteps of his father and his eldest brother, a military career. He had received the rudiments of his formal education in Richelieu, probably from the age of six to about nine, at the hands of the prior of an abbey in nearby Saumur, Père Hardy Guillon of Saint-Florent.[2] The decision to appoint this tutor had presumably been made by Suzanne. Richelieu's mother's success in preserving the family heritage was attributed by a contemporary not only to her good management of property but to the "attention she gave to the education of their children," a tribute not uncommonly paid to conscientious noblewomen of Poitou.[3] Suzanne, too, probably in concert with her brothers and other relations, was influential in assigning careers to her children. One report maintains that she was forced to play a decisive role when family opinions conflicted.[4]

When Armand was still very young, perhaps even before he showed precocity as a pupil of the local priest, it was intended by his family that he become Bishop of Luçon. This office had been, as we have seen, in the gift of the Richelieus since 1584. Unless one of their family occupied it, its revenues, such as they might be, were subtracted from their income, while the costs attached to the diocese continued to be charged to them. Alphonse, however, Armand's nearest older brother who, no doubt through the sponsorship of Amador de La Porte, had been destined for the naval career of a chevalier of Malta, came to find the prospect of this vocation uncongenial.[5] Since he seemed to be of a studious and retiring nature, this son was reassigned to theological studies in order to become Luçon bishop. Thus it came about that, at an early age, Armand himself was diverted from clerical to military preparations.[6] Some years later, in 1602, Alphonse decided, after all, to renounce a career in the regular clergy in favor of monastic life. It is then that his brother's aspirations were once more directed towards becoming Bishop of Luçon.

In thus twice changing his aspirations to fit the family's interest, Armand's behavior contrasted strikingly with that of Alphonse: "Although

Richelieu had a strong interest in his own kin, it was not the same with his brother, who always remained indifferent to their fate and professed little sympathy for them."[7]

Alphonse's failure to comply, as a child, with the expectations of his family may have been the cause of disputes while Armand was still very young. As will be discussed later, this elder sibling took drastic measures to escape his destination for the Order of Malta. According to Pure, his subsequent "melancholy" caused "reproach" from his family. His later decision to enter a religious order may have caused like reproaches from his mother and other relatives. Such possible causes of family dissension, like the ones earlier ascribed to Françoise de Rochechouart and her La Porte in-laws may be the source of a contemporary report that the household was ridden by strife.[8]

Richelieu left a written record of his general views on the family. He believed it has total rights over its individuals. One member's title to call upon another in the name of the good of the whole is virtually boundless. In one of his earliest theological writings he finds this principle to be sanctioned by the Gospel. Discussing the Decalogue, he goes into unusual detail on the obligations of sons to protect the family name through obedience to the father. While, he claims, children should not normally be forced to marry against their will, a son could be forcibly prevented from marrying against the father's desires, no matter how strong the inclination, if the girl chosen is of a lower status. This is a mortal sin, for it threatens the honor in which the family is held.[9]

In the same early work he appears to be applying the principle of a filial obligation which he would later put into practice in Alphonse's case. This obligation is so compelling, he notes, that a monk can obtain release from his vows to come to the aid of his parents. Further—and here Alphonse's defiance of the family plans may have played a part in his brother's thoughts—a son may not enter religion if the father refuses permission on grounds that the material need of the family forbids it.[10]

In the two brothers' lifelong relationship Alphonse provided as good an example of recalcitrance in lending himself to family interests as Armand did of assiduity on their behalf. When the younger brother was moving towards the center of power in 1622 he became concerned lest Alphonse's conduct reflect unfavorably on the Richelieu public image. As a Carthusian, Alphonse's ill health was causing extra expense to his monastery. Richelieu, solvent at last, was in a position to defray these costs, but his brother made objections. Alphonse's scruples obliged Armand to request the head of the Order for "a word in writing for the discharge of his conscience . . . because otherwise he would not wish to accept the intention I have to underwrite his indispositions."[11]

In the contrast between Armand de Richelieu's concern for and Alphonse's indifference to family interests, it is Alphonse's behavior which was exceptional, Armand's normal. Nor did this rather eccentric older

brother ever become easily accommodating to family demands. In spite of
this, Armand continued throughout his life to call on his brother to serve
in support of himself and the family interests, just as though Alphonse's
commitment to the norm of solidarity were as firm as his own. Soon after
the younger man became the king's prime minister in 1624, he moved to
extricate Alphonse from the monastic life he preferred and install him in
high clerical office. First he had him accepted as Archbishop of Aix en
Provence, then as Cardinal Archbishop of Lyons. Not long after Alphonse
had reluctantly adjusted to the last role, his younger brother dispatched
him to Rome as a special emissary to the Holy See. Alphonse accepted
none of these assignments gracefully.

A self-proclaimed stoic, it was characteristic of Alphonse de Richelieu to
protest the splendor of his office as Archbishop of Lyons. A typical remark
was, "The posture in which I like myself best is that of Stoic Philosopher,
protesting to you that I would have great trouble to catch myself even
once a month in that of Cardinal."[12] Yet, when he was assigned to Rome,
he lamented sacrificing a Lyons living, remarking, "It annoys me a bit to
see myself . . . without a retirement place," and claimed that the appointment as ambassador required him to take "a sort of second vow of poverty."[13] Richelieu had little empathy with his brother's tastes and little
patience with his humors. Nevertheless, his trust in Alphonse's loyalty
seemingly remained intact and he demanded and expected useful service
from him as long as he lived.

While the youngest Richelieu brother accepted every change in plans for
his future that family needs dictated, his final destination for the bishopric
evoked a response which was far more than mere acquiescence. He threw
himself into theological studies that were beyond the *pro forma* prerequisites
for filling the office.[14] His unusual enthusiasm for this particular assignment, like Alphonse's persistent recalcitrance, was a personal characteristic. As such, it calls for investigation in later chapters. But the enthusiasm
had also social and cultural determinants visible in the influence on the
young bishop of his family's history.

2. Juridical Perspectives

In the spring of 1617, when Richelieu was exiled from the court, he had
been Bishop of Luçon for nine years and served for more than one year
as close advisor to the crown. In 1618, still in exile, he drafted, with his
secretaries, notes for an *apologia* of his past performance. It makes the
following self-description:

> Son of a father who always served kings and, in what small way
> he could, had always done so himself. In his diocese, from the
> beginning, the late king had confidence in him. After that the
> queen continued it.[15]

The implication that Richelieu makes here that his model was his own father is by no means fully confirmed by François de Richelieu's actual role. For the father's example of commissioned officer and man of military arts was one that the son had had little opportunity to observe and had, in fact, renounced to follow an ecclesiastical career. It is true that Henri IV had nominated the son to the bishopric, and supported his appointment before he reached the canonical age of eligibility for the office.[16] It is true that, even as a cleric, Richelieu would conceive of service to the king as his primary duty. It is not that he did not recognize his obligation to God and the church; only that in his mind no possible conflict could exist between enhancement of the authority of the crown and divine aims. Yet, for him, this service would take a form different than that performed by his father. As Bishop of Luçon, first preaching occasional sermons at court and later representing clerical and royal interests at the meeting of the Estates General in 1614, Richelieu was not the "strong arm" of royalty that François de Richelieu had been. Rather he was, like François de La Porte, his maternal grandfather, a "mouthpiece" for the crown.

Thus, a clue to explaining the zest with which Richelieu threw himself into the study of theology is that the opportunity to enter the clerical profession gave more scope than the military to skills and habits of thought he possessed through affinity with his mother's family. For a young nobleman, of course, professionally exercising these juridical skills of the robe was difficult without derogating one's noble status. In another, more elevated station, however, the same skills had a highly acceptable use. As a cleric, Armand's outlook on the world showed itself to be colored by a juridical viewpoint.

It is doubtful that Richelieu ever knew his renowned grandfather La Porte, the lawyer. But it is clear from Suzanne's letters that he met in his own mother those abilities to describe reality succinctly and to select rules applying in particular cases that characterize the legal outlook. Moreover, there are apparent in Madame de Richelieu's correspondence the verbal and intellectual skills of legal argument; her values showed the influence of standards of equity applied in law courts.

Even before Richelieu came near the seat of state power he had acquired not only a juridical outlook but much experience of actual legal processes. The tangled web of lawsuits, prosecutions, leasings, foreclosures and forced auctions surrounding the Richelieu estate has been noted in an earlier chapter. The cardinal's correspondence shows him to have been occupied frequently, from the beginning of his career, in attempts to influence the course of justice as it affected both his personal and his professional life. But legalistic habits of thinking penetrated his religious as well as his secular outlook, and it is in the theological context that they will first be examined here.

Theologians who have evaluated Richelieu's religious sentiment generally agree that, while his faith is unquestioned, it lacks a personal apprehension of the sacred.[17] He sought to become a notable preacher but, as such, "his tendency was to convince rather than to move" his listeners.[18] "He lacked," observes an ecclesiastical authority, "many of the essential qualities of the evangelical orator."[19] To Richelieu, the opportunity that the bishopric presented was that of advancing his own and his family's position by mastering the art of religious controversy:

> Controversy was his principal object. It was at that time in great vogue against the Protestants; it had brought the Purple to Du Perron and to Bellarmin. He wanted to follow the same career.[20]

Skill in controversy uses the training of a lawyer to vanquish the opposition by the lucidity of argument, not the light of inspiration.

Richelieu had been prepared by home experience for adversary situations. Later, as a theology student, he continued his apprenticeship under Gabriel de L'Aubespine, a cleric about six years his senior, whose family of high royal officers and magistrates seems to have had connections of long standing with Armand's family.[21] L'Aubespine, consecrated Bishop of Orléans in 1604, two years before Richelieu himself became a prelate, earned a reputation as a learned controversialist. He was admired for his "erudite wisdom (*docte sagesse*)" by Du Perron and was an author "much to the taste" of the learned Peiresc.[22] Indeed he became, in effect, the successor to Du Perron as the leading choice to defeat the Protestants in debate.[23]

L'Aubespine gives information on the debating strategy he counseled his pupil to adopt: "to learn their opinions thoroughly before commencing to read our own." It may be, however, that even this practical advice was not worldly enough for the ambitious younger cleric. Richelieu has withdrawn in order to draft a polemical work against the Huguenots and L'Aubespine complains to him in this letter "that you have set yourself to controversy and have told me nothing about it, . . . having brought two Englishmen to help you."[24] For the bishop of Orléans's strategy seems to aim at changing the "hearts and minds" of the dissidents; Richelieu, on the other hand, prefers to point to the pernicious consequences of religious dissent for civil society. Thus, in his first polemical work, he observes that those of the reformed religion "are only a tiny part of France, half of Germany, and Switzerland and England." While Catholics have preponderant support almost everywhere else, the Protestants "do not even agree among themselves."[25] In this work designed to encapsulate Christian doctrine for the layman, he seems not to base the case for Catholicism on its Christian verity, but on the verdict of public opinion. His appeal is not to the conscience of his readers but to their fears of disorder.

Like his view of the basis for acceptance of the faith, Richelieu's interpretation of doctrine itself often shows his habit of thinking in juridical analogies. Recalling the Protestant charge that the Catholic cult of the Virgin Mary was idolatrous, he transposes to the celestial arena—as, of course, one current of Christian thought always has done—the image of a court of law:

> If the Church, in addressing the Virgin to ask her assistance, sometimes uses terms which may be hyperbolic, as when it prays her to save us, it is not that it believes that she is able to save us by virtue of her own power, but only by her intercession with her Son. We ask that she protect us by means of her Son who, no doubt, always has a high regard for his mother's prayers.[26]

Thus the mother of God is invited to act on our behalf as a Friend of the Court. While this explanation is standard for the time, and may even come from Richelieu's "workshop" rather than his own pen, it exemplifies the kind of phraseology that caused a modern writer on theology to assert that his arguments were "cold" and "legalistic" and that with him, "religious virtue does not appear as an act of love but as the means to fulfill a law."[27]

The view that men are related to God as are petitioners before a reasonable, but all-powerful magistrate, is applied in Richelieu's personal life as well. On one occasion, tormented by an exceptionally severe and persistent headache, he prayed God, by the intercession of Saint John (his patron) to cure him "within a week" on the promise that he would repay the saint by hiring a chaplain to celebrate a weekly mass at Richelieu.[28] "He gave God only a week," wryly observes Abbé Lacroix; "After that interval, if he feels no relief, he will consider himself free of all commitment."[29]

With his usual attention to practical questions, Richelieu makes exemptions for lawyers in the requirement of church attendance on Sundays: their absence is permitted if it might prejudice a case for them to have to come.[30] Judges themselves violate the Fourth Commandment if they fail to give due process to those before the bar in certain kinds of cases. For, indeed, the judge's role is like that of the confessor: "because the spiritual life, like the natural one, requires a tribunal of judges who decide differences and settle (reiglent) everything." No wonder, then, that bringing lawsuits frivolously is also considered by Richelieu to be a violation of the same commandment![31] As a priest Richelieu also performed the duties of a director of conscience. In this role, too, his approach to theology resembles that of a legal counselor. In a letter consoling the comtesse de Soissons on her new widowhood, he begins by pointing out that for her own good "it is better that you have a lawyer (avocat) in heaven than a husband on earth." He continues with words that are, presumably, designed to reconcile her to the ways of divine justice in removing Monsieur le Comte:

> If you experience pain because he is absent from you, you must experience happiness that he is present to God. Just as you possessed him on earth, equity requires that God have him in

heaven; that if he is your husband he is God's son; that God is preferable to His creatures and that therefore it is more reasonable that He have His son than that you, Madame, have your husband. These reasons must have great power over an afflicted soul.[32]

A.   Equity

Richelieu's mention of "equity" in the passage just quoted calls attention to a further characteristic of his religious thought that shows the imprint more of early modern legal reasoning than of the inspirational message of the Catholic counter-reform. One looks in vain in his writings for the concept of the equality before God of all believers. The Council of Trent, for example, arbiter of reformed Catholic teaching, found the appeal to "Our Father" in the Lord's Prayer to signify this message of brotherly equality:

> All the faithful are brothers and . . . must love each other as brothers. The Apostles, too, give the name of brothers equally to all the faithful.[33]

Richelieu, on the other hand, discussing the same passage, omits reference both to the sentimental tie and the equalitarian message. For him the phrase conjures up a class action brought before the bar of justice. "We say," he writes, "*our* . . . " to show that we act not only on our own behalf but also on that of . . . our brothers." Indeed, the Lord's Prayer itself is a brief with particularly strong powers because of the high status of its Author. It is the best form of appeal to higher authority because it is drafted not by "mere men," but by "Jesus Christ himself," making it a privileged communication, "not only more noble but . . . more efficacious."[34]

In Richelieu's social perspectives, as in his Christianity, equity, not equality, is the rule. Human justice, like divine justice, is distributive: women, legitimate children, bastards, foreigners, soldiers, aristocrats and commoners are entitled to treatment befitting their status and performance.

This nicety of discrimination he applied in small as well as great affairs. For example, he introduced an innovation at the first performance of *Mirame* in his Palais Cardinal—assigned seating arrangements. "One could enter there only by tickets," writes an ecclesiastical author, tickets being given only to those on a list drawn up by the cardinal himself, who had arranged everyone "according to his status, for there were some for Ladies, for *Seigneurs*, for Ambassadors, for Foreigners, for Prelates, for Officers of Justice, and for military men." Finding himself among the "Ecclesiastics," the abbé de Villeloin, who recounts this event, was able to see the performance with ease. At a later ballet performance presented by Richelieu the discrimination was nicer still: "There were places for Bishops, for Abbots, and even for Confessors, and for the Almoners of Monsieur le Cardinal."[35] Equity (*équité*) consists in thus subtly discerning the rules appropriate to each category in a particular situation and apportioning benefits accordingly.

B.   Reciprocity

Above all, the principle of equity requires reciprocity. Among supporters outside the family circle it is based on the obligation to return *quid pro quo*. For Armand de Richelieu, this principle ruled even in the most sublime circles. In a sermon which is as good an example of Richelieu's prosaic view of the divine as it is of his belief in the principles of equity, he preaches, on Assumption Day, that God "receives today the Virgin in heaven . . . because formerly she received Him on earth."[36] He who goes, owes.

In his personal dealings Richelieu was scrupulously attentive to both sides of the *quid pro quo* equation.[37] When someone did him a service, he became, in turn, a debtor. A writer who observes the "extreme ease" of Richelieu to "have recourse to others," also notes this tendency is balanced by his quickness to "become protector in turn." He was extremely "active in soliciting favors." But he regarded debts thus contracted to bind him to reciprocate with equivalent service or benefits. His friend Madame de Bourges, for example, from whom he borrowed money and took such services as her intervention in a lawsuit involving his interests, so that the judge "may return to me an effect of the good will that he bears you," could expect to receive comparable benefits in return. Richelieu wrote her of his search for a suitable husband for her daughter—"On my faith, I think daily about marrying Magdelaine"—and, on learning of financial reverses she had suffered he remarks, "Although my purse is not furnished as well as it should be, nevertheless I beg you in offering what little I can, to dispose of everything that is mine."[38]

To Richelieu, a benefit rendered was a solemn obligation incurred. Thus a debt he owed from 1616 to Claude Barbin, the minister of state who championed his entry into the inner councils of the queen mother, was not immediately repayable when Barbin fell out of favor with the king in the following year. It remained on Armand's "books," however, even after the disgraced one's death. It was eventually repaid by a legacy Richelieu assigned, in his last illness, to "Baron de La Broye, heir of the late sieur Barbin, whom I have learned is in need." The sum was 30,000 *livres*—three times as much as he assigned to any gentleman among his close personal retainers.[39] It was not self-flattery when Richelieu claimed, as a young man, that he was "a person entirely opposed (*du tout ennemi*) to ingratitude."[40]

The same strong feeling of obligation also prevailed when, in 1632, the duc de Montmorency was about to be executed for undoubted treason. The duke had given staunch support to Richelieu when, in 1630, the latter's fate seemed to be in the balance. Despite the young duke's fall from grace the cardinal—quite remarkably "while in the bath"—admitted an emissary from him to plead for his life. Richelieu was "seized with pain and grief," according to the unpublished manuscript of a personal attendant who was present. "Sighs, and even a few tears" testified to the cardinal's distress when Saint Preuil proceeded, "on behalf of Monsieur de Montmorency, to recall to his memory what had happened at Lyons"—where the duke had come to Richelieu's defense. The witness of this scene is confident that this reminder "was enough to say to this great man"—that is, to the cardinal—"for him to commit himself to risk everything of the favor he enjoyed [with the king] if he could have seen the slightest possibility of success."[41] The private character of this first-hand testimony gives it a verisimilitude that will later be reinforced by considering the motives of the other party to Montmorency's death warrant—Louis XIII.

C.   Inducements

In his first addresses to the people of Luçon, Richelieu presented himself as the secular agent of the king seeking to promote the political unity of a family divided by beliefs. He would strive for, he promised, the worldly welfare of Protestant and Catholic alike, letting the "poor people" of his new town "taste the fruit of the relief that I want to procure for them."[42] Responding to the welcoming party he promised that all his efforts would "strive only for your welfare . . . there being nothing I want more than to be able to be useful to all, both collectively and individually."[43] In return he hoped to win a reputation as a reforming bishop, enforcing the resolutions of the "sacred Council of Trent," restoring order to the church, probity, zeal and learning to her priesthood, and right beliefs to her children.

He would have liked to win popularity with a splendid generosity, but his material resources were inadequate to this aim. Not only the region but he himself was poor. His family had struggled for years against demands from the cathedral chapter of Luçon that the Richelieus pay for needed repairs to church property in the diocese. He was aware that his family's delinquency in this matter lessened the enthusiasm with which he was received.[44] In his own words the new bishop was more a "beggar" than the *"grand monsieur"* he thought his poor parishioners considered him.[45] The rewards were few that he could offer in exchange for the many benefits that he sought for his region and its constituents. Thus among the justifications he advances for granting his many petitions to persons in a position to help him, the welfare of the church and the peace of the community frequently figure among inducements. He assures one whose favorable action on a certain matter is requested that this "will, in time, bear great fruit in my diocese." Appealing to a tax official for a reduction in the tax load on Luçon, he appeals to the principle of equity: the people of his poor town are taxed as heavily as those of a nearby prosperous city.[46] His appeal to justice from this tax collector is given additional force by a threat to go to law if reason does not prevail, but in two letters to more august personages he does not add threats to his appeal for justice. Instead he promises future courtesies and considerations. He will owe the one petitioned a "private obligation" which, since he is a "not ungrateful person," will make itself felt by "all the effects you could possibly desire."[47] Apparently he does not consider an increment in inner sense of merit as sufficiently alluring.

For it is typical of Richelieu that the rewards for compliance that he offers are both temporal and tangible. From the time that, as a young student, he suggested to his mother that her creditor would appreciate a gift of greyhounds he was most likely to be quite explicit concerning proffered indulgences. It was not his habit to suggest that a correspondent would pile up pennies in heaven, even though this suggestion was a common one in the correspondence of contemporary clerics. In other such petitions of the time salvation was likely to figure prominently; in Richelieu's writings such mentions are rare. When he does cite possible supernatural intervention, he is more likely to invoke the wrath of God than His less discernible grace, perhaps another residue of his mother's religious perspective.

D.   Beyond the Law

In Richelieu's mind, neither equity nor reciprocity applies to a relationship with a monarch. As will be seen later, the king feels an obligation in return for services rendered to himself, but his failure to discharge it does not release the servitor from his bond, as it does in ordinary *quid pro quo* relationships. Hanotaux thinks "striking" a passage from Richelieu's *Instruction du chrestien* which shows that "to explain the power of God, he finds nothing better than to compare it with that of the king: 'As a sovereign King in France bears witness to the fact there is no one equal to him, and that all those there are his inferiors, so God, sovereign King of the world, bears witness to the fact that he has no equal and that he is unique.'"[48] In fact, in Richelieu's view the king stands with respect to his subjects in the position of the father to his children. In this relationship solidarity and obedience, not equity and reciprocity, are the key words.

3.   Richelieu's Royalist Tradition against the "Grands"

If an equalitarian message was lacking when Richelieu wrote of the relationship among men before God, it was often present when he spoke of their relationship before the king. To the cardinal the monarch was not *primus inter pares;* he was the supreme temporal authority before whom even the least of subjects was as the greatest. Few who have considered the regime of Louis XIII have failed to stress Richelieu's exaltation of kingship. In raising royalty to a level where it became "the living personification of public salvation," as Thierry writes, it is necessary that all be reduced "to the same level of submission." The nineteenth-century historian identifies this "fidelity to the royalist principle" as a Richelieu family characteristic.[49]

In seeing the Richelieu royalism in this light Thierry was at one with the cardinal himself who claimed, in his devoted service to the crown, to have followed in the footsteps of François de Richelieu as "son of a father who always served kings."[50] If one listens only to what Richelieu says of it, one may overlook the fact that Richelieu's service to the king was as much in the tradition of his La Porte antecedents, the advocates, as in that of his militarily trained father. In fact, too, his interpretation of his father's performance was not entirely realistic. For while the elder Richelieu had reached the summit of his career in the personal service of Henri IV, he had not always so directly "served kings." His first military service was as an ensign in the army of the duc de Montpensier's son. Indeed, a *maître-fidèle* relationship had bound the Richelieus to the rich and princely house of Montpensier for several generations. It was through service to this family of overlords that François first attracted the attention of Henri III.

As one of the most powerful families of Poitou, however, the Montpensiers were allied with the royal cause against the Catholic League. Local history puts this alliance in a context that throws further light on the Richelieu tradition of passionate royalism. In the district, supporters of the anti-monarchical League "came principally from below" in the social scale, comprising "artisans who organized against the gentry."[51] For upwardly striving families like the Richelieus and La Portes, these elements were not only the forces of disruption but also of social inferiority. As allies of the pro-monarchical Montpensiers, Richelieu's father and uncles were, locally, on the prestigeful side.

Recall, too, that once introduced into Henri III's retinue, François de Richelieu had faithfully "served kings" to the exclusion of lesser loyalties. On behalf of the interests of his royal master he was able to treat princes of the realm summarily, even, as in the case of the Guises, callously or brutally. Nor had loyalty to his own former employer deterred him from servicing the king to the disadvantage of the duc de Montpensier's interests. On March 20, 1586, a court correspondent reports, "the sieur de Richelieu, Grand Provost, has sent the heads of certain captains who were roaming the fields without authorization," adding: "Some of them confess to belonging to Monsieur de Montpensier."[52] Thus had François become, as an agent of the king, superior to his former lordly masters. Furthermore, as we have seen, his transfer of allegiance from Henri III to Henri IV, unlike that of many Catholic noblemen, was exceptionally swift and unhesitating.

In Richelieu's personal experience of his family history this royalist tradition may well have been understood as a loyalty to the crown at the expense of deference to the *grands*—the great nobles of France—who so often threatened or undertook rebellion against the royal power. His paternal grandmother, Françoise de Rochechouart, may have been linked, in this experience, to those haughty princely families in whose households she had been reared. Although there is little direct evidence on the point, biographers have often presumed that Françoise, of lustrous social origins herself, looked down on her daughter-in-law, Suzanne de La Porte.[53] It has been supposed that the dowager's sense of social superiority to Richelieu's mother gave rise to ill will and possibly to conflict between the two women during the youth of the children. It may be, therefore, that Richelieu actually had to witness the humiliation of his mother by a woman of the high nobility. A curious early unpublished letter from him could signify indignation at a slight given his mother by another great lady, Madame de Chappes, wife of a high officer of the sword.[54] The baroness had preferred lodging in a hostelry to the château de Richelieu. Richelieu's comment, weighted with irony, is no doubt intended to seem facetious. He complains of "your present signs of contempt" which belie the honor she previously paid him and says that were it not for the promise he has made to her of eternal attachment, "I would be unable to suffer the insult you have given Madame de Richelieu."[55] In later years, after genealogists employed by Richelieu had taken pains to establish the ancient noble lineage of the Du Plessis-Richelieus, it may have been on Richelieu's behalf that Du Chesne claimed still higher origins for Suzanne's maternal ancestors, linking them to the royal house of Dreux. It was, perhaps, a late vindication of earlier slights.

In any case, as a young adult Richelieu had good reason to resent the heedlessness of great princes in what concerned his mother's welfare. In 1614 and again in 1615 the armies of the prince de Condé overran Poitou, "committing excesses" and leaving a trail of "fire and blood" worse than any the region had experienced in the wars of religion.[56] It was on the second of these occasions that Suzanne wrote her daughter-in-law of the destruction wrought in her parish by Condé's army.[57] It was news of which her son Armand, in nearby Coussaye, was well aware.

Richelieu's fury at these developments may be imagined from a letter he addressed to a third person complaining of the duc Du Maine, one of the commanders in Poitou. Asking that his mother's parish be exempt from the lodging of troops he concludes with the icy comment: "I would gladly have written him myself had I not seen plainly, by the treatment he has given my mother, that he either believes me no longer among the living, or that he at least believes me incapable ever of returning him a service."[58] Richelieu leaves no doubt that he takes as a personal affront the damage inflicted on his mother's household, more especially, as he says in another letter, because he himself had advised her not to leave her home before the advancing troops.[59] This, and other felt humiliations and injuries received at the hands of the great nobility were to have important sequels.

It may be partly a result of the impression made on him by his mother's experience that he was known by his friends to have a special loathing for the depredations of an undisciplined military force. Some years later one of his most intimate associates, Sébastien Bouthillier, Abbé de La Cochère, wrote to him recommending a certain Poyane, governor of Navarre, whom he was sure Armand would appreciate because, "being of the disposition you are to hate pillagers . . . you would like the man who of all the world is that the least, albeit very courageous and valiant."[60]

A.   Career Impediments

Arriving in western Poitou as a young bishop of twenty-three, Richelieu found many obstacles to his ambition to make his mark as a reforming bishop. Primary among these was the fact that his region was in large part populated by Protestants and therefore nominally outside his ecclesiastical jurisdiction. The privileges of Henri IV's former co-religionists were not only guaranteed by the Edict of Nantes but also by the fact that Henri's personal friend, the powerful Huguenot duc de Sully, was governor of Poitou and hence chief civil administrator of Richelieu's territory. As such, as well as in his capacity of finance minister for all of France, this great nobleman's support was necessary for local projects. Yet he had been for some time unfavorably disposed toward the Richelieu family.[61] Moreover, of all the *grands* who found favor with Henri IV, Sully was notorious for exercising his powers with the least graciousness.[62] Not only this highly placed lord, but many lesser local *grands* presented impediments to Richelieu's early professional success. Of the assets the new bishop possessed, one of the most important was his power to make ecclesiastical appointments. The effect of his authority, he was aware, depended in large part on putting the right person in the right job, and he was conscious, as he was later to say, that "everyone knows the best affairs are not always accomplished by the grandest persons."[63] Awarding church offices on the basis of merit was a prime objective of the Catholic Counter-Reform. This was a policy consistent with Richelieu's view that merely ascriptive claims to privilege, based on birth or status alone, were dysfunctional to achievement. Tridentine policy, therefore, was not only congenial to his ambition to make his mark as a reforming bishop; it probably also gave the additional gratification of strengthening his hand against the importunities of local nobles. These were accustomed to placing their clients and relatives in clerical posts and to receiving the income from benefices whose duties were performed by others.[64] In one letter from this period Richelieu explains to a noble lady of his diocese that he refuses to appoint a certain curate she has proposed unless he agrees to be examined on his ability. He suggests, perhaps with tongue in cheek, that her candidate "will be received at the competitive examination if he deems his capacity great enough to compete for this benefice on the basis of merit."[65]

His concern to resist such solicitations is indicated by a few notes in his hand written toward the end of his tenure in Luçon. When he was made representative of the clergy of Poitou at the Estates General Assembly of 1614 he studied the list of complaints drawn up by his colleagues for presentation to that body. Most items are concerned with protecting the rights, privileges and possessions of the Catholic church of France against Protestant incursions and usurpations, and against undue royal influence. Concerning these issues he makes no comment. In marginal notes, on the other hand, he stresses the need for residence of bishops and archbishops in their cures[66]—a point with personal meaning for him. He expands most, however, on items dealing with the intervention of the gentry in clerical staffing. Opposite a remonstrance against bestowing clerical livings on laymen and Protestants he notes "unworthy distribution of benefices," and emphasizes "*pensions.*" Elsewhere he stresses a point by declaring, "gentlemen who possess abbeys will no longer present the *curés.*"[67] The pressures from gentlemen—and ladies—presenting incompetent *curés* for Richelieu's approval was a particularly disagreeable problem of his episcopacy. The emphasis he gave to the Poitevin clergy's list suggests the centrality for him of obduracy in the face of such demands.

B.   A Bourgeois Mentor

The reverse side of Richelieu's dislike for heedless military leaders under the command of princely rebels, for importunate local *grands,* and for arrogant nobles in general, was a tendency to sympathize with those of lower status who were victimized by them. This sympathy seems incongruous in one so often described as cold and haughty. But, for example, when Richelieu made a visit to Rheims in 1638, a spectator was surprised to find him "full of commiseration for the *bourgeois* who were suffering from the lodgment of the troops." One of the victims, a certain Coquebert, had been injured by them and Richelieu tried to make amends by dispatching his personal surgeon to care for his wounds.[68] These unexpected feelings may also have had their origin in the influence exerted on the cardinal, as a youth, by a family member—his uncle.

Amador de La Porte, Suzanne's younger half brother, was, in the absence of Richelieu's father, the most influential adult male presence in the future prime minister's boyhood.[69] He was, according to all reports, the financial sponsor as well as the intimate friend of the Richelieu children.[70] This distinguished lawyer and *Chevalier*—later *Grand Prieur*—of the Order of Malta is said to have remarked to the prince de Condé that "he had greatly assisted his sister" in her widowhood. As for Armand de Richelieu, "he had supported him at college at his own expense."[71] Amador seems to have been a Godfearing, good-humored bourgeois who made no attempt to dissemble his origins. "The Commander," as he was called in his family, had so wide a reputation for virtue that it had reached even Tallemant Des Réaux, who rarely has anything favorable to say about persons to whom he is not personally indebted. "This *grand-prieur*," he notes, "was a good man and a man of honor." As governor of La Rochelle, continues the usually malicious gossip-monger, "I have found he was much beloved"—a striking tribute.[72]

Armand de Richelieu's correspondence with his uncle shows the latter to have had high respect for his nephew's ability and confidence in his good will. The younger man reciprocated Amador de La Porte's devotion and, as his own career advanced, insured that the uncle's fortunes improved apace.

These promotions were sometimes a problem for the increasingly influential minister. In important ways La Porte's personality differed from that of his austere, correct, cautious and dignified nephew: the older man was jovial, somewhat impulsive, kindly, and outspoken. Armand's letters to him occasionally seem to suggest, with delicacy, that he is too indulgent towards those who have broken the law. As the cardinal acquires new responsibilities he tries to moderate—rather than suppress—his uncle's spontaneity. He warns him, for example, not to express openly the displeasure that he assumes he has with Marie de Medici after she has disowned Richelieu on the Day of Dupes: "I know your frankness," he writes, "which might be given free rein because of the affection you bear me." On another occasion he reminds the older man, whom he has made governor of Brouage, to show sufficient "solemnity" with the bourgeois of that city. His respectful solicitude for his uncle's feelings is as marked as any sympathetic sensitivity he would ever show. It is apparent when he declines to intervene in La Porte's jurisdiction in order to administer a justified reprimand to an insubordinate soldier. Though the offender deserves punishment, he believes, anticipation of his uncle's reaction deters him from administering it. It is "consideration of this great man, whom I respect," he writes, which "restrains me."[73]

Despite their differences in temperament the two men shared important political perspectives. A letter of the uncle to the nephew soon after the latter entered the government for the first time shows common themes in their thought ranging from matters of style, through positions on tactics, to fundamental beliefs. Concerning the first, we find in Amador's "salty" self-expression the probable model for Richelieu's proneness to use seagoing jargon and nautical metaphors. As for tactics, the uncle commends his nephew, who is pursuing a stern course to subdue mutinous nobles, for having adopted techniques he himself has always recommended. In his devotion to the principle of royal supremacy, in his belief that the welfare of the state depends on a single authority and an unbroken chain of command, and in his opposition to the disorder fomented by unruly nobles, the older man shows himself to be at one with his nephew's basic political inclinations:

> You are embarked on this ocean of confusion without a needle and without a compass. And what is worse, with heaven justly irritated with us. What labor, what strength, and what good luck are necessary to guide one's vessel and one reputation among so many obstacles! Nevertheless, there is always a remedy, and honor lies in vanquishing these difficulties. But what use is an experienced pilot if the whole crew conspires against him? You and your friend[74] will do well, but the others will spoil everything.

Going on to report that he has won his case for the grand master of his Order in Rome, he regrets that "we are just as ill-assorted a crew here as you are there—bad administration, leaders apparently without masters and without judgment. May such a people as ours love the leader and justice— you know if I know what I'm talking about in this matter." He continues:

> This remedy of conferring together, as I used to tell you, will do much good, bringing lasting peace to the virtuous, instruction to the people, and recompense to the nobility—always understanding that we do not mean that vain nobility which is good for nothing but bringing disorder wherever it sets down its foot. For the Lamb wants obedience and order in all things, and above all in what affects the king.[75]

In this letter Amador de La Porte is recalling lessons that his nephew must have received in his early youth: political order is all-important; consultation and discussion are useful in settling issues and contributing to public instruction, the *grands* are likely to be vain and seditious. In various forms each of these lessons would be important for shaping the cardinal's career.

This member of Richelieu's mother's family was, then, apparently an influential and admired mentor in the statesman's boyhood.[76] In the bourgeois origins of his uncle, as in those of his own mother, is a further reason also for Richelieu's enormous satisfaction when the bishopric of Luçon offered him a clerical career. Not only did the post open to him the chance of advancement by the use of skills not honorably employed by a young gentleman in any other profession; it offered also the only avenue by which a man from such a family as his—certainly regarded by the princes, if not by the Richelieus as "*très petite noblesse*,"[77]—could reach the pinnacle of honor in the state.

With the elevation of the territory of Richelieu as a duchy, in 1631, Richelieu brought to his father's name an additional lustre. But, in the son's eyes this temporal honor, which his father might have won had Henri III lived, was surpassed by his own great post in the church. For the clerical hierarchy was both outside and above caste. The prelate was exempted from deferring to noblemen. Indeed, he could lecture and reprimand them virtually with impunity.[78] As a bishop, moreover, the distance between Richelieu and the monarchy was appreciably diminished. As such, representing a clerical delegation in the Estates General of 1614-1615, he argued the special status of his order vis-à-vis the king.[79] Before he was inducted into the government in 1616—considerably before he himself became a cardinal—he supported an argument on behalf of the precedence of cardinals over princes in the king's council.[80] As cardinal, a prince would be "My cousin." After this promotion to the purple, as a prince of the church, he was not obliged to defer to any other man in France save the king and his brother.[81] Thenceforward he was in a position to "return the service" of the *grands* many times over.[82]

6 Tradition and Innovation in Richelieu's Family Performance

I forbid my heirs to ally themselves with houses that are not truly noble, leaving them well enough off for them to have more regard for birth and virtue than for comforts and possessions.[1]

This inquiry into Armand de Richelieu's personal history has the aim of throwing light on his public performance. But there is much in the record of his life that shows him implementing policies designed to further family goals. Sometimes this activity was separated from, sometimes it coincided with, service to the crown. In either case many features of his behavior show him to have been, though unmarried and without descendants, a family man.

As such, Richelieu saw himself as a member of a kinship group that preceded him in time, surrounded him in his lifetime, and would continue after his death. The acts which he performed as a member of this group give important clues to his character. For these acts were sometimes traditional and their meaning evident in the expectations and models set by family members, living and dead. At other times, however, no precedent for his behavior can be found in family history or tradition.

The present chapter aims to distinguish what was conventional from what was original in Richelieu's family performance. In chapters that follow, the origins and development of his innovative behavior will be sought in his childhood experience.

1. Family Norms

The little that is known about how Richelieu's view of his own role in family life was shaped in these first years at home allows identification of two features of his environment as significant: on the one hand, much was expected of this youngest son; on the other hand it was neither expected nor desired that he become politically eminent.

Hindsight alone does not entirely account for the many attributions to Richelieu of expected greatness by those close to him in his youth. By his own report there was consensus on his promise as a boy. In a fragmentary note he writes, "from his youth, that one will find to have been accompanied by good omens (*présages*)"[2]—a description that seems to refer to the views of those around him in his childhood. The existence of this belief in Richelieu's early promise is confirmed by the testimony of family members and their friends. Sébastien Bouthillier, long intimately acquainted with the family, was Armand's would-be biographer many years before the young man's aspirations for power became a reality.[3] Le Laboureur, who was in possession of contemporary documents, credits Henri de Richelieu with an awareness of Armand's early "designs for greatness"—an awareness that is believable, as will be seen later, in view of the self-subordination of the marquis to this youngest brother's interests.[4]

But if the family and their friends had great expectations of the third Richelieu son, it is just as clear that they did not encourage him, either by example or by their comments, to set his sights on gaining political power. That aspiration cannot be seen as a family trait.

Armand de Richelieu's father, François, was close to two kings. In spite of his assiduity and skill in implementing their designs, there is no evidence that his aims ever went beyond enriching himself and his family and bringing military and social distinction to his name. He was an effective, but silent, adjunct of royal power.

Alphonse, the elder brother closer in age to Armand, was to go to great lengths to avoid becoming a public figure.

As for maternal influence, it is not to be expected that a woman of that era would express ambitions for herself from which Armand's high aspirations might take their cue. Even so, it is noteworthy that the usual worldly shrewdness of Suzanne's letters seems actually to give way to other-worldly thoughts when she contemplates court life and, perhaps, her youngest son's rising influence in the highest councils of the state. Around the time of royal negotiations with the rebellious princes—negotiations in which Richelieu was playing an important role—we find his mother reflecting with resignation rather than enthusiasm on current events:

> They tell us here of so many changes that we are all astonished. That is why I do not see that there is great security in anything in this world. It is a truly fragile building that is based on such foundations. He who may must build on high, and hope from it whatever it may please the good Lord to arrange for us.[5]

In the light of Suzanne's customary impulse to activity, her fatalism here is worth noting. One may speculate that her youngest son's increasing involvement in the most important worldly affairs helped inspire it.

Another letter from Madame de Richelieu, dated near the end of her life, is written just after Armand, on a royal mission, has succeeded in inducing Condé to return to Paris. The prince was causing considerable disquiet in the capital, however, by his attempts to rouse popular opposition to the government. Suzanne writes to sympathize with her daughter-in-law who must endure the "disorders" of the court which have forced Henri to remain in Paris. "I pity him, and you as well, for the unpleasantness I know you experience in seeing so much confusion."[6] Apparently this former lady-in-waiting to the queen had little taste for political life and few expectations that it would make the fortune of her children.

Unlike his half-sister, Armand's maternal uncle, Amador de La Porte, was an important figure in worldly affairs. As a lawyer he undertook cases at court; as counsel to the Order of Malta he represented French interests in negotiations abroad. He did not, however, see himself as a political man, but merely as a docile officer of the crown. A few years later Richelieu would reflect his uncle's self-estimation. Instructing Amador, in 1619, on a speech the commander was to make, Richelieu suggests he say, "I am a bourgeois who does not concern himself with great affairs."[7]

Like so many, Amador de La Porte expected great things of his nephew but, like his sister, he looked with concern on Armand's entry into the political struggles of the day. In the letter written to Richelieu on the occasion of the latter's first appointment as minister of state, the older man seems to echo Suzanne's apprehensions, as well as her otherworldly perspective on embroilment in court affairs:

> I do not know if I ought to rejoice with you at the charge with which the King has honored you, in view of the current climate. I know that God has, by His grace, made you capable of the very greatest things. But these turbulent times, so full of disloyalty, where justice but rarely appears, make me think them unworthy of you, for in God alone is to be found all happiness, and your health, and all peace of mind. . . . Therefore resolve, Sir, that to cope with affairs of state one need concentrate only on appeasing God, for all our problems arise from our irreligion.[8]

In Amador's warning that true peace of mind lies in resigning oneself to the divine will, he repeats his sister's recent admonition to the same effect: it is better to build "on high" than to base one's hopes on things of this world.

Such philosophy was never to be within Armand de Richelieu's power[9]— burning ambition, albeit justified in terms of divine as well as human purpose, insured that he would never passively accept an adverse verdict of fate so long as any strength remained in him to challenge it. The uncle's disinterest set no precedent for the nephew's aspiration.

Unlike Amador de La Porte, most of the cardinal's intimate family died early in his lifetime. Foremost among those early departed was, of course, Richelieu's father. But it was characteristic of early modern practice that, as family members vanished, others replaced them. The replacements did not necessarily continue the affective roles of predecessors; they did carry on their functions and duties. Thus when François de Richelieu died, a boy of ten replaced him, both in family position, as Marquis de Richelieu, head of the household, and in professional function, continuing the dead father's personal service to the monarch in a military capacity. This was Suzanne's second child and the first of her sons. In his new relationship with his youngest brother, Henri de Richelieu's role was a distinctive one—both important, and replaceable.

2.   Henri de Richelieu: An "Alter Ego"

When Armand de Richelieu was sent, as an eight- or nine-year old boy, from rural Poitou to school in Paris, the transition was less drastic than might be supposed. Like most such student migrations of young aristocrats in early modern times, the change was attenuated by integration into a home away from home. The boy brought with him a lackey and perhaps other family retainers. Many more of these last were to be found in the capital. There were there, in particular, family allies of long standing, such as the Bouthilliers, associated with the La Porte law practice in the days of Richelieu's grandfather. But most important for Richelieu were the close relatives already in Paris. Chief among these, in addition to his uncle Amador de La Porte, whose normal residence was in that city, was his eldest brother. At about the age of fifteen Henri was considered adult; he was already a military officer and gentleman courtier.

More than any of the Richelieu children, Henri had been acquainted with the personal example set by their father, the grand provost and captain of the king's guards. Many of the reports on the father resemble those on this son: like François Henri was brave and able, but inclined to resort to violence. Apparently also his ambitions were military and not political; his letters express a personal *ennui* with court affairs. In one letter to his brother Armand, for example, he regrets he cannot come to Poitou, being in the midst of "settling up all my affairs," but hopes that, this done, he will be able to come and stay three or four months, "in order to restore my spirit a bit, away from the anxieties of the court."[10] His later reports to Armand on political matters are entirely devoted to that young brother's prospects and interests.

The young marquis was unlike his father in one respect: his manners seem to have been graceful and agreeable. When Armand arrived in Paris,

Henri was already installed at court in an intimate circle—the so-called "Seventeen"—of those whose society was personally pleasing to Henri IV. We have a glimpse of his skill as a courtier from Héroard, who shows him joking pleasantly with the seven-year-old future Louis XIII.[11] He was a young man who impressed many not only with those qualities his father had possessed of straightforwardness and valor, but also with warmth and charm[12]—attributes with which the grand provost had not been credited. In these years the easy, agreeable personal impression he made on others may have contrasted with his youngest brother's sobriety. It may be significant that, in 1618, while both brothers were together in exile, Louis de Marillac wrote of his "esteem and inclination" for this older Richelieu brother, but merely of his "obligation" to Armand, Bishop of Luçon.[13] Furthermore, he seems to have been highly esteemed by certain Catholic zealots as one of high religious integrity. Père Anselme describes him as "an extremely sound man."[14]

The marquis became Armand de Richelieu's informant at court, the champion of his career, and his most faithful friend and supporter. He was, however, more than these. After their father's death and Armand's assignment to the clergy, Henri embodied all the hopes for survival of the Richelieu lineage. As his wife, Marguerite, was to be "another myself" to her mother-in-law, Suzanne,[15] Henri was in some respects "another myself" to his youngest brother.[16]

As the eldest brother, the bearer of the family name, and the only son not in orders, the long-term preservation of family interests seemed to depend on Henri's prosperity and posterity. When he first assumed these responsibilities, various difficulties had to be overcome in order to discharge them. The legacy of debt left by the grand provost made it necessary for Henri to extricate his property from the family community in which it was held by his mother while he was a minor. On one occasion a suit was actually brought against Suzanne in his name, apparently in order to salvage inheritances from the many encumbrances attached to them which otherwise would have made them worthless.[17] Some have interpreted this process as an unchivalrous action directed at Madame de Richelieu, but there is no suggestion of a strain between her and Henri in family correspondence. On the contrary, it seems that all family members cooperated in helping the eldest brother detach what property he could from the hopelessly mortgaged patrimony.

The death of his widowed aunt in 1611 put Henri in a position to marry: as Françoise de Marconnay's heir he was able to win Marguerite de Charmeaux, a rich widow and heiress, a match in which all the Richelieus rejoiced.[18] The hopes thus raised for a Richelieu heir caused Suzanne to write Marguerite, in one of a series of very warm letters, that Henri was now "a husband to me as well as to you."[19]

The correspondence between Henri and Armand de Richelieu testifies to the close collaboration and affectionate relationship between the two.

Their aunt had made Armand executor of the will by which Henri became her heir. The latter's letter to his youngest brother asking him to discharge this responsibility gives evidence of the mutual sympathy animating their feelings of solidarity: "Forgive me, if I am so bold as to beg you to do this in the state of health you are," Henri writes, "but I believed you would not take it amiss," and would act "all the more willingly because you have my interests at heart." He is, he says, reassured by confidence that the tiresome part of the work can be done by others, but he expresses concern for his brother's state of mind since the aunt had died while Armand was with her:

> I know that that event will have touched you greatly. Take care
> that this pain doesn't intensify the melancholy state of your
> mind and, as a consequence, your fever.[20]

This was not the first time one brother had seconded the other in legal matters. In 1604 Henri had signed for Armand in a settlement of a contest the latter had had over delinquent payments for the upkeep of the bishopric of Luçon.[21]

The inheritance of Madame de Marconnay's estate brought a train of further legal actions in its wake and it is possible that the bishop of Luçon's agents acted on behalf of Henri de Richelieu in these processes too. Relatives of the aunt's second husband claimed a share of Henri's inheritance, requiring several hearings before the seneschal of Saumur in September of 1613.[22] This may be the "annoying lawsuit" to which Suzanne refers in one sympathetic letter to Marguerite.[23]

If Armand de Richelieu supported Henri in his business and personal affairs, the older brother participated in the younger's political ambitions. When the latter, as Bishop of Luçon, was seeking an entrée to power, Henri was his faithful informant and advisor.[24] When the bishop followed the queen mother into exile in 1617, his elder brother acted as his representative and informant at court. Banished himself in the spring of 1618, Henri was ordered by the king to accompany Armand to Avignon. In October of that year, however, the marquis's wife died at Richelieu after giving birth to a son. Although Henri appealed to the king in order to be permitted to return in order to attend to urgent affairs in Richelieu and in Paris,[25] and although this permission was granted, Armand had in the meantime fallen ill in the papal state. Henri seems to have delayed his departure on account of this illness of his brother, as he suggests in a letter to his sister Nicole asking her to go to the side of his newborn child.[26] In any case, his baby son died in mid-December, 1618, and Henri did not arrive in Paris until early February, 1619.[27]

Henri carried on the role of François de Richelieu, his father. With the death of his only child, hopes that he would succeed, as his father had done, in perpetuating the line were only temporarily at ebb. But his performance, as his father's son, threatened family continuity in another way. A propensity to ready violence was demanded of noblemen in military service by the code of honor. This frequently triggered this eldest brother to challenge those he considered had insulted him, and involved him in armed encounters that could be fatal for him and for the chances of a Richelieu descendance. It was, as Georges d'Avenel has pointed out, "good form to play with death,"[28] and the sensitivity on points of honor of such an otherwise prudent and sensible gentleman worried the family, and with good reason.

Henri's dangerous bellicosity was a tendency which his brother, the bishop, was bound by his profession and, later, by his commitment to the king to frown upon. Yet he could not, in his capacity of family member, condemn it wholly, since he himself shared the concern for Richelieu honor. He did, however, attempt to restrain the marquis's tendency to risk his life in duels. A letter written in 1611 by Armand to his brother is clearly designed to discourage Henri from challenging the neighbor who has destroyed a Richelieu tenant's wall.[29] He suggests Henri make use of the excuse for conciliation afforded by his own intervention, as Bishop of Luçon, in the matter:

> I have not committed you to anything, but have put the affair in
> a state in which there is more disposition to get out of it by
> peaceful means, it seeming, in my small judgment, that you can
> be satisfied with less, in consideration of me, than you could if I
> had not mixed myself in it. That is to say, you can say that for
> love of me you close your eyes to many things which you would
> scrutinize more closely were I not involved. In a word, if one
> does not get out of this affair peacefully, always assuming that
> nothing rightfully yours remains in it, it seems that there is no
> other way to get out of it except with a sword, which you must
> not do according to God and may not according to society, as
> much because of the Edicts . . . as because you have to do with
> a man of sixty years, and such a one as you know, that is to say,
> a real peasant.

Richelieu's aim is to make it possible for Henri to withdraw without its seeming that his honor has been compromised. To this end the bishop promises that their correspondence will be secret. He concludes with an assurance of solidarity:

> You may be sure that I know what courage you have; that I be-
> lieve it as whole-hearted as any in the world, and consequently
> that I say nothing with the thought of encouraging your disposi-
> tion, but on the contrary of preventing it from following the
> paths to which it tends of its own accord. We are brothers; I
> speak to you as such with an open heart. I beg you to find this

acceptable and to believe that no one will ever wish for your happiness and your honor with as great a passion as I.[30]

Apparently Richelieu was successful on this occasion in restraining his brother's impetuosity, but a few years later he was unable to prevent an armed confrontation between Henri and another antagonist. The bishop had the thankless task, no doubt after consultation with the culprit, of presenting the *fait accompli* in the best possible light to Henri's new wife. Presumably, Armand's clerical position and his rapidly increasing influence at court earned him this assignment. He adopts a facetiously light tone to make the marquis's sin and his own complicity in it seem of little moment. Although the affair is regrettable, he tells his sister-in-law, there is for it as there should be for "bad meat," a "good sauce," which is the fact that Henri unhorsed his adversary without killing him. Hence there will be work for the tailors—"the jacket of Mr. de Blet," the antagonist, "being cut up in a way not presently in fashion"—but not for the surgeons. Personally, he avers, he condemns such actions, but assures her that Henri has since made peace with God and with his adversaries.[31] Suzanne, evidently writing to Marguerite about the same event, strikes a similar note. "Except for the interests of God," she tells her, "the outcome should give us nothing but joy."[32]

The cheerful face Henri's brother and mother put on his disposition to become involved in such deadly games disguised an anxiety which proved to be justified. About four years later this head of the House of Richelieu was killed in a duel over another point of honor.[33]

Armand felt the loss of Henri as a disaster for himself. The sense of misery he expressed privately to Père Coton, himself an exile from court and a friend of the dead brother, was unlike any he had experienced before. He wrote to this confidant, "Grief at the loss of my brother, who died a few days ago, holds me so much in its grip that it is impossible for me to speak or to write to my friends."[34]

Among papers found in Richelieu's office after his own death are several notes that appear to be attempts to express this sense of loss. The death of his brother seemed to him to be a partial death of himself: "I never received a greater affliction than the loss of that person. My own loss would not have caused me more pain."[35] In another of these fragments he likens his feeling of loss to a feeling of his body being separated from his mind: "Separation of the body and the mind cannot take place without a great effort of nature, and that of two minds which have always lived together in close friendship cannot occur with less pain."[36] Henri's death also seemed disastrous for the career of his youngest brother. For on the eldest had depended many Richelieu hopes. In the letter already quoted, to Coton, the king's former confessor, the bishop makes the avowal, "I must confess to you, Father, that aside from the interests of our good mistress [the queen mother] nothing in the world could bring me more trouble than this disgrace which has befallen me."[37]

Richelieu had just been recalled from exile to rejoin the queen mother. He had recommenced his rise to favor at court with his brother's fortunes closely linked to his own. The mutual support of the two brothers in exile had promised to become a close collaboration at the apex of power. The threat of disgrace compounded the disaster, for royal edicts affirmed that a duel between noblemen was a crime against the king. Even though, in this particular affair, Henri's assailant had clearly provoked the showdown, Louis XIII did not look as tolerantly on transgressions of the prohibition of duels as his father, Henri IV, had done. Moreover, the slain marquis's successors, formally at least, could not inherit the family estate; the crime of the transgressor entailed punishment to his whole family. The *seigneurie* of Richelieu reverted to the crown. This soon had, however, an outcome favorable for Richelieu: the property was awarded to Marie de Medici from whom he was able to repurchase it in 1621.[38]

Other consequences were more lasting for Richelieu. Thenceforward it was necessary for him to play Henri's role in the family as well as his own. For, in view of the incapacity of Alphonse, the youngest brother became head of his house. Contests in court arose over Henri's property in which Richelieu was obliged to act as the family representative.[39] As the new owner of the family estate he became the *seigneur* of Richelieu that Henri had been. His now was the responsibility for perpetuation of the family lineage and honor.

Thenceforward, therefore, survival of his *ligne* became one of Richelieu's persistent concerns. The failure of the direct male line, with Henri's death, meant that the title of Seigneur (and later Duc) de Richelieu could descend only through his sisters' sons—in the first instance through Françoise's only surviving son, and after that through the sons of Urbain de Brézé, husband of Nicole de Richelieu, the youngest of the family. Richelieu made the welfare of his nephews and grandnephews an important preoccupation, although his family affections were, in later years, reserved chiefly for his niece, Marie de Vignerod, Duchesse d'Aiguillon.

At first Nicole had been made responsible to her brother Armand for looking after the dead Françoise's children. Later Richelieu was perpetually concerned to insure that the widowed Marie would stay out of a convent in order to perform the same function for her nephews, Françoise's grandsons.[40] On Armand's deathbed, a witness testifies, he reiterated this exhortation to her, "having expressly forbidden her to retire after his death into a cloister, and that if she wished to displease him after his decease she had merely to entertain the thought of it, that she could be more useful in the world, where he asked her to take care of the education of his Du Pont nephews."[41]

As in the case of brothers' roles, one cousin could be substituted for another to the *n*th degree. Thus a testament clause provides that, in case of attrition of the descendance from nephews, the title will devolve upon sons of Armand's nieces in order of primogeniture. By these means the dying cardinal hoped to compensate for his own celibate status, providing for almost every contingency that could threaten the Richelieu family's survival.

Inheritance of the Richelieu title was to be, by terms of the cardinal's will, exclusive: those who received it were to bear the "sole name and none but the arms of the house of Du Plessis de Richelieu." The compass of its territorial domain was to be kept intact: if any part held as security for a loan should be forfeited, the proceeds must be reinvested in substitute real estate.[42] The sentence at the head of this chapter shows that a principal benefit, as Richelieu saw it, for his accumulation of fortune was to make it unnecessary for his successors to make any but "truly noble" alliances of marriage. As head of the family he tried to arrange both for its territorial integrity and the purity of its nobility. Significantly, these were two important requirements of family status which François de Richelieu, his father, had signally failed to meet.

As the cardinal grew in influence and power he found himself in a position to glorify his family's reputation in another way. He commenced—to use Suzanne's hopeful words, "to restore this House"—in a literal sense. That is, he began to reconstruct the family château at Richelieu. This undertaking, first projected in 1629, had barely gotten under way in 1630 when its gigantic scale and grandiose conception furnished grounds on which Richelieu's government was attacked for extravagance in an anonymous, but widely circulated, political pamphlet. A prompt response was published, undoubtedly drafted under the cardinal's direction.[43] It includes a defense of the Richelieu château constructions, condemning critics of the cardinal's buildings, "as though, instead of stones, they were made of diamonds, even though, as for him, all he is doing is to finish his house on a much smaller scale than it was begun, and much advanced, by his father more than fifty years ago."[44] Despite the fact that the enterprise Richelieu brought to completion in his native hamlet surpassed in splendor most of the royal palaces of Europe, he claimed that, in erecting it, he aimed only to implement the modest designs of his father—indeed, on a smaller scale—in fulfilling his duties as head of the household.

With Henri's death, not only the perpetuation of a lineage, but the honor of its name became the responsibility of this youngest Richelieu brother. Henri, as we have seen, had been quick to resort to the sword: "Men of the sword feared to be taken for cowards," a modern writer notes.[45] Richelieu's oldest brother had done everything required to dispel such an idea. After he died, the youngest surviving brother, like Henri, was a subject of the king and as such prohibited from resolving private disputes by force of arms. As a clergyman, moreover, Armand was professionally obliged to be "something of a 'coward.'"[46] He was forbidden even to be a party to violence without a dispensation. Yet with Henri gone, it was no longer possible to leave to another the task of defending family honor. In years to come the incompatibility of this task with the status of cleric would occasionally appear.

On two such occasions responsibility for filling Henri's shoes fell upon Armand in disputes in the neighborhood of Richelieu in Poitou. In the first, readiness to use private violence was endorsed by the cardinal. He intervened in a Poitevin legal process to have a sentence suspended against a local ally who had violated the edict against duels.[47] A second affair concerned a dispute which would have threatened to provoke Henri to violence, had he lived. Towards the beginning of 1623, the nominal suzerain of the Richelieu estate—overlord of the county—put a stop to the practice of praying for the Richelieu family that had been established in the parish church of Nueil-sous-Faye. Further, this nobleman caused to be erected to himself in the village square a post and pillar symbolizing his own judicial supremacy in the territory. Partisans of the Richelieus tore down the offending challenge. The suzerain countered by bringing a legal action, aimed at identifying and prosecuting the culprits.

Richelieu became involved in defense of the vandals. In a letter to the governor of the district he expresses his desire to live in peace with these neighbors, as did "my father," and "my predecessors," in spite of the plaintiffs' desire to give him offense.[48] Coming in this order, his "predecessors" can only be his mother and his brother. In fact, it was Suzanne to whom the suzerain had shown complacency in a relinquishment of his rights in 1608.[49] But Richelieu prefers to see himself as his father's successor. He trusts the arbiter to whom he has appealed, he says, to settle matters amicably, yet his sense that he must defend family honor leads him to set the following limits to his submission on the legal charges:

> Once again I tell you that I did not have the post torn down . . .
> although the offense I received from these gentlemen by their
> having implanted it is very great. . . . I am sorry that it hap-
> pened, but without knowing who did it (as on my honor I know
> nothing about it), it would not be reasonable that I abandon
> those who, albeit with an imprudent zeal, did this deed out of
> consideration for me.[50]

Since the relationship of suzerain to vassal was largely a formal survival, there is more than a little irony in these sentences from a later letter of the powerful cardinal to the same governor:

> As to the issue in question, I shall be delighted to resolve it by
> your agency, asking for nothing but friendship and concord with
> those whom I recognize for my overlords. But you will admit, I

am sure, that it is not reasonable that they devour their little
vassals who humiliate themselves before them as I do. I have no
doubt whatever that you will contribute all that you can to this
end.[51]

The same mixture of ultimatum and ironic self-abasement occurs in his
response to the suzerain's claim of the right to force others to inform on
those who tore down the controversial post:

In my judgment those gentlemen give little consideration to my
poor, miserable person. . . . I am obliged to guarantee those
who committed the deed.[52]

Certainly, if Henri had lived, it would have been his youngest brother's
task to try to restrain him from taking action in response to provocation
like that in Neuil-sous-Faye. But now Richelieu had to assume the family
role that Henri, and his father before him, had played, as well as continuing
to perform the peace-making function of man of the cloth.

3.   Filling Henri's Public Role

Henri de Richelieu not only played a central role in the Richelieu family;
he was also Armand's supporter in politics, subordinating any personal
ambition he may have had to his younger brother's star. When the fatal
duel took place in the summer of 1619, Marie de Medici had just appointed
the marquis governor of Angers on his brother's recommendation. His
sudden death deprived the future cardinal of his most loyal, ardent, and
effective collaborator. It deprived him also of a trusted advisor—a senior
person of independent judgment who did not stand in awe of him.

In addition, Henri had personality characteristics that complemented
those of his youngest brother. The bishop of Luçon seemed scholarly,
serious, and reserved. The marquis was gay, spontaneous and outgoing—
qualities that gave him popularity with his peers and gained him favor
from the king and queen. Now it was Armand de Richelieu's task to supply—
by himself or through others—these qualities of the missing adjunct.

In the years to follow, Richelieu would attempt to fill the gaps his brother's loss had created by appointing other family members to important
posts. Notably, he assigned his uncle Amador and his brother Alphonse
to important offices and missions. As has been seen, however neither of
these was suited to replace the oldest Richelieu brother. A brother-in-law,
Urbain de Brézé, was also chosen for, and often brilliantly discharged,
important and demanding services for the cardinal. On several personal
counts, however, Brézé was in striking contrast with Henri. From an ancient
noble family in the neighborhood of the Richelieus, he was by far their
social superior. To Armand de Richelieu he seems often to have exemplified

that arrogance of the high-born that claimed the right to withhold services from the monarch if personal conditions for rendering them were not met, and that felt no solemn obligation to reciprocate for services rendered. Periodically preferring private gratifications, such as going hunting at his country château, to public duties, Brézé received chastisements from his brother-in-law for being deficient in that honor "which men prefer to their lives," and in gratitude for "the great benefits I have bestowed upon you" since allying himself with the family. When Brézé married Richelieu's sister, the cardinal reminds him, he was indeed possessed of "those fine titles you speak of, but so few possessions that between what you now enjoy and that which you had then there is the difference between much and nothing."[53]

There was another group of supporters, however, that was as attached to Richelieu public interests as the Richelieus themselves. These were the Bouthilliers, who faithfully and intimately served the cardinal's purposes from his early youth.[54] The father, Denis, had been an associate in the law practice of Richelieu's maternal grandfather, François de La Porte, inherited his practice, and helped protect the young children of Suzanne de La Porte after (and perhaps also before) her husband's death. There were four sons in the Bouthillier family. Sébastien, the second, was four years older than Richelieu and seems to have been his devoted familiar since their school days in Paris. After taking orders he acquired the modest abbey of La Cochère but when Richelieu took up his bishopric his older friend became a canon of the cathedral chapter of Luçon and remained wholly absorbed in his superior's career until his death, in January, 1625.

In 1610 Sébastien was dispatched by Richelieu to Paris, not only to pursue a suit in canon law against another cleric,[55] but also to carry out certain personal missions on behalf of his bishop. Letters from this Bouthillier to Richelieu in Luçon show the intimacy of their relationship. Armand had made the abbot the confidant of his ambitions. Thus, when two other bishops who are on the scene are chosen to deliver the funeral orations at joint interments of Henri IV and Henri III, Sébastien writes that the assignment would have been "worthy of you had you but been here." But, seemingly to diminish the keenness of Richelieu's regret, he continues, "It is a great honor to those gentlemen to be hired for that; nevertheless, I do not think it will bring them great advantages." The bishop of Luçon is, in turn, the confidant of his canon's hopes. Bouthillier reports in the same letter that Gilles de Souvré and the Marquis d'Ancre have had the "spoils" of Henri IV's half brother (who has recently died). These are the abbeys of Marmoustier and Saint Florent "which are two very beautiful abbeys,"— much finer, one is certain, than Sébastien's own La Cochère.

The older cleric's great affection for his bishop is shown towards the end of this same letter:

> I cannot help writing you these long accounts—I ask forgiveness for it. I should be longer still if I set myself to telling you the extreme regret I feel at being so far from you.[56]

Bouthillier's esteem for Richelieu was unbounded. As his would-be biographer he assured the twenty-five-year-old bishop, "You are known to surpass in merit and virtue the worthiest prelates in this realm."[57] Richelieu's successes were Sébastien's. He seems to have lived more through them than on his own account. Thus when the bishop was finally elevated to the cardinalate, an event for which Bouthillier had lobbied in Rome, the abbot wrote to his brother Claude, "Now that Monsieur de Luçon is cardinal . . . it seems to me that I no longer have anything to wish for in this world."[58] Richelieu repaid him for his devotion with the most conscientious thoroughness. A letter from Sébastien thanking his friend for his election as Dean of Luçon recalls that Richelieu had told him—apparently at the start of his own incumbency—that he wished the abbot to have "the first dignity of your church after yours." He gives the bishop all credit for the strategy that brought it about—"for having long ago taken care to lay the basis for it [and for] . . . having brought, entirely on your own, all that was necessary to make it succeed."[59] Having won the deanship for Bouthillier, Richelieu enlisted many others to secure his appointment as canon in the cathedral of Paris. Although his candidacy was supported by Marie de Medici as well as by the bishop of Paris himself, the nomination was successfully opposed by the rector of the Sorbonne, Edmond Richer.[60] The bishop of Orléans, Gabriel de L'Aubespine, was one of those whom Richelieu recruited to make an effort on Bouthillier's behalf. That prelate had to write Richelieu "Your good friend has lost his cause . . . against Richer." But he assures him, "I believe I did not fail him in any way."[61] Once cardinal, Richelieu was quick to obtain the nomination of Sébastien as Bishop of Aire, an appointment approved in the year after his own great ecclesiastical success. He had not failed to make sure that his faithful supporter's church career followed as closely as possible in his own path. Had Sébastien Bouthillier lived longer, it seems likely that some of the honors and responsibilities that Richelieu insisted on heaping on his surviving elder brother Alphonse, often with unfortunate results, would instead have gone to that old family connection who had acted, in so many ways, as the cardinal's other self in church affairs.

Close ties linked the entire Bouthillier family to the Richelieus. Victor, like Sébastien a priest, was also advanced to the episcopacy by the cardinal and became useful to him in church matters.[62] Sébastien thanks Armand for his message of condolence to another brother and sister-in-law on some loss they have suffered, and remembers to report—no doubt in answer to an inquiry from the bishop—that his mother and father are beginning to feel quite well again.[63] When Henri de Richelieu and his brother are exiles in Avignon, Sébastien, striving for their recall in Paris, does not forget to write Marguerite a sympathetic note, lauding her husband's merits and decrying the injustice of his punishment, and, a few months later, congratulating her on her pregnancy.[64] Two other Bouthillier brothers became important adjuncts to Richelieu during the administration that began in 1624. Both Claude (close in age to Sébastien) and Denis served in the highest official posts under the cardinal and Claude's son, Léon, was groomed to carry on his father's faithful service. Even more than Sébastien, however, their careers advanced in the wake of Richelieu rather than abreast of him; despite their intimacy with him, they were his creatures, and their status, like that of their parents with respect to his grandfather, one of *fidèle* to *maître*. This was not the case with another intimate of Richelieu whose unofficial title of *Eminence grise* reflects his social and affective relationship to the cardinal as one of equality rather than dependency.

Shortly after the duel that had been fatal to Henri, Richelieu linked himself more closely than before to the man who was to be his deputy and close collaborator for the next two decades. In July and August of 1619 the aristocratic Capuchin François Leclerc Du Tremblay began to replace Henri de Richelieu in his youngest brother's entourage. Père Joseph, as the monk was known in religion, had been known to Richelieu at least since 1612.[65] It was now that he began to assume the position of *alter ego* to the bishop of Luçon.

In several ways Père Joseph was suited to replace Armand de Richelieu's older brother. The Du Tremblays and the Richelieus had similar social and geographical origins.[66] Born in 1577, François Du Tremblay was about the age of Henri de Richelieu; like him he had begun active life in a military career. In this expectation, he had spent several years in Italy, mastering military arts, but also learning languages, pursuing studies in ancient Greek, and, especially, in the law.[67] Just as Henri had preceded Armand at court, Père Joseph was known to have been respected there before the bishop of Luçon arrived on the scene. He was said, by his attributes of the "perfect cavalier," to have won the favorable attention of Gabrielle d'Estrées, mistress of Henri IV. Later his charm made an impression on Louis XIII's mother.[68]

Père Joseph was himself the elder of two brothers. His cadet, Charles, also long known to Armand de Richelieu, had been the one sent by Louis XIII to recall the bishop from exile, in order to rejoin the queen. Like Henri de Richelieu, Père Joseph apparently lacked personal ambition, zealously putting himself in the service of other persons, causes and institutions. It may be too, that the Capuchin monk was, like Henri, a personal solace to Armand: at least he was capable of mitigating the wounds inflicted by the outlawed death of the marquis de Richelieu. Towards the end of August, 1619, Richelieu was describing him as the director of his conscience—his confessor, as Fagniez believes—a person "seeing clearly to the very depths of my interior," and "with a knowledge of the interior of my conscience."[69] The piety of this Capuchin may have helped relieve a sense of shame felt by Armand on account of the circumstances of his brother's death. This feeling has been noted in the letter the bishop wrote to his old confidant, Père Coton, referring to the "disgrace" brought upon him by Henri's duel and its disastrous consequences. So severe was the stigma that the cleric Bérulle, who reached Henri soon after, if not before, he expired, is said to have expected that Armand de Richelieu himself would retire to private life as a consequence.[70]

Towards the end of 1638 Père Joseph suffered a stroke whose sequels would soon prove to be fatal. The scene in which, according to Aldous Huxley, Richelieu took his dying friend's limp hand and reflected, *"Mon appui . . . Où est mon appui?"* seems fictitious. Dedouvres, apparently the source of Huxley's notion, ventures that, after the funeral, "In fact, several times, when pressed by affairs, he was heard to say, 'Where is my support! I no longer have my support.'"[71] These legends, nevertheless, point to Père Joseph's performance vis-à-vis the cardinal in a role which was perhaps held by only one person at a time: that of the selfless adjunct who was yet the equal of his principal and could act, on his own authority, in his place.

There is evidence, however, that several years before his death the Capuchin had been replaced in this *alter ego* role by a younger man. As early as 1629, Giulio Mazzarini had attracted Richelieu's favorable notice. In 1630, having met him in person, the cardinal seems to have been confirmed in his good impression of the young papal attaché. By 1635 Mazarin himself was aware that Père Joseph took umbrage at his eclipse by the newcomer.[72] At the time Père Joseph was dying of a stroke in December, 1638, Richelieu was arranging that the application for a cardinal's hat which he had made for his old collaborator be transferred to Jules Mazarin.[73] In 1640, in a letter congratulating Mazarin on the negotiation of a treaty with Savoy, Richelieu used words very like those with which so many had commended his own promise, as a young man: "God has allowed you to show, by this sample, what you can do for the greatest and most important negotiations for which you are destined." Mazarin, exulting in this letter, thought its praise sufficient to "raise the dead."[74] Richelieu may, indeed, already have decided that Mazarin would succeed him as prime minister.[75]

Part 3   CONDITIONS

7 Father of the Man: The Shaping of Richelieu's Character

> I speak not of his childhood because none was ever observed in him, and one may say . . . that he was a perfect man from the cradle.[1]

Whatever were the experiences of Armand de Richelieu's earliest youth, they presaged an adult ambitious for power and capable of achieving and wielding it. With prodigious, unflagging energy the grown man sought constantly to influence events in the name of the king and of the church. All the powers of his mind were enlisted in this striving to control. His vast output of communications included not only his work as state propagandist, strategist and administrator, but also the theological writings and preachings and the ecclesiastical activities which caused his admirers to marvel at "the passion that he had to make God reign in the hearts of those over whom he had made his Prince rule so absolutely."[2]

1. Richelieu in the Eyes of Others

If passion underlay Richelieu's desire to rule it was well disguised in his personal contacts. Du Grès's observation that the cardinal fully commanded his passions[3] represented an assessment that was general. This ability to dominate his own impulses seemed salient, for example, to a close collaborator who ranked the virtues that were personified on Richelieu's tomb:

> Up in front prudence appears;
> Strength is at her side.[4]

So strong was the rein of prudence Richelieu imposed upon himself that he gave familiars the impression of a kindly, gentle master. *"Doux"* was a word that was often used by the cardinal's *fidèles* when they described their chief to others. Thus one who had seen him often in many situations could claim at his funeral that he was "gentle and mild." Whatever anger the cardinal may have felt towards others was almost always under strict control, concealing the extent, according to this confidant, to which he was "bothered by annoyances," in order that "no weakness would appear in his acts."[5]

It was rare for Richelieu to utter words that expressed aggression, even towards avowed enemies of himself or the regime. When he complained of someone to a third person his hostility was usually either heavily clothed in irony or belied by positive phraseology. To injuries from the powerful he sometimes responded with apparent submission, while he devised means to protect his own power.

Still less than aggressive drives did he directly gratify erotic inclinations in his personal life. One devoted collaborator combined praise of the cardinal's purity with that of his control of his aggression, lauding, after his death, "the sweet glances of his innocence (*l'innocence aux doux regards*)," that made his company highly enjoyable.[6] A drive to dominate replaced intimate relations in Richelieu. In particular, evidence that he had any overt sexual life as an adult—whether homosexual or heterosexual—has always proved to be chimerical. Indeed, the very absence of rumors of impropriety in his lifetime was noted as significant by one contemporary historian who remarked that the purity of his personal life was so great that no one ever impugned it.[7] Long before he rose to power in the state, his choice by Henri IV to be Bishop of Luçon was interpreted by a fellow Poitevin as a response to the "scandal in the habits and morals of ecclesiastics" because the young prelate was one of those who were "very notable . . . in integrity of morals." The circumstances under which this tribute was published suggest that Richelieu had a youthful reputation for chastity.[8] Another early apologist calls him a "prelate highly renowned for the innocence of his life."[9] Richelieu's own earliest published work was in large part a lesson to curates to exemplify a life so blameless that it could withstand any amount of scrutiny.[10] And in a defense against a pamphlet attack it is probably the cardinal himself who mentions "the purity of his life" first in a list of his virtues.[11]

No contemporary ever successfully challenged Richelieu's reputation for lifelong chastity. After his death legends of romance multiplied, but the only color of verisimilitude given to such stories during his lifetime was the report of his bitter enemy, Mathieu de Morgues, that "in his youth" Richelieu liked unnamed "*voluptés*." Even though the term by no means denotes only sexual indulgence, one of the cardinal's collaborators discusses this charge in a 1631 rebuttal of a series of accusations made in Morgues's pamphlet. After observing that any such transgression could have subtracted nothing from Richelieu's reputation, and that indeed God himself enjoins that youthful sins be forgotten, yet he demurs:

> The accusation is, withal, false, and the cardinal's reputation for
> piety commenced at the age when he became capable of vice
> and virtue and it is evident that the calumniator speaks falsely
> because he cites no example.[12]

In fact, every posthumous rumor of Richelieu's sexual indiscretions has
been thoroughly canvassed and dismissed.[13] The only plausibly documented tale of a youthful "misdemeanor" was one allegedly told forty
years later by the gardener at the Collège de Navarre where, as a student,
the future cardinal was supposed to have pilfered fruit from the trees.[14]
Even that report may have been invented to "humanize" the austere prime
minister; evidence will later be presented to show why he was not likely
to have engaged very often in boyish pranks.

In Richelieu, then, energy more usually used for satisfying libidinal drives
was directed towards other aims. His aggressive impulses, too, were inhibited in personal contact and converted into fuel for his striving to rule.
Seeking the sources of these transformations in his childhood experience
is a first step in understanding his adult behavior. Tracing his development
through his early years will offer clues to the statesman's performance.

2.   Outward Conditions of Richelieu's Early Rearing

The fragmentary evidence on Armand de Richelieu's first months of life
points to a closeness between mother and infant which was rare for families
of noble rank at the end of the sixteenth century. The baby's weakness at
his birth, on September 9, 1585, apparently delayed his church baptism
for eight months and made the relationship between Madame de Richelieu
and her third son one of interdependence.[15] Indeed, according to one whose
information came from reminiscences of his older brother Alphonse, Armand's condition procured him such intense attention from his mother
that her exertions on his behalf were almost fatal to her. François was
absent during Richelieu's first months of life, Pure tells us in his mannered
Latin style, and "divided by a double fear"—for him and for her newborn
son—Suzanne finally "took heart as she became . . . accustomed to the
pressing stings of fate" and learned to cope with the difficult situation,
"restraining and tempering her vexations."[16]

François de Richelieu's absence from his family was habitual long before
his premature death. Even while the Richelieus were lodged in Paris during
Armand's early months, the father's absences must have been more extended than his infrequent visits. As a chief officer of the king's household
he was supposed to accompany Henri III (and later, for a shorter time,
Henri IV) on the itinerant path a king of France was obliged to follow in
those days of uncertain royal authority. Furthermore, like that of many
courtiers, the elder Richelieu's amorous life excluded his wife some part

of the time.[17] Distance between the couple widened further when, some time before midsummer 1590, Suzanne removed to the family seat of her husband, taking Armand with her. It is quite likely that this move took place considerably earlier than that year, not only in view of the family's straitened circumstances,[18] but also because Suzanne felt distaste for court life and always regarded the château at Richelieu, not Paris, as her home. Her statement, in 1615, "I have lived forty-nine years in this house,"[19] indicates that the country estate was her customary residence from the time of her marriage.

The composition of Richelieu's family in their country home was predominantly female. Henri, his oldest brother, probably was entered at court in Paris as a royal page while the future cardinal was still a baby. The second son, Alphonse, would before many years leave the family house in order to prepare for the church in Paris. He was a shy and taciturn presence during Armand's infancy. There remained, in addition to his mother, the paternal grandmother, a widowed aunt, and the first of the Richelieu children, Françoise, seven years older than himself. Hanotaux believes there may have been still another female Du Plessis relation in the household during the 1580s and 1590s.[20] To reinforce the femininity of the environment, sometime around 1590—possibly even after the death of his father—the last of Armand's siblings—a girl, Nicole—was born.[21]

On July 10, 1590, separation of the father from his family was made final: François died of illness on the battlefield of Gonesse. Suzanne was left at the château of Richelieu to raise her children. Here Armand would remain until the age of around nine, his rudimentary education directed by his mother with the help of a clerical tutor. Pure summarizes: "Educated through the care of his mother alone, he was above all directed by advice of his relatives in whom his mother, who mistrusted the errors that one of her sex might commit, confided."[22] Chief among these advisors was probably Amador de La Porte, Suzanne's half brother.

These facts are virtually all those on Richelieu's earliest years to which creditable contemporary witness testifies. They tell little about the inward development of the future prime minister. What do they suggest about the conditions of his rearing as they may have affected his early conflicts and their typical resolutions? It is with this scant information that we must sketch a plausible reconstruction of the paths taken by his development that resulted in some of the distinctive features of his personality already identified.

3.   Nurturing and Hatching: Clues to Early Patterns

The highly effective adult that Richelieu became—mostly realistic concerning the world around him and able, with few signs of inner conflict, to influence that world according to his aims—does not allow him to be considered, in any important way, as a case of "failed" development. Nor did his emotional life show significant pathology—especially not in the context of his particular culture. He was able to see others as real individuals, to love some of them and to be loved in return, again seemingly with little conflict, in ways apparently satisfying to him, however restricted such gratification may seem from a modern vantage point. Together, these capacities of working and loving bespeak an infancy that was, on essential points, "successful." There is every reason to assume that his early nurturing was "good enough."[23]

Psychoanalytic inquiry into infant development has disclosed that a first stimulus to intellectual effort may come in reactions to disappointment at the absences of the mother (or nurturing figure). By repeatedly experiencing separation from what is at first felt to be part of the self, followed by its restoration, the infant comes to apprehend the existence of objects in the outside world. Not all infantile responses lead to realistic thinking, however; one reaction may be to hallucinate the missing object, imagining omnipotence. Transforming such illusory satisfaction into anticipation of the mother's future return—realistic thought—requires confident expectations. Such confidence, in turn, is based on secure bonds tying mother to child in the earliest days of life. The mother accedes to the child's needs— perhaps expressed in crying—by a prompt and satisfying reappearance. With her renewed presence the nursling actively takes in, through the mouth, the reward he has been stimulated by her absence to imagine. This happy outcome of temporary absences, repeatedly reenacted, establishes in the child the capacity to defer gratification by anticipating it. And with the mother's prompt and sensitive response to his signals the infant is encouraged for later efforts to control her movements.

Influences that heighten the deprivations or satisfactions of these experiences will leave their marks on thought patterns formed in the first months of life. For example, physical pain experienced by an infant may serve to intensify the aggressive feelings with which it responds to separation from the mother. Such feelings may overwhelm the child and lead to despair. On the other hand, less severe discomfort may instead speed up thought processes through which the mother comes to be seen as an object separate from the self, and thus quicken the pace of the infant's progress towards mastery.[24] And, of course, overlong deprivations of the necessary presence, too often repeated, may soon not be followed by its successful restoration. The infant may become depressed, increasingly withdrawing from contact with the outside world, rather than progressively reaching out towards it.

That close bonds linked Suzanne to her youngest son during his first months has been affirmed by Pure. We do not know, in Richelieu's case, who may have shared nurturing functions with Madame de Richelieu, nor whether, in fact, his mother was also his earliest nurse. We do learn from Pure, however, not only that she was closely involved with Armand as an infant but also that she experienced conflicts connected with this involvement owing to the absence of her husband and, perhaps, the difficulties of the family's situation. Her anxieties, we may surmise, may have made her occasionally "not there" for her infant, despite usual closeness to him. What is more, the fact that the future cardinal had, as an infant, greater possession of his own mother than was common for a child of his social level may mean also that he had the painful experience of her physical absence more frequently. An upper class child cared for entirely by a hired nurse has claims on her continual attention; such could not be the case for Armand's right to his mother, a busy *châtelaine* with responsibilities to many others. Furthermore, more prolonged absences must have occurred in Richelieu's early life at those times when François made one of his appearances.[25] Possibly, also, Armand's early illness served to heighten the impact of such absences and to intensify the rage animating his responses to them.

Another probable feature of Richelieu's care in his first year may be mentioned. The wrapping and handling of an infant, it has been suggested, is a further important influence on how that infant first experiences and apprehends the outside world. Infant swaddling was, of course, a near universal practice through centuries of European history. In the France of that era it was variously applied, depending on the season, the resources of the child's family, and the needs of the child as they were perceived by adults. When a reason for swaddling was given it was that the fragile bones of a newborn needed support in the first few months. Protection from cold, too, was an unspoken advantage of wrapping; often swaddling was continued during the night long after it had been abandoned in daytime hours.[26] Since Richelieu was, by all accounts a delicate and sickly child, born at the beginning of the winter, he was probably allowed less freedom from bindings than most infants, and thus prevented, for a longer period than was customary, from tactile exploration of his own body and of the world around him. Such a limitation, one may speculate, could have helped to sharpen, by way of compensation, the efforts of his mind to understand and master his environment. It could also have stimulated the faculties of other organs of his head in taking in and expressing impressions.[27]

When an infant's experiences of possession and loss of his mother and of his own physical distress are overwhelming, he may respond by withdrawing from an outside world too difficult and painful to confront, turning inward for an imaginary, more indulgent version of reality, or, despairing of his helplessness, he may succumb to depression and apathy. When circumstances are favorable, on the other hand, a child may be able, through mental effort, to overcome the obstacles of his environment, reaching out to influence it in an increasingly effective way.

Father of the Man

For adults, most such infantile experiences are beyond recall. The memories of dependency on an all-important nurturing figure, and of those first human relationships that laid the groundwork for all subsequent ones, are buried too deeply to be accessible to the conscious mind. But in the symbols of art, the substance of dreams, and the imagery of fantasy some of the feelings that accompanied such primitive processes can often be glimpsed. Such imagery is, perhaps, the passage considered in the second chapter here—Richelieu's musings on the means for conquering the sea. The *"mer océane"* was, as I suggest there, an object that seemed to be particularly laden with affect for the adult cardinal, as well as a symbol very commonly associated with the mother. In Richelieu's reworking of this passage, it was noted, the sea became progressively more like a capricious woman, infinitely desirable, passionately loved, but vain, jealous, fickle, and subject to being lured away by others.[28]

It seems justified at least to speculate that among the unconscious memories associated with such striking analogies are those of an infant—in Richelieu's case one weakened by illness and immobilized in bed—who sought to master the incomprehensible comings and goings of a woman necessary to him. His control over her could only, at first, be won by converting into tears the rage he experienced at her absence, and by using his head in other ways to subdue some of his wants in order to gratify more urgent ones. At the same time we may have a glimpse here of another fantasy—the ultimate means to gain the longed-for object—her possession by violent force.

Richelieu's later techniques of domination would show all these strategies: his eyes, his ears, and his powerful mind were enlisted in devising means to gain control over the realm of which he was leader and over that sea that was so alluring to him. And, as the king's surrogate, he would gain also, at last, that *puissance* which brought what may have been primordial dreams of violent conquest within the realm of the possible.

4. **Developing an Active Disposition**

If Richelieu's experiences during his early months were something like the intense ones that have been sketched, what indications in his adult character give clues to the ways in which his responses took shape?

No trait is more characteristic of Richelieu than a deprecation of words and thoughts in favor of a constant striving towards action. Cerebral processes alone are variously characterized by him as "mere chimeras," "vain imaginings," "idle dreams," "sterile thoughts," or "facile meditation." He contrasts these with the outwardly directed *actions* that alone produce the behavior he desires in himself and others. *"Effets"*—variously translatable as effects, actions, deeds, or results—is the key word of a phrase that appears again and again in his writings. Early in his career he remarks in a letter to a friend, "You know my nature, preferring to speak by actions (*effets*) than by words." Another version is, "being accustomed to give much more [weight] to results (*effets*) than to appearances, I would rather seek occasions to show you how much I honor you . . . than to confirm you in this belief by words."[29]

The glorification of action and the view that words and ideas were vain if they produced no tangible effects were as characteristic of his theological beliefs as of his thought on mundane matters. In a work designed to convert Protestants to Catholicism he seems to deprecate all those inward-turning tendencies characteristic of a contemplative life: "Action is worth more than contemplation; it is worth much more to love God than incessantly to consider whether or not one loves Him." A work on Richelieu in his priestly role as director of consciences, which quotes this passage, observes, "Richelieu understands the meritorious life for a Christian to be a perpetual will to action."[30]

In thus deprecating mere words and thoughts, and in extolling action Richelieu may also have been, consciously or not, extolling the virtues of an idealized paternal model. François de Richelieu's duties had called for action to a high degree, and it was as a man of action that he had acquired a distinctive, if not very savory reputation.

There is, too, something in this emphasis on strong and sustained momentum towards results that reflects the example Suzanne de La Porte set for her children. High expectations for a happy outcome if intense and thorough efforts are sufficiently persevered in were, as has been seen, characteristic of Richelieu's mother. Like her, the cardinal was continually alert lest a battle "well begun" be lost for want of maximum effort and whatever additional expenditure might be needed for victory. Like her, he repeatedly expressed, as an adult, the purpose of leaving no stone unturned in pursuing the goals he resolved upon. A phrase that recurs in his letters articulates the principle justifying this dogged persistence: "He who leaves the game, loses it—*Qui quitte la partie la perd*."[31]

The example of parental models, real or fictitious, may be important in shaping the style of behavior of a son or daughter; it may be important also in influencing the moral and practical value that is consciously attached to various options in conduct. But basic orientations, such as those to activity or passivity, *élan* or depression, do not originate as late in the life of the child as the possibility for perceiving such models, or learning the relevant family history. Rather, they originate even before the acquisition of language makes explicit communications possible. The individuality of each person's response pattern is owed not only to his or her particular genetic inheritance, but also to the interaction between this inheritance and a unique experience within a family context. When several children within the same family can be compared as adults, insight into the dynamics of each individual's development can sometimes be gained.[32]

5.   Contrasting Personalities: Two Richelieu Brothers

Armand-Jean de Richelieu was not the only boy raised in the family château. For his first few years he shared the household, and his mother, with a brother, Alphonse-Louis, probably two to three years older than he, but possibly even closer to him in age.[33] While the eldest Richelieu brother, Henri, was already attached to the court in Paris when Armand was born, Alphonse presumably remained at home until Armand was at least six or seven years old. Since the two boys were therefore raised in the same family environment it is possible, by comparing them as men, to determine what characteristics were personal to Armand and which ones he shared with Alphonse, presumably on account of their common inheritance, or like experience of nurture, or both. The ways in which the two adults were different, as well as similar, helps reconstruct the distinctive path of development taken by each.

As men, these two brothers differed fundamentally in their perspectives on life. Armand de Richelieu first embraced a career as a political clergyman, actively seeking to widen the scope and force of ecclesiastical and royal authority. His scholarly pursuits were directed toward finding workable formulae that would solve any doctrinal problem likely to trouble the minds of parishioners or their vicars or disturb the peace of the realm. No theological inquiry could have put less emphasis on soul-searching than did the body of his religious writings. Far from being a mystic, like many of the increasingly influential "new wave" of theological reformers, an analyst of the cardinal's religious thought finds him instead "practical."[34]

Alphonse de Richelieu, on the other hand, rejected the role of professional cleric, choosing a life of self-mortification and contemplation. His taste in philosophy confirmed his fight against worldly concerns: he was a student of Seneca—reportedly he had committed much of that philosopher's work to memory[35]—and called himself a Stoic. His choice of retreat from the world was a monastic order that not only imposed restrictions on conversation but also on the consumption of meat—a deprivation considered in that era more severe than it is today. Alphonse did rejoin the world at his brother's insistence, but kept his preferences, declaring that it would be better for him to die on the "straw pallet of Dom Alphonse the monk than on the magnificent bed of the archbishop of Lyons." After he had been confirmed as Cardinal Archbishop of that city he continued to lament the uncongeniality of such a splendid office to a person of his tastes.[36] Even after his release from monastic vows, he persisted in renouncing meat.[37]

The youngest Richelieu brother's care for splendor of appearance stands in bold relief against Alphonse's conspicuous simplicity. It is in the prime minister's early writings that his concern with outward show appears most clearly; in later years arrangements designed to make a public splash were handled through administrative channels.

Arriving in 1609 in his remote Luçon diocese, Armand was dismayed at the poverty of his personal accommodations: impossible to build a fire because of smoke, grounds so poor that one could not take a walk. His disappointment, however, was secondary to his concern that he might make a shabby appearance in the midst of such a dilapidated setting. He is thus delighted to have hired as *maître d'hôtel* the gentleman servant of the late duc de Montpensier—in short, a butler from the richest princely family of the realm[38] to "serve me extremely well, in your style," as he writes Madame de Bourges in Paris. Thus we glimpse a further motive for relying on the taste of that lady in selecting his personal and household accessories: she is familiar with the ways of the rich. So is the butler: "Whatever company comes to see me," he continues, "he knows exactly what must be done."[39] He asks the same lady to order for him two dozen silver plates, "of a good size, as they make them nowadays." As a "beggarly" bishop in the most "mud-encrusted, unpleasant bishopric in France," he writes, "I cannot pretend to too much opulence; nevertheless, when I have silver plates my nobility will be much heightened." Madame de Bourges's skill and knowledge were congenial to Richelieu's bent for conspicuous consumption: "I know very well," he comments concerning the cost of these plates, "that you would not want me to have something skimpy merely for the want of one hundred *écus* more."[40]

Projecting regular visits to Paris in 1610, Richelieu asks advice of the same consultant on the possibility of having his own establishment there (rather than taking furnished rooms) in spite of the cost and his meagre resources:

> Being of your disposition, that is, a bit vainglorious, I should
> very much like, it being more comfortable, to make a better ap-
> pearance. It's a great pity—impoverished nobility.[41]

To give the appearance of splendor was important for Richelieu. This concern included his personal attire. Missing the white taffeta clerical vestments Madame de Bourges was supposed to have included in a shipment to him at Luçon, he has had to have others made ("otherwise I could not have officiated" at Easter), but in a different color, so that in case the first set is found, "I shall have them in two colors."[42] In his list of synodal rules for the clerics of his diocese he stresses details of personal appearance as well as church adornment.[43]

His vanity concerning his public appearance included his mode of travel. About to return from exile in Avignon in 1619 he writes his brother Henri: "Please send me a beautiful hackney—but altogether beautiful if possible." And the appearance made by the gifts he presents to others is similarly important. The marquis de Richelieu was also to send:

> Two pieces of gold jewelry that I want to present in the places
> you know about . . . I should like something suitable to my po-
> sition. . . . It's better to give nothing than to give a meagre gift.[44]

The skills, as well as the tastes, of the two younger Richelieu brothers
also contrasted strikingly. Perhaps the most obvious of the differences was
that with respect to verbal mastery. Conflicts and failures in the use of
words partly explain why Alphonse chose to renounce the family bishopric
in favor of joining an order which committed its members to vows of
silence. He was reported to be an "extremely poor" speaker,[45] while his
cadet, succeeding him as prospective Bishop of Luçon, sought out opportunities for public speaking and achieved his first signal success as a preacher.
One rare report by a witness to his public performance tells us that Richelieu's style of delivery was dramatic and fluent. In discourse, writes
James Howell, "he had a pressing way of eloquence and exaggeration of
speech which came from him in such a grave serious accent that it moved
all along."[46]

The writing styles of the two men also contrasted in a manner that seems
significant for their diverse characters: Richelieu's style was spare and to
the point; his calligraphy angular and strikingly economical. One of its
distinguishing features is the almost complete absence of punctuation and
other marks—accents, dots on *i*'s, crosses on *t*'s—although the expression
is so concise and skillful that the meaning is almost always plain.[47] Alphonse's letters, on the other hand, are verbose in the extreme. An elaborate, elongated, curvaceous handwriting corresponds to a message that
usually contrasts, by its circumlocution, with his brother's succinctness. In
contrast, also, with Armand's straightforwardness, the older brother's style,
more often than not, only partly masks hostile feelings which it seems
intended to deny. Consider, for example, this letter to his sister-in-law
which has the manifest purpose of apologizing for delay in writing:

> The letter with which you have honored me gives me a true rea-
> son to acknowledge my neglect and to repent of it. I offer myself
> for everything which you may find necessary to atone for this
> crime. But permit, I beg you, since I frankly recognize my fault
> in good faith, that I also tell you that you have given me too
> much reason to pity myself for me not to express my resent-
> ment.[48]

In these contrasts of perspective and performance a pervasive difference
in moods between the two men may be perceived. Alphonse himself referred to his own "melancholy temperament."[49] A contemporary portrait
of him as Cardinal Archbishop of Lyons is almost a caricature of profound
gloom.[50] In contrast with his younger brother, who, despite melancholy
moments, consistently expresses optimism concerning the possibility of
changing the world to make it conform to his desires, Alphonse's words

frequently reflect the deep pessimism that his face seems to express. Thus, in a letter from Rome, he complains of a lack of good men who live in "fear" or "love" of God. He knows, he claims, none of the former kind; there *are* none of the latter.[51]

In infancy, too, are formed basic conceptions of one's own body and patterns of movement that persist into adulthood. As an adult Alphonse de Richelieu apparently had certain motor disorders that may be traceable to that earliest period. "In walking," it was reported by contemporaries, he had what was described as a "tic"—he "swayed from side to side."[52] As far as can be determined, on the other hand, the youngest Richelieu brother was graceful and easy in his movements. During his period at the Academy in Paris, while training for a military career, he apparently had no difficulty in mastering horsemanship and fencing.[53] He continued to love exercise, in the country, and in public appearances was given to making flamboyant, theatrical gestures with his whole body.[54]

The impression of sadness given by Alphonse de Richelieu's portraiture is strengthened by one of homeliness: "His physiognomy is displeasing," as Deloche sums it up; "He is ugly and awkward."[55]

All in all, Alphonse de Richelieu seems to have been a plain and unappealing figure. If other circumstances had tended to determine that Suzanne would prefer Armand, as a child, to her second son, these characteristics may have reinforced that preference. In a family letter written after Alphonse became a monk his mother names him "my poor *chartreux*."[56]

There is, indeed, more direct reason to believe that Alphonse felt himself to have been disadvantaged, as a child, in the competition with Armand for his mother's favor, and that he emerged from childhood with bitter resentments. As an adult, for example, he was fiercely misogynous. The concealed hostility suggested by a letter to his sister-in-law has already been mentioned. The terms of a later letter concerning the women of Lyons, written when he has just arrived as Archbishop, are still more revealing. He has been told, he says, that this region is "the province of women, at which I am astonished, for they are animals." Further,

> Their occupation is to do nothing. . . . If certain persons were banished . . . this would be an agreeable place to live . . . harpies . . . created to torment poor strangers . . . spiteful women . . . some whose bodies and faces seem . . . models for monsters.[57]

Indirect evidence that a dislike of women was linked to resentment of Suzanne could be seen in omission of any mention of her in Pure's biography of the Lyons cardinal. That book, based on information given by Alphonse himself, alludes neither to Madame de Richelieu nor to her forebears.[58] This contrasts with Pure's laudatory treatment of Suzanne in his fragmentary account of Armand de Richelieu's life, published after Alphonse's death. In that work he claims that the qualities of the human foetus are determined by the mother's contribution as well as the father's, rather than only (as was commonly believed) by the father's, and praises Suzanne's virtues and those of her ancestors. These, it will be remembered, he links to a royal house.[59]

Alphonse de Richelieu's self-deprivation where eating was concerned and his difficulties with speech have also been noticed. There is, further, fragmentary information on a curious minor conflict with his younger brother, that seems to hint that these difficulties date from an early stage in life. After Alphonse had been made Archbishop of Lyons, Armand, fearing that chocolate, a new substance that his brother had been "using often" was a dangerous drug, sent a court physician whom he thought Alphonse respected to try to persuade him to depend, instead, on the "regular medicines" prescribed by doctors for "maladies." Alphonse's response suggests not only an emotional dependency on foods that may be related to very early deprivation, but also that he obscurely felt Armand was responsible for that deprivation. The older brother wrote his cadet, "My best friends"—by which he meant chocolate and pepper—"have abandoned me because you outlawed them, whether with knowledge of the reason or on account of professional convention I don't know."[60] The words he chooses evoke, whether significantly or not, the feelings of many small children whose "best friend" abandons them for a new arrival in need of the nurture they still crave.

In any case Pure depicts Alphonse as a melancholy schoolboy who tired easily and whose difficulty in learning caused him to weep when his peers surpassed him in their studies. Armand, on the other hand, astonished everyone with his precocity, outdistancing his elder brother with little difficulty. Alphonse is described as showing a sadness beyond his years. He had a meditative nature, read much, and was taciturn and rough in manners. This inward turning, we are told, was the reason a naval career was at first selected for him—presumably because it was thought to be a *métier* compatible with a love of quiet solitude. The ability to swim was required for this profession, however, and this Alphonse was unable to master, either because "he lacked sufficient zeal or perhaps his fear was too great." The biographer then reports an incident which surely was told him by Alphonse himself. Fearing that others would think he was dissimulating in order to avoid naval service, the seventeen-year-old boy went alone to the lake and threw himself into the water in order to prove his incapacity. Had not some boaters happened by at the time, he would certainly have drowned.

Alphonse's self-destructive gesture in plunging into the "sea" can possibly be understood, in view of the infantile deprivation he may have experienced, as acting out a fantasy of merging with his mother, while his usual horror of water might have reflected the fear of such reabsorption. Such tendencies would represent a "developmental deficit"—owing to an incomplete separation from a nurturing figure that had been, for him, inadequate.[61] Certainly they contrast with his younger brother's later ardent aspirations and active efforts to master the sea.

For two years afterwards, Pure continues, Alphonse was meditative, feverish, and "lost in reading." This episode, seemingly the depressive aftermath of an adolescent suicide attempt, caused his family to "reproach" him for his "silence and sadness," the author relates.[62]

This Richelieu brother's tendency to depression continued in adulthood. Sometimes he was melancholy and silent; sometimes he directed anger outward. His younger brother, whose subordinate he had become, was an occasional target for that anger. In his letters Alphonse shows how much he feels himself to be slighted by Armand. During a mission to Rome he writes to Claude Bouthillier complaining that the prime minister does not appreciate him: "I may say without vanity that I have always been worth more than he has estimated." Again, he writes ruefully of the "melancholy which he caused to be born in me," and "the small esteem he has shown up until now for my person."[63] Although he ostensibly refers to contemporary neglect in his reproach to Armand for valuing him insufficiently, his resentment may be linked to feelings that date from much farther back in time. "I have found my consolation," he writes, "in the belief that he will regret me when he has lost me." He hopes only that "he will realize after my death what I was worth."[64] Is he here expressing a grievance from a childhood in which he had felt himself forsaken in favor of a newcomer whose weak condition attracted the loving attention of the adults? In any case, his fantasy seems to be one of taking revenge on his brother by means of damage to himself. Perhaps the same motive in part accounts for his self-destructive plunge years before.

In later years Alphonse's special skill, applied first within the confines of the Carthusian Order which he joined as a young man, and years after that when the plague gripped Lyons where he presided as Archbishop, was that of a nurse. In thus nursing the sick he may have been reproducing an actual situation of his childhood, consoling himself by taking over the nursing role performed by women in his family who, once his own caretakers, were now caring for his brother. Indeed, during Armand's last illness Alphonse longed to nurse him and the dying man had steadfastly to decline his brother's petitions to be allowed to come care for him.[65] Nor did the younger one have any sympathy for Alphonse's wish to be allowed to minister physically to the suffering of his diocese at the risk of his own health. From Paris the prime minister sent a message refusing permission for so hazardous an effort:

> I have learned that now that the plague is at Lyons, you have
> some thought of helping the sick yourself. . . . You will do much

better to have them helped by people you assign to that end . . .
God will see your intention and the sick the effect of your charity much more efficaciously employed for them.[66]

As an adult Armand de Richelieu was much interested in medical matters. Like many others of that age, too, he was given to medical analogies
in his written work. The personal role he adopted, however, was that of
the doctor who prescribes strategies, from a distance, for coping with the
ills of the body—human and politic. Alphonse's interest in taking on the
task of physical care of the sick was not his brother's.

In manifest ways, then, these two brothers stood, as adults, in striking
contrast. Alphonse was homely, awkward, withdrawn, contemplative, mo-
rose, and self-mortifying, while Armand was attractive, graceful, outgoing,
active, optimistic, and splendid. Some of these obvious differences may
have been due to genetic predispositions. Some, however, seem to be
traceable to differing treatments the two received in infancy—Alphonse
perhaps neglected by nurturing figures, displaced by a more favored newcomer who received sufficient empathic attention to enable him to reach
out, with hopeful expectations and enormous energy, toward the surrounding world. But still other elements in the contrast between the two
may have developed, or been reinforced, later, as the children grew up in
a common family setting.

8 Gaining Self-mastery

> I know, thank God, how to govern myself, and know moreover
> how those under me should govern themselves.[1]

Richelieu's drive for achievement earned him the reputation, in the eyes
of Louis XIII, for being able to accomplish in one day what others needed
months to do.[2] The prodigious, unflagging energy and the thorough, persistent method with which the cardinal strove to influence events are most
often cited as remarkable in his career.[3] In the passage above, Richelieu
himself makes a connection between his drive to control others and his
own self-control. His declaration is confident. There are, however, signs
that his self-mastery had been hard-won. His progress in the struggle to
achieve it can be partially traced to that early period of life after infancy in
which the child brings what resources he has available to the task of beginning to conform to the expectations of adults.

1.   Growing up at Richelieu

In the family in which Richelieu was raised, he and his brother Alphonse
were outnumbered by at least three adult women and two sisters. Occasional visits by uncles, male cousins, and, perhaps, a brother-in-law, probably did not replace the authority of a father who was usually absent.[4]

It is likely also that the absence of men had consequences for the techniques used to control the boys. The two brothers may have escaped the
severe kinds of physical punishment that were characteristic of the epoch.
It was customary to start applying *verges*—or switches—to chastise boys
about the time of weaning. This form of punishment may intensify a fear
of castration; applied for the first time at a time in which the child is

struggling to gain sphincter mastery, such a fear may be repressed and transformed into fantasies of beating and being beaten.

If the two younger Richelieu boys were less subject than most to switching and beating, this would be owed to the deference shown by women of that time to males of all ages.[5] Richelieu's supposedly delicate health, as a child, would further have protected him from such harsher forms of discipline. And, indeed, Pure claims that, as a schoolboy, Armand was swayed by praise but would do nothing if threatened with whipping.[6] It seems likely that such adamancy in a young scholar had been encouraged by experience at home. In Richelieu's own later discussion of the duties of parents, he cautions that "extremity is always pernicious" in disciplining children.[7] In a later work he again warns against excessively severe (*outre mesure*) punishment of children, even if there seems to be good reason for it.[8]

That there was such respect for the physical integrity of the youngest son in the Richelieu household seems confirmed by his adult character. Signs either of pleasure in inflicting harm or enjoyment of being abused are largely lacking in him in later life. Even those who have stressed the brutality of the policies which he underwrote as prime minister have acknowledged the apparent lack of pleasure he took in causing damage to others. He usually absented himself when punishments were administered and tried to avoid witnessing the effects of war's violence. "Anyone," writes Avenel, "who has thoroughly studied Richelieu knows that cruelty was one of his political methods rather than an instinct of his character." He finds "no indication which could give the impression of a merciless spirit or cruel instincts."[9]

Another kind of disciplinary method is, however, suggested by forms that were often taken by both brothers' aggressive and submissive urges. These bear the mark of such controls being imposed as teasing, shaming, and ridicule. These are child discipline methods typically used by the weak— such as women—who are unable or unwilling to apply physical sanctions. Reinforcing this age-old tendency were the "progressive" influences in French education of the Counter Reform movement (in which women played a newly important role) stressing the preferableness of shaming over violence in securing compliance from small children.[10]

Armand de Richelieu's sensitivity to shame, his strategies to avoid ridicule as an adult, his intense sense of personal dignity, have variously been noticed by one or another of his biographers. Such sensitivities are shown explicitly in the instructions to confessors prepared under his direction, in which the danger of shaming is frequently stressed. If absolution is withheld, Richelieu warns here, it must be so "discreetly, so that no one is aware of it" if the priest is in any doubt. He must be "cautious and restrained" in questioning those under his direction about lechery, especially women, who are timid about confessing sins of the flesh. One can be

Conditions

tactful: it is not necessary to ask for details or explicit avowals. The priest is forbidden to exact public penitence for private sins and he is instructed to take care that feelings of shame are not so intense that they deter the penitent from making future confessions. While those of humble station are less sensitive, for those who are "in society (*du monde*)," "gentle and suitable" penances must be exacted that do not humiliate the sinner.[11]

Evidence suggests that, as a boy, Armand avoided the possibility of being shamed by shunning the company of his agemates. According to the contemporary storyteller, Charles Perrault, Richelieu's childhood fellows reported that, as a youth, the future prime minister would not join them in play because "he was destined for occupations which did not permit him to waste his time."[12] Raconis, closer to the event, similarly avers that the future cardinal's schoolmates at the Collège de Navarre attested to his continual and successful ambition to be first in every class. As in the case of John the Baptist, wrote this admiring friend, "there was nothing childish in his childhood."[13]

While these anecdotes may be more imaginative than factual, they evoke a picture of a young man whose fear of ridicule dictated self-isolation. Through hindsight this may have appeared to his peers as concentration on self-advancement. But his former intimate, and later implacable enemy, Mathieu de Morgues, understood, according to Deloche, that Richelieu was more vulnerable to ridicule than to direct attacks.[14] It may be noteworthy that there is no story that depicts him taking part in pranks, either as a boy, or in that court of Louis XIII where practical jokes sometimes afforded the king a welcome amusement. Although, as an adult, Richelieu loved to be amused, in the strictest privacy, by various jocose friends, and occasionally indulged, with such intimates, in a certain levity,[15] his own reserved and sober manner was almost always maintained in public.

Richelieu's habitual seriousness was of concern to his friends, who feared that his worry about great affairs might impair his health. One of his closest confidants wrote to him when, for the second time, he had been inducted to the king's ministry, that on this occasion he did not pray God to give his friend the blessing of a conciliatory spirit, nor of a strong nor wise one, "with which you are, by His grace, sufficiently provided, but rather a joyous one (*spirituum gaudii*)."[16]

Richelieu's customary gravity was only rarely described as melancholic, as when, after a death or disappointment, he was temporarily unable to devise strategies to surmount problems in the outside world. More usually it seems to have reflected an anxiety lest he be shamed before witnesses. As a schoolboy, Pure claims, he would never venture a response to a question without knowing the right answer: "If an instructor interrogated him he . . . anticipated, by intelligent questions, the dangers of a rash response."[17]

Throughout his life Richelieu was wary lest he act unguardedly or impulsively and thus expose himself to humiliation. On a trip to Rheims with

Louis XIII in 1641, for example, he was invited by town representatives to give his name to the great bell which was soon to be installed there in a baptism-like rite. Characteristically, he did not assent spontaneously, but took the matter under advisement, "saying that it would be the first to which he had given a name and he wished first of all to inform himself about the ceremony." Later, "he sent word that he accepted." The same report recounts that the cardinal was careful not to select a house to stay in where he could be seen from neighbors' windows.[18] Such a desire for privacy was not characteristic of seventeenth century notables.

In personal relations Richelieu was still more cautious of familiarity. Before he gave way to any demonstrativeness he first assured himself of the other's deference. A sign of favor was given to a company commander, for example, after the latter had given extreme and repeated marks of respect to the cardinal. At first the courtier was treated brusquely—"I was only La Hoguette"—but after the prolonged courtship the minister signalled his appreciation by calling his subordinate "Monsieur."[19]

A rare instance of a misstep in protecting his personal dignity shows Richelieu's vulnerability to humiliation. A retainer recalls how the cardinal had been so charmed by the comte Du Plessy Praslin that "he had let him enter his carriage twice," and, on the second occasion,

> slapped him on the shoulder and said to him, 'Count, let us serve the king well and he will reward us well.' This affectionate gesture, which was not habitual to the cardinal, persuaded the count that he was really in his good graces.

Accordingly, Praslin thought to take advantage of his favor by appealing to Richelieu for appointment to the command of a company of carabineers. This upset the delicate balance which had been struck: "His Eminence, drawing himself up with coldness, said to him, 'The king will take it under advisement,' and after that never had him enter his carriage, although he presented himself there often."[20] The icy *hauteur*, often attributed to the cardinal, seems here to be self-protection against embarrassment resulting from excessive impulsiveness.

Alphonse de Richelieu, like his younger brother, was preoccupied with questions of dignity to an exceptional degree. In him, however, the concern usually took quite a different form. As newly appointed Archbishop of Aix, for example, he provoked a quarrel over precedence with town leaders. His position was considered so petty and ill-founded that even his well-wishers were embarrassed by his insistence.[21]

This older Richelieu brother did not always react against slights with such vehement protest of his worthiness. Instead, he often took real or supposed humiliation "lying down," possibly relishing it. In reproaching his younger brother for harboring contempt for him, he warned that his own premature death might be the consequence "because a person of pride cannot endure an unjust scorn without . . . great changes in his physique."[22] In Alphonse's mind these fantasies were sometimes accompanied by thoughts of inflicting harm on others, especially on Armand. When he muses of his melancholy, "I nurture it . . . with care," he is anticipating with satisfaction the remorse that his own death would cause his brother.[23] The plaintive and vindictive notes so often struck by Alphonse were different indeed from the recoiling and coldness with which Richelieu met lack of deference shown to him by others. But the vulnerability to humiliation which both men showed may plausibly have had its origin in experience they shared as children.

Other historians have seen in Armand de Richelieu's insistence on the trappings of personal dignity a defensiveness concerning his insufficiently exalted social origins. Inversely, his occasional diffidence towards, or exaggerated deference to the high-born has been interpreted as revealing feelings of shame about his own modest status.[24] It is indeed quite possible that Richelieu did, as a child, apprehend unfavorable judgments made by others on his social position. It could be supposed, for example, that the reputedly haughty Françoise de Rochechouart may have humiliated her daughter-in-law Suzanne de La Porte. Armand's sensitivity to shame may well have been reinforced in childhood by such scenes. It is also likely that ridicule and humiliation afflicted the children in the wake of their father's heedless dissipation of the family's fortunes. But the study of child development—not to mention everyday observation of children—seems to show that such experiences would neither be early, nor intimate, nor profound enough to produce the trait that the two brothers shared—high sensitivity in matters of personal dignity—or at least, not the highly individuated form taken by this trait in each one. For more satisfying explanations of this aspect of Richelieu's adult character it is necessary to seek in it clues to his unconscious mental life that may be linked to his private responses to these outward influences of his youth.

2.   Ambition

"Ambition," writes Fenichel, "represents the fight against . . . shame."[25] While a drive for achievement as powerful as Armand de Richelieu's is doubtless determined by many influences, evidence has already been cited that suggests that he did, as a child and youth, struggle to ward off the experience of shame.

Freud was apparently the first to observe that the reaction of shame is "intimately connected with involuntary emptying of the bladder."[26] Through his and successors' research, links between the etiology of shame and processes associated with urinary incontinence have been further elucidated.[27] Fenichel summarizes: "*Shame* is the specific force directed against urethral erotic temptations; *ambition* . . . an outcome of urethral-erotic conflicts."[28] In Richelieu, both the timidity before possible shame and the

118

ambition that countered it may point to traces of the early struggle Fenichel describes. Here it is the task to consider whether this struggle was an important one for Richelieu, and, if it seems so, how he transformed feelings originally associated with it.

A.   Signs of Conflict

The distinctiveness of Richelieu's ambition in his own time consisted in the exceptionally concentrated way in which he used his mind to anticipate and plan the future and the methodical purpose with which he developed strategies intended to put his plans into effect. This singleminded purposefulness, however, had another side. Richelieu's proneness to anxiety, his periodic apprehensiveness of catastrophe, his bouts of uncertainty before decision-making, hint that his characteristic confidence and determination indicate an overcoming of opposite tendencies in himself, just as his powerful energies and persistent, active inclinations may represent resolutions of even earlier conflict over the fear of damage—to himself, on the one hand if he surrendered passively to the many causes of his infantile distress, and on the other hand, to the one who nurtured him if he gave vent to his violent feelings.

Anxiety. Richelieu was fond of saying that his was a timid nature, a confession that no doubt seemed disingenuous to those who feared the redoubtable cardinal. As a statesman his reputation for personal bravery was scarcely ever questioned. Nevertheless he remarks, in a letter to his sister-in-law, on his "rather cowardly temperament (*mon humeur un peu poltronne*)."[29] His strong impulse to act, and his ability to do so forcefully, are the other side of this version of himself as a "poltroon." He could disclose to his secretary, "I am indeed one of those who is frightened by everything (*à qui tout fait peur*) even though they wish to fear (*craindre*) nothing."[30]

Richelieu's "timidity" is the anxiety he experienced before he determined on an effective means to control himself and others. It appears typically as he takes stock of a situation, canvassing expedients before finally deciding on plans.

One student of Richelieu shrewdly observes that the cardinal was "incapable" of improvisation. In another place the same author remarks, "Surprises frightened Richelieu."[31] This antipathy to improvisation suggests a desire of the cardinal to avoid taking chances. A more recent inquirer, analyzing the prime minister's use of words, notes the rich variety of terms he employed to denote bad surprises.[32] Seemingly, what was unforeseen could never be pleasant.

Once a course was decided upon, however, Richelieu was resolute, by his own report as well as the evidence of his deeds. He himself is said to have confided to a friend "that he was timid by nature and that he dared undertake nothing that he had not thought about many times, but after having resolved upon it, he acted boldly."[33]

Aware, as we are, of interpretations made by Freud and Fenichel, it becomes significant that these emotions that Richelieu says accompany his planning are similar to the anxiety of a small boy who is still unsure of his physical self-mastery.

And, indeed, the prime minister's word associations sometimes seem to betray origins in such childhood experience. The following passage from a letter to his cousin is a particularly striking example:

> I owe the good outcomes that I have had in my life primarily to the blessing of God and, in the second place, to the care I have taken to anticipate unfortunate events (*mauvais accidens*), and to a certain prudence—timid perhaps, but useful—which, in preventing me from persuading myself that I was sheltered when, while it was not raining in my bedroom, a rain-gutter could be filling my office with water, has contrived that I shall not forget to make sure of getting as well under cover from the one as well as from the other.[34]

By the use of his mind he is able to forestall "bad accidents" and thus to avoid getting wet from the "rain" entering his bedroom. This wisdom of the statesman may succeed the triumph of the three-year-old who surmounts his anxiety and devises a strategy by which he may reliably avoid embarrassment by using his head. In this passage, as in another one we have considered, the prime minister describes the consummation of his ambition as achieving power over water.[35]

A sense of urgency. It has been noticed that Richelieu's dogged perseverance in the projects he undertook may have been an aspect of his style of action that dated from his overcoming of tendencies to depression in early infancy. Equally characteristic of his mode of pursuing projects on which he had decided was a sense of urgency, as though he feared that the slightest weakening of persistence would open floodgates through which overwhelming forces would surge. Thus, however long the projects he undertook might be in progress, he endeavored not to allow the *élan* with which they were launched to subside, nor his own sharp attention to them to languish.

It is not clear that this sense of urgency was much affected by what the objective of any particular enterprise might be; any "game worth the candle" was worth pressing forward as though the next moment might be the very last opportunity for success. In his early years as a political figure he "runs and gallops" ahead at such a pace, in Hanotaux's words, that he ignores developments at court that should have warned him of impending disaster from another quarter.[36] Later, at the height of his power, he would use the strong imprecation of "shame" against one who had merely failed to produce on time a certain report Richelieu had requested as source material in a work of historical writing.[37]

From the scant traces that survive of his diocesal administration an early example of his sense of the pressure of time can be followed. It concerned a project in his diocese to serve an evangelical cause. Soon after he arrived there he issued an invitation to the commissioner of the Capuchin Order in nearby Fontenay to found a monastery in Luçon. To inaugurate his campaign he proposed that this officer sponsor a forty-hour prayer meeting, "judging that it will heat up the devotion of souls that may otherwise cool down." The effectiveness of this strategy, he thought, would be increased because it would be timed shortly after Easter while "devotion is still fervent (*vive*)."[38]

Correspondence concerning this project continued for four years, into 1613, when Méry de Vic, Keeper of the Seals, warned Richelieu of the queen mother's concern lest such a monastery become a charge on the state exchequer.[39] By the end of 1617, foundation of the religious house was still an issue. At this time Richelieu, now in exile, wrote to the head of the Capuchins suggesting that the proposed institution be founded "as soon as possible." He continues in almost the same words of urgency he had used more than eight years before: Unless there is haste, he warns, "the fervor . . . presently heated up . . . might cool down."[40] According to records of the Capuchin Order, the Luçon establishment was not, in fact, finally inaugurated until 1619,[41] yet every communication on the matter from Richelieu suggests that the very next moment is the time to strike while the iron is hot—that with one more effort a decisive victory will be won.

B.   Symptoms

Richelieu's ambitious planning and the anxiety and sense of urgency that accompanied it contributed to the impression of powerful thrust given by most enterprises he undertook. It has been suggested that these tendencies may have been importantly shaped by a struggle for bodily self-mastery that took place after his emergence from infancy. The struggle itself could have been intensified by physiological obstacles to urinary control, such as the feverish illnesses from which Richelieu suffered as a small child. Enforced bed rest, too, could both have impeded facile self-conquest and increased the concern of adults in a way that aggravated the young patient's anxiety. And, in fact, certain behavior of the adult Richelieu seems to bear marks of a conflict that once took place in an interior arena.

Insomnia and illness. As an adult, Richelieu's frequent serious illnesses were apt to involve the urinary tract, ending in an obstruction of urine. He himself describes, during a visit to Bordeaux in 1632, how an innovative surgeon has devised a catheter which "has now made me void all the urine which was in the bladder, which was killing me, which gives me inde-scribable relief."[42] This may not have been the first such episode; it certainly was not the last. In 1635 he mentions that he is suffering for the third time from an illness "like that of Bordeaux." At that time, as in the weeks preceding the earlier attack, Richelieu's ailments seem to have been ag-gravated by anxieties concerning the course of political affairs. As so often, he himself voiced his awareness of the relation between mental and phys-ical states. The experience of this last illness, he wrote, has "made me realize how the outbursts of my blood come from the agitations of my miserable mind."[43] In each case of illness one of Richelieu's concerns had been the development of conspiracies against his leadership in which the king's brother was an unacknowledged participant. After the last bout, Alphonse, in professing his happiness to learn of his brother's recovery, voiced to Bouthillier his "lingering apprehension that that organ [partie], so often weakened by vexatious obstructions, may finally become like the drainpipe into which . . . an infinity . . . of putrid substances are dumped"— that is, blocked altogether.[44]

Another indication that the urethral tract may once have been a focus for intense inner conflict is given by evidence concerning the adult Richelieu that was known to contemporaries: he suffered from chronic and intractable insomnia, a symptom which may also be a residue of a childhood struggle against enuresis.[45] It was the prime minister's habit, during his habitual bouts of early morning wakefulness, to use the time thus abstracted from sleep for work with a secretary. Because of this arrangement, the pattern of his insomnia is well-documented; he often awakened around 2:00 A.M. and worked until about 5:00.[46] Many of his letters and dispatches are dated with the time of these early hours. On other occasions, finding himself thus wakeful, he would have an attendant read to him. Among such at-tendants was, before he elected to follow the queen mother into exile, the writer Mathieu de Morgues, Abbé de Saint Germain. After becoming Ri-chelieu's enemy, this former familiar addresses the prime minister, in a hostile pamphlet: "Thou who art always listening and who never sleep except the Devil rock you."[47] And Richelieu himself, in giving advice to the king, may be revealing an unconscious function that night wakefulness performed for himself: If Louis wishes to "maintain his authority," he warns, "one must have an eye perpetually open." Otherwise, he concludes, "One is assuredly lost."[48]

Tears. For a child who has struggled to control it, urination may have an aggressive meaning. It may even be directed, in fantasy or fact, against others. Later, hostility expressed in such aggressive gestures can be con-verted into other, more acceptable forms of behavior, such as weeping.[49] As an adult, Richelieu was much given to tears. Even in his time, when crying was more acceptable for men than it is today, the cardinal's prone-ness to weep was notorious.[50]

A compliment paid to Richelieu by a royal confessor stressed his readiness with tears: "Those who, like me, have had the happiness to know Your Eminence will stand witness to the tenderness of your heart, as evidenced by the tears which flow from your eyes at the sight of the miseries of others."[51] In fact, however, it was not primarily the sight of the miseries of others that seems to have evoked Richelieu's tears. On the contrary, the best-documented occasions of the prime minister giving way to floods were ones on which he suppressed angry feelings or "turned the other cheek" to those toward whom he felt strong resentment.

Charles de Montchal, the archbishop of Toulouse, describes a scene in which he had been strongly opposing Richelieu on a certain policy. The latter, "trying to conquer his hostility," pressed the archbishop "to promise him his friendship, which he had desired for a long time." The observer continues: "And as he said these words he pulled out his handkerchief and wiped his eyes, which were moist, saying, 'I am suddenly overcome by affection (*tendresse*).'" Montchal reported himself "extremely surprised" at this speech and this demonstration, "knowing that the cardinal had a long-standing antipathy towards him."[52]

The most famous scene of those in which Richelieu's tears flowed copiously was that on the Day of Dupes when he was the object of Marie de Medici's unbridled wrath. This occasion, on which his favorite niece was also spurned and humiliated by Marie, was probably one on which the cardinal felt the strongest feelings of anger towards the queen mother. These feelings were repressed and, evidently, converted into streams of tears. Mathieu de Morgues, who apparently received a first-hand account from Marie herself, accused Richelieu of "throwing yourself at her feet," and "heaving," with the "crocodile tears abundantly distilled by your eyes."[53] Often thereafter Richelieu's tears flowed when he thought of Marie de Medici. When this was reported to her she was said to have commented that "he cried when he wished to."[54] It is, however, doubtful that the tears which Richelieu released when he contemplatd the queen mother were consciously hypocritical. It is as likely that they represented, instead, the rage he could not allow himself to express directly.

In attempting to reconstruct the process by which these patterns became established, it is helpful again to compare Alphonse de Richelieu's behavior with that of his younger brother. As a small child, it has been conjectured, Alphonse was not as much indulged by his caretakers as his invalid sibling. In a letter to Henri, the oldest Richelieu brother, on the occasion of the death of Henri's wife, Alphonse shows that he considers tears an enviable privilege: he counsels the marquis to "shed torrents of them"—bizarre advice for a man of religion at that time—although he avers that in giving it he may be like the "too-indulgent surgeon who, in poulticing the wound of his patient, infects him with gangrene." Presumably tears were a solace that this brother could not, as an adult, permit himself, although he seems to have made a point of admitting to Pure that he had been prone to weep, as a schoolboy, at the frustration of being outdistanced in scholarship.[55] Moreover, as we have seen earlier, he feared water, could not learn to swim, and made an attempt to drown himself on the pretext of demonstrating this to others. Armand de Richelieu, on the other hand, according to all reports a precocious, energetic, and adaptable scholar, seems to have resolved childhood conflicts in a manner more conducive to worldly success.

A child's weeping, according to findings of psychoanalysis, sometimes originates just after he or she becomes *visually* aware of the mother's departure. Before this stage, absence is experienced only by tactile impressions. Tears are a response to the mother's loss that express, "I do not see you."[56] The proneness of infants to crying may be further accentuated by physical pain.[57] Persistence of frequent tear-shedding in later life may partly reflect its early success in forcing the loved one to return—a success which, I have surmised, was more frequent for Armand de Richelieu, as a child, than for his brother Alphonse.

From the first, Suzanne de Richelieu's responsiveness to her youngest son may have encouraged in him an active reaction. Given this favorable condition, he may have been further disposed to an ocular form of discharging emotions, especially if, as conjectured earlier, his bodily movements were rather thoroughly restricted in his early months. In any case, his response to frustration seems to have been instrumental: in our hypothetical reconstruction this response took the form of converting rage into angry crying in order to recall his mother rather than, as in his brother's case, into mortification of himself. An early, sympathetic relationship of Armand to his mother might help explain how he could overcome early obstacles to maturation which, in the older brother, seem to have evoked developmental disorders and later neurosis.[58] The statesman's effectiveness in coping with the outside world may have had its precursor in an infantile pattern of interacting with his caretakers. Later, in gaining control over his own bodily processes—possibly pressed to do so by the fear of shaming—previous rewarding experience could have reinforced a tendency to express fury in tears, a fairly risk-free way to show hostility. While Alphonse's anger was sometimes turned against himself, sometimes released in letters of complaint and recrimination, Armand's rage was directed outward, sometimes disguised by a mode of reaction that had, as surmised here, sucessfully served him in infancy.[59]

The day that Richelieu was, as he probably felt, betrayed and abandoned by the queen mother is not the only occasion on which history records that he wept at a woman's "departure." He shed, according to a witness, "tears of sympathy" with Louis XIII when Mademoiselle de La Fayette, the king's inamorata, abandoned the court for the cloister. The hostile spectator who observed this thought the demonstration faked,[60] but it is perhaps as plausible that it represented an infantile reaction to this kind of withdrawal, now evoked in the adult Richelieu. If in these two instances his tears no longer aimed to force the departing ones to return, at least they could still be instrumental in disguising feelings of rage.

Richelieu's feelings on the Day of Dupes may have been those of rage, but, if so, they led only to an outward show of tears and submission. The next day his triumph over the queen mother was confirmed: the king renewed his confidence in his prime minister at Marie de Medici's expense. Yet even then Richelieu did not allow any show of anger to emerge undisguised. In a letter to his sister Nicole he edited every trace of resentment towards the queen mother that appeared in the first draft. In his own hand he *excised* the phrases which are emphasized in the following passage:

> My sister, I did not want to delay telling you that, the queen
> having let me know that she no longer wished to make use of
> me . . . we have been obliged to obey her wishes. I do not
> doubt that this news will astonish you, *because it is most extraordi-*
> *nary;* nevertheless, I call on you, insofar as I may, not to be too
> upset at it, as its only cause is our misfortune *and not any fault of*
> *which we are guilty.* . . . Time will show the queen *my innocence*
> *and* that, whatever treatment I may receive from her, I shall al-
> ways acknowledge publicly the great obligations I have to her
> which constrain me to live and die her servant.[61]

The cardinal's fury at those who had power to constrain or humiliate him might be expressed by tears, but his words were almost invariably reviewed to harness them to his ambitions.

Headaches. In contrast with the brother nearest to him in age, Armand de Richelieu was usually able, as a young man, to direct his energies outward. Unlike Alphonse he was not inclined to be self-pitying, carefully monitoring, throughout his life, expressions of complaint and usually trying to stress the positive aspect of most misfortunes that befell him.[62] "It's a great pity, poor nobility. However, the only remedy to [bad] luck is a stout heart." Nor, so far as is known, did the cardinal ever try, as his brother did, to inflict damage on himself, and, also unlike Alphonse, he usually combatted tendencies to become deperessed with concerted, effective action. His strategies, however, especially in his youth, were not always successful. When his actions failed to produce the effects he desired he sometimes developed a characteristic symptom: he fell victim to a severe headache. Sometimes his headaches lasted for weeks or months.[63]

His descriptions of these ailments are not detailed—"My headache is killing me," or "I have the worst head in the world," or "Great pains in the head." Some of the headaches were, as has already been noted, most likely associated with fever and chronic infection. Others, however, may have been migraine.[64] While much remains unknown about the physical and psychic etiology of migraine symptoms, they have sometimes been found to be associated with rage and with sphincter spasms.[65] One who responds to stimuli with such headaches has been seen as expressing an "identification of himself with a long-suffering mother" who is regarded as "abused and depreciated." The head is, thus, felt "unconsciously as a female organ," and the pain conceals a longing to surrender to an over-powering father.[66]

It has been seen that Richelieu did see his mother as abused and de-preciated—the victim, in his words, of "frustrations, afflictions and bitter-nesses." And it seems to have been on occasions when he himself felt victimized, as he conceived his mother to have been, that his head was most likely to become the site of suffering instead of the source of active mastery.

The onset of some of Richelieu's most severe attacks of headache—before he left Paris for Poitou in 1608, in 1611 after he had been rebuffed at court, during exile in Avignon in 1618, during his subsequent exclusion from power in 1621, while he was having reason to believe his nomination to the cardinalate was being sabotaged in 1622, at the beginning of the first open opposition to his policies in 1625, and at the time of the discovery of the king's brother's conspiracy against him in 1626—came during periods when he was thwarted, threatened, or subdued by other men.[67] His head-aches became rarer or disappeared after he reached the heights of power at the end of 1630.[68]

3.   Early Coping Techniques

Stages of development in the first years of life are marked by progressive acquisition of the skills and the force to transform old methods of wresting gratification from the environment into new, more socially rewarded tech-niques. When a successful transformation is achieved through great effort, the techniques that contributed to the triumph over difficulties will prob-ably show traces of the conflict they resolved. I have suggested that, for Richelieu, a particularly powerful effort may have been required to gain control over certain functions of his own body, and that the outcome of the struggle was to redirect forces in himself that were thus subdued to-wards the goal of dominating others. These transformed energies, however, seem in some ways to bear the mark of the stage in development at which they were successfully applied.

A.   Using Words

The time at which a child is expected to acquire sphincter controls usually coincides roughly with the time in which he or she is also learning to master the organization of words in speech. The intensity of the conflict in acquiring the first type of skill, therefore, and the method of resolving it, may influence the mode in which the second type is developed.[69]

It has already been shown that Richelieu was much given to deprecating the significance of "mere" words and thoughts. Bent on action as he was, it is ironic that his performance has become memorable to posterity as much on account of his words and his thoughts, as because of his deeds and results.

Even so it is not difficult to find evidence that Richelieu linked the skillful use of words to effective wielding of power. Thus, during a period when he was excluded from the government, he expresses the feeling that he has lost his capacity for eloquence as a consequence of being powerless:

> He protests his devotion to the archbishop [La Valette, of Toulouse] and regrets not being able to prove it to him . . . being useless for any good purpose. . . . You will recognize that I am neither Demosthenes nor Cicero since I have so much difficulty expressing myself.[70]

There is no mistaking the energy Richelieu invested in selecting the right words for the right purposes. Thus, as the former intimate, Morgues, describes him:

> He is busy night and day . . . searching for the words to use . . . to the king . . . to all the *grands* with whom he must deal . . . even to the point of thinking about the compliment he must pay to the least important people.[71]

Furthermore, despite the cardinal's conscious and often expressed view that words are of no consequence unless they produce actions, it often seems clear that, at another level of belief, words, of themselves, had a powerful, aggressive potential. When wielded by high authority they are more powerful still. He is credited with the maxim, "The blows from a sword are easily healed, but it is not the same with blows of the tongue, especially if they be from the tongue of a king."[72] Certainly, as prime minister, he credited the king's words with immense power, as when he advised the stuttering Louis XIII, "It is vital to shut up (*fermer la bouche à*), those lords by a tongue-lashing (*incartade vigoureuse*) such as your majesty knows how to give."[73]

Perhaps an adult belief in the damaging potential of words had its precursor in childhood experiences of being wounded or frightened by adults' words of ridicule or menace. And perhaps his own skill in the use of words originally took form as a means of defending himself against such hazards. In any case, as a statesman, Richelieu's high estimation of the importance of well-chosen words, his great investment of time and thought in selecting them, and his skill in organizing them were all exceptional for his time.

In his view on clerical strategy, the power of words was conditional upon their being used sparingly, by design. Releasing too many at one time was likely to make them ineffective. Thus, as bishop in an era of mannered, highly embellished preaching he advises his curates to cut sermons in half if they become overlong, in order that the congregation may receive them "with pleasure."[74] An ecclesiastical historian finds this precaution extraordinary, since "the longest of his instructions is no more than ten or twelve pages"—far shorter than the normal sermon of the day.[75] He prepared an innovative catechism for his diocese, radically abbreviated—"reduced . . . to the least quantity" to make it possible for the "simplest among you to master it."[76] Thus also Richelieu finds the power of the Lord's Prayer to lie in its brevity and succinctness. It is not only the "noblest" but also the "most effective," because "complete," "in few words," and "made with such order that it leaves nothing to be desired."[77]

In instructions to his favorite uncle, recently promoted to high office, he advises speaking to the queen with "beautiful phrases" (belles paroles), but "in few words" and warns that everywhere La Porte appears he must "speak little and bridle his liberty [of tongue]."[78]

Written words usually flowed easily from Richelieu. When he wielded the pen himself their stream was, as we have seen, almost entirely unimpeded either by punctuation, dots and crosses, or by accents. A further curious idiosyncracy of his handwriting seems to express an unwillingness to accept the limits imposed by the boundaries of the page. Where his secretaries, although otherwise quite convincingly imitating his script, invariably contrive neat and uniform terminal margins, their master, rather than cut off a word, crowds his letters together to squeeze them in and, if it is necessary in order to complete them on the same line, runs the final syllables up the side of the page.[79]

The pleasurable feelings Richelieu sometimes gained from writing are occasionally clear, even when the activity also seems to have a serious purpose. An intimate's report shows what is an apparent function of writing down words to discharge tension:

> While conversing with personal friends at times when they were seeking to give him a bit of relaxation, one often sees him take pen in hand and make notes in order to lose nothing of what his fertile mind produces for him, and every night waking several times he does the same thing[80]

It may be that the aggressive significance words sometimes had for Richelieu influenced his marked preference for employing others to do his writing for him when it came to implementing decisions he had made. Even at the very beginning of his career, at Luçon, much of his correspondence was carried on through two secretaries. Despite the fluent ease and high legibility of his hand, and the obvious pleasure that writing afforded him under some circumstances, he habitually dictated his official letters, or the ideas to be conveyed in them, to others whose task it then was to produce a written draft. Richelieu was the editor, pruning the text as much as possible and usually, as we have seen, eliminating aggressive expressions. Avenel notes the cardinal's care, in editing a secretary's work, not to "irritate" the recipient.[81] In his later career, of course, he removed himself still farther from the aggressive significance of his words when he spoke through the king.

While Richelieu's own words are carefully chosen to minimize their wounding import, the words he uses to refer, indirectly, to halting the speech of others are quite aggressive. A favorite phrase is *"fermer la bouche"* (shut the mouth) of someone. The necessity of shutting up others is mentioned early in his correspondence, as when he commends an author for a work which will "shut the mouth" of certain adversaries, "if they do not wish to increase the shame (*honte*) they have already received."[82] Shame, apparently, is the consequence of loose talk. When he is exiled Richelieu writes to Père Joseph asking him to intervene on his behalf with Déageant, an ally at court, because he himself has done that courtier services in the past: "I have often shut the mouth of one of those who are most incensed (*eschauffés*) against him."[83] The phrase recurs throughout his career; in later years he could call on the king to do much of the "mouth-shutting" he thought necessary—censorship practices of the regime were many, and inventive.

B.   Teaching

For Richelieu the power of words did not lie only in their damaging effect. Their potential use for control of others was attractive to him. The desire to dominate by *teaching* was characteristic of him throughout his life.[84]

Richelieu's interest in educational institutions of all kinds first took on a public character when he arrived in Luçon as bishop. Convoking a meeting of his synod he was concerned to "exhort and conjure" the clergy of his diocese "by what is most holy and sacred . . . to study and bring all the effort and diligence required to acquit yourselves 'worthily.'"[85] Not content to entreat and enjoin by word of mouth, he put his lessons into writing. His first published work directed his priests to "study in order to acquire the knowledge necessary in [its correct] order."[86] The teaching methods of the clergy as well as the content of their instruction were objects of his detailed concern in this manual: brevity, simplicity, regularity, were the recommended ingredients of successful communication.

At Luçon, instructing the instructors—the clergy—became a primary objective of Richelieu's policy. This preoccupation caused him to take the innovative step of attempting to found a seminary in the town at the time there was no such institution in France.[87] He called upon the new teaching order of Oratorians, headed by the mystic Bérulle, to implement his design of establishing a school for priests in Luçon. It was a project in which he was to persist for many years.[88]

Discussion of the public policy objectives of Richelieu's later foundation of groups such as the Académie Française, the Bureau d'Adresse, the *Gazette*, and many other organs designed to influence opinon and culture directly belongs in another place. Here it is merely noted that one aim in his sponsorship of all these institutions was to *teach*. Even in a cultural medium as far removed from the schoolroom as the drama, of which he became a chief patron, "the orientation that Richelieu meant to give . . . was instructive." The stage was to him "a book for the ignorant which gives affecting lectures through which the ignorant may be informed of and instructed in virtue."[89] Any planned and systematic use of words held out the opportunity to dominate others.

In 1618 Richelieu separated himself finally from his diocesan duties. In that same year he published an "instruction book" to direct, in his absence, the "souls" with which he was charged. The work begins with a catechism so notable in its simplicity that it became a best seller. Thus, "away from his diocese," writes Raconis, "he continued to teach it."[90]

In this catechism, Richelieu's explication of the *credo* is followed by an exposition and discussion of the Ten Commandments, which he introduces as follows: "Having taught you what you must believe, it is fitting that you know what you must do."[91]

He had already departed Luçon, but he left his teaching behind to carry on his domination.

C.   Seeking Respite

If, in political relations, words had an aggressive meaning for Richelieu and if their educational potential served his drive to control events, in other contexts they had a different purpose—they were means for obtaining relaxation and amusement. Richelieu's work in the world of politics was characterized by high anxiety and intense, serious activity. He found relief from the stress of these efforts by turning to certain kinds of cultural activities which, in his view, had little political significance.

Playing. Psychoanalysis has seen in play an essential bridge between the self-absorbed state of the infant and the capacity of the growing child to relate creatively to the outside world. Observation of babies suggests that the original setting for play is a reliable relationship between mother-figure and child. In the "potential space" between them—a space that takes form only gradually—the child "gathers objects or phenomena from external reality and uses these in the service of some sample derived from inner or personal reality."[92] The conjecture that Richelieu's childhood opportunity to manipulate his physical environment may have been for long hampered by restrictions on his body and limbs would, if it is correct, help explain why, as an adult, the objects of his play were usually not tangible ones. Nor were they, on the other hand, speculative flights of fantasy or otherworldly artistic constructions. The "chosen external phenomena" invested with "dream meaning and feeling" by Richelieu were, primarily, earthbound thoughts and words.

Richelieu's biographers depict his youth as one of exceptional sobriety, distinguished by intellectual precocity. This characterization followed him into adulthood. Accounts are lacking of his use of hand skills, except for writing.[93] As for gross motor activities, although the grown man was said to be an able horseman, and occasionally took exercises for the sake of his health, these were not, apparently, recreations that he invested with passionate enthusiasm. The chief amusements in which he regularly engaged as an adult were not physical but mental: he enjoyed games of wits and words.

Foremost in material for providing such play are the dramatic arts. But the theater became Richelieu's chief recreation only in his last years, barely discovered as a respite until he reached the height of power. Until then his pleasures were simpler: he liked to engage, in private, in contests of wits and words with a few chosen companions. Sometimes he would demonstrate a levity in these sessions that contrasts with his usual public manner of decorous sobriety. Notebooks that survive, apparently drawn up at his instructions, include a collection of puns and plays on words.[94] He was himself capable of low puns.[95] His appreciation of such double meanings was not necessarily in particularly good taste. An example, "very much to Richelieu's taste," as Avenel remarks, was the intended ironical comment on Prince Thomas of Savoy, who had been acting against French interests in 1640: "The insolence . . . of this prince leaves nothing to be done except to pray God that, through the power of His Holy Spirit (*Saint-Esprit*) he gives him a sound mind (*sain esprit*)."[96]

One type of play that has been described as a favorite recreation for the cardinal was a game of wits like "Can you top this?" In a sort of conversational sparring match, Richelieu took delight in vanquishing a competitor. Desmarets de Saint-Sorlin recounts how, after enjoying a theological discussion amidst congenial company, Richelieu would take a favorite aside privately, "in order to divert himself on gayer, more delicate matters." Never, reports this literary collaborator of the cardinal, did he tire of such efforts of the intellect:[97]

His greatest pleasure came when, in our conversation, he improved on thoughts beyond my own; then if I produced another thought on top of his, his mind made a new effort, and with extreme satisfaction, in order to improve still farther upon that thought. He savored no pleasure in the world more to his taste than that one.[98]

In these encounters it was the play of minds with words that pleased.

Richelieu's realism in political matters, the gravity with which he regarded royal authority, and his innovativeness as a statesman and propagandist, contrast with the peripheral and superficial character of the theological work attributed to him and the reported banality of his artistic and other intellectual views. The contrast could be explained if, for him, activities in these areas were not serious, but instead, play.

In fact contemporary descriptions of Richelieu's interest in religious thought show it to belong to the less serious part of his life. In times of stress, we are told, Richelieu turned to theological writing not for moral guidance, but for respite from the real cares of the world. In a preface to one of the two posthumous religious works that bear the cardinal's name his confessor, Jacques Lescot, recalls:

> Many people know that amidst the weightiest of state affairs . . . working at the clarification of certain disputed points of the Faith was one of his pleasantest pastimes (*ses plus agréables occupations*). . . . It was in that work that he relaxed (*se délassoit*) from all the others.[99]

Although Richelieu's religious treatises, particularly the early ones, served his political as well as his private aims, their reasoning on sacred subjects has a quality that has evoked negative comment from many writers on theology. La Fontenelle, for example, regrets that the "solidity" of Richelieu's theological work is "slight."[100] Dhotel finds his discussion of the sacraments lacking in "firmness" and containing "doubtful approximations" to dogma.[101] Orcibal, in particular, suspects "laxity" in Richelieu's treatment of some central doctrinal issues of the time and "cleverness" in his evasion of others.[102] He examines at some length inconsistencies in the cardinal's positions that suggest, according to the reasoning here, their function as play rather than as matters affecting the immortal soul.

As a reformer, Richelieu represented himself always as a champion of the decisions of the Council of Trent. Yet that body had rejected the argument that, in the absence of true love of God, mere *attrition*—fear of punishment—may suffice for salvation. As a provisor of the Sorbonne, Orcibal is sure, Richelieu could not have been ignorant of this rejection; therefore it is a "real abuse of language" for him to aver, as he does in the *Perfection du chrestien*, that attrition is sufficient. He finds *"laxisme"* in a thesis advanced by Sirmond, writing at Richelieu's bidding. Expressing his master's "entire thought," Orcibal thinks, Sirmond commends absolution *in articulo mortis* on what are apparently expediential grounds of an amoral kind: since there is always danger of backsliding if submission to God is based only on fear, persons of doubtful faith had best delay deathbed repentance and confession until the ultimate moments of life.[103] It is easy to see that in disregarding the intentions of the Council of Trent, Richelieu may have been expressing his own legalistic bent for manipulating the letter of the law. Since the spirit of contemporary religious tendencies was mostly a closed book to him, he was presumably unaware that his use of the terms of the argument was "abusive."

In Richelieu's personal correspondence there is a hint that his unorthodoxy was apprehended with some misgivings by his close friend and former teacher, the bishop of Orléans, Gabriel de L'Aubespine. The bishop of Luçon had not informed this erudite prelate when he recommenced intensive studies in order to produce a work of theological controversy; the older man had learned of it only indirectly. He writes Richelieu reproaching him for not consulting him and comments, "I have always had high regard (*fait grand estat*) for your *courage* in spiritual and ecclesiastical things,"[104] a compliment that may be thought rather ambiguous. Indeed, Richelieu rushed into a doctrinal fray where many *doctes* feared to tread.

Few critics believe the cardinal was lacking in faith. They have therefore been at some pains to account for the *légèreté* with which he offered his theological contributions. Orcibal explains his conflicts with accepted doctrine as in keeping with the humanist tradition of a Renaissance outlook that split off other-worldly concerns from those of a terrestrial order.[105] These last, seen as basically beneficent, could be considered unhampered by religious strictures.

Yet Richelieu considered himself a proselytizer in the vanguard of the Catholic Counter-Reformation. Indeed, says the bishop of Chartres, so great was his evangelical fervor in his last years that he regretted losing the use of his arm in his final malady chiefly because it interfered with what he regarded as his mission—writing works to convert the Huguenot separatists.[106] A humanist duality does not explain Richelieu's enthusiasm for religious argument as a pastime, nor his apparent unawareness of the opposition of his approach to accepted doctrine.

Inconsistency of Richelieu's views with the reformist doctrine he claimed to espouse is understandable if the unconscious function of his theological explorations was in truth a playful one. When, on the other hand, important unconscious aims inspired his speculations, he could manipulate, with no apparent sense of hypocrisy, particular elements of dogma to fit these more serious dispositions. Thus, the lightness with which he regarded learned theological opinion allowed him to issue the following confident, *ad hoc* assurance to Louis XIII on a matter of utmost importance to the cardinal—the status of kings:

I do not doubt that God, for Whose glory [Your Majesty] patiently bears this suffering, will console him *promptly*. Kings who submit to His will and prefer His glory to their happiness not only receive rewards in the other world, but also in this one, and in truth I hope for no small temporal benediction for Your Majesty.[107]

Here Richelieu seems to elaborate a new theme; kings receive quicker, on-the-spot service from God than do lesser mortals.

The playful function of religious speculation is shown also by Richelieu's unrealistic appraisal of doctrinal disagreement. His capacity for correctly gauging opposing political demands and expectations was legendary, but he often regarded the theological convictions and aesthetic preferences of others as malleable like his own. Thus, as will be seen later, he frequently underestimated the stubbornness of religious dissent; what was not serious in himself he could not take seriously in others.[108]

The aspect of Richelieu's approach to religious thought that seems most clearly to reveal its playful quality is its stress on the *ease* of finding and following the correct path to salvation. In contrast with his view of temporal matters, where correct behavior is chosen only after anxious reflection and enforced only through painstaking, constant effort, grace could be sought calmly and with assurance. The view of contemporary Catholic reformers was exactly contrary to this. It held that the passage to heaven was strait indeed, and while this world's affairs could be regarded with indifference, anxiety was justified in contemplation of the means to enter on high.

One popular Reform writer of the epoch, Père Grenade, was better attuned to the contemporary temper when he stressed the *difficulty* of following the religious precepts of the Lord's Prayer. Citing the affirmation "His will be done," as a case in point, he notes, "Our nature experiences a great repugnance in submitting to God."[109] Richelieu approved of Grenade's work, emulating some of its forms in his own,[110] but when he considers this same text he takes a view contrary to that of the Spanish Dominican. He pronounces it "impossible, in my opinion, to consider that God is our Father . . . without wishing to go to Him . . . and accomplish His holy will." Indeed, compliance is "assured," as Richelieu "believes with *certainty* . . . that you will do this *without difficulty,* judging that in what concerns your salvation you are like starving children for whom it *suffices merely* to present the breast for them to take it." Note, too, that one is deterred "easily" from usurping others' rights on earth by the "hope of being rich in heaven,"[111]—an opinion entirely at variance with Richelieu's observations in the practical realm of politics. Apparently reality-testing—a painful and anxiety-fraught necessity in serious affairs—could be suspended in pleasurable sallies into the world of religious speculation.

Nor in Richelieu's missionary designs to restore unity to the church did he anticipate much stubborn opposition. In his posthumously published treatise designed to convert the separatists it is remarked, "the controversy that *may be* between us and the Protestants"—on the issue of transubstantiation—"is *easy* to resolve." Lescot reports that at the end of the cardinal's life, he had a "confident certainty" that he would be able to reunite Christian believers.[112] He was, of course, entirely mistaken if he believed this. His confidence was capable of dimming even his usual astuteness concerning the state of mind of his aides on such points.[113]

As Bishop of Luçon, Richelieu's first printed religious work was a contribution to the small book published under the name of his grand vicar and former Sorbonne instructor, Jacques de Flavigny. Its title may reflect the bishop's inspiration: *Brief and Easy Instruction for Confessors*. Indeed, Richelieu regarded all doctrinal questions as subject to brief and easy solutions. In his own *Instruction of the Christian* he writes, "All that a Christian is required to know may be reduced to three points . . . what he must believe . . . and . . . do, and the means . . . for doing and believing it." Going on to discuss the proper interpretation of the sacraments, he concludes that it is "impossible really to have this knowledge without carefully practicing all that one knows to be necessary."[114] Therefore, we may conclude that in fact the first point—what we must believe—is, after all, the only one required to be learned. Problems in compliance have been reduced to a minimum by an act of the bishop's imagination.

Richelieu's writings often reflect his naif perspective on learning in general. Those who were "simple" or "ignorant" needed to be carefully instructed, as he himself undertook to do in his *Instruction du chrestien*. For the others—the *doctes*—erudition was a possession that made the solution of intellectual problems self-evident. It is to these that he and his vicar address themselves in the *Briefve et facile instruction*. In case these favored readers find in doctrine "some obscurity or other" he strives to enlighten them so that they can serve, for their flocks, the function of "stars lighting the firmament." To these vicars he can be "succinct" for they are able to "understand much in few words."[115] The stark contrast between the *doctes* and the *simples* applies to aesthetic as well as scholarly perceptions. For example, years later, Richelieu saw the problem of evaluating Corneille's theatrical innovations merely as one of the "*doctes*" enlightening the "*ignorans*" on correct form for theatrical presentation.[116]

Some playthings. After Richelieu's ordination and consecration as bishop he set out to take his *grades*—the second degree in theology—at the Sorbonne. This was a move not requisite for filling his position.[117] The step seems to have been motivated partly by his enjoyment of association with that center of theological learning.

"He took a great liking to the Sorbonne," observes Louis Batiffol.[118] It was a strong taste indeed. Lacroix notes that he had a "very particular attachment to the doctors of the Sorbonne" and "always sought out their conversation, their friendship, and their concourse."[119] The same year that he became a bachelor of theology Richelieu petitioned for admission to the small confraternity of *sociétaires* of the university. One of his very first acts after entering the ministry in 1616 was to sponsor the founding of a new royal chair of theology in that venerable academy.[120] To Jacques de Flavigny, the Sorbonne professor whom he chose as grand vicar at Luçon, he wrote of the favorable reception of his book by the faculty, "I am delighted . . . since it is the gentlemen of the Sorbonne, a group that I esteem so highly that I judge the honor that I have to be a member of it one of the greatest which I . . . may ever have." In the following year he set forth his claims to favor from the king in an *apologia*, noting as one of his special distinctions, "the Sorbonne is honored to have him in its Society."[121] When, in 1622 Cardinal de Retz, who was *proviseur*—equivalent of president—of the institution, died, Richelieu had his friends lobby to secure the succession for himself. He was received as cardinal a few days after his appointment and is said to have declared that the provisorship gave him more satisfaction than the cardinalate.[122] It is a curious feature of Pure's biography of Cardinal Richelieu that it contains, as an appendix, a list of provisors of the Sorbonne since its founding—a feature that may reflect the charm that this school and its dignities had for its most powerful member.

After the professorship, Richelieu's next gift to the university was, fittingly, a building to house a new hall of debates, begun in 1625. The last structure he sponsored for it was one in which he intended to be buried— the chapel—begun in 1629.[123]

Richelieu's interest in the Sorbonne was no doubt related to his political designs to control others by "teaching." But the Sorbonne was also his "pet"; he was its patron and in return enjoyed the dependence of this institution upon himself.[124]

Related to the gratification Richelieu derived from the Sorbonne was the pride he took in authorship and the pleasure that the sponsorship of books and authors gave to him. Throughout his life major works on history and religion were planned under his direction and material collected for them. Actually, however, he can be credited with sole authorship only of the very earliest, short theological works. The books on religion attributed to him in his later years and published posthumously may contain very little that is his. If he was principal author of any long published historical work, it was of little more than short sections of what was to appear in various forms, posthumously, as the *Mémoires* or the *Journal* of Richelieu.[125] Elsewhere I have discussed the probable special circumstances of his authorship of the fragmentary history that was first published as a preliminary to the so-called *Testament politique*.[126] Entitled *Succincte narration des grandes actions du roi Louis XIII*, it is usually preceded by a dedicatory letter that is also attributed to Richelieu. While that letter, too, may not be entirely in the cardinal's own words,[127] it expresses, nevertheless, an enjoyment of authorship that he was known to have felt:

> It gave me no little pleasure to describe what was accomplished only with pain. . . . I savored the sweetness (*goûtais la douceur*) of this labor.[128]

Not for Richelieu the travail of the creative writer!

Richelieu's ambition to produce a history of the reign of Louis XIII has often been interpreted as an aspect of his aim to justify the policies of his regime and to vindicate his own role in it. But another element in this desire was less realistic: He wished to be credited with published works. His ambition for authorship had an unrealistic quality which distinguishes it from his more usual objective orientation to politics.

Lavollée remarks the "literary vanity" of the cardinal. "We know," he writes, "how Richelieu liked to give himself credit for literary works for which he often had done no more than trouble himself to pay those who composed them for him."[129] This vanity was known to the literary men who surrounded him and comprised his favorite company for private relaxation. One of these, Chapelain, seemingly is aware that the cardinal is under the illusion that he himself is the author of the *Comédie des Tuileries*, the work of others. In writing to the abbé de Boisrobert, Richelieu's factotum for literary matters, he actually gives credit to the prime minister for the work, engaging in extravagant flattery of a kind the cardinal would have discounted from a political colleague: "Seeing the contrast between my usual productions and these extraordinary marvels," writes the future head of Richelieu's Academy, "if people think me the author they will believe a miracle has been wrought in me and that my customary weakness is suddenly converted into great power."[130] Boisrobert himself was a jocose figure whose company Richelieu enjoyed during his later years. In his flattery of the cardinal he seems to have developed a formula that would prevent his master from feeling guilt over idling away his time with "mere" words. In a eulogistic address he told Richelieu, "Your words are deeds (*effets*)!"[131]

In his role of *amateur* of literature, too, Richelieu's behavior contrasted with his careful habits as a political man. Where literary decisions were concerned he could act, as he strove never to do in politics, on impulse. Two instances are reported in which he rewarded authors, on the spot, for verses that had caught his fancy. The lines themselves were half-facetious, suggesting that in this realm of action he could suspend his usual care to avoid appearing ridiculous.[132] Another impulsive act is related by Claude Courtin, of Richelieu's household staff. During an insomniac episode the cardinal asked his valet to read to him and the servant obliged with a work of Mézeray, then beginning his career as a historian. The dedication (to himself) "pleased him greatly," and, doubly pleased by recalling that the writer's father had been in the service of his own father, he forthwith dispatched a gift of money to the son, then residing in a college of the Sorbonne.[133]

In the same realm of pleasurable, anxiety-free activity was Richelieu's interest in acquiring books and building libraries.[134] On two occasions, feeling himself near death, he executed a last will and testament. In each of these documents his desire to establish a library figures importantly. On the first occasion he connected the library with his projected school for clergymen: he exhorts the bishop who will succeed him to "kindle, by his example and teachings, those under him . . . to maintain and augment the seminary begun at Luçon, to which I leave a thousand *livres* and my entire library to give more reason for people of merit to stop there."[135] This is but one example of an occasion when his designs for promoting education seem to have as much in common with carefree enjoyment as with that ambition to dominate which also often characterized his teaching schemes. Perhaps it was because academic, literary and scientific endeavors seemed to him "untainted" by that passionate striving for power that constituted the usual substance of his preoccupations that they could provide him with "pure" relaxation. In associating himself with them he acquired a dignity without risk.

Avenel is aware of this pleasurable aspect of Richelieu's educational plans. He accepts Tallemant's report that, at the beginning of Richelieu's last illness he took time daily for planning a new Parisian academy that was to attract the "great men of the century," and is not surprised that this should be the occupation in which the cardinal sought relief when he was "torn by his most acute anxieties and burdened by the gravest matters."[136] Hippolyte-Jule P. de La Mesnardière, who accompanied the prime minister on that last troubled voyage to Catalonia, confirms the story:

> I had marvelous, long audiences with His Eminence. . . . during the Roussillon trip, whose serenity was troubled for him by so many storms. He put in my hands memoranda, made by himself, for the plan that he ordered me to draft for that magnificent and rare College that he was meditating for *belles sciences* in which he intended to employ all that was most outstanding in Europe in literature.[137]

In Narbonne, far from the capital, the worried, dying man sought surcease in innocent, grandiose dreams.

Twenty-three years after he had drafted his first will and testament, his desire and means to make a library available to the meritorious have become sufficient to fill three printed pages of a new will. His instructions include keeping the library's location intact (in the precincts of his own Palais Cardinal). It is to be catalogued under the supervision of "two doctors of the Sorbonne, deputized by their colleagues."[138] Here the charm of libraries is linked to his happiness in associating himself with that academy.[139]

In this last provision for a library, Richelieu goes into remarkable detail. He makes an allowance for new acquisitions, since this is "necessary to maintain a library in its perfection," and stipulates that no books are to leave the premises. He specifies further an annual inventory, the terms of appointing a librarian, and the duties of the custodian who "will sweep every day" and "wipe the books"—or the cases in which they are contained.[140] The language he uses to insure cleanliness of the books is reminiscent of his words, written many years before, instructing his curés on the proper care of artifacts used in church rituals. No corporals will be used, he wrote then, which are not "clean and white," and after the last ablution the platinas and chalices are to be wiped with "*purificationes* or little white cloths . . . which they will provide and will be careful to have laundered."[141] Libraries, like churches, are to be stocked with objects of spotless virtue and high purpose.

Not himself a serious intellectual, lacking in a sense of the mystery of religion, possessed of conventional aesthetic standards, for Richelieu the vehicles of worship, art and learning had more the quality of pristine objects of intrinsic worth than of means for discovery of or communion with the divine, the beautiful, and the true. He was concerned, as a child may be for toys, to protect the paraphernalia of literature, scholarship and religion with loving care.

9 Transforming Childhood Experience

Even had this man not had despotism in his heart, he had it in his head[1]

As Richelieu's development has been reconstructed here, his earliest experience prepared him better than his brother's had done to surmount the next major problem of maturation, gaining self-control. His success in overcoming obstacles at this second stage of childhood, I have surmised, reinforced a confidence he already possessed to some degree in the powers of his mind to overcome disappointment by subduing some of his impulses and enlisting others in the service of his deepest needs. If both Armand de Richelieu and his brother felt strong impulses to aggression, if both were sensitive to shaming, Alphonse's solution was inward-turning, while Armand, with growing confidence of self-mastery, reached out to influence the world around him. As I have projected it from what evidence is available, Richelieu's second triumph confirmed the effectiveness of the first one's *modus operandi:* in his play as well as his work the experience of his earliest years predisposed him to the active use of his mental powers. His intense ambition to control himself and others was served by using his head: anticipating contingencies and taking precautions against untoward events. His means of seeking relief from anxiety that accompanied this press towards mastery was also primarily cerebral: plays on words, games of wits, and collection and sponsorship of objects associated with the intellect gave him pleasure and relaxation. Only when his mental powers failed to ward off humiliation or domination by others, I have speculated, did he direct anger against his "miserable head" and fall victim to incapacitating headaches or lapse into temporary gloom.

1.　Richelieu at Five: The Family Setting

The Richelieu household, as has been seen, included no resident adult male figures. At a very early age, moreover, almost certainly by the time he was five or six, a profession had already been chosen for this youngest Richelieu brother which would commit him to a celibate life in which the powers of his intellect would be central to success. This was a life, furthermore, for which there seem to have been no precursors in family history or legend.

It is in circumstances something like these that a change that took place in Richelieu's family situation around his fifth birthday may be considered. In 1590 Armand's father died and sometime near that year his mother gave birth to a baby girl.

In Armand de Richelieu, the normal curiosity of children to determine "where babies come from" must have been unusually challenged, if not confounded, by Nicole's arrival. The appearances at home of François de Richelieu, the baby's father, were infrequent and unpredictable. There is no record of any personal contact between the grand provost and his youngest son; it may be that for the latter the former had always been a figure of imagination rather than of personal experience. The occurrence of the father's death, unseen and in a distant place, at about the same time as the sister's birth may have added to the mysteriousness of the second event.

The other man with a close relationship to the family at Richelieu, Suzanne's half-brother Amador La Porte, seems to have resembled François in a habit of suddenly appearing and then, as mysteriously, disappearing. Apparently he astonished Suzanne's daughter-in-law, soon after her marriage to Henri, by departing, after a visit to the young couple, without giving forewarning. Madame de Richelieu explained in a letter to Marguerite that this was his normal procedure:

> I see that you were not accustomed to the *adieux* of my brother,
> the commander. He always makes them to us in writing to show
> us that he puts his heart in them.[2]

Yet Amador, as has been seen, had few of the professional or personal characteristics attributed to François, his brother-in-law. He had apparently never married and he had no children of his own. Furthermore, aside from the fact that it is not likely that he seemed, as a father is likely to do, the sons' rival for their mother, he probably also did not inspire on other grounds the ambivalence that a father's more assertive side is apt to arouse in young boys. His role for Armand, for example, seems to have been entirely benign.

Taken together, these facts contribute to explaining, although by no means fully, why the birth of Nicole, puzzling as it may have been, and the death of Richelieu's father so early in his life, seem to have aroused few of those conflicts characteristic of the Oedipal phase of a boy's development in the modern, nuclear family. It is far from clear what all the mental processes could have been that may have enabled this Richelieu brother to resolve problems that often cause lifelong stress for other sons. It is possible, however, to discover clues to some of them by examining two aspects of his family relations. First, his actual relations to the women in his family may be traced; secondly, patterns in his relations to his father may emerge through considering his theological interests, particularly those focussing on the holy family.

2.   Mother, Sister, Niece

The behavior of Armand de Richelieu towards those women in his family for whom his father, had he lived longer, would otherwise have been responsible discloses an apparently conflict-free assumption of the paternal role. It was seen in an earlier chapter how elated the young Richelieu seemed at the opportunity to rescue his mother from the financial difficulties in which his father had left her. Apparently he welcomed eagerly, as Bishop of Luçon, the chance to provide her with the shelter of her choice, at his own expense. His relations with the little girl born to Madame de Richelieu about 1590 were also to show a tender, protective concern. Those few letters which survive from him to or about Nicole show him acting, apparently without anxiety, in the role of a father towards his sister. Her letters to him, in return, exemplify reverent devotion.[3]

Although in 1617 Henri was head of the Richelieu family, it was the exiled Armand who acted in the place of their long-dead father to arrange the marriage of Nicole to Urbain de Maillé, Marquis de Brézé, of the neighboring terrain of Milly. Apparently the bishop of Luçon had also chosen the bridegroom. We do not know what else he may have done to implement the marriage; Nicole was already beyond an optimum age and the match was sufficiently advantageous to her as to remain, to this day, rather puzzling. Disgraced as the bishop was in that year, and disadvantaged as the Richelieus had always been in money, it is not clear what the alliance had to offer the much younger, impecunious, and very high-born Brézé, except that there had been earlier marriages between his family and that of Nicole's paternal grandmother, the Rochechouarts, thus establishing a pattern.[4] If, as was frequently the case in alliances of this period, it was the family connection that the bridegroom sought, he must have been unusually discerning about future prospects, for at the time Armand and Henri were virtually powerless. Brézé was aware of close ties between his fiancé and Armand: before the marriage he wrote to his future brother-in-law that

Nicole "must be more attached . . . to you than to anyone in the world."[5] In the years that followed Richelieu would call on his brother-in-law for exacting and devoted service, and Brézé, though often able and effective, would not always be willing to conform to his brother-in-law's expectations.

Nicole's sickness of soul may already have been apprehended when, in 1621, Richelieu expressed solicitude for her *"délicatesse."*[6] His tender concern for her continued during the mental illness which was to afflict her during much of her married life. He wrote Brézé in 1631: "I don't know how to express to you the joy I feel from what you tell me of the health of my sister. I pray God that your hope may be well-founded.[7] Nicole incarcerated herself in the country house of Milly and was fearful of leaving. A series of letters from Armand to his brother-in-law show that the cardinal's feeling of responsibility for his sister resembled the concern he had once had that his mother find suitable shelter, as well as the sensitivity he had shown to Suzanne's anxieties and wishes. He tells Brézé to persuade Nicole go to Saumur "or another place she might prefer to live" on account of the plague in the neighborhood of Milly. He warns his brother-in-law, "You will give me great displeasure if you leave before my sister has departed," continuing:

> In my opinion she will agree to this without repugnance, not being able to refuse to do something which she can no longer resist doing unless she wishes to be lost. Make her, then, change location . . . as gently as you can.

But Nicole begs Armand to allow her to postpone her departure until spring. Although the danger of plague is past, her brother is adamant, "knowing full well that by then too she will be in the same difficulties that she is now." He tells her husband, "Nothing bad will happen to her in Saumur; on the contrary," she will find there "every solace, should she only wish, however little, to help herself." He asks that she be assured that she will have "full powers there, and in case she doesn't find it to her liking she can have herself taken to l'Ile Bouchard in the spring."[8]

Nicole was apparently unable to resist these solicitations, and was removed to Saumur as her brother had instructed. From there she wrote to her brother expressing once more the depth of her feelings of devotion and submission:

> Monseigneur,
> Your eminent goodness never ceases to oblige us continually, both infinitely and also because of obligations so personal (*particulières*) that if there remains to me still some tiny desire to conserve my life among so many languors and continual and distressing illnesses, I can only desire it for love of you, Mon-

seigneur, and for as long as it pleases you to do me this honor of desiring that I conserve it, wishing it only for the favor of being, really and truly,
Your very humble and very obedient servant,

N. de Richelieu[9]

Richelieu's accounts for 1635 show his reimbursement of a man who had been charged to ride on horseback from Saumur with news of Nicole in her last illness.[10] Nicole died soon afterwards, mourned, as her husband wrote her brother, by almost no one but the two of them.[11] Richelieu was apparently concerned that Nicole's death be duly noticed in the newly burgeoning town of Richelieu which he was creating. His deputy, there, a retainer from a family long attached to the Richelieus, wrote to tell him that everyone was sad to learn of the event and to assure him that all proper observances of it would be made in the "chapel of your château and in the churches throughout your duchy."[12] The prime minister played to the end the part of father to the sister born to his mother in his father's absence. Perhaps too, as a little boy, he had played the same role in his imagination.

A further clue to Richelieu's imaginary links to family members is offered by another real relationship—in this case with a niece, Marie de Vignerod, later Duchesse d'Aiguillon. This lady was the daughter of Armand's older sister, Françoise, and of an old family friend and ally, René de Pont Courlay. As some feelings a young boy may have for his mother are often transferred to an older sister, Marie's mother may once have stood in a relationship to Armand in some respects like that of his own mother. Françoise died early in 1616, the same year that was to see Suzanne's death. Marie had been born to her marriage in 1604, while Richelieu was in adolescence, beginning to prepare for another change in career. This birth, coming at such a time in the uncle's life, may have revived in him some of the feelings which had been inspired by the birth of Nicole years before.

In any case, as with Nicole, Richelieu stood in *loco parentis* to Marie de Vignerod. As with Nicole, also, his assumption of paternal functions seems to have caused him little or no conflict. Apparently he arranged for Marie an early education like his own.[13] He was concerned that she marry well and contrived to ally her with the family of Albert de Luynes, the king's favorite, who at the time held the greatest political influence in the kingdom. After she became a young widow he pressed her repeatedly to resist the temptation to enter a cloister, predicting, "I believe she will allow herself to be persuaded to be of the religion of her mother."[14] The "religion" of her mother, Françoise, had been the same as that of Richelieu's own mother—the secular life of the mother of a family. In the event, however, Marie did not remarry and had no children of her own. Instead she devoted herself exclusively to her uncle, the cardinal, perhaps gratifying a wish of his that had remained unexpressed. In 1638 this commitment was ac-knowledged in a dramatic way by Richelieu: through the king's unusual action he had her made, widowed and childless as she was, a duchess in her own right. This also showed, writes her biographer, "that the cardinal had finally given up the idea of remarrying her."[15]

Richelieu, now himself a duke and peer, was thus able to have conferred on his niece the honored title of Peer of the Realm which he had not had, before her death, the power to confer on his mother. It seems that with Marie, probably more than with Françoise, Richelieu otherwise recreated features of his relationship with his mother.[16] Playing the role of *ménagère* that Suzanne had played when he was young, the duchess took respon-sibility for supplying her uncle's household and personal needs. It was she, for example, who ordered the "very-fine cloth" for his litter, colored with a new scarlet dye of Holland, and the fine linens and the down filled cushions for his bed.[17]

This well-educated niece had a mind of her own that seems to have inspired in her uncle a respect for her judgment, as well as for her man-agerial ability. One of her letters to him reflects his concern for her good opinion of him. On learning that he has been told by others that something he had done had displeased her, Marie reassures him as follows:

> [Your] last letter would have pained me greatly had I not already been assured that you were, more than ever, in good standing with me (*mieux . . . dans l'esprit*) and with more affection than you could imagine. . . . I feel very resentful towards those . . . who have tried to perform bad offices towards you, since the honor you have always paid me of giving me a share of your good graces and counting me among the number of your very particular servitors obliges me to make no distinction between your interests and mine except that of being much more sensi-tive to what affects you than to what touches me. I shall talk about this matter with you on your return. I await it with impa-tience as well as the means to show you that I am, with more fidelity than anyone in the world . . .
> Your very humble and very obedient servant. . . .[18]

As far as can be determined, the duchess was the only one among Riche-lieu's intimates whose moral judgment on his political acts he sought. Thus, when she expressed doubts about his justification for imprisoning Duver-gier de Hauranne, the highly reputed Jansenist abbé de Saint Cyran, the cardinal took pains to convince her of the need for his action by sending her to consult the pères Condren and Vincent de Paul.[19]

Richelieu made this niece heir to a large part of his fortune and—more significantly—executor of his papers. He put her in charge of her brother's sons—the grand-nephews who were to carry on Richelieu's name—as

Nicole had been charged with responsibility for her dead sister's children.[20] On his deathbed, according to a credible eye-witness, the cardinal told Marie that he had loved no one as he loved her.[21]

Feelings which Richelieu may originally have had, as a child, for his mother, I have surmised, may have evoked fantasies at the time of Nicole's birth when he was about five that made this youngest sister a special object of his affections. The same feelings may have been rekindled by the birth of the niece who would become his favorite in later years. If, however, erotic, incestuous fantasies or castration fears like those that often accompany, after like events, such feelings in little boys, ever had played a part in Richelieu's imagination, their transformation seems to have been so complete, and to have caused so little conflict, that traces of them rarely appear in the imagery he used later to describe related events.

3.   Father, Sons, and Holy Ghost

If, as conjectured here, the birth of Nicole evoked in Richelieu the fantasy that he and his mother had, in some largely problem-free way, engendered this child, how did he understand the relationship of his father to himself and to his mother?

Richelieu gives us little direct information on his view of his father. There is, however, another source for discerning his feelings and beliefs. In several religious writings he elaborates on family relations in ways that may be connected with his personal experience.

Consider the bishop of Luçon's explication of the text of the Fourth Commandment, "Honor thy father and thy mother." In the Council of Trent's official commentary we find no sentence comparable to the following condemnation by Richelieu: "Those who disinherit . . . their children without legitimate cause, who deprive some of the property which is fairly owed them in order to give it to others, violate this precept very notably."[22]

In fact, if not in law, François de Richelieu had, by his indebtedness, disinherited his children, depriving them of the property due them. This deprivation was likely owed to gambling losses and to the costs of at least one mistress—both examples of the transgression to which his son refers here: squandering an inheritance upon those not entitled to it.

In the same unusual context of considering the honor children owe to parents, Richelieu seems again to consider the relationship of his own father and mother. As unprecedented in this context as his first stricture is the warning that "husbands who live always absent from their wives on account of some distaste they may have for them" are in transgression of the commandment, while "he who is absent on account of matters important for the household is absent legitimately."[23] The test, applied to François de Richelieu's absence from Suzanne, might have found him sometimes wanting.

Alongside such worldly considerations of a father's place in the family, Richelieu's discussions of the holy family and the Trinity may express feelings towards the Richelieu family. In the earliest of his extant religious commentaries, a sermon of 1608, he raises the question of the incarnation:

> Perhaps you still are desirous of knowing why the Word took
> . . . the form [of flesh] rather than the Father and the Holy
> Ghost. . . . I shall not hesitate to tell you that it was appropriate
> (à propos) that He who had in heaven a father without a mother
> have on earth a mother without a father.[24]

The same prosaic imagery, suggesting that temporal analogies were in his mind, is repeated later in the first book to bear Richelieu's name. In it, he begins in standard fashion, Jesus, the Son of God, was a real human being "formed out of the blood of a woman, since all men are thus formed out of their mother's blood." Then, departing from the usual formulation, he explains that, as a divinity, it was "appropriate" that Jesus have a "father without a mother," but "according to his humanity he needed only to have a mother, without a father."[25] The familiarity of this language may be compared with the Council's words:

> It is the property of every human body to be formed from ma-
> ternal blood. But that which surpasses the forces of nature, and
> even of human understanding, is that . . . Jesus Christ . . . was
> in a single and same moment . . . at the same time a perfect .
> God and a perfect man.[26]

The mystery of the incarnation was linked to the mystery of the Trinity. But that this trinitarian mystery should have captured the young cleric's imagination, while the religious sentiment of his family was, in effect, unitarian, seems to indicate a special, personal interest. On the first occasion Richelieu had to establish his credentials as a theologian, he turned to the problem of the tri-partite character of the divinity. When the time came in 1608 for the young bishop to launch himself on his career, he chose to defend as his thesis in a public session at the Sorbonne a treatise "on the most difficult of our mysteries, which was that of the adorable and ineffable Trinity"[27]

The thesis which Richelieu defended has not been rediscovered, but in it his interpretations were probably little different than they were ten years later when he wrote his first full length discussion of the question. This was *The Christian's Teaching*, destined for the parishioners of Luçon. To these simple folk, their bishop thought, the problem is to explain the essential unity of what is manifold. He begins with the different forms which *water* may take.[28]

> A fountain produced a stream; the fountain and the stream to-
> gether, a lake. The lake, the stream and the fountain are three

different things; nevertheless, the water which is in them is of the same kind.[29]

How does it happen, he asks, that God and Jesus (the "fountain" and the "lake") both have "proper names," while the Holy Spirit has none? To clarify this he turns to a family analogy:

> The same happens every day in houses where there are several brothers all with the same surname. When some are called by the names of particular *seigneuries,* one among them can be sufficiently identified by their surname.[30]

This was the situation of the Richelieu brothers, of whom Armand was one. Henri, the eldest, was the marquis de Richelieu. Alphonse was at first presumably designated, as was his younger brother, by the name of some property belonging to the family. Armand himself was called, until he became Monsieur de Luçon, the marquis Du Chillou after a territory that his mother had added to her husband's resources. All were Richelieus, though only one was called by that name. Henri and his infant son had both died by the end of 1619, leaving only Armand to act, in their place, as bearer of the family name. In 1622, when he acquired the cardinal's bonnet, he chose to become, like the Holy Spirit, the "stream" through which the family name was conserved.[31] There is evidence, however, that the *Saint Esprit* already had, in his mind, particular applicability to himself.

4.   Powers of the Mind

At least one contemporary saw some special relationship between Richelieu and the Holy Ghost. Pure makes the tortuous observation that the future cardinal was born in the same year that the Order of the Holy Spirit was established—a coincidence so unremarkable, had it occurred, that it suggests a significance linked to family lore.[32] It may be that this was one of the "good omens (*bons présages*)" that Richelieu claimed "would be found to have accompanied him" from the time of his youth.[33] His uncle and his father had, of course, been early members of this exclusive royal chivalric society.

In French, the word *esprit* denotes both faculties of mind, such as intellect and wit, and also the less definite quality, spirit—the mental energy which animates action. To his contemporaries, admirers and detractors alike, Armand Du Plessis de Richelieu exemplified the operation of mind —*esprit* —on politics. His head—as collector of information and producer of strategies dominated the picture others formed of him.[34]

Even at a tender age, writes his intimate, Raconis, he confounded the elders with his learning and perspicacity. He showed a "firmness of judgment" and a "liveliness of mind" that were extraordinary.[35] Fifteen years after his death a former intimate thinks it enough identification to mention the "most marvelous *esprit* in the world."[36] Another contemporary also lauds the "liveliness" of his *esprit*.[37] His last confessor talks of his mind's "prodigious vigor" as well as of its "force."[38] Others further note the *powerful* impression given by his mental capacity—"this force of mind . . . that one and all perceive in him"—the "warmth" and the "extreme force of his mind."[39]

The *Saint Esprit* embodied powers of the mind. A modern writer sees the Holy Ghost of Christian thought as the successor of other mythical personifications of wisdom—the crocodile, the serpent—exemplifying the omnipotence of thought.[40] In the views of Richelieu's contemporaries, too, wisdom was foremost among the "particular gifts" of the Holy Spirit:

> The gift of wisdom is an appreciative knowledge of God, of his
> attributes, mysteries. . . . When a soul abandons itself to the
> conduct of the Holy Spirit, He raises it . . . and little by little an
> interior light makes clear its way.[41]

Richelieu, as has been seen, attributed his worldly success to his care to anticipate events and devise measures to meet them. To him, wisdom, or knowledge—that special gift of the Holy Spirit—was power.

In crediting Richelieu's mental energies with exceptional power to apprehend the outside world, his contemporaries tended to merge their imagery of his faculties of mind with that of the organs of his head. It was as though he "possessed binoculars," writes a devoted servant, and the "eyes of an eagle," so far could he "penetrate into the most secret affairs."[42] The binocular analogy also suggests itself to another observer of Richelieu. La Hoguette believes that his "foresight brought future success into his view as do binoculars," and believes his mind had "lights" which "caused his eye to see the possibility" of the remarkable ventures he undertook.[43] Another intimate recalls his "exact vigilance," his "lively and piercing eye," his "foresight."[44] One propagandist for the cardinal actually equates the cardinal himself with the powers of an all-seeing *verge* —a word used both to signify a whip and the penis: "He is truly that *verge* covered with eyes, watching."[45]

Ever alert, with ears as well as eyes attuned, is the picture of Richelieu painted by his former familiar, Mathieu de Morgues, a mortal enemy.[46] The cardinal himself sometimes likens persistence in error to failure of occular power. Correct beliefs derive from the power to *see*. Thus he explains the persistence of the Rochellais Protestants in heresy:

> I found that it came undoubtedly from the fact that the objects
> which one wants to be seen one does not present in the full
> light of day, or that people do not wish to look at them, or that
> they see them only through a veil, and from too great a dis-
> tance, or that they do not take time to consider them, or that he

who looks, being incapable of seeing the object he contemplates by himself has not the help which is necessary for him to understand it well.

His task, he believes, is to heighten the visual powers of others by efforts of his own mind: "It is therefore up to me, in this work," he continues, to present the truth so well in its full light that it may be easily seen."[47] The need to "lift a veil" that hides the truth is mentioned in the earliest of Richelieu's published works: "Our clergy," he writes, "must truly be the light which illumines others, not merely by their doctrine but also by their conversation."[48] Through reason and words others will be made to *see*.

The hallmark of Richelieu's strategy in the planning stage of any enterprise was to "penetrate the designs" of others. Typically, what must be anticipated are their *intentions* and *sentiments;* their power and resources rarely are difficult to discern. Others stressed the *penetrating* quality of the cardinal's intellect when it was used for this purpose. His admirer Raconis, for example, claims, "He knew how to unravel the most tangled matters and, from a single word, immediately penetrated what I had in my heart."[49]

From the earliest years of his career there remain only traces of his efforts to discern and interpret the designs of others, as when an ally writes to report on the "perfidy" of a witness who did not testify as Richelieu had foreseen in favor of a certain campaign, or an agent writes to ask for new instructions because the one whose intentions had been predicted "played it entirely differently than you had projected it."[50] A rare confidential letter from the bishop to his faithful secretary, Charpentier, who is with the court at Tours, acting for his master, shows the customary straining of Richelieu to discern the intentions of others and their possible consequences for his strategy. He believes he understands the aims of one figure whose behavior has worried his subordinate, "although it is true that people sometimes have two aims (*desseins*)," but as for another, "I don't penetrate his objective too well (*je ne pénètre bien son dessein*)," and the intention of a certain pair is particularly "what seems to me to be feared." In fact, "I confess to you that, however stoical I try to be, that matter agitates me." Hence he develops an elaborate strategy "to try to get some clarification of it."[51]

The passion Richelieu invested in such efforts of his mind to "penetrate the designs of others" seems to be signalled by physical symptoms which appeared in the head itself—tears and headache—when reason and vision failed in their aims. Raconis reports an instance of Richelieu's recourse to tears during the last months of his life. As the prime minister struggled against a spreading illness, writes the bishop of Vaur, one often saw "fat tears flow from his eyes in abundance" when he contemplated the mystery of the passion of Christ."[52] Raconis's report is unusual, for Jesus makes few appearances in Richelieu's writings. His attention seems not often to have been captured by the still "lake" into which flowed the "stream" carrying water from the "fountain" of God the father. While the observer thought his tears indicated a "tender" love for Christ, they were perhaps rather an expression of rage on account of his own increasing helplessness. Contemplating the passion of Jesus and feeling himself to be crucified like him (indeed he suffered from "wounds" caused by lanced abscesses on his arm), his tears may have been tears of anger directed at the One who had inflicted a torment upon him against which he was, finally, powerless.

In the modern nuclear family setting, normal phallic strivings of boys typically reach a crisis at two points in life. First, around the age of five, genital primacy and love for the mother come into sudden conflict with the power of the father and the fear of castration he inspires; second, in adolescence there is a renewed surge of genital desire and the original choice of the mother as sexual object threatens to become conscious once more. In Richelieu's case, the emphemeral, ambiguous and elusive character of a fatherly presence contributed to a family situation very different from this "classic" picture. The evidence, discussed above, does no more than suggest that, at the time of the first "Oedipal crisis," as it appears in this picture, whatever may have been Armand de Richelieu's phallic impulses towards women in his family, they were largely transformed into strivings of the mind. Such drives seem mostly to have provided additional energy for the ambition to dominate by the power of his intellect; sexual curiosity may have reinforced a pressure to penetrate the secret designs of others.[53] I have suggested, also, how Richelieu may have been particularly predisposed to such a conversion by still earlier circumstances of his rearing. First experience in gaining control over his bodily functions could already have conditioned him to seek discharge through his head. The arrival of Nicole at a time when Oedipal curiosity and phallic interest are supposed to be at their height could have, in her brother, reinforced an already strong tendency to transform bodily strivings into cerebral activity.

Some of Richelieu's imagery suggests the possibility that on some level he imagined himself, perhaps as the father of Nicole, the vessel receiving the "stream" from the "fountain," seemingly putting himself in the place of his mother vis à vis his father. Viewing or imagining the primal scene, he could have imagined receiving the father's semen.[54]

Later, in his priestly capacity, Richelieu would picture himself as a mother who gives Gospel milk to her children. The Word, he writes, is a *nourriture céleste* like the "milk that one gives to babies without any additional seasoning." His parishioners are infants, taking this nourishment from their protector:

> Our lord bishop . . . teaches you in a manner that the most childlike among you, that is to say the most imbecile, will be able to . . . convert the meat that he gives you into so mild a milk that the weakest stomachs can digest it. . . . It remains for

151

> you, like good children, to tread as you ought the paths that he
> has traced for you and to receive with conviction the food that
> he gives you.[55]

In thus ministering to his diocesan children, Richelieu may possibly be
replacing a dangerous, passive role of a woman by a satisfying, active one,
as well as converting base and impure aims of the father into high and
innocent ones.

At about the time whatever conflicts of an Oedipal nature that Richelieu
experienced were resolved, it will be recalled, he began training for the
life of a cleric under the tutelage of a local priest. It was also at about the
time some kind of second, adolescent crisis might be supposed to have
taken place, in 1602, that Alphonse de Richelieu renounced the bishopric
and his younger brother was called from military studies to resume preparation for the priesthood. According to all accounts, as will later be seen,
the seventeen-year old accepted this opportunity with extraordinary energy
and enthusiasm. At adolescence, then, he could have transformed whatever resurgent incestuous impulses might have troubled him by assuming
the priest's cassock:

> Object-love for the mother is replaced by a regression to the
> original identification with her, so that incest is avoided and the
> father pacified; further the opportunity is given of winning the
> father's love by the adoption of a feminine attitude towards him.
> Peace of mind is purchased by means of a change in heart in the
> direction of a change in sex.[56]

The role of Holy Ghost in mythology, too, Jones has concluded, is in
some respects a feminine one. In earlier religions this middle figure of the
Trinity was a woman; in Christianity alone has a purified spirit replaced
the older, mother goddess. But "the mysterious figure replacing the mother
is a male being, who symbolizes the creative elements of the Father," Jones
continues. While, in Richelieu's words, the *Saint Esprit* is the stream issuing
from the fountain of life, He also actively transmits the holy water. Moreover, the Holy Ghost, as contemporary iconography depicted it, impreg-
nates the mother with its breath. The dove, its symbol, may be, as Jones
maintains, the most effeminate of all the phallic emblems; nevertheless it
does represent the phallus of the father. The Holy Spirit appears, he writes,
"where we would . . . expect to find a phallus and semen."[57] Perhaps, in
Richelieu's case, his head became a phallus; by this transformation his
ambitions might have been further voided of guilt and enlisted in the
service of the king and God. Thus, in a partly feminine guise, masculine
drives could have been at work.

Historical writers have occasionally attributed femininity to Richelieu.[58]
Yet, in the light of recent research, femininity in men (in contrast with that
effeminacy which is hostile miming of female characteristics) seems to arise

from a failure to sever symbiotic bonds between a mother and her boy infant.[59] In such cases, the "normal" Oedipal conflict fails to develop, since separation from the mother, necessary for the rise of drives directed towards her as a desired object, has not taken place. In Richelieu's case, however, there are substantial indications that he separated himself exceptionally early, as a male, from his mother and other female caretakers. What evidence subsists indicates the *transformation* of those libidinal and aggressive energies which may reach a first crisis in the Oedipal dilemma, not their failure to appear. The adolescent's zest for his clerical role and the imagery he associated with it were masculine; femininity appeared chiefly in power failures.

Richelieu's experience of his own cerebral drive seems to have been phallic. He attributes to women a weakness in just those regions of his greatest strength—learning, reasoning, and foreseeing contingencies. The capacity of women for these is slight, he believes; the best that can be hoped for from female intellects is "judgment" while the "learning of a woman ought to consist of modesty and restraint." "Great knowledge" is a capacity "employed for the good by men"; women generally put it to bad use.[60] As a young bishop he is consulted by a woman on how to avoid headache as a result of protracted prayer. His advice is that she should cease to strain towards "understanding" and that she should avoid "inventing" more than she finds outlined in books of guidance already given her.[61]

Nowhere does Richelieu's view of thought as a masculine activity appear more clearly than in letters he drafted to be sent by women over their signature. In one of these he puts himself in the place of the duchesse de Chevreuse, composing a letter he wishes her to send to the duc de Lorraine to discourage him from supporting the king's brother. He has her say, "A woman's brain not being too good, I don't want to interfere by giving him advice, but . . . ."[62] Only a male has a head.

5.   E Pluribus Unum

The Holy Spirit is a link; it unites the family by binding the Father in heaven to the earthly mother. From the moment that Richelieu took up the clerical profession we find evidence that this function of unifying the family took possession of his imagination. It has already been noted how he sought, before the elders of the Sorbonne, to explain the unity in diversity of the Trinity; probably his rationale was the same as the one he used later to explain the identity of family membership among brothers of different names.

The theological profession seems to have offered Richelieu an opportunity to unite divided families. His first address to inhabitants of his diocese at Luçon was a secular one, taking account of the disunity in the temporal domain. Although he admits that the Protestants are "divided from us as to beliefs," he minimizes the importance of this. What is important is "that we be united in attachment" to the crown—a goal he promises to do all he can to promote and which will be agreeable to the king, "whom we must all please."[63]

The chief message of the Christmas sermon which he delivered to his congregation a few days later is only slightly less secular than his lay address. While this second audience presumably consisted only of Catholics—indeed he addresses it as "Peuple Catholique"—his remarks seem aimed as much at non-Catholics as at his co-religionists. Here, as in his secular address, he emphasizes that strength lies in union. He exhorts his hearers to be like the philosophers' stone which floats on the water when it is whole, but sinks when shattered. It is not clear whether an analogy is intended with the civil union of diverse sects or with solidarity among Catholics, but the context suggests that it is the first which is meant. Certainly, Richelieu does not intend that those separated merely by belief escape his influence. It is by increasing the king's power that the unity God desires is achieved. What He demands of us is, like that which is required by the king, our cohabitation in peace. In fact, in the following passage king and God are rather curiously intermingled:

> God in his goodness has favored the arms of our king to such an extent that by pacifying the disturbances (*troubles*) he has ended the miseries of his state and we no longer see France armed against itself, nor its children's blood spilled.[64]

But it is not sufficient that peace prevail throughout "France;" it must also reign within cities, households, and, "principally in our hearts." In cities, peace reigns when there is compliance with the "laws and ordinances" of "those in authority;" in households, "when those who dwell together live without envy, without dispute, without enmity one towards another." And in discussion of that most important location of peace, the *heart*, he places there a quality which is more usually viewed as belonging in the *head:*

> Peace is in our hearts when reason commands . . . when inferior parts, which contain the seditious people of our appetites, obey; and when both submit to eternal reason, from which our own has borrowed what light it possesses.[65]

At every level, peace is equated with subordination to authoritative reasoning and compliance with its commands.

The nation becomes a household by the equation of "people" with "children" and this equivalence will appear again and again in Richelieu's public pronouncements. Writing more than a decade later, on the occasion of reunion between Louis XIII and his mother, Marie de Medici, he condemns those who "pull from their brain obvious falsehoods to glorify themselves," and sow dissension between the king and his mother. Out of *his* brain he pulls the strategy of punishing promoters of disunion with a policy through which "the public . . . would see . . . proofs of good understanding between their masters."[66] In a later sermon he dwells again on the theme of family unity with probably impressive effects on Louis's rebellious brother Gaston.[66] As prime minister, the unity not only of the royal family but that of French Christians was to be the object of his policy; on an ever wider scale he strove to "contain the seditious people of our appetites" by commanding that they submit to the reason he imposed in the name of the king and of God. The "family" harmony desired by God is achieved by working the designs of Richelieu's brain through the king's will.

6. Master and Model

A. Father and King

In discussing the myth of the birth of the hero, Freud remarks, "The inner source of the myth is the so-called 'family romance' of the child, in which the son reacts to the change in his inner relationship to his parents, especially that to his father." At first the father is over-estimated—a king— in the imagination of the child. With the later influence of rivalry and disappointments, "a critical attitude towards the father sets in."[68]

In contrast with the myth of the hero's royal origins, the humble family of his rearing includes the downgraded, disappointing father. In Armand de Richelieu's writings we have found traces both of his idealization of and disappointment in his own father. We have seen, often disguised, his critical attitude toward François de Richelieu for abusing and neglecting Suzanne, abandoning his family, depriving them of their due inheritance, and committing other sins. At the same time, fears of possible dangers from rivalry with this figure may have been attenuated by his habitual absence. Moreover, at about the same time that his disillusionment might have set in—when Armand was almost five—his father died, becoming what might have seemed for his youngest son, like the Father in heaven, an absent "spirit."

As in the myth of the hero's birth, too, the image of the kingly father of infancy persists in the mind of the adult. For Richelieu, this attribute of his father may have been confirmed by the fact that François had "always served kings." Thus his father's majesty was linked to real majesty. For the Catholic boy growing up at Richelieu, however, the king in whose service his own father died may have seemed in some ways like François not only on account of persisting infantile awe, but also on account of Henri IV's very human imperfections. For "Le Grand Henry" as Richelieu would later call this king, was, in the early years of his reign, not merely a sinner but also a heretic.

When Richelieu, about six, commenced his studies, destined, as it then seemed, for the office of bishop, the authority of the new king was still uncertain, partly owing to his Protestant religion. Both this uncertainty and a widespread hatred of the Huguenot "heresy" inspired prayers throughout France for Henri IV's conversion. Possibly even then Armand, son of the Catholic, but loyalist, François, also joined at Richelieu with his clerical tutor to pray for Henri's return to the faith.

Soon after this time, Alphonse's defection from a naval profession caused Armand to change his plan of becoming a bishop and, instead, to direct his steps towards a soldier's career like his father's.[69] Not until adolescence was he able, through Alphonse's second withdrawal, to resume training for the bishopric of Luçon.

In thus striking out towards a clerical career, Richelieu took a path with few family precedents. Neither the Du Plessis-Richelieus nor the La Porte-Meillerayes had followed careers in the church. Even Jacques Du Plessis, who had briefly held the bishopric of Luçon for the family, had not been consecrated. The violent traditions of Armand's father and other paternal antecedents contrasted especially strikingly with the commitment to peace entailed by the clerical profession,[70] a commitment that Richelieu himself would later stress repeatedly. This contrast leads us to look elsewhere for models in real life from which the future cardinal might have formed an idea of his role in the career before him.

B.   A Forerunner: Du Perron

Armand de Richelieu's tutor, Père Hardy Guillon, may have been an important early model for his youthful pupil, but nothing is known of the personal qualities of this priest. By the time Richelieu changed back to a clerical future at adolescence, however, there was on the national scene a conspicuous example of the glory and power to which an ecclesiastical career could lead. This figure was Jacques Davy Du Perron, Bishop of Evreux. It was of this cleric that Richelieu wrote, two decades later, when he affirmed his love "of the name of him of whom all Christianity reveres the memory." Du Perron, he wrote, was the one "whom I should be delighted to set as a model for myself."[71]

Du Perron's peculiar suitability as a model for Richelieu lay first in the fact that he had achieved great fame by ministering to kings. In the 1580s he had concealed and defended the excesses of Henri III.[72] Later he had contributed signally to the salvation of Henri IV—and in a popular view, to that of France itself—by helping the Bourbon king to convert. In a speech he would make shortly before his death, Du Perron resumed his political career in words that Armand's own would later echo:

> I am a Frenchman and son of a Frenchman [detractors had de-
> nied this] and have never looked to any but kings. In matters of
> state I have never cast my eyes on others and, if it pleases God
> to keep me in sound mind, I shall never turn them elsewhere. I
> was nursed and raised under the wings of Henri III and re-
> mained constantly attached to his fortunes while he lived. After
> his death . . . I followed Henri le Grand . . . in good conscience.
> . . . I brought him back to Catholicism by the grace of God.[73]

Indeed, after the Vert Galant's renunciation of Calvinism, Du Perron had
stood at his side, defending the king's new faith before the bar of public
opinion and successfully seeking Henri's absolution for his sins from the
pope himself.

It was at about the time when the boy Armand de Richelieu first arrived
in Paris to begin his studies that Du Perron figured dramatically in Henri
IV's fate. The king's decision to become a Roman Catholic was the strategic
move that put his reign on the road to success. The counsel of Du Perron,
himself a former Calvinist, was supposed to have helped the Protestant
Henri to make this conversion. In July, 1593, Henri formally abjured Calvinism and espoused the Catholic church. It was a momentous, festive
occasion, celebrated as the essential condition for French domestic peace.
If it symbolized, as Jean H. Mariéjol holds, "the wedding of the king and
France,"[74] then Du Perron was best man: he presided, before hundreds of
Frenchmen, over a solemn ceremony at Saint-Denis as the sponsor of the
king.

Two years after this event Du Perron was sent to Rome to obtain absolution for Henri IV. This mission, too, he accomplished brilliantly. His signal
success, from the French point of view, consisted in refusing to surrender
any of those of the king's prerogatives that the pope had initially claimed
in exchange for his blessing. Such a defense of majesty would favorably
have impressed the royalist young Armand, as it did Henri himself. With
absolution from Clement VIII, Henri IV's legitimacy as ruler of France was
confirmed.

Five years later the same Bishop Du Perron was the leading figure in
still another important event—a doctrinal confrontation between himself
and Du Plessis Mornay, the Protestant leader. By this time Armand de
Richelieu was a fourteen-year old Paris student. It is likely that he was
among the more than two hundred spectators who witnessed the bishop's
triumph over his Huguenot antagonist.

Staged by Henri IV himself, the debate took place at Fontainebleau in
the presence of the king and a host of princes, lords, scholars, and magistrates. Armand's eldest brother, Henri de Richelieu, was one of seventeen
seigneurs who comprised the king's inner circle of companions. Pont Courlay, Henri's friend and his and Armand's future brother-in-law, was one
of those who inspired the public confrontation. François Pithou, a lawyer

colleague of François de La Porte, the brothers' grandfather, was one of the judges appointed by the king to determine the winner on each point debated.[75]

The outcome of the disputation was a theatrical success for the king and for Catholicism. In this exciting confrontation Du Perron "convicted" Du Plessis of misquoting and citing out of context arguments of the Christian fathers. The king was able to profit politically by his sponsorship of a debate that presented Catholic doctrine in so favorable a light: he made public a letter in which he announced that the "diocese of Evreux has beaten that of Saumur"—Saumur was the Protestant stronghold of which Du Plessis was governor—and claimed the event to be one of the "greatest blows for God's church which has been struck in a long time." Henri professed to foresee that by such peaceful means as these more conversions to Catholicism would be effected in one year than by other, warlike, ones in fifty.[76]

Du Perron's performance in this encounter brought him dazzling personal acclaim: "It was to his high reputation as the laurels of Miltiades were to Themistocles," judged a contemporary cleric.[77] It brought also a more worldly honor: soon after the debate Henri IV nominated the bishop of Evreux for the cardinalate. In 1604 Du Perron became a prince of the church.

In observing the prizes that Du Perron was able to grasp in the service of goals so close to Armand's heart, the young man may also have sensed in the older one a personal affinity with himself that made him believe his own burning ambition could be justified and implemented by following the same path. Cardinal Du Perron's writings encouraged a belief that his religious perspectives were "more in the mind than in the heart,"[78] a description that was, as we have seen also apt for Armand de Richelieu. Further, Du Perron's skills were more those of the courtroom than of the pulpit of his day. He was, like Armand, a debater, not an inspirational preacher. He introduced into the church "a new kind of eloquence," inaugurating in the pulpit "a polemic founded on discussion and reasoning."[79] This cardinal had, moreover, an exalted notion of the position ecclesiastics ought to take in the councils of the king—a notion particularly alluring, perhaps, to the ambitious young student. It was characteristic of the ex-Protestant prelate to observe that less than two hundred years before his own time, bishops were being honored by being given precedence even over sons of the kings of France.[80] Indeed, at the public abjuration of Henri IV, Du Perron the bishop took precedence over peers of the realm—the princely *grands*. Such a prospect of preeminence would surely have appealed strongly to Armand de Richelieu.

Thus when Richelieu was offered, through his brother Alphonse's withdrawal, the chance to become a bishop, Du Perron's example could have been fresh in his mind. A later contemporary claims that he actually confided to his friends his intention to acquire the cardinal's proficiency in theological controversy.[81] It was, in fact, at about the same time as Du Perron's nomination to the purple that this youngest Richelieu brother left the Academy in order to prepare at the Sorbonne for his ecclesiastical career.

Following in Du Perron's footsteps, Richelieu set out with energy and determination to learn the art of theological controversy. He immersed himself in private study in the company of a doctor of the celebrated school of Louvain "to bring himself to complete perfection in the study of holy letters." This account, probably ratified by Richelieu, since republished several times in his lifetime, continues, "After that he threw himself into controversy with so much application and assiduity that he gave it regularly eight hours a day for four years." It is easy to believe that one so motivated to action would become ill, and perhaps depressed, through leading so interiorized, receptive a life of study. Indeed, we are told that this hard scholarly concentration "so altered his constitution . . . that his body feels to this day the efforts of his mind."[82] Aubéry pronounces it a "certainty that the languishing health, which he had almost always thereafter, was principally caused by this contention and this extraordinary labor of the mind."[83]

The prospective bishop showed that he chafed at this bridling of his impulses towards action. In 1604, before he had won any theological degree, he asked the Sorbonne to authorize a public debate on philosophical issues at the university. This was refused, on the grounds that it was a thing that "was never done." Nevertheless, Richelieu was so impatient to make a name for himself that the contest actually took place, under irregular auspices, at his old college of Navarre.[84]

It was probably late in 1603 that Richelieu was formally nominated Bishop of Luçon by Henri IV.[85] The nomination had to be ratified by the pope. Moreover, since the candidate was short of the canonical age for the post, Henri sought a dispensation from this requirement as well as approval of the appointment.[86] Such exceptions were frequently made; the king requested this one through Cardinal Du Perron himself who was in Rome at the time on another royal mission.

While the nomination was pending, Richelieu succeeded in winning the certificate of completion of the first course in theology, an achievement also requiring an exemption—in this case a dispensation from university residence requirements. His petition, presented in June, 1605, already describes him as bishop-designate. Only a month later the degree was awarded to the prospective bishop on account of his "status (*dignitatis*), knowledge of doctrine, and ability (*capacitatis*)."[87] The first mentioned attribute is likely to have been decisive; the significance of such recognition of his scholarship should be discounted, inasmuch as a mere formality now stood between the young man and the high status of bishop.

With his diploma in hand, Richelieu set out for Rome to further the cause of his own appointment. There seems little doubt that it would eventually have been confirmed without this step; he therefore risked no danger of

Conditions

humiliation by taking it. Most likely the young man was attracted by the chance for vigorous action and perhaps by other opportunities a visit to the holy city offered. Furthermore, Italy itself may have had its own appeal for the future prelate: in later years he would show that he found Italian manners and tastes especially congenial.[88] Du Perron's presence in Rome, too, may have made the trip attractive. Once in Italy, Richelieu is said to have become fluent in spoken Italian and Spanish, the secular languages of the *curia*. The knowledge that he would subsequently show of papal politics may have been acquired during this visit. It is certain that he improved his political connections, acquiring or strengthening at least two highly influential friendships, those of Du Perron himself and of the marquis d'Halincourt, son of Villeroy, one of Henri IV's chief advisors.

Over the years, legend has tended to exaggerate the figure cut by the twenty-one year old Richelieu in Paris and at the papal court.[89] According to several—much later—reports, he made a strongly favorable impression on many Roman clerics, including Pope Paul V, on account of his character and ability. In Rome, it has been claimed, he demonstrated eloquence and a formidable memory in addresses to the papal conference *De Auxiliis*. Avenel, however, has shown such an appearance to have been highly unlikely.[90] Probably Richelieu's history in the matter has been merged with that of his model Du Perron, who did, in fact, participate in that congregation. A similar confusion may account for the story that Armand, in a conversation with the pope, defended Henri IV's sexual morals and religious faith against criticisms.[91] Du Perron, after all, had sought and obtained absolution for his ruler's sins from an earlier pope. It seems quite unlikely, on the other hand, that a very young clerical novice like Richelieu should have been called upon to discuss the sexual conduct of his own monarch, Henri the Great, in a confidential interview with the Italian pontiff. Yet publication of this report by Pure suggests that it may have been circulated during Richelieu's lifetime—perhaps even encouraged by him after Henri's death had made it harmless. Defending an errant master—king or father—against a higher authority could well have been an appealing role that Richelieu would gladly have assumed had he been able to do so, and thus later, at least, might have failed to discourage its attribution to himself. The accounts that were published while King Henri still lived, however, make more modest claims.[92]

Richelieu's mission to Rome was soon successful and, in the spring of 1607, he returned to Paris a consecrated bishop. By October of the same year he had, through further suspensions of rules, succeeded in hurdling remaining academic formalities; he became a bachelor of theology and a few days later was received into the Society of the Sorbonne.[93]

Du Perron returned to Paris towards the end of 1607. As Grand Almoner of France it was he who scheduled sermons at court and preached regularly there. He could and did bestow patronage on Richelieu. The young bishop was invited to preach at court in the lenten season of 1608 and planned to give the sermon at Easter of that year, although it is not known whether or not he actually did so.[94]

It is probable that Richelieu hoped at this time that still more doors at court would open to him. Yet apparently his entrées did not lead to any further opportunities. Conditions for his advancement in political influence were not propitious. Even if Henri IV had formed a particularly favorable impression of the new bishop's capacities, circumstances at court were not conducive to the advancement of clerics in royal councils. Henri was jealous of his power and it was no accident that his chief advisors were laymen dependent for their status on himself alone.[95] Even Du Perron, whose services had been well-tried and appreciated by the king, was to progress no farther in governmental influence. Moreover, as long as the Calvinist Sully was foremost in the king's administration, there was no chance for ecclesiastical preponderance in policy making. This Protestant finance minister probably looked upon the new bishop of Luçon with little favor; he had already formed the view that Henri de Richelieu and his brother-in-law Pont Courlay were part of a faction allied with Père Coton, the king's Jesuit confessor, against himself.[96]

Moreover, times were becoming difficult for clergymen who preferred court life to diocesan duties. The Catholic reform movement demanded new attention to pastoral assignments, a demand that Henri IV, the new convert, was no doubt happy to encourage. A recent papal order had ruled that even cardinals charged with bishoprics must either reside in them, resign them, or provide substitutes who would perform their functions. The command caused concern to Du Perron himself during his mission to Rome. At the time of Richelieu's consecration he was writing to one of the king's ministers that his means were insufficient to make it possible to forego the income from the diocese of Evreux, yet that income was not enough to cover the salary of the required coadjutor.[97] The impecunious bishop of Luçon was under much more pressure on account of this new ruling enforcing residence requirements.

Since 1583, when the bishopric of Luçon had come into the family as the gift of Henri III to Richelieu's father, the Richelieus had drawn income from its properties without returning either clerical service or contributions to the upkeep of the church buildings and grounds. Two family representatives had been designated by them to act as bishops before Armand was assigned the post, but neither of these had been resident, nor had either one been consecrated bishop. The second, in fact, one François Hyver, was not even an ordained priest.

By 1604, discontent among the officers of the Cathedral Chapter of Luçon had gone so far that they declared the office of bishop vacant and initiated lawsuits against Suzanne de Richelieu intended to oblige the family to pay its share towards restoring cathedral buildings. Thence came the Richelieus' haste to provide a genuine incumbent for the bishopric and to substitute Armand when Alphonse declined the assignment. In 1608 the chapter was actively pressing its claims for restitution against the new bishop.[98]

It seems indubitable that Richelieu was reluctant, at this time, to exile himself from the center of power, especially to such an isolated little town as Luçon. His disappointment at this necessity may have contributed to the "annoying illness" which kept him in bed in Paris for several months in 1608. His departure seems to have been postponed several times.[99]

Several years later, in a set of requests drawn up for Richelieu to present on behalf of the clergy of Poitou to the Estates General of France, he was to stress the moral obligation of all clerics to meet the residence requirement—with one significant exception. Only "those who are employed in Their Majesties' service on account of their outstanding learning" were exempted.[100] When, in the autumn of 1608, his own outstanding learning had not been recognized by a call to the service of Their Majesties, he prepared to make the long journey to Luçon in order to take up residence in his diocese.

When Richelieu had assumed the feminine robes of a priest he had, I have hypothesized, hoped to gratify a profoundly masculine ambition to surpass his own father. François de Richelieu had served kings in a profane, warlike role. Armand de Richelieu, too, was called to his task by the king, to whom he owed his nomination. But he was called to a higher, holy task that gave zest to his clerical assignment.

In words he would later use, he came to the rescue of the "downtrodden" church, the "holy bride of the sovereign monarch of the world." For she— église of course is of feminine gender—like his own abused, afflicted mother, was "dishonored . . . despoiled . . . frustrated," and "profaned," her altars in shambles and her children divided.[101] Richelieu's duty, as bishop, was to restore her physical and moral integrity and the unity of her children by the exertion of his mind. Thus what might have been a dangerous ambition to replace the father became, in the young man, a sacred mission.

Part 4   PREPARATIONS

10 The Queen's Bishop: A Courtship

Crowns ought only to descend upon those women capable of supporting them and of acquitting themselves well of the power that the character of sovereign attributes to them.[1]

Richelieu arrived in Luçon, at the end of 1608, swearing fidelity to the Catholic church—"holy bride" of the Monarch of the world. By the spring of 1610 he was already burning to go to the rescue of another "bride" of a king—the newly widowed queen mother, Marie.

1.   Richelieu to the Rescue

On the afternoon of May 14, 1610, Henri IV was stabbed to death in Paris by an assassin. An eight-year-old boy was declared to be Louis XIII, King of France. The following day an *arrêt* proclaiming Marie de Medici Regent was confirmed in the Parlement de Paris in the presence of various peers, ecclesiastics, other notables, the young king, and the queen mother herself. At this ceremony Marie's formal status was affirmed but her lack of real authority was betrayed by the absence there of several of the *grands* whose support she would need in order to rule.[2]

The bishop of Luçon is said to have wept on learning of Henri's death, to have conducted a mass for the repose of his soul, and then to have hastened to write the queen a letter of condolence.[3] No such letter is known, but another document written by Richelieu may be the one recalled in that report—a "*Serment de Fidélité*" to the new king and the new regent. This oath of allegiance, drafted within three or four days of the time news of the regency reached Richelieu in Coussaye, is a clue to the electrifying effect produced on him by the changed situation in Paris. In what has been described as an "extraordinarily confused style,"[4] it declares his unbounded loyalty to the new regime:

> Although it may seem, after the tragic misfortune dealt us by a homicidal hand, that we could no longer experience happiness, nevertheless we feel an inexpressible satisfaction that it has pleased God, by giving us the queen as regent of this state, to bestow on us following . . . extreme evil . . . the most effective and necessary good that we could have wished for . . . hoping that the wisdom of so virtuous a princess will maintain all things at the point to which the greatest king ever covered by the heavens has brought them, we swear . . . to bear her all obedience and pray God that He may send us death rather than permit that we be wanting in the fidelity which we owe and now swear to the king her son and to her.[5]

Richelieu attested personally to this oath and also had it promulgated in the name of the cathedral chapter of Luçon. He dispatched a copy of it to the governor of Poitou and another to Paris for his brother personally to present to the queen. He required the townspeople of Luçon, of both religions, to bear witness "in writing" of their loyalty to the crown.[6]

The bishop's eagerness to affirm a loyalty that no one questioned by an oath that no one had solicited from him was odd. The gesture was especially inappropriate coming from a cleric. The devoted Sébastien Bouthillier in Paris wrote back that Henri de Richelieu had not offered the document to the queen as he had learned that "such a practice has not been followed by anyone here, as for my part I have taken special pains to find out for myself."[7] Historians have wondered at this ill-directed move of the usually circumspect young Richelieu. Erlanger finds it "unbelievable," the sign of an "overexcited mind." Another student of the cardinal's early career writes "This precipitateness even has something inexperienced about it which is astonishing on the part of such a man as Richelieu."[8]

The precipitateness is understandable as the effect of several elements in the new political situation that strongly stimulated Richelieu's imagination and caused him to act, exceptionally, on impulse. He did nothing to restrain the urge to go to the rescue of the queen mother and her little boy, the king. Words written by Bouthillier in his first letter, announcing the assassination, may have specially excited him: The queen, reports the abbot in terms very like those Richelieu would use in his vow to her, was "very wise" and "very virtuous." As for young Louis, "everyone noticed that the king has an infinitely good and assured manner and that his demeanor and actions in no way reflect his age."[9]

The powerful effect of these reports on the bishop may have been due to parallel events in his own history. It is likely that this picture of a precocious, royal son, in the care of a wise and virtuous mother whose husband has suddenly died, evoked in Richelieu associations with the situation he and his mother Suzanne had shared on the death of his father, the grand provost. The queen, like his own mother, had suffered "afflictions and bitternesses" at the hands of her husband; her present dangerous position inspired in Armand the wish to rescue her and her little boy, thus taking the place of the great Henri and, perhaps, in his imagination, his own father. It may have seemed to offer to him an opportunity, formerly denied him, to be a better husband to his mother than his father had been.

The new royal predicament, furthermore, had parallels in several features of the Richelieu family's past relations with the monarchy that were sufficient to confuse an excited mind. François de Richelieu had first been attached to the court as page during the minority of Charles IX who was then guarded by another Medici regent, Catherine. François had won favor with this first Florentine regent of France as well as with her favorite son, later to be Henri III. The situation produced by that monarch's death, in turn, was a potentially revolutionary one; Henri III's apparent successor was a heretic from a new and untried dynasty. On the morning after the murder of the last Valois king, the grand provost had hastened, with other high officials of the crown, to swear loyalty, in a solemn oath, to the insecure new regime of Henri IV. Now, with that king's death, Armand de Richelieu's oath showed that he was, like his father, ready to offer himself— body and soul—to the crown. Henri IV himself had had little need for the services of Captain Richelieu's youngest son, but his widow, menaced from all sides, might well stand in need of fidelity from her loyal subject, the bishop of Luçon.

The uncertainties of Marie de Medici's position were real ones. While Bouthillier's letter has reassuring words—"everyone seems to breathe nothing but service to the queen and the wish to make her happy"—it also alludes to circumstances likely to arouse anxiety in Richelieu lest the queen's happiness be jeopardized. The abbot announces the arrival, on the previous night, of the arrogant, reckless comte de Soissons—from the crown's point of view one of the most unruly and factious of all the princes. It was he, explains Bouthillier, although the facts were no doubt already known to his correspondent, "who withdrew from the court on account of a certain dissatisfaction because the king did not find it good that Madame, his wife, wear *fleurs de lys* [sign of a royal princess] on her ceremonial cloak."[10] In a subsequent letter the abbot reports the disquieting news that the prince de Condé, first among the *grands* outside the nuclear royal family, has written his mother that he is planning to return to Paris within three weeks.[11] Condé had left the realm to escape Henri IV's reach; his imminent return held special menace of disruption. In a letter to his father-in-law the prince expressed his hope that the new king and the queen would accept his "exercise of the charges that my rank and my birth give me in the government of the state." About this time, too, Richelieu could have heard the further rumor that the Spanish king proposed to sponsor Condé as "rightful heir" to the throne of France.[12] A few weeks later he received information from a Provençal correspondent that seditious talk was circulating in that province in favor of Condé's title to the throne.[13] To Richelieu, these reports could well have meant that Marie's position was soon to be challenged by rebellious *grands* unwilling to subordinate themselves to a weak princess. It was perfectly possible that they would challenge even their legitimate monarch, the little king.

Richelieu's ill-conceived oath reveals his urgent desire to be the defender of the queen and her son. Within a month of Henri's death he was not only planning an early trip to Paris, but hoping also for a permanent residence there. As he writes Madame de Bourges, "Henceforth I hope to make a tour in Paris every year."[14] He lost no time in setting off for the capital.

Richelieu had reasons to believe that his presence in court might be more welcome than it had been during the lifetime of Henri IV. Bouthillier's letters after Henri's death suggest some of those considerations that could stimulate his friend's calculated ambition as well as excite him to impulsive acts. In one, for example, the abbot reports to him that Cardinal Du Perron publicly lauded the young bishop of Luçon as a model to all other young prelates in France. In another he names two bishops from the neighborhood of Luçon who are to have great honors in the impending funeral ceremonies because they happened to be near Paris at the time. A few days later he reports a conversation with Cardinal de Sourdis who, as Archbishop of Bordeaux, was Richelieu's own metropolitan, and who held much patronage in his hands. This dignitary, the abbot writes, "asked several times for news of you and one day . . . said to me that he wished that you might have been in Paris."[15] It may have been in Bouthillier's mind, as well as in Richelieu's, that political conditions at court had changed in ways that were likely to improve prospects for the bishop of Luçon.

Under Henri IV's rule, church and other religious figures had had little part in political decision-making, but with his death their influence could be expected to increase. The queen, unlike her husband, was known for her piety. Père Coton, Henri IV's confessor, was a friend of both Henri and Armand de Richelieu. It was good news when Bouthillier wrote that Marie had decided to keep the Jesuit father with her. Coton was, indeed, one of those to whom Armand himself had written immediately, upon learning news of the assassination, and the abbot reports that upon receiving this letter the priest had "promised you much service."[16]

Gilles de Souvré, the young king's governor, was also friendly to the Richelieus. Henri IV was well-known for leaving little discretion to the officials charged with his son's tutelage, but now arrangements could be expected to change. Souvré was trusted by the queen. Bouthillier only regrets that it is difficult to get a word with the governor because he is now always near the king. Nevertheless, when the abbot has a chance to talk a bit with him he tells him that Richelieu has commissioned him to salute him. Souvré declares himself "very pleased to hear news of the bishop of Luçon," and speaks highly of him, Sébastien writes, "because of the reputation your merits have earned you all over France."[17]

The queen herself was quite likely to seek advice in new directions. Sully, the chief of state finances, had been Henri IV's right-hand man, used by him even to control Marie, but the queen had no love for the Protestant duke. In the autumn after the assassination, rumors were already circulating that he would soon be dismissed.[18] This prospect was a further favorable sign for Richelieu fortunes.

Richelieu's correspondence shows that he had no difficulty gaining an audience from Marie de Medici and her ministers. Soon after his arrival, in the summer of 1610, he personally recommended, before the king and queen and in the presence of two ministers, the petititon of one of his acquaintances for a son's commission as company commander. In the same audience he received assurances that the favor would be bestowed at the first opportunity.[19]

Despite this early success, it is not reported that the bishop of Luçon played any further part in the court politics of 1610. He could have attended nine-year-old Louis XIII's coronation at Rheims on October 17—a place was reserved in the cathedral for bishops who did not officiate at the ritual *sacre*[20]—but if he did so his presence was merely ceremonial. His popular brother Henri had been sent on a foreign mission the week before and hence was, for the time being, not available as a champion at court.[21] In any case Armand was back in Poitou before Christmas of that year,[22] suffering from a feverish illness accompanied by headache and, apparently, dejection. It is at this time that he complains of the "sterility" of his surroundings.[23] It is at this time, too, that Henri, now back in Paris, apologizes for requesting a favor and expresses the hope that the recent death of their aunt has not aggravated his brother's "melancholy mood." Henri hopes he himself can also return to the family home "in order to improve my spirits somewhat, away from the anxieties of the court."[24] Auguries were not yet propitious for the Richelieu brothers.

2.   Shifting Political Sands

After the public torture and execution of Henri IV's murderer, Ravaillac, an atmosphere of supicion prevailed in Paris. Rumors of sinister developments circulated and evil portents were discerned in everyday events.[25]

In the mind of a public that felt itself sorely bereaved, the possibility that the assassin had had accomplices could not be ruled out. In some circles a favorite candidate for scapegoat was the Society of Jesus whose close link with the papacy, reputation for secrecy, and sudden rise in power inspired envy and resentment, especially among representatives of older influential institutions. The Jesuit, Père Coton, whose favor with Marie was one of Richelieu's best connections to inner court circles, was himself in a precarious situation in the summer following Henri IV's assassination. The Sorbonne, intellectual center of French Gallicanism, issued a denunciation of the work of the Jesuit Juan de Mariana's work that seemed to justify tyrannicide.[26] This action ended in nothing more serious than the faculty's official condemnation and an *arrêt* by Parlement for a ceremonial book-burning, but Coton, as royal confessor very much in the public eye, was put sufficiently on the defensive that he published a disavowal, on behalf of his Order, of Mariana's doctrine. In this *Lettre déclaratoire* he dated his own opposition to *De Rege* to a conference in 1606. There, he claimed, the work had been repudiated by French Jesuits.[27] He may have justified, by this means, his reputation as a loyal supporter of the crown, but this was no time for the queen to draw attention to herself as a defender of Jesuit and papal interests. In spite of this, when the papal nuncio, "whom the queen would have liked to please," complained of Parlement's order, Marie attempted, albeit unsuccessfully, to have it suspended.[28]

Marie's position was delicate. In Paris, conditions were propitious for witch-hunting. The queen had been crowned, partly at her own instance, only the day before her husband's violent death. To some this seemed a suspicious coincidence. An upsurge of xenophobic and Gallican feeling among Parisians would make precarious the position of an Italian princess with Ultramontanist connections.[29] Perhaps Marie herself understood this; more likely she was advised of it by councillors. In any case, she did not immediately change her official advisors. Sully, Villeroy, and Président Jeannin—all chief councillors of Henri IV—continued, at first, to surround her.

With Henri gone, however, the old cabinet was disunited and indecisive. The new weakness of the government compelled a strategy of propitiating the *grands* in order to prevent them forming a coalition against the regency. With Marie as nominal leader, the policy of pacification entailed heaping on one after another of the great princes and lords subsidies, benefices, and advantageous marriage alliances. As each one's benefits swelled, the next one demanded even greater favors and, as often as not, demonstrated still less deference to the crown. The comte de Soissons was at first the most openly demanding but, at various times, the dukes of Epernon, Guise, Vendôme, Nevers, Mayenne, Longueville, and others, alternately competed and collaborated to share in state power, while the queen "devoted her efforts to keeping equal the balance of her generosities."[30] Meanwhile the Protestant duc de Bouillon sought to form a coalition among the discontented lords.

Most menacing of all was Condé, who had arrived in Paris—on July 18, 1610—at about the same time as Richelieu himself. As the highest ranking prince outside the immediate royal family he had a large independent following. He had links with two interests capable of subverting the regime—Spain and the Protestants. Although raised a Catholic, Condé's antecedents had been Protestant rebels. Adding danger were his Spanish connections, formed during his sojourn in exile. Bouillon, "an old conspirator," thought of forming an alliance with him that would at once win over the Huguenots and all the other *grands*. It was suspected that Spain might secretly help Condé to exploit his influence with Protestants in order to spread insurrection in France.[31]

The nervousness of the Huguenots contributed to general fears of disunity. Henri IV's personal history and sympathies had been guarantees for Protestant liberties. Despite early reassurances from Marie and her ministers, many Calvinists feared that their privileges would be less secure under the new leadership. These anxieties turned the thoughts of Protestant leaders to self-defense. Huguenot cities whose citizens had felt safe under the previous regime now considered measures to protect themselves. Attacks on their religious autonomy might come from the crown, or, more probably, from ambitious *grands* against whom the regency would not or could not protect them. Fears were rife of the revival of those civil wars that Henri IV had subdued. To many Huguenots, therefore, it was an ominous sign when, on the twenty-sixth of January, 1611, the duc de Sully, guardian both of Protestant rights and fiscal integrity, obtained the consent of the queen to withdraw from the government.

Marie, too, was apprehensive. Negotiations were under way for the assembly, in May, of Protestant leaders at Châtellerault, a city under the governorship of Sully himself. Convoked under a law giving the Huguenots the right to petition the crown for a redress of grievances, the prospect of this meeting "gave much anxiety and embarrassment to the new government," which feared it would become the rallying point for political separatism.[32] Late in Lent the court repaired to Fontainebleau for the spring season. It was here that Richelieu found a new occasion to approach the queen.

3.   Armand's Courtship Renewed

Since the beginning of the year the bishop of Luçon had resided in his priory of Roches, near his mother's home at Richelieu. Also in the neighborhood, at Chinon, lived François Le Clerc Du Tremblay, the Capucin monk known as Père Joseph. The two men had in common the friendship of Antoinette d'Orléans, reformist acting head of the great royal abbey of Fontevrault—a landmark in that part of Poitou. Madame d'Orléans had been coadjutrix of the monastery with her aunt, Eléanore de Bourbon, a royal relative like herself. Madame de Bourbon died at the end of March, 1611, and now Antoinette, who had distinguished herself by introducing a reformed regime at Fontevrault, wished to withdraw to a less worldly religious community. Père Joseph, the "spiritual father" of the coadjutrix, asked Richelieu, who was also on good terms with her,[33] to help persuade her to remain as the new abbess and, when this failed, to help bring about the selection of another reforming Bourbon family member, Madame de Lavedan-Bourbon. The two clerics' mission to Fontainebleau during the spring had the purpose of announcing Madame d'Orléans's resignation to the queen and gaining Marie's support for the edifying aim of securing a worthy successor.[34]

The pious mission succeeded, bringing credit to all concerned. Marie agreed to allow the Fontevrault religious to elect their own abbess, a discretion arranged in advance to result in selection of Madame de Lavedan-Bourbon. This was accomplished at the queen's direction, in the presence of the two priests, on June the twenty-eighth.[35] Antoinette d'Orléans, though continued as coadjutrix, withdrew to Lencloître, near Poitiers, where Père Joseph and Richelieu attended her installation later in the summer.[36] The new abbess of Fontevrault, too, continued the cordial relations of her predecessors with the bishop of Luçon: early in the following year she is found to be gladly postponing her formal benediction in the post in order that Richelieu may officiate at the ceremony.[37]

The sojourn of the two clerical colleagues at Fontainebleau marked a turning point in Richelieu's political fortunes. The circle around Marie had recently changed in such a way as to make the young bishop's presence more welcome, in the spring of 1611, than it had been in the preceding summer.

Even before the departure of Sully, L'Estoile, the Protestant diarist, had complained that the queen was taking private counsel on high politics from her intimates—the "council of the little writing-desk"—before conferring with her official *conseil*—those "good old French statesmen of the great sword."[38] With the Huguenot duke's withdrawal the actual visible intervention of this kitchen cabinet in state affairs increased. There were three outstanding attributes of the group that differentiated it sharply from Henri IV's intimate circle of advisors: Figuring prominently in it were Italians, clerics, and women. As it happened, each of these features was one for which the bishop of Luçon had a special affinity.

The figure in the unofficial council that seemed most detestable to L'Estoile, as to many other Parisians, was Concino Concini, who had been appointed a councillor of state soon after Henri IV's death. Shortly afterwards he received the title of Marquis d'Ancre. His influence on the queen, however, was derived entirely from that of his wife, Leonora Galigai.

Marie de Medici's strongest affection—perhaps her only strong affection— was for the marquise d'Ancre. This woman, a Tuscan commoner by origin, had been Marie's intimate companion since childhood. In 1601

The Queen's Bishop

Leonora was married to Concini, a Tuscan nobleman from a family of counselors to the Medicis. He had been a member of the suite that had accompanied Marie to France in the preceding year. Thereafter, the queen's attachment to Leonora remained unchanged. A representative of the Florentine court who arrived in Paris in 1610 was an eye witness. According to him, "Her Majesty loves Leonora in an extraordinary fashion; she is, as it were, enamored of her."[39]

Marie's passion for Leonora did not diminish in the ensuing years. She showered her with gifts of the kind that attentive lovers bestow, confided her intimate needs to her care, and depended on her daily companionship. After his marriage, Concini's access to the queen increasingly reflected his wife's relationship with her. He too learned to serve Marie to her taste.[40] His skill in pleasing the queen, however, reflected his broader interests and a social standing and cultivation superior to Leonora's for, contrary to contemporary rumors, Concini was a well educated gentleman.[41]

The femininity of the new ruler and of her favorite had significance beyond the mere change in gender of personnel with whom she associated; it penetrated the atmosphere of the entire court. Henri IV's surroundings had been highly masculine: sports, military arts, and adultery had been the leading recreations of that ruler and his entourage. Such a setting was perhaps congenial to Armand's brother, the marquis de Richelieu, who had been raised in Henri's court to be a soldier. But Richelieu himself, brought up in a feminine household, favored by sisters, aunts and mother, might well have felt more at ease in the new milieu than did his brother Henri. Certainly, he had the capacity to make himself more welcome now than he could ever have done in the secular, rough court of Henri IV.

The queen had one definite interest which Richelieu shared—decorative arts. The attraction for Marie of the Concinis lay partly in their skill at serving this interest: they were "good domestics."[42] Like Marie, Richelieu was experienced and interested in details of jewelry, dress, interior and exterior decoration—in everything to do with domestic and institutional ornamentation, especially in the Italian manner. He, like the Concinis, was capable of serving the queen in ordering decorative objects to suit a fastidious taste.[43] It is possible that their affinity was discovered at the 1611 meeting. Certainly it became evident later.

Besides these temperamental characteristics that made Richelieu congenial to the queen mother, there were family connections that gave him an entrée to her inner circle. The Richelieus had had direct links to the queen's private cabinet under Henri IV, when such connections were of little political value. Madame de Guercheville, a Poitevine relation, had been matron of honor to Marie since the latter's arrival in France.[44] She remained close to Marie after Henri's death. More important was a link to Leonora herself. Claude Barbin, a colleague and friend of Denis Bouthillier, had been a Richelieu family friend since Armand's youth. As government

173

prosecutor, Barbin's base was near Fontainebleau where in previous years he had formed close personal relations with Madame Concini and thus had gained access to the queen. With Sully's retirement Barbin was given new responsibilities for financial management, and, although not yet a minister of state at the time of Richelieu's visit to Fontainebleau in 1611, he was already influential. Barbin admired the bishop's merits and later championed his advancement with an avuncular concern, even to the point of deprecating his own qualifications.[45]

In his new approach to the regent Richelieu had a collaborator whose welcome from her was already well-established. In his days as a layman Père Joseph had been a familiar at the court of Henri IV. Sébastien Zamet, Florentine merchant friend of Henri and Marie, was the long-time lover and later husband of Père Joseph's aunt. After Henri's death Zamet continued to be one of Marie's preferred companions.[46] In addition to this connection, Père Joseph's piety, social facility, and renown as an eloquent preacher were recommendations to the queen.

The queen mother's interest in religious matters was not political, as had been the case with her husband, but personal. She prided herself on her blood relationship with cardinals and popes. She had a high tolerance for long sermons. An exceptionally constant churchgoer and frequent monastery visitor, she apparently considered it a recreation to attend a session of debates on the issue of papal versus conciliar supremacy in the company of her nine-year-old son.[47] Those aspects of religious belief that have a superstitious quality—relics, shrines, sorcery and possession—were of special interest to her, as the ladies around her were well aware. Leonora seemingly shared this interest. Malherbe relates the eagerness with which the princesse de Conti and Madame de Guercheville seized on a letter to him from Peiresc giving an account of the Gaufriddi affair, a lurid precursor of the case of Urbain Grandier. Cardinal Gondi was asked by the queen to read the account to the assembled group of her intimates.[48] Père Joseph had the interests and the abilities to cater to these tastes.[49] Thus, Richelieu's new ally was a further reason for expecting a better reception at court in 1611 than had met him in the preceding year.

Whatever were the crucial factors in his success, contemporaries agree that Richelieu did win the favorable attention of Leonora, and, through her, the less acute appreciation of Marie, as well as the favor of Concini himself.[50] With all of these, the bishop's fluency in Italian was no doubt helpful, as was that of Père Joseph. Perhaps Richelieu's ease in Italian company, possibly based, as we have seen, in his family's history, was supported by a belief that outside nationality could be a sign of independence from seditious French *grands*. Later, in the name of the king, he would denounce the princes for holding Italian birth against the Concinis— "as though this were a crime, and none of them had ever been seen to advance outside of their countries."[51] As a French prelate conversant with

Italian ways Richelieu was in a good position to impress favorably the Italian clerics who were close to the queen, notably her grand almoner, Cardinal de Bonzi, Bishop Gondi of Paris, later Cardinal, and the papal nuncio, Ubaldini, in whose good opinion she seems to have been particularly interested.[52]

Although direct evidence is lacking it is unlikely that Richelieu left Fontainebleau in the spring of 1611 without a commission from the queen to report on Protestant activities in Poitou. At Roches, the priory where he habitually resided, he was midway between Châtellerault, the city originally selected for the projected Protestant assembly, and Saumur, the site finally settled upon.[53] Saumur was a center of Richelieu's territory. His customary eagerness to collect and report information would surely have been expressed in an offer to Marie or her aides. Moreover, the queen was nervous about the upcoming meeting; when the assembly finally adjourned a confidence overheard by Malherbe reveals the unease the proceedings had caused her.[54] Contributing to the queen's fears, no doubt, was her lack of sympathy for "heretics." Possibly she even regarded them with a horror that was politically impermissible to express. Those around her, moreover—especially the Italian prelates—did not understand and had no commitment to the principle of religious toleration. The failure of the Saumur assembly to cause any kind of disruption was regarded by the government, therefore, as a triumph of recent policy. Sully, whose appearance there had been feared by the crown, had been seen to behave in a distraught and bizarre manner, due, as a government observer believed, to the frustration of his political ambitions.[55] The dukes of Bouillon and Rohan, as well as Sully, all suspected by the court of fomenting rebellion, had been expected to be agitators at the Saumur assembly. In the event, however, the meetings adjourned having taken decisions reassuring to the crown. The Protestant *grands* had been held in check by the prudent Du Plessis Mornay—a venerable leader now exempt from being suspected of mutinous ambitions. The following year would see Richelieu reporting to the queen's secretary on his own close contact with Du Plessis.[56]

Richelieu may actually have shared credit for what was regarded as the successful outcome of these meetings for the cause of Catholicism. During the year just past he had devoted some efforts to earning a reputation for religious zeal in Luçon. Finding a thriving congregation of Protestants preparing to construct a new church there near his Cathedral residence, he immediately took exception to the plan, writing early in 1609 to Sully proposing a relocation.[57] To such pressure he added inducements—700 *écus*—for moving the site of the temple, as well as, according to the indignant Protestant pastor, engaging in harassment and provocation:

> He sought opportunities to complain of us; had some [of us] threatened, saying they hadn't bowed to him as his procession

passed. . . . He discharged a good old man from his office as
keeper of his precincts on [religious] grounds . . . and forbade
his seneschal to employ any but Roman Catholics for his civil
officers.[58]

Apparently this strategy of carrot and stick was effective: the Huguenots
accepted the offer of money and agreed to move as desired by the bishop.[59]

Episodes of this kind may have helped Richelieu acquire the renown
with which Méry de Vic, the government mediator of inter-religious conflicts in the region, credited him later, comparing the sorry state in which
the new bishop had found his diocese with the extent to which "thanks
to God, it was improved by your labor, industry and residence."[60] Furthermore, as has been seen, Richelieu had at court several clerical colleagues—Du Perron, Père Coton, L'Aubespine—to recommend him for
religious zeal and skill in combatting heresy. It was later during this same
summer that the crown issued the official papers he needed to establish
his Luçon seminary—another indication that his merits had been recognized by the queen during his visit to Fontainebleau during the spring just
past.[61]

During the autumn and the winter of 1611–1612 fragmentary surviving
correspondence of Richelieu allows a glimpse of his rising ambitions. A
marginal comment in the archives for these months notes the "grandiose
perspectives (*grandes vues*)" of the young prelate who has sent an emissary
to Rome, ostensibly on diocesan matters, to present his letters to Cardinals
Barberini and La Rochefoucauld, as well as the French ambassador. The
correspondent also reports the news that Cardinal de Joyeuse is now dean
of the Sacred College.[62] Of Cardinal Sourdis, his metropolitan in Bordeaux,
he requests appointment as regional representative to a clerical assembly
to take place in Paris in the following year. A letter to Méry de Vic, Keeper
of the Seals, seems to show his eagerness to appear active in claiming
Catholic rights.[63]

Richelieu reappeared in Paris early in 1612.[64] In February he took part in
an important *ad hoc* assembly of leading prelates called by Cardinal Du
Perron, held in his residence, and chaired by him. It had been summoned
to consider an issue of doctrine raised by a faction of the Sorbonne faculty,
and deeply interesting to the court. The object of controversy was a recent
work by Edmond Richer, Syndic of the Sorbonne, declaring the clergy of
France to be exempt from temporal control by the papal see. The book,
entitled *Libellus de ecclesiastica et politica potestate*,[65] was not only a plea for
the Conciliar movement, but also for *episcopal* Gallicanism; Richelieu was
already committed to support of the first, and one may imagine that the
second had for him, as a bishop, potential appeal.[66] Richer, kept informed
by insiders of the progress of this conference, was convinced that Du Perron
was acting under the inspiration of the Curia, mediated by Ultramontanists

in the French court. The papal nuncio's periodic appearances at the sessions, as well as those of Bishop Gondi and Cardinal Bonzi, made it clear to the Gallican Richer that prompting of the conference had come from the pope himself, in collusion with the Jesuit apologist, Bellarmin, object of the syndic's denunciations.[67] Bonzi, Marie's grand almoner, was a relative of Pope Paul V, and did not hesitate to put direct pressure on Richer, by calling him in and asking him, in the name of the queen, to recant.[68]

Apart from Marie de Medici's actual sympathy for papal interests, it is easy to see why Richer aroused her suspicion. The syndic's attack on Jesuit doctrines and Cardinal Bellarmin found no support among her own councillors at the time, except, as Richer tells us, for that prince of doubtful loyalty to her authority, Condé. Outside the court Richer's cause was vigorously seconded by the Parlement de Paris. The prospect of an alliance between Condé and the Gallican Parlement against the regent and her government raised fears of sedition that were strengthened by an apparent disposition of the comte de Soissons to make common cause with Monsieur le Prince on Richer's behalf. Chancellor Sillery accused Condé of having sponsored the publication of Richer's book, a notion, Richer himself believed, that came from Du Perron who took the lead in organizing moves to censure it.[69]

Richelieu's position at this special February meeting could not have been an easy one. Du Perron, one of his earliest and most important patrons, was the ardent sponsor of the anti-Richer campaign. According to the syndic himself, some of the prelates attending there were facetiously equivocal in their response to Du Perron's insistence on condemnation of the book in question and the bishop of Luçon's friend, Bishop L'Aubespine, expressed reservations concerning the total iniquity of the work and devised a ruse to evade Du Perron's pressure to sign the censure motion that emerged.[70]

According to Richer his book was the subject of recrimination in Paris pulpits "during all of Lent" of that year. But the priests whom he mentions as his persecutors were Gondi and the Jesuits, especially Coton. He does not describe any part played by the bishop of Luçon in the secret conclave nor identify him as having played a role in the general denunciation in church. It seems likely, therefore, that Richelieu was careful not to take a public stand on the questions being debated. Certainly, he had an opportunity to do so: this was the first season in which he played a prominent role as a Paris preacher.

On Sunday, March 18, 1612, as Jean Héroard, first physican to the ten-year-old Louis XIII tells us, his young patient attended a sermon of "Monsieur de Richelieu, Evêque de Luçon," at Saint-André des Arts. This explicit identification from the Protestant diarist indicates that Richelieu's reputation was now rather widely known. Louis was in the company of Marie who most likely had heard the bishop of Luçon preach before.[71] A writer later to be employed by Richelieu assures us that it was in this chapel of Saint-André that "the king, with his mother the queen, very often honored him with his presence."[72]

Richelieu was scheduled also to have the distinction of preaching the sermon on Easter Sunday, April 22, in the chapel of the Louvre, but it was announced on that very day that he would be unable to do so and that Père Coton was available to take his place.[73] It is possible that the bishop had left court suddenly or was making preparations to leave, for a Protestant uprising was threatened in his diocese; the duc de Rohan had taken possession of Saint Jean d'Angély, a city between Luçon and La Rochelle.

Richelieu was back in Poitou within a few weeks of Easter. He would necessarily have asked the queen's permission to leave court. Perhaps he represented to her his need to take action on behalf of peace in his own territory. In any case, according to his letter to Phélypeaux, her secretary, she "commanded me, when I left, to let her know what was going on around here."[74]

The queen had threatened, with Catholic zeal, to lead, together with her young son, royal forces into Poitou if Rohan persisted in his secession. Thus, in returning to his diocese, Richelieu may once again have been acting as Marie's protector.

The news he relays to Paris is good. Most of the Huguenots are loyal, he reports, and even "admire the courage of the queen and the resolve she has taken to set out with an army, if need be." He has had several conversations with Du Plessis Mornay, who "always has great credit and authority among the Huguenots," and who disapproves of Rohan's rebellion and plans to try to dissuade him from persisting in it. Du Plessis has talked to the bishop "frankly," and "of many things, contrary to his usual habit." Furthermore Du Plessis is said to believe that Rohan will not depart further from "the obedience and respect owed their majesties."[75] Thus in bringing news designed to please the queen, Richelieu also preempts some of the credit of the loyalist Protestant.

As in his earlier rescue mission, the young prelate's eagerness for the role of the queen's protector leads him to an inappropriate gesture of devotion. In a letter to another loyalist Protestant he expresses a grandiose bravado that is incongruous both with the political situation and his own relation to it:

> The wise conduct, attachment and fidelity of many good servi-
> tors will protect us against evils within [the state]. For those evils
> outside, I shall christen them with another name if they engen-
> der opportunities to expand our boundaries (*accroistre nos limites*)
> and to heap honor upon us at the expense of France's enemies.[76]

These letters mark the beginning of Richelieu's secular political correspondence. There follows in the next months a number of exchanges showing him to be in regular contact with the court on matters related to the unrest in Poitou. On August thirteenth he writes to Méry de Vic, the other crown official besides Phélypeaux sent by Marie to negotiate with dissident Protestants, that the "neighborhood moods" favor peace. He assures him of the loyalist sentiments of such Protestant leaders as Bouillon and Lesdiguières, another message to reassure the queen.[77]

Despite Richelieu's growing attention to political alignments during these months, the activities he reports to his friend L'Aubespine, who is at court, show him still also directed at his earlier goal—winning preeminence through controversy with the Protestants. It is during this period that the bishop of Orléans hears that Richelieu has buried himself in the country with two Englishmen to advance his mastery of theological disputation.[78]

There were good reasons for Richelieu to be absent from court during these months. The news sent him by his friends was such that an ambitious young cleric might well see least jeopardy in devoting himself to the one cause on which all those who were most influential in Marie's circle could agree—combatting Protestant heresy. For the bishop could not but have been aware, by this time, of problems in gaining and keeping the favor of the queen.

4. The Regent Marie

Marie de Medici had a short attention span for most affairs of state. It was generally easy to divert her by raising questions more to her taste, such as those concerning household and personal adornment.[79] We have already seen her complaining of the fatigue caused her by the assembly of Saumur; in many other public matters she showed her limited capacity to concentrate.

The queen's limitations were perceived by her compatriot, the Florentine ambassador Bartolini, who had a close personal relationship with her. After a conversation during which she assured him of her agreement on a proposal he had made, he observed to a correspondent, with undiplomatic frankness, "but she is a woman who remembers things only while one is talking about them to her."[80]

The queen's inconstancy made her decisions unreliable. Thus her official secretary comments, "They put it into the queen's head to create . . . new chevaliers of the Ordre du Saint Esprit." L'Aubespine, writing to Richelieu, describes the turmoil caused by the hastening of hopeful *chevaliers* back to court: "The rush and the uproar were so great that everything was dropped there." The queen abandoned the plan.[81] Robert Arnauld d'Andilly recounts how his uncle told Marie, after a crisis meeting of the council on finances, that "the whole of her authority depended" on making economies to reduce a staggering public deficit. She responded, "Well, what must be done then?" The Draconian plan with which Isaac Arnauld responded met with her instant approval—she "said it had to be done"—but might just as well not have been offered, for her agreement had no consequences. A few days later, when further drastic cutbacks were proposed, she "approved everything extremely," with like lack of effect. When the duc de Nevers followed other princes in leaving the court to pursue mutinous purposes, the queen asked a supporter, "Well then, what must one do?" The courtier offered to try to negotiate, if she wished him to do so. "She said she found that a very good idea." But when he arrived at Nevers's headquarters in Champagne, orders reached him countermanding this approval. Even one close to the queen's inner circle of clerics, Bishop Miron of Angers, complained of "the ease with which the queen was led."[82]

Personal accounts of the time show that Marie's volatility was a key to understanding the political role played by the Ancres. It was Leonora whose company had the power to give the queen pleasure and, through this, the power to vouch for her firmness on any decision. Thus a participant in some important negotiations describes how the nursemaid's daughter stood as guarantor of the queen's word:

> The queen . . . ordered me to . . . assure the duc de Bouillon of
> Their Majesties' attachment to him and to exhort him to peace,
> which she seemed to me to desire with much fervor. . . . [Leo-
> nora] who had an apartment next to the queen . . . repeated
> what the queen had told me and promised me that she would
> be guarantor (*seroit caution*) in regard to the duc de Bouillon for
> all Her Majesty's promises.[83]

The marquise d'Ancre could be persuaded to exert her influence if a project seemed to contribute to strengthening the queen's authority, on which her own family's security and wealth depended. Contesting claims of the *grands* had to be played off against one another, lest any faction bring Marie under its control.

The contemporary view of the Concinis was that they were avid for personal gain in fortune and status; developed stands on political issues were not attributed to them. This is consistent with a modern biographer's judgment on the maréchal: "He might perhaps be a costly parasite for France; never a man to fear."[84] Acting from material interests, not from political ambition, the couple would mediate between the queen mother and others on behalf of projects compatible with these aims. Leonora then would keep Marie confirmed in the resolutions she had been persuaded to take.

Although the queen's commitments to policy were often ephemeral, she could harbor personal likings and resentments for prolonged periods. She had felt, for example, greatly injured by pretensions of mistresses of Henri IV; after his death she persisted in seeking vengeance against them.[85] The maréchale's role as an intermediary was given further importance by the transparency of Marie's emotions and her lack of control over their display.

Everyone was aware of the queen's tendency to reflect her anger by changing color. Robert Arnauld d'Andilly, a witness of some of her frequent rages, even attributed a violent episode of stomachache and diarrhea she suffered to the previous day's fury.[86] In one letter of Richelieu he is at considerable pains to work out the wording of a compliment to Marie in which he wishes her good health, revising with apparent caution his references to the disposition both of her body and of her mind.[87]

As has already been seen, Richelieu had no high opinion of the mental powers of women. The queen lacked that "judgment" which he thought the best distinction of a feminine mind. She was even lacking in the financial sense characteristic of women in his own family. Marie was extravagant, as well as impulsive. In Richelieu's haste to go to her side at the beginning of her widowhood he may have been unaware of these failings. By now, however, he could have formed the idea of supplying that "head" that the queen lacked and in substituting his own self-discipline for her impulsiveness.

If he did have an ambition of this kind, he dissimulated it. In one of the first of his letters to her that survives, written after he had served her for some time, he attributes to her exactly that capacity in which she was most conspicuously deficient. Apologizing for being too ill to join her he continues:

> What consoles me is the knowledge that I have of not only not being necessary, but what is more, not useful; the help which your majesty can draw from her own head in her affairs being more than sufficient, and the best there could be to make them succeed.[88]

It is impossible to know whether this compliment was conscious hypocrisy. It is plausible, however, that such flattery may have made a queen "who remembers things only while one is talking to her" at least momentarily aware of the services she was missing. In fact, also, Richelieu's practice of coping with Marie's inconstancy by withdrawing from the scene and courting her favor by indirection may replicate a technique for winning women in his own family that he had learned at an early age.

In praising to the queen mother the very qualities she lacked, Richelieu's letter is reminiscent of two others, written earlier, to another powerful woman, the comtesse de Soissons. In the first one of those he lauds the count, her husband, as one for whose health "all France has prayed." In the second he tells the recently widowed countess that her arrogant, quarrelsome and unpopular husband had a "merit that assured that he would be useless to no one, esteemed by everyone, and loved by all those capable of loving goodness and virtue in a prince."[89] Blatant flattery, so markedly at variance with the facts, seems to have been reserved for those *grands* over whom Richelieu felt he had gained the upper hand. Sully, for example, received a sycophantic and self-deprecatory letter from Richelieu after Henri IV's prime minister had been released by Marie. At the height of his favor the Protestant duke had been known for his arrogance. Since his withdrawal from court he was said to have become more polite and affable. This was explained, in reports probably known to Richelieu, by Sully's reputed conviction that those now seeking him out no longer did so only on account of his position. This is exactly the argument that Richelieu uses in soliciting a favor from the former minister; in doing so he may be twisting the knife in the wound. He avers that those "whom one can truthfully call great, even more for their inner qualities than for their positions, are happy to have the chance to oblige their inferiors in order to show that, if their power makes them admirable, their benevolence makes them still more so."[90] In this unusual posture of abasement one may suspect Richelieu is guilty of *Schadenfreude*. More than once the bishop uses his most flowery compliments to those who no longer hold power over him.

For Marie, realistic appraisal of power consequences of decisions seems to have been impossible. Personal inclinations determined the views she would take of public affairs. Her own life history may partly account for her "mania for marriages" as instruments of statecraft.[91] Her high status had been acquired by her marriage with the king of France. Now, in widowhood, the arrangement of matches as a means of influencing policy was a favorite project.

Soon after Henri IV's death Marie conceived a desire for marrying her two eldest children in Spain—a project that entailed overturning affiliations with Savoy that had been arranged as part of her husband's long range strategy.[92] Her ardor for this plan is understandable in terms of her family experience: it was through her mother's Habsburg antecedents that the house of Medici had acquired royal pretensions. There were also, of course, important political reasons why a weak regency such as Marie's would seek protection, in outside support, against challenges from within. Yet the queen mother's eagerness for renewing the affiliation with Spain through her children was so great that when she learned that, contrary to her more modest expectations, King Philip might allow Louis to marry the eldest infanta, Anne, rather than the younger one previously destined for him, Marie was observed literally to "jump for joy," declaring to her familiar, the Florentine emissary, that she herself had always been, as it were, "in love" with this princess.[93] Indeed, for Marie, alliance with the Habsburg Spanish monarchy was the pinnacle of achievement. Leonora reflected her mistress's pride when she declined a proposal for Elisabeth to participate in a court dramatic production after her engagement to the future Philip IV had been formalized. "Madame," she explained, "being a princess of Spain, no longer ought to do anything that is not wholly magnificent."[94]

The queen mother herself clearly lacked a consciousness of the historic French enmity towards Spain. She allowed herself to confide indiscreetly in the Spanish ambassador. When the marriage alliance finally was approved by some of the *grands* she rejoiced with that emissary and said, "Don't delay informing the king of Spain, my good brother."[95] On at least one occasion she contemplated seeking help from the king of Spain in repressing French dissidents.[96]

In her intimate circle, as has been seen, the queen mother had a predilection for the company of Italians, especially those (except for the Concinis) with important ecclesiastical connections. In addition to these, her preferred female companions were selected from the house of former Leaguers—the dowager duchesse de Guise, the duchess's young daughter-in-law, and her daughter, married to the prince de Conti. The duc d'Epernon, Henri III's old favorite, now allied with the Guises and closely connected to Jesuit circles in Paris, was rarely far from the queen's side.

Marie's liking for this society was in contrast with policies of Henri IV. As leaders of the Catholic League against Henri III and his successor, the Guises had been a source of subversion and a threat to royal stability. They were still linked to the Spanish monarchy and imperial interests. As with external policies of her late husband, Marie was indifferent to his position on these internal matters. Instead she reveals her self-conception by a comment about an earlier Medici regent, Catherine. That queen, like herself, she notes, was left without any but a duc de Guise to support her during the trials of her regency.[97] The Guises, moreover, together with Epernon, reinforced the queen's attentiveness to Ultramontanist counsel. The cabal set an example for the quarrelsomeness—often murderousness— that was associated with rivalry among the *grands*.

5.   Biding Time

Richelieu's views on court affairs during this time may be inferred: except for the Concinis there were few in the queen's preferred circle whose presence augured well for his advancement in her favor. His perspective may be glimpsed through the letters written to him by the bishop of Orléans, who kept him well informed on court happenings. L'Aubespine takes for granted that his own mistrust of the *grands* who were then competing for favor from Marie is shared by his friend. With a family background of experience in royal service, the bishop of Orléans chronicles the machinations of the Guises. Early in 1613 a feud broke out between these *grands* and a young nobleman who they thought had betrayed their confidence. The chevalier de Guise murdered the young baron de Luc near the Louvre— a proximity insulting to royal authority—on the pretext that the latter had claimed credit for participation in the murder of the former's father thirty-five years before. The bishop of Orléans gives Richelieu a shrewd account of the affair, explaining that the "Guisards" have taken revenge for more recent disservices from Luc. He affirms that "the queen is very annoyed";—

"more so than she has been by anything that has happened since the late king's death." He predicts with evident satisfaction:

> After this there will be some changes around here—and very great ones. *Audere didicerunt et docent*—I say this because you will take it for good French (*du bon françois*).[98]

The political affinity between the two bishops—as *bons français,* in contrast with the Guisard record as Leaguers—reflects shared hopes of future posts at court.[99] The Guises' disfavor could be expected to lead to greater credit for Richelieu and his friend. In this event, however, the queen was no more persistent in her indignation than she had been before. The offenders were soon reconciled with her. A few months later she astonished the Venetian ambassador by her signs of favor towards them: on holiday at Monceaux she had the Guise ladies lunch and dine at her table, departing from the royal custom of solitary repasts.[100]

News of these developments must have confirmed Richelieu in his strategy: by staying away from court, ostensibly to devote himself to word combats with heretics, he could avoid contact with the Guise circle in which he might well find himself *persona non grata*. Members of that clan were descendants of his father's enemies who were apt to use ancient family history as an excuse for outbursts of hostility. Additionally, by not being there, Richelieu could escape taking sides in the still ongoing controversies, in which L'Aubespine was perforce involved, among Sorbonne factions, the court and Parlement, over the doctrine of papal supremacy and the rights of the Jesuits.

L'Aubespine himself loses out by remaining at the scene of these struggles. He has hoped to become Marie's first almoner, but he is disappointed. Cardinal de Bonzi, who is the queen's grand almoner and has himself recently been made a prince of the church, has secured the first almoner's post for Dominique de Bonzi. This nephew—"Big Foot" as the bishop of Orléans nicknames him in his letters to Richelieu—is also coadjutor-bishop of his uncle's diocese of Béziers and, according to the bishop of Orléans, "aspires to higher things still."[101]

In spite of his own poor success, L'Aubespine is aware of the growing favor Richelieu's services are winning from Marie. Big Foot "will put us in the good graces of the queen," the older prelate writes his friend, but adds, "if you have need of it." He has reason to doubt that Richelieu needs this additional advantage, for he has learned that the queen is already considering the bishop of Luçon for an important mission. The Protestants had recently assembled at La Rochelle without royal consent. L'Aubespine reports that Marie is considering sending Richelieu to that city "to harangue those larcenous gentlemen (*messieurs larsins*)"—that is, to reprimand the Huguenots who have usurped Catholic sanctuaries and rights.[102] The bishop of Luçon's reputed skill in controversy had already brought him a high—and non-controversial—reputation.

By the beginnning of 1613 Richelieu's practice of remaining at a distance has won him acceptance as an adjunct to crown policy. Méry de Vic has learned to appreciate his value in the terms Armand himself likes to describe it. The secretary of state writes:

> I cannot sufficiently praise . . . the devotion and care that you demonstrate every day for the Catholic religion . . . since beyond what redounds to the honor of God, the king's service and authority are enhanced by it.

More important than Vic's admiration for Richelieu's religious zeal is the fact that he has learned to make use of him as a trouble-shooter. In the same letter he asks him, "while you are near Poitiers," to stop in that city to settle an ongoing dispute between the bishop there and the dean of his chapter. He leaves no doubt that the matter should be settled in favor of the bishop rather than of the dean "since the cause of the latter is so much worse than that of the the former."[103] The assignment was probably both welcome and easy for Richelieu since the bishop of Poitiers, Chasteignier de La Rochepozay, a militant royalist, was his close personal friend and ally.[104]

6.   Success

The remainder of 1613 has left almost no record of Richelieu's activities. But an important political change took place at court: toward the end of the year Marie marked her continued favor for the Ancres by promoting Concini to the rank of *maréchal*. Barbin, Leonora's friend (and Richelieu's) was appointed *intendant* of the queen's household at New Year, 1614.[105]

The majority of princes and great lords at court found Ancre's growing favor disagreeable. Condé, although at first on good terms with the Florentine, now saw in him a further obstacle to his own preeminence. He withdrew from court in January of 1614. This time his withdrawal coincided with the exodus of Nevers, Longueville, Bouillon and others, including the duc de Vendôme, a favorite half-brother of the young king. The court was virtually emptied of *grands* except for the Guises and their allies. Meanwhile the maréchal d'Ancre, solicitous of his status, repaired to Amiens to protect his newly acquired frontier fief from possible depredations by inimical lords.

Richelieu arrived in Paris early in 1614, perhaps summoned by one or more of his friends at court. It seems to have been at about this time that he acquired an appointment in the private service of the queen. A royal historian, writing during the bishop's exile, pictures him as having entered the inner councils of state soon after Barbin's induction.[106] One letter written by Richelieu apparently confirms the belief that he began acting as one of Marie's secretaries before October 2, 1614. In it he refers to the "assignments" (*charges*) with which the queen has honored him.[107]

Soon after his arrival at court Richelieu reaffirmed, in no uncertain terms, his loyalty to Ancre. "Honoring always those to whom I have once vowed service," he writes, he will continue to reciprocate unconditionally as long as the *maréchal* continues to patronize him. "I beg you only to believe," he tells him, "that my promises will always be followed by good effects, and that as long as you do me the honor of liking me I shall always find a way to serve you worthily."[108] Thus the bishop expresses his solidarity with the Italian *parvenu* against the discontented princes of the realm.

Meanwhile most of the dissident *grands* collected in Mézières whence, on February nineteenth, Condé sent a letter to the queen containing a list of complaints and demands. Its contents quickly became known in Paris. It is probably evidence of Richelieu's close attention to affairs at this time that there are copies in his files of the exchange of letters between Marie and the prince.[109]

While Richelieu had been absent from Poitou, La Rochepozay, the militant royalist bishop of Poitiers, had taken a lead in preventing Condé's supporters from gaining influence in that city's administration by barring entrance to the prince's partisans in a heated confrontation there.[110] Although the bishop of Luçon was not present on this occasion, it is likely that his supporters gave La Rochepozay more than moral support, for the latter, and his vicar, Duvergier de Hauranne, were later to exert themselves so vigorously on behalf of Richelieu's interests as to give the impression of close collaboration and repayment of a debt of gratitude.

This uprising of the princes was short-lived. On May 15, 1614, after a minimum of combat, a peace treaty was signed at Sainte Ménehould.[111] Richelieu, though now back in his diocese, is nevertheless in close touch with the court. He sends news of the truce to his chapter at Luçon. The terms of the treaty were generous towards Condé and the other *grands*. But they also contained an agreement that was to give Richelieu himself his first opportunity to play an important public political role: The queen promised the princes to convoke an assembly of the Estates General of France.[112]

Since early in 1612 there had been discussion of a plan to summon delegates of the three estates of France. At first promoted by Condé as a way to contest Marie de Medici's position as sole regent, it was later also furthered by the government as a means for rallying support. The regency's intention to summon the assembly before declaration of the king's majority was averred in early February, 1614.[113] Thus Richelieu, then at court, was aware of the plan.

The bishop's correspondence shows that he was interested, from the first, in representing the clergy of Poitou at the national gathering. Before conditions of the forthcoming elections were officially announced, Sébastien Bouthillier, who was in Paris, obtained through an informant the news that convocations of electors will only be in "principal *baillages* and *sénéchaussées*," thus, "in Poitou, by the only seneschal who has that status."[114]

Richelieu had a bitter opponent in the region. For reasons not clear he had covertly sponsored legal proceedings against the seneschal of Fontenay, chief town in the region of Luçon. The case was to be heard in the court of the Parlement de Paris. In mid-April the bishop wrote to Madame de Bourges in the capital asking her to intervene on his behalf with Monsieur de Courtin—one of the hearing officers of that court—on a matter "which is of such importance to me that it is impossible for me to describe it to you, judging that I have never had one in which so much of my interest was at stake as in this one."[115] Thus the question seems to involve more than money; it is likely that the interest at stake is Richelieu's chance to represent the clergy of Poitou.[116]

Richelieu succeeded in defeating any move to block his nomination and the seneschal's animus did not prevent the bishop's friends from naming him, in mid-August, 1614, to represent the Poitou clergy in the meetings scheduled for the autumn.[117]

During the summer of 1614 Richelieu seems to have had another opportunity to strengthen his favor with the queen and her advisors by renewed personal contact. While announcements of terms for electing representatives to the forthcoming assembly were being sent out, the queen determined to undertake a trip through the Loire valley to Bretagne in order to rally royal support in the face of continuing challenges from the princes. One purpose of the journey was to encourage popular confidence by putting the health and vigor of the young king on display; another was to contribute to selection of Estates General delegates who would be favorable to the crown. At the time this trip commenced, Richelieu was resident in Poitou.

Héroard chronicles the peregrinations of Louis and his mother and their retinue: setting out on July the fifth they proceeded from Orléans along the Loire to Tours, then by way of Châtellerault to Poitiers, arriving there on the twenty-eighth. After a week in that city, only a few days before delegates to the regional selection council began arriving there, the royal party moved on to Mirebeau, the small town neighboring Richelieu's residence of Coussaye.[118] Although no record is known to confirm it, it seems likely that the bishop of Luçon was one of those who paid court to the queen and the young king as they passed through his home territory. His commitment to the crown's interests was well known by now; his selection as clerical representative for Poitou may have been directly influenced by signs of approval from Marie de Medici on this journey.

Richelieu's nomination a few days later in Poitiers was actively supported by La Rochepozay. This prelate had benefitted from the bishop of Luçon's help in the contest with his dean the year before; now he received Richelieu's sympathy for his struggle with Condé's partisans over the past five months. Correspondence shows the bishop of Poitiers kept his Luçon counterpart informed on efforts to make the latter sole representative of the Poitou clergy at the upcoming meetings. Also active in pressing this candidacy was Duvergier de Hauranne, La Rochepozay's vicar, and Richelieu's own devoted *fidèle*, Sébastien Bouthillier. In the end it was necessary, as La Rochepozay explains, to give Richelieu a coadjutor; otherwise the citizens of Poitiers, accustomed to representation, would have grumbled. A capitulant had to be chosen for this because it was these chapter officers "who alone make the difficulties," complaining that "the bishops take too much for themselves." Even so, the news that Richelieu would be the delegate "served greatly to satisfy them"—a report that suggests that the bishop of Luçon enjoyed a certain popularity with the lower ranks of the local clergy. Moreover, La Rochepozay assures him, the deacon from Saint-Hilaire who has been selected as Richelieu's coadjutor is "as peaceable a man as you could possibly desire."[119] Thus was Richelieu's dominance over his colleague assured.

Poitou's clergy had chosen the queen's candidate as its representative. During that summer the triumphant parade of the royal family had swept all before it: opposition from the *grands* melted away. In Richelieu's case, Deloche is sure, "the favor of the court designated him in advance as the choice of his order."[120]

Even at the time the Estates General Assembly was convening, in October, a letter from an old family acquaintance shows that Richelieu was already in a position to dispense a certain amount of royal patronage. The army officer, Louis de Marillac, asks him to make good on a promise, writing, "I do not doubt that . . . you will protect me and procure for me the honor that you yourself proposed to me in regard to Monsieur Praslin, unless you employ me in some other way."[121] Richelieu probably also had a house in Paris by this time. A letter to Madame de Bourges that may date from the summer of 1614 shows him arranging, from out of town, to have repairs made to his own dwelling in the capital.[122] Such a purchase would confirm his commitment to residence there.

Soon after his election to the Estates, in August, Richelieu arrived in Poitiers to participate in determining the articles to be presented by the Poitevin clergy to the assembly of the First Estate. He did his homework with his usual diligence: his copy of the final document is annotated in his own hand. Most of the items decided upon by the group are concerned with the protection of the rights, privileges, and possessions of the Catholic church of France against Protestant incursions and usurpations, undue royal influence, and intervention by temporal lords. Richelieu's marginal notes emphasize, as has been seen, the need for residence of bishops in their cures and for resistance to the importunities of the nobility in demanding church patronage for their clients.[123]

Like any special interest group, the clergy of Poitou were interested in preserving and enhancing their rights and privileges. But the man they had selected to represent them at Sens, where the assembly was scheduled to convene, was preparing to be a star, rather than merely a spokesman for his provincial order.

As the date for convening the Assembly approached, Richelieu's favorable publicity preceded him. A royalist pamphlet singled him out as "very distinguished in doctrine and virtuous in *moeurs*," and thus a stellar representative of the reforms through which Henri IV had aimed to elevate the learning and morals of the Catholic clergy. Richelieu himself may have had a hand in composing this work, attributed to an anonymous author who calls himself a "poitevin." It is dedicated to the bishop of Poitiers, the friend who organized Richelieu's election as delegate, and includes paeans of praise to "Blanche de Médicis"—that is, to the queen, who is thus compared with the revered mother of Saint Louis.[124]

The representative of the clergy from Poitou, it is true, owed his nomination to the queen. Yet he could already have been aware that his scope for action was limited by the need to adapt to Marie's desires. In this same year of 1614 his words give a clue to his deeper feelings. The queen has, he writes, "through her prudence, kept vigil in order to assure our repose; all we desire is the continuation of this benefit."[125] The image is consistent with his earlier view of Marie as the good mother, fending off dangers besetting the fatherless family. Now, however, when he is about to assume a place at her side, it is not certain that Richelieu, the man of action, feels the need for "repose" to continue much longer. The queen, furthermore, had just consented to a treaty making concessions to the *grands* so extensive as to make it seem that her desire was for peace at any price.

In weeks to come the bishop of Luçon would give a performance that would show him to be confined neither by the role of clerical representative nor of queen's protector.

11 A King's Man: Overture

> I have never done anything that I did not believe with certainty, in my conscience, to be advantageous to the king, and I may say before God that I have always had a very great passion to please him; I mean not only him as king, but as Louis XIII.[1]

On October 2, 1614, just after his thirteenth birthday, Louis XIII delivered a short speech to Parlement. "Loudly, firmly, and without stuttering," he declared himself to be, legally, an adult in whose hand God had placed sovereign power and royal authority. Then, turning to his mother, he thanked her for having taken such good care of his interests in the past and asked her to carry on as before, serving as chief of his council in his absence. He told her, "I wish and intend that you be obeyed in everything and everywhere."[2]

It was the hope of the queen's government that the assembly of the Estates General, to convene three weeks after Louis's declaration, would strengthen the crown and increase the likelihood that royal authority would be obeyed. In particular the queen sought from the upcoming meetings endorsement of her policy of the last few years and confirmation that the power she had had as regent would continue until that unspecified time when the king would be, in practice as well as name, capable of conducting the government.

1. The Setting

Ultimately, the 1614–1615 Estates General Assembly was without political effect. The delegates were unable to induce the government to implement those few reforms on which all three orders were able to agree—reduction of crown expenditures and of venality in office, increase of representation in overseeing financial administration. This very lack of consequence, however, was a success for the crown. It was able to ward off demands that would have been costly or threatening to its authority. At the same time it was able to secure endorsement of the only programs for which *Etats* support was sought—continuation of Marie's government and effectuation of the Spanish marriages. For Richelieu, however, the sessions of the Estates General were consequential indeed. For the first time his political skills were demonstrated in a national context.

Insofar as the regent's government had followed a consistent policy in the four years since Henri IV's death, it had sought to pacify potential opponents by temporizing and propitiating. Outside France's borders, former allies were put off with reassuring words. Those who had previously been supposed to be likely enemies were promised hostages and territorial benefits. Thus the queen, reversing the policy of Henri IV, had actively pursued marriage alliances with Spain, both for her son Louis and her eldest daughter. The treaty arranging these marriages had been signed in 1612 and Marie now sought approval from the Estates of the realm for honoring it. Within France, in exchange for loyalty to the crown, the Protestants were promised protection, the *grands* wealth, honors and influence, the office-holding class security in office, and the rest—the "little people (*menu peuple*)"—a domestic tranquility that would allow for improvement of their lot.

The regency's strategy had been costly: since the departure of Sully, controls over disbursements had weakened and expenditures of many kinds had greatly increased. Now, delegates from throughout the realm were to meet to expose their discontent with these policies and to petition for a redress of their grievances.

Long before the meetings began the court had intervened to influence selection of the deputies in order to insure that results favorable to the regime would emerge from the assembly. The government's confidence that it had succeeded in this was demonstrated when it granted permission to transfer the upcoming sessions from Sens, where they had been scheduled, to Paris, and gave consent to a request to allow all three orders to meet under the same roof—that of the Augustinian convent near the Louvre.

Despite the loyalty that was expected of most delegates from each order, there was yet a possibility of significant opposition to certain government policies and personnel. This possibility was particularly high among delegates of the Second and Third Estates. The nobility were strongly opposed to the increasing influence and pretensions of the merchant and magisterial classes, from which they were excluded by legal, financial or customary barriers, and they were seriously adversely affected by the secular rise in price levels. Thus they asked abolition of the *paulette*—the annual tax payment by which families of magistrates were able to monopolize and inherit their offices. Many Third Estate delegates had serious grievances against the government on account of the high pensions being paid to buy off the *grands*—pensions financed mainly by revenue from taxes from which the nobility were exempt. In both bodies there was apprehension about what was seen as increasing papal and other foreign influence on the new regime. This was especially strong among the Huguenots, who had representatives in both chambers.

In the wings, as a menace to the crown, stood the prince de Condé. He had arrived in time for the declaration of the king's majority. Now he held the potential for uniting opposition against the government. While he openly flattered and courted the bourgeois of the Third Estate, his position also made him capable once again of organizing the *grands* and a "whole band of gentlemen who were young, ardent, and not inscribed on the pension roll,"[3] with the aim of overturning the government and installing himself in place of the king's mother, her chief councillors, and possibly even of the king himself.

Thus, from the monarchy's point of view, the clerical order was truly first, in more than name, of the Estates.[4] From ecclesiastics Marie had little to fear. There was not, as there was in the other two delegations, any possibility of the detested Huguenots exercising influence. The dominant view of the clerical deputies at the assembly was sympathetic to the queen's own respect for papal authority and Jesuit rights in France.

Henri de Loménie, a young secretary of the queen, was one of those sent by the court to help insure that presiding officers favorable to the regime were selected in each delegation's chamber. He encountered problems in the Second and Third Estates, but there was none in the First. There the cardinals were appointed *présidents* more or less *ex officio*, together with Denis de Marquemont, Archbishop of Lyons and Primate of France.[5] All believed themselves to be strongly favorable to the queen's interests. Cardinals Joyeuse, Du Perron, Sourdis and La Rochefoucauld were closely allied with her intimate circle—the Guises, the duc d'Epernon, the nuncio Ubaldini and Cardinal Bonzi. The cardinal-delegates saw the Estates General as a means of strengthening the alliance between the church of Rome and the French state. Their behavior through the sessions showed a license with the crown and with the other orders that reflected their sense of superiority and consciousness of power. Du Perron, for example, would take it upon himself to threaten opponents of the clergy's position among the other companies with fire and brimstone, "excommunications and anathematizations." The bishop of Angers, Charles Miron, who was Du Perron's prospective successor as Archbishop of Sens, would speak "extremely boldly" to the queen. On another occasion a deputation consisting of La Rochefoucauld, Sourdis, Du Perron, Bonzi, and Miron spoke with "frightening insolence" to the king.[6] The princes of the church were confident of their right to dominate the proceedings at the Grands Augustins.

At the sessions rules were adopted which gave the clerical chamber the task of mediating among the three orders. Thus they largely controlled conditions under which deliberations took place and the form in which they emerged. In the plenary sessions at the beginning and end of the assembly, clerical speakers had precedence.[7] In between they set the rules of discussion and themselves acted as agents of communication between chambers. Thus Condé's opportunity to take advantage of discontent between the Third Estate and the nobility was minimized. From the first joint session he found himself outmaneuvered by the court and clergy together. Although he arrived with a speech in his pocket, ready to attack the queen's government,[8] he found no opportunity to deliver it. He was forced to bide his time.

2. The Diplomat

So favorable had been reports of Armand de Richelieu's ability, and perhaps of his royal favor, that he was almost chosen by his order to deliver its opening address at the initial convocation of the Estates. Instead, Denis de Marquemont, as Primate of France a less surprising choice than the young bishop, was selected for the task by six votes to five.[9]

After the first plenary session, held in the presence of the king, the queen, and many *grands* and dignitaries, the delegates of the three orders withdrew to meet regularly in their respective chambers. Any hope of effectiveness depended upon concerted action. It was, as has been seen, the clergy that drew up rules and procedures that would make this possible. Richelieu was selected to head a delegation to the Third Estate to present the scheme that had been decided upon. The mission was innocuous, but it was one that gave the bishop an opportunity to present himself to this most royalist body of the assembly in a role that could bring him nothing but credit.

Richelieu advised the delegates of the Third Estate that the clergy had taken an oath "to conduct themselves in all their actions" in such a way as to contribute to "the honor of God, the rule of the king, and the welfare of his state, and not to reveal anything of the proposals they might make nor of discussions they might conduct that could do harm to the whole, or to any particular member."[10] The chamber of the Third Estate was primarily composed of high judicial and financial officers of the crown, garnished by a few barristers and merchants.[11] Richelieu's appearance gave him a chance to be gracious to them: they suggested exceptions to the schedule that would better fit their needs and habits; he assured them that they would be accommodated.[12] This was but the first of several deputations Richelieu would conduct at the sessions. In each, though he represented the clergy, his mission had a secular aim.

A few days after Richelieu's first visit to the Third's chamber, the king's council of state affirmed by an *arrêt* that the Sénéchaussée of Poitiers, rather than that of Fontenay, was the legitimate electoral agent for Poitevin representation at the Estates. The rival groups that had come from Fontenay and Niort were to return home. It was the bishop of Luçon who took it upon himself to ask for and obtain the official publication of this decision. His initiative in this matter, thinks Deloche, shows a conspicuous respect for formality in procedure—a "scrupulous concern for observing the regular forms of public life."[13] However this may be, it certainly served Richelieu's own interests: those who challenged his authority were routed and he himself displayed his competence in manipulating the secular bureaucratic structure.

The central contest of class interests that developed at the sessions was one between the Second and the Third Estates. The nobles, excluded from the magistrature and the state administration by the rising cost of high office, asked the king to suppress the *paulette* that effectively made government posts hereditary property over which the newly affluent bourgeoisie had monopolistic rights. To this an eloquent representative of the Third Estate, the Auvergnat official, Jean Savaron, responded on behalf of his order. In a speech to the king he attacked the multiplication of crown pensions and gifts to the nobility. He depicted the misery of the "poor people," obliged to suffer the runaway costs of a nobility whose loyalty had to be bought with money. He suggested that if aristocrats were excluded from high office it was not because of the cost of such positions but because of a dearth of capable men in the ranks of the Second Estate.

We may imagine that Richelieu, to whom these remarks were certainly reported, may have given them at least some silent concurrence. When the *sieurs* of the chamber that housed the nobility learned of them, however, their indignation was fierce. This reaction could not be ignored, for, in unwitting support of the truth of Savaron's charge, the *noblesse d'épée* was much more likely to seek redress by arms than by reason.

The clergy, as the self-appointed agent of peace, stepped into the fray. It was the bishop of Luçon who was selected to remonstrate with "those of the Third" in the interests of Christian conciliation.

Richelieu's mission was a personal success even if it did little to heal the mutual dislike of the two orders. The matter pertained to questions of personal and group privilege that had been the business of his first visit to the same chamber. Now he transmitted the complaint of the nobility but disclaimed any recrimination on his own part or that of his order. In terms that conveyed both his benevolence towards them and his own indispensability as a mediator he virtually forgave Savaron in advance:

> Monsieur de Luçon said that he knew very well that no word
> could be uttered by him [Savaron] that was not worthy and well

said, either orally or in writing, but that sometimes there escapes
from our mouths, without intent to offend, certain things that
nevertheless do have the effect of striking an offensive note; that
in such cases all that was needed was a little amends (*satisfaction*)
to those persons, or a declaration that one had no intention to
offend them.

The report of this witness, an Orléanais official, also conveys the impression
that Richelieu gave his audience a sense that they were indebted to him
for this generous indulgence:

As for them [the clergy] that it seemed that they too might have
a slight cause for taking offence, in that we [the Third] had gone
to the king alone—that that was not done—and one might get
the idea from that that there was some disrespect, but, as for
them, they would make nothing of it and would ask no amends,
and believe themselves obliged to forget all kinds of offences.
Furthermore, they will never take amiss (*en mauvaise part*) anything that might come from this Company.[14]

With these reassuring demurrers Richelieu now invited an explanation
from the "very mouth of the sieur Savaron . . . that what had been said
was . . . without intention to offend anyone."[15] Whereupon Savaron took
the floor and, assuring the bishop that he was innocent of any such intention, gave an "explanation" of his remarks that amounted to a recapi-
tulation of his original charges:

He had criticized the unmerited usage of pensions, not people
who were qualified for them; that the habit of paying them out
as debts of the state meant that instead of feeling gratitude for
them, as would be done if they were paid according to merit,
there is merely competition for favor . . . that loyalty . . . ought
not to be bought with money.

To the nobility's complaint, as relayed by Richelieu, that Savaron had cited
Charlemagne as an example of a ruler who rewarded those of high rank
only as long as they were capable, otherwise seeking meritorious recruits
farther down the social ladder, Savaron "explained" that not everyone
inherited the virtues and generosity of his ancestors, and that he was
criticizing merely the "ordinary corruptions" of those possessing commissions, and not "what had to do with the honor and preference of the noble
order."[16]

This argument for the merit system and the removal of preference for
"incapable" sons of the nobility was one to which Richelieu, as a leader
of Catholic Reform, was committed for posts within his own order. In
Luçon he had, as we have seen, attempted to practice what Savaron now
preached. In the margins of the *cahier* of the Poitevin clergy he had personally emphasized, as we also noted, the points Savaron was presently

making concerning secular recruitment to office.[17] The bishop now responded to the speaker in gracious terms:

> After having thanked the company for having permitted, in his presence, that the sieur Savaron describe the affair as it had taken place, and that they had allowed him to share in the secret of the matter [Savaron's audience with the king and queen, like the deliberations of his order *in camera*, had been confidential], [he] invited the said Third Estate to send to the chamber of the nobility either the said sieur Savaron or another . . . to make a like declaration; that that would satisfy the *sieurs* of said order and would absolve said company of the calumny that might be cast at them of causing strife and dissension in the holding of the Estates.

Since Savaron seems merely to have repeated the remarks that had originally inspired the nobility's ire, it is difficult to see how the new version could appease it. Yet Richelieu assured them that "giving this satisfaction and contentment to the nobility, everything would come out better (*tout s'en porteroit mieux*)."[18]

Richelieu's soothing appreciation was well received by the presiding officer of the Third, who thanked him for "this opinion," which "indeed demonstrated a great benevolence on the part of the *sieur Evesque*."[19] Richelieu in due course reported to the nobility that the Third Estate was ready to give them "satisfaction" for the offending remarks.[20]

After the bishop withdrew from their chamber, the Third Estate deliberated on their next move. Members were divided between two courses of action: to take Richelieu's advice and send representatives to the nobility—a course they quite reasonably feared might be "perilous"—or to ask the clergy to send the good bishop himself to represent them to the nobles.

Richelieu would have been in an awkward position had he been asked to make the case for the Third to the belligerent chamber of nobles. He managed to escape being asked. Eventually one of the deputies of the Third went to the chamber of the nobility and, in arguing for mutual confidence among all three orders, suggested that the Third Estate, as the "youngest" order, might, as commonly happened in the case of the youngest child of a family, restore the integrity of a household that had been ruined by the older children![21] Such an "explanation," too, might have been satisfying to Richelieu, who, as the youngest son in his own family, was trying to restore family fortunes. It only served further to enrage the Second.

If Richelieu really believed that Savaron's first demurrers, much less this latest one, would satisfy the injured noblemen, he was, of course, disappointed. Word soon got back to the third chamber that the Second Estate had let out that "no satisfaction was necessary except to put the said sieur Savaron in the hands of pages and lackeys" who would, presumably, give him the thrashing he deserved. What a contrast in this insulting response with the *bienveillance* of the noble bishop of Luçon! The *robins* and their fellow delegates in the third chamber were "so offended" by this message that they decided to send no one to the nobles. Instead they determined to send deputies to the clergy to thank them for their good will in trying to pacify the other two orders, and to ask those who had paid them this honor to pass judgment on the matter themselves, "according to what Monsieur de Luçon had heard."[22]

The nobles complained to the king that the Third Estate's reference to "the youngest sons of a house often restoring houses destroyed by the oldest," was "an insult." The king put an end to the matter, replying that he "knew quite well what esteem he ought to give and did give to the nobility," and that it did not depend on the opinion of the Third Estate. He agreed with the Third, however, in expressing his intention "that this matter be composed by the intervention of the clerical order."[23] Despite the king's command the sessions did not end without one officer of the Third Estate being attacked and beaten by a bellicose noble,[24] a form of satisfaction with which Richelieu was familiar through his own family history.

In reconstructing the bishop of Luçon's appearance before Savaron's chamber, Hanotaux imagines him as "cold and elegant."[25] But the *procès-verbal* of Clapisson, recording secretary of that body, shows him rather as the beguiling figure who was later described as "so charming" that he "stole everybody's heart through the ears."[26] A member of the Third Estate records, for example, that their chamber sent a delegate to the clergy "following their advice brought by Monsieur l'Evesque de Lusson, who had, as it were, drawn us there by his eloquence."[27] Manifestly, the Third Estate derived little tangible gain from the bishop of Luçon's intervention; nevertheless his manner with them was so ingratiating and confident that the personal contact was followed by their trust and satisfaction.[28] Years later one who had first-hand experience of Richelieu's personal tactics observed that "his aspect was so charming that of all who have approached him, none has ever left him without being well satisfied, even when they had not obtained . . . what they had hoped for."[29] The delegates of the Third Estate certainly did not obtain what they hoped for. Yet Richelieu's effect on them seems to have been powerful—the first instance to be reported by witnesses of his power to turn face-to-face encounters to his advantage in this way.

Richelieu's success at the sessions of the Estates is marked as much by the quarrels he managed to avoid as by the tasks he undertook. In his first important assignment there he calmed the Third Estate and ingratiated himself with its members without having to make good on his assurances by bearding the hostile Second order on behalf of their "younger brothers."

Thus he risked neither rejection nor ill-will. This skill in avoiding controversies that might be problematical for his career is demonstrated in a more complicated strategic problem raised by the second great issue to agitate the assembly—papal powers over the king of France.

The disagreements between Gallicans and Ultramontanists in France were prolonged over centuries; in the assembly that met in the winter of 1614-1615 the argument came to focus on an article proposed for adoption in the chamber of the Third Estate. This declaration—the Third's "first article"—proclaimed that it was a fundamental law of the kingdom that no earthly power whatever was superior to the king of France, nor could any consideration release a French subject from obedience to his monarch. It condemned regicide under any and all circumstances and banned all works that justified it in any manner.

The French clergy's position on the general issue of political Gallicanism was that a legitimate king was independent of the pope's temporal authority; only in matters of religion did Rome hold sway over monarchs. Yet the papal power to excommunicate heretics or apostates was a religious power. And what was the obligation of a citizen whose ruler, anathematized by the church, sought to force his subjects to depart from grace?

The question was an awkward one. Du Perron and other leading French theologians usually tried to evade it. Their practice was to condemn such justifications of regicide as Juan de Mariana's, and to emphasize a *positive* duty of the church to protect the lives and temporal rights of legitimate kings—even heretic kings. They tried to avoid the problem of apostate monarchs who persecuted Catholics. Nevertheless, in their view the pope's power to excommunicate a ruler was a sanction required for the continued influence of Catholicism itself. Not to acknowledge this power seemed to them to invite a French schism like that of England. Therefore the leaders of the First Estate could not accept the Third's declaration. Yet it was difficult to argue against it without seeming to degrade royal authority and somehow, thus, to justify regicide.

This difficulty exacerbated a tendency on the part of some leading clerics to indulge in suspicious recrimination of fellow subjects who were seen as dupes of subversive foreigners. James I of England was accused of promoting schism to undermine the forces of Catholicism in Europe. Cardinal Sourdis, for example, maintained that *"pensionnaires"* of the English were the instigators of the Third's article.[30] Such suspicions were given substance by the fact that the English ambassador was frequently seen at social gatherings sponsored by the prince de Condé. This prince, in turn, was suspected of having helped the members of the Third to draft the controversial declaration.

The article was introduced in the chamber of the Third Estate towards the end of the year 1614. The leaders of the first chamber tried to persuade the third to suppress it. The controversy that followed in some ways reenacted the Richer affair of 1611-1612. As clerical emissaries from the court had then sponsored censure of the syndic's Gallican work, *On Ecclesiastical and Political Power*,[31] so several of the same figures, now members of the First Estate's body, tried to suppress debate of this new Gallican resolution. The militant clergy were particularly incensed by the thought of papal authority being questioned in state assemblies that comprised Huguenot members. The First Estate's official position was that the substance of the Third Estate's first article concerned religious matters only and should not even be discussed by any but clerics.

In the Richer affair Richelieu had been present at the meeting of prelates assembled by Du Perron to condemn the offending book but, as far as the record shows, he had been inactive there. He had also been a non-combatant, so far as is known, in the attack on Richer from Paris pulpits in the spring of 1612. In the campaign now launched, with support of the court Ultramontanists, against the first article of the Third Estate, the royalist bishop of Luçon seems once again conspicuous by his silence.

The clerical assembly decided upon a deputation to the Third's chamber to admonish them to cease deliberations on the proposed article. A bishop other than Richelieu was sent to speak in "silken words" to the company of officials.[32] He was unpersuasive; the Third refused to bow to the First Estate's admonitions. Du Perron, although ill, was summoned. After addressing the nobility, who received him cordially, he delivered a long harangue to the Third with no more success than his predecessor. Most likely Richelieu would have been no luckier than this most famous orator of France. It was fortunate for him that he was able to avoid the thankless task. The fact that he could do so suggests that he had both the wish and the strategic skill to escape being appointed to propound the Ultramontanist view advocated by the majority of his order's delegates, and by the court.

Even less congenial to Richelieu's inclinations, one may imagine, was the task the most militant clerics—Du Perron, Sourdis, and Bishop Miron—took upon themselves to bring pressure on the king and his mother in the interests of the clerical position. The royal council first advised Louis to reserve to himself the right to make decisions on articles such as this first one that pertained to the crown's rights, thus denying the Third Estate jurisdiction in the matter and removing it from their agenda. But this was not enough for the militants. They wanted the king to renounce his own claim to a right to rule upon the question the Third Estate had raised. Supported by the Ultramontanists close to the queen they made themselves an embarrassment both to Louis and his mother by an insistence that many considered insolent. By some means Richelieu avoided being associated with these delegations championing ecclesiastical rights over the rulers of France.

The embarrassment of the crown was further increased when the Parlement de Paris, as many supposed through Condé's machinations, took up the cause of the Third Estate with a new *arrêt* condemning works of Suarez and Bellarmin that justified papal authority over temporal rulers. The King in Council, under the same Ultramontanist pressure as before, prohibited publication of the declaration. The First Estate chamber supported this prohibition, holding, further, that the sacred nature of the king's person and the authority of the pope were exclusively religious questions. It passed a resolution to this effect, to be presented to the king for his public agreement.

This time Richelieu was recruited to support the dominant position of the clerical order. But he was selected not to solicit acquiescence in it from the Third Estate, where opposition would have been fierce, but from the chamber of the *noblesse* where both Condé and Parlement were regarded unsympathetically.

Even among these noble delegates, however, there was a significant group that had seen no obstacle to affirming the sovereign independence of the king in temporal matters, as the first article of the Third Estate had done. A distinguished *parlementaire* maintains of the nobility on that issue that the "sanest and largest part of that order" did not want to join with the clergy in removing the article from the *cahier* of the Third.[33] In Richelieu's appeal to the nobility he seems to have avoided all discussion of the merits of the parliamentary *arrêt*. Nothing that is reported of his address to them suggests that he is sympathetic to the Ultramontanist position. Indeed, he refers to an earlier harangue of them by Du Perron as "the beautiful and learned reasons you have heard from the mouth of the greatest figure of Christianity,"[34]—a designation that might be considered implicitly Gallican because of rival Italian claims—at the same time making no pronouncement whatever on the merits of those reasons in the case before them. Instead, his argument rested entirely on the privilege the clergy claimed to be arbiter on all religious matters—a legalistic point—and the advantage the Second Estate could expect to reap from respecting this claim of the First. With the business-like strategy of a modern parliamentary log-roller he mentioned the "mutual help that the noblest parts render each other," and promised that if the nobility supported their distinguished counterparts in the clerical chamber, "when you judge certain requests . . . particularly [advantageous] to your order . . . [the clergy] will never make less of a case for your interests than they do for their own." Richelieu's appeal carried the chamber by six to five, the secretary reports, but there was "a great contestation" from delegates of Provence who tried to call attention to the substantive import of the matter. They pointed out that "it was a question of nullifying *arrêts* that had condemned those who had made attempts on the sacred person of our kings."[35] Their protests did not prevail against a presentation by the bishop that referred only to jurisdictional issues. No wonder that some noble members complained of the "glib tongues (*langues disertes*)" and "subtle persuasions" by which their company was inveigled into supporting the clergy's pretensions.[36]

Richelieu's personal views of the merits of Du Perron's position on papal limitations to the temporal powers were not made public here nor anywhere else. Nevertheless a curious confirmation of his private dissent from Du Perron's position has survived. In his files are papers, apparently collected at the time, that contain a digest of some of the arguments Du Perron made to the Third Estate to persuade its members to renounce their doctrine that the king was independent of the papacy. Three notes in Richelieu's hand can still be clearly identified. In each one the young bishop's comments on his mentor's words are counter to Du Perron's argument for the subordination of rulers to earthly agents of divine power.

In the transcription in question Du Perron is recorded as beginning with the observation that "this opinion that it is just to depose kings when, being obstinate heretics, they persecute Christians and impede practice of the true religion . . . has been held by most doctors of the church, by all the theologians and jurisconsults of France." After several historical examples of his point, the cardinal proceeds to scriptural justifications for the right to depose kings. He states these as affirmations. But in some cases the arguments cited by Du Perron are countered by Richelieu. Thus when the cardinal related, "Samuel deposed Saul; he was declared deposed because he had violated the laws of the Judaic religion," the bishop demurs in the margin:

> Samuel was a prophet who might have had (*pouvoit avoir*) a revelation to [do this][37] depose Saul, just as he had it to subrogate David in his place.

Again, from Du Perron:

> The prophet Ahra deposed Roboan from the royal right he had over the ten tribes of the people of Israel because his father Solomon had apostasized.

To this Richelieu responds marginally with a reservation:

> The prophet Ahra was sent expressly by God to make this change.

And where, on the reverse side of the page, Du Perron cites the case of Mathathras who, "seeing that Antiochus who reigned in Judaea wanted to force the Jews in their law, took arms and delivered the people from his yoke," Richelieu dissents. "Antiochus," he argues, "was not a legitimate prince but a tyrant . . . by force."

Finally, when Du Perron responds to the argument that Saint Paul commanded the Christians to obey pagan emperors with the qualification that this was required only until they had sufficient numbers to be able to install Christian princes, Richelieu, in a tiny interlinear note, qualifies with the words: "without . . . causing a shipwreck of state."[38]

Thus the young bishop reveals his view, in private, that only superhuman authority is sufficient to justify overturning a legitimate ruler. No power on earth, we may conclude from his interpolations, is entitled to dispense subjects from their duty to obey their ruler. Revolution can *never* be justified for mere humans. He was, in fact, in secret agreement with the substance of the first article of the Third Estate, seconded by Parlement. He supported the principle in Richer's position and opposed the Ultramontanist argument.

"Men of the robe in France have never loved Rome," Hanotaux remarks,[39] and the Third Estate delegation, composed overwhelmingly of *robins*, was ardently Gallican. On this point of papal authority as against the absolute requirement to obey kings, Richelieu too, descended as he was from illustrious men of the robe, and closely allied with them, took the side of the Third and of the court of Parlement. He was willing, in a speech to the *noblesse*, to ask agreement to a prohibition of lay discussion of religious matters, but his private comments show that his opinion on their substance was different from the one that Marie and her ecclesiastical supporters thought correct. "Good Frenchmen (*les bons françois*)," averred Monsieur de Thou in 1616, "who know what they owe to religion and to the Republic, have always believed that this matter concerned the state more than it did religion."[40] Once in power Richelieu's actions would exemplify his agreement; secretly he seems always to have shared this view.

On another article advanced by the clergy, too, the bishop of Luçon was able to avoid being labeled as a militant. This was the proposal to adopt the decrees of the Council of Trent in France. Insistence that the king sponsor Tridentine reforms aroused opposition both from ardent royalists, who thought this would limit the powers of the crown, and from Protestants, with whom the decrees pronounced binding agreements impossible. Thus the Third Estate opposed the proposal overwhelmingly, and among the Huguenot nobility it aroused opposition and resentment. Richelieu was also fortunate in being able to avoid being chosen to champion this article in the clerical deputations sent for that purpose to the chambers of the other two orders.

The equivocality of Richelieu's position may have been discerned by Ubaldini, the papal nuncio, who watched the proceedings carefully. In a dispatch to the Holy See, Richelieu, together with his friend L'Aubespine, as well as their colleague Marquemont, Bishop of Lyons, were rated in the second rank of merit, below the most aggressive champions of papal authority—Joyeuse, Sourdis, Du Perron, La Rochefoucauld, Bonzi, and Miron.[41] Richelieu was not the only cleric in the first chamber to oppose Ultramontanist views. Within the order, even so prestigeful a figure as Du Perron was challenged by a monastic delegate for wishing to treat an issue by authority rather than reason. The leading Ultramontanist princes of the church assured themselves of an uneasy welcome at court by their arrogant militancy in the presence of the king and queen. Robert Arnauld, an out-raged witness of their behavior, probably reflected the indignation of the upright Catholic *robins* in Parlement and in the Third Estate's delegation at the temerity of the advocates of the extreme clerical stand. He impugned the motives of the cardinals and their supporters: none was a disinterested advocate of the papal position on monarchy, he claimed, since each might become a pope or a pope-maker. When some clerics sought to exempt themselves from the jurisdiction of the parliamentary court in personal matters, he felt solidarity with his juridically trained fellows in the Parle-ment de Paris. Their outrage was so great that the attempt to win such a privilege had to be disowned in the chamber of the First Estate.[42]

Richelieu's abstention from these activities was an advantage to him. Nor did his dissenting private opinion harm the esteem in which he was held by his clerical colleagues. When it came time for each order to choose a delegate to represent it in the final plenary session, the Second and Third Estates chose their respective presiding officers. In the case of the First Estate, however, this would have been Cardinal de Sourdis. Of all the princes of the church he was the one who had spoken with the most freedom before the king and his mother—so much so that the "queen showed herself piqued at so many insolences." According to one report, Louis himself rebuked him. Sourdis was, of course, anathema to Condé and all who supported him; with the arrogance befitting a prince of the blood, this *grand* Condé later told Marie and the king that he had been on the verge of threatening to "run his sword through" the cardinal.[43] Riche-lieu, on the other hand, though inferior to Sourdis in the ecclesiastical hierarchy, was benignly regarded by the queen. Furthermore, thanks to his careful performance, the *noblesse* had no reason to bear him ill will. The respect given his oratorical skills by his clerical colleagues had been dem-onstrated. He was thus an ideal compromise candidate for spokesman of the First Estate.

On January 23, 1615, the secretary of the order reports, the company of clergymen chose, "by common consent," the bishop of Luçon to take charge of preparing that body's address to the king at the final session of the estates.[44] It has been said that the queen took a hand in selecting Richelieu for this role,[45] although it seems as plausible that her direct intervention was not necessary under the circumstances.

3. The Innovator

The secretary of the First Estate tells us that Richelieu at first modestly tried to beg off, but "pressed by the company said that he would render it obedience."[46] Exactly a month later, on the morning of the day on which he was to present his harangue, the bishop made a move that has seemed puzzling to some. He requested the company to tell him what were the "principal points" they wished him most to stress. Since his speech must already have been written and memorized, Deloche finds the request "bizarre."[47] Nevertheless, an outline was produced, its contents adopted by resolution, signed, and turned over to the bishop of Luçon. It seems clear that any such outline must have been drawn up by Richelieu himself, along with his request for last-minute instructions from the clerical body. The circuitous tactic, it seems, was "for the record." The probable reason for it is that the bishop's harangue deviated considerably, in substance and emphasis, from the long list of points in the *cahier* already approved by the First Estate chamber to summarize its views. In presenting a summary of the address he had prepared, Richelieu arranged authorization for the personal position he was about to present. The agenda adopted on this day at his suggestion is a short list of the chief points in his speech. Both this list and the harangue itself differed, in topics, priorities, aims, and justifications, from the list in the *cahier* of the clergy which Richelieu's speech was allegedly designed to introduce.[48]

Richelieu's harangue for the First Estate was the first address at the final plenary session; hence it could adumbrate all the complaints of the three orders. It did, indeed, largely preempt the *noblesse's* chief points and anticipate the Third Estate's more considered criticisms of government policy.

In style as well as substance the bishop's presentation gave signs of being designed to appeal to the two orders not his own even more than to the clergy. It was couched in terms that showed a political, rather than a spiritual orientation. It contrasted with contemporary speeches of clergymen and with the harangue given by Marquemont, Bishop of Lyons, at the opening session of the Estates, in citing secular considerations far more than clerical ones.[49] Infrequent allusions to rectitude and salvation were invariably reinforced by reasons of equity, or state, or both. Indeed the word *équité* itself—not a term frequently encountered except in legal writers of that day—appears three times in the speech. The first three citations Richelieu makes are of the political philosophers, Aristotle, Plato and Bodin, and the first empirical example he gives is from the history of pagan Rome. Representative of the legal and political cast of reasoning in the harangue is an argument against bestowing benefices on laymen who then appoint clerical surrogates to perform their duties:

> There is . . . no reason, since it is against equity, to give a share of the fruits [of a post] to those who do not share its labors (*peines*) . . . and . . . very shameful experience teaches us that to deprive a man of what belongs to him legitimately sometimes causes him to take illegally (*injustement*) that which is not owed him.[50]

The first complaint Richelieu mentions does not concern the Catholic church in France—as did the first item in the *cahier* of the clergy as a whole—

but instead the heavy burdens placed upon the "people"—the "poor and afflicted"—for whom the church, as their mother, must have special care. The source of their misery, as of "most of the ills of all the communities of the world" is not moral, but economic: "excessive expenditures," "enormous gifts," distributed "without restraint or reason." Thus the chief grievance in the *cahier* of the Third Estate is the one mentioned first by the bishop of Luçon. He goes on to urge abolition of the *paulette*, a demand dearest to the Second Estate in which the clergy had joined, as had, finally, the Third Estate as well, for the sake of reciprocity on other matters. Accordingly, Richelieu uses a tactful, general term, referring to "venality of appointments and offices," whose main dangers, he avers, come from multiplying the number of government posts, thus draining the poor of their resources.[51]

After having denounced venality in office in terms to which the Third Estate as well as the nobility could subscribe he goes on, in two longer passages, to denounce evils chiefly identified by the Third Estate: "exemptions from subsidies and taxes," "great expenditures, immense gifts and profusions" from the king. These he represents as damaging not only poor people who are the chief resources of government, but also "ordinary noblemen (*commun des nobles*)" who are as "poor in money as they are rich in honor and courage." Such a description fits the Richelieu family—not those who have recently benefitted from royal largesse. He refers to benefits dispensed only to "those nearest the king"—that is, by clear implication, the *grands* of the realm.[52] The *cahier* that had actually been adopted by delegates of Richelieu's order had interests of the Catholic church at the head of the list. Their demands were first for reestablishment of Catholic primacy in historic jurisdictions, restoration of Catholic liberties, especially in Béarn, and royal promulgation of the decrees of the Council of Trent. This was followed by a request—aimed at the Jews—for expulsion of non-Christians from the realm. The next item—included to exonerate the clergy from the charge of encouraging regicide—was a call to declare those who perpetrated this crime outlaws. Following this came an exhortation to the king to remain in close alliance with the pope. In Richelieu's harangue, on the other hand, Catholic ecclesiastical rights as against those of Protestants do not appear until the secular topics already mentioned have been discussed. When they do appear they do so in conciliatory form. His allusion to Béarn is brief; he makes no general references to threats from the Protestants, and no allusion whatever to the clergy's demand for expulsion of non-Christians. Instead, he dwells at some length on a church desecration that had recently occurred in the Auvergne. During deliberations in the chamber of the Second Estate, a haranguer from the first chamber had charged Huguenots with perpetrating this incident. A bitter confrontation between Protestant noblemen and the visiting churchman had ensued.[53] Richelieu, by contrast, does not specifically attribute the desecration to the rival confession. Instead, he qualifies his denunciation with the soothing comments: "I speak only of those who have committed such a barbarous act." As for the others who, "blinded by error"—(a milder term than heresy)—"live peacefully under your authority, we think only of converting them" by example, instruction and prayer—"the only arms with which we wish to combat them," and "do not doubt that they themselves detest so strange an impiety."[54] Richelieu makes no mention of regicide in his speech. It may have seemed poor policy to him, in an address designed to exalt the monarchy, to protest what should have been self-evident. Moreover, since the regicidal doctrine was chiefly associated with Jesuit theorists, he may have wished to avoid raising an issue that could weaken the effectiveness of his own ecumenical stand.

Perhaps the most conspicuous indication of Richelieu's desire to conciliate the Gallican sentiment of the Third Estate is his treatment of Rome. Despite its prominence on the list of desiderata of his order, current relations with the Holy See are not once mentioned in the bishop's harangue.

Another issue that called for delicacy was the clergy's advocacy of royal promulgation of the decrees of the Council of Trent. This was in the first article of the First Estate's list. The *noblesse* had joined with them, not without Protestant dissent, in including this article in their *cahier*, but the Third Estate had refused to assent, not only because of objections from their Huguenot minority but also because, from their Gallican position, the Tridentine reforms posed a danger of subjecting French royal authority to constraints from Rome. It is, on the other hand, fifth on Richelieu's "morning list." In the harangue he actually delivered, however, Trent is not mentioned by name until the beginning of his conclusion, although reforms contained in the Council's decrees are advocated earlier. And in introducing the need for such reforms he is cautious, pointing out that the "reestablishment" of the church "conflicts in no way with present necessities of affairs"—that is, one may presume, with interests of state. Even more significantly he makes a notable exception: "If there are certain articles in this Council which, good in themselves, seem less useful to this realm on account of being repugnant to its ancient usages, we agree very willingly to ask their modification."[55] Richelieu has, seemingly, agreed by this to any amendments to Tridentine decrees that seem incompatible with French practice.

Historians have given little attention to those innovations in substance and order that Richelieu made in the agenda presented to him by the *cahier* of the clergy.[56] Their attention, on the other hand, has often been captured by another aspect of his address: throughout the harangue Richelieu makes a bid for power on behalf of the clergy and, by implication, of himself.

Richelieu's plea is for greater influence of clerical advisors in government, not on account of their spiritual qualifications, but because of their special aptitude for public affairs deriving from the disinterestedness, skill, and learning peculiar to their condition. A personal characteristic in which the bishop himself took special pride is adduced as a virtue of clerics in general: "Their profession . . . obliges them particularly . . . to conduct themselves (*se gouverner*) with prudence."[57]

The plea for ecclesiastical preeminence in councils of state was one that had been made by Du Perron. He had argued, as Richelieu now argues, that the celibacy of the clergy made them specially qualified to advise the king without regard to personal interests. He had also denounced, as Richelieu now denounces, the practice of giving precedence to laymen over ecclesiastical dignitaries. Du Perron had, in fact, specifically criticized the queen for allowing Condé to precede Cardinal de Joyeuse in the council.[58]

Richelieu, of course, tactfully does not mention names. In elaborating on the disinterestedness of clergymen, however, he seems unintentionally ironic as he, the strong family man, argues that "keeping celibate as they do . . . obliges them not to think of anything here below in serving their king and their fatherland, except for acquiring forever, up high in heaven, a glorious and all-perfect reward." He does, however, broaden Du Perron's case for clerical aptitude for state functions by claiming that the special training and status of churchmen equips them not only for validating laws and guaranteeing agreements, for negotiating and arbitrating disputes between states, for educating princes, superintending financial management, and counseling kings on every matter, but also for another role. They may be surrogates for kings:

> The belief that is held that religion, which links them to God, makes their faith inviolable, results in their word being desired as security for their masters' promises; they are asked to be, and they are accepted as hostages for kings, together with their children, as though their status (*dignité*) somehow made their persons royal.[59]

The distinctive link is not only with God, but with the king, for whom they serve, like his own children, as another self.

Richelieu's characterization of a cleric's person as the God-given *alter ego* of the monarch is followed by an implicit description of his own role at the moment, in this last session of the estates. Using medical analogies he visualizes his potential part in the king's councils. He speaks first of the ills of the church itself because "when there are several sores on the body, reason dictates that one concentrate most on those that are in the noblest parts."[60] In parlance of the time it was usual to compare the state to the body, but it was usual also to depict the king as its "head." Here Richelieu seems to be attributing that role to the church, since this is the usual meaning of "most noble parts."

It is difficult for the church to play this role for she is "so prostrate (*tellement abbatue*) that she would scarcely have powers to complain, feeling herself on her last legs (*aux dernier abois*), were it not that, seeing before her the only doctor from whom she can receive a cure, she makes a last effort" to induce him to revive her.[61]

Most often in this speech Richelieu depicts Louis as the absolute master with *power* to apply medication to remedy his realm's afflictions. By implication, Richelieu himself is the consulting physician who prescribes the cure:

> You command us to propose remedies to our ills and counsel
> you for our cure. . . . We reveal our ills to you in order to permit
> Your Majesty to accomplish his design, bringing remedy to
> them.

In this process, diagnosis is the first step:

> And, inasmuch as one does not reach an objective except by the
> means which conduct to it, and among those which are suitable
> to cure an illness, one of the chief ones is to know its cause, we
> will first represent to you what ours proceed from in order that,
> informed, you may entirely tear out their roots and dry up their
> springs.[62]

Here, it seems, the king is the surgeon who applies the cutting edge of his instruments at the directions of the doctor. There follows the list of *plaintes* and proposed cures that, as we have seen, concern not only ills peculiar to the clerical order, but also those in the rest of the body politic. The exposition complete, Richelieu summarizes: "There, Sire, are . . . our ills and our complaints . . . that I have reduced to the fewest possible counts." But diagnosis is only half the game, and the doctor is powerless alone, "inasmuch as a doctor vainly orders what has already been prescribed by another," and it is not so much a question of making new ordinances "as to guide the hand in observing the old ones." The work of the medical advisor, however valuable, is validated only by royal *enforcement*. Here is Louis's chance for greater glory than his antecedents achieved:

> Your Majesty, having executed religiously that which has been
> holily ordered by his predecessors, will surpass them to the ex-
> tent that results (*effets*) exceed words, and the execution of good
> things, the proposal which has been made of them.[63]

In retrospect, Richelieu seems to have innovated, in presenting an agenda of clerical complaints, for the sake of casting himself as a spokesman not only of his own order, but also of the Second and, especially, the Third Estates. Was the strategy detected? The absence of clerical protests over his departure from prescription would indicate it was not. Witness the commendation of Pierre Behety, secretary of the clerical order:

> Monsieur the bishop of Luçon . . . made the remonstrances,
> complaints, and supplications that he had been ordered and re-
> quired to make, but with so much judgment and eloquence that,
> acquitting himself worthily of his duty, and representing every-
> thing with which he had been charged with extreme discretion,
> he must have satisfied everyone without offending anyone.[64]

Perhaps, as far as the First Estate was concerned, possible resentment was forestalled by Richelieu's appeal to the vanity of the churchmen, for whose capacity he claimed so much. There was enough also to ingratiate the young bishop with the other two orders: Richelieu's picture of French society comprises the poor but brave nobility, the hardworking afflicted people, the solicitous powerful monarchy. There is only one group not conciliated by his harangue: in no context are the *grands* of the realm—the princes of the blood, the dukes and peers not directly represented at the Estates meeting—mentioned in a favorable light.

Moreover, the monarchy depicted by the bishop of Luçon is not plural but unitary: it centers on the king alone. Louis's mother seeks her son's glory and that of his realm because she is "full of love for his person and of zeal for his state."[65] Nor is there any reference to others in the royal family. Even Louis's brother, the seven-year old Gaston who, as the heir apparent, had significantly strengthened Marie's status as regent, gets no attention, although he was present at the final session.

4.   The Courtier

When Richelieu prepared his address, he was already assured of the confidence of the queen, insofar as this could be assured. The objectives most important for Marie were endorsement of her continued leadership and of her implementation of the Spanish marriages. These were agreed to by the *cahiers* of all three Estates.

Endorsements of these two policies are also the first two items on Richelieu's morning agenda. In the speech itself they appear at the climax, rather than at the beginning.

The bishop praises the queen in one address to her son:

> Among an infinity of graces that Your Majesty has received from
> heaven, one of the greatest for which you are indebted to it is
> the gift and the preservation of such a mother, and, of all your
> actions, the worthiest and most useful to the reestablishment of
> your state is that by which you have committed it to her care.

Turning to Marie, he avers: "All France knows itself, Madame, obliged to award you all the honors that in olden times used to be accorded to guardians of the peace, public calm and tranquility." His appreciation of Marie is practical, in terms of past and future benefits for France, and while fulsome, it avoids the extravagance of the addresses and pamphlets of others which habitually compared her to the venerated and self-sacrificing mother of Louis XIII's namesake, Saint Louis. His moderation may be an implicit concession to those who criticized many particulars of her rule. He promises Marie that if, in continuing her administration, she enacts the reforms for which the estates petition, "your merits, adding a thousand crowns of glory to the one which crowns your leader, as crowning recompense the king will add to the glorious title you have of being his mother, that of being mother of his realm." Still, after favorable comments on the Spanish marriages and a plea for enactment of the petitioned reforms, "which your honor and that of the king, who is so dear to you, require," he has addressed the queen directly for only four paragraphs before turning back to Louis, to whom, with these exceptions, he has spoken from the first.[66]

Among the exhortations Richelieu directs at the king, first in order of presentation is one appropriate to his clerical profession: he warns Louis of the risk of damnation: To award church benefices to those unworthy of them is, "Sire, . . . a great abuse, which entrains in its wake the loss of an infinite number of souls, for which your own will one day answer before the Sovereign Judge of humans."[67] Further references to the risk of perdition, even as delicate as this one, do not appear in the speech. Richelieu is usually concerned for Louis's earthly status. Furthermore, the worldly inducements he holds out are lures rather than menaces. As before, in Luçon, Richelieu accents the positive: the carrot is preferred to the stick.

The chief inducement put before Louis is the prospect of earthly glory, "glory being a spur that sharply pricks (pique) generous minds." He seems to link his own ambition for earthly distinction to the king's by using the same words for the clergy's motivation: were the king to bestow honor on those who show the merits called for by church reforms, he would give the clergy "a new spur"—"worldly honor"—"to impel us more strongly to that end."[68]

One possible spur to Louis's performance is noteworthy by its virtual absence from the bishop's harangue. Neither to the queen nor to the young king is Henri IV held up as an example for political conduct. The unusualness of this omission is put in relief by the fact that the queen's regency as well as her son's succession were legitimated by Henri's intentions and actions. That monarch, by common consent declared "Henri le Grand" the day after his death,[69] was still very much alive in the hearts of his subjects. The Third Estate and Parlement were still actively seeking scapegoats for his murder. The public at large cherished his name. Even ten years after the Vert Galant's death a foreign visitor reports that popular recollection of him is still green:

> Never was any king so lamented as this. There are a world not
> only of his pictures, but statues, up and down France, and there
> is scarce a market town but hath him erected in the market place
> or over some gate.[70]

Yet the only clearly favorable reference Richelieu makes to Henri IV in his harangue is a plea for his "prudence" in financial matters to "serve as our rule."[71]

In contrast with a plethora of harangues, addresses, and pamphlets exhorting the young king to follow in his father's footsteps, Richelieu's speech, by implication, cites a number of shortcomings of the "Great Henri." First, of course, is the necessity for praising the regency's foreign policy. In the bishop's text the regent's record is made to compare favorably with that of her predecessor, for not only has she, by "so many miracles to this very moment kept us in that repose which the invincible arms of the Great Henri acquired for us," but, beyond this, "because you wished to attach peace to this state forever," she has arranged by, it is implied, a better means than Henri's arms, "the gentlest and strongest tie that can be imagined," that is, the Spanish marriages. Thus the link that Henri, preferring bloodshed, refused to forge with his rivals, has now been arranged by the queen "between the two greatest realms of the world, which have nothing to fear being united while, being separated, they can receive injury only from each other."[72] Henri's strategy, of course, had been to maintain the separation.

Other allusions to Henri's shortcomings are clearer in Richelieu's speech. In his complaints concerning the low condition to which ecclesiastics have fallen in the councils of state he comments, "the greatest of our kings are those who made the greatest use of them, which is clearly shown by the fact that the great prince"—Charlemagne is identified in his footnote—"never did anything in peace or war without the advice of bishops."[73] But, as the queen, Louis and Richelieu were well aware, Henri IV had not regularly sought the counsel of ecclesiastics, and his chief advisors were laymen.

In similar vein Richelieu recalls that Henri III had promised, in the last meeting of the Estates (in 1588) to abolish the practice of selling survivors' rights to offices. That king had, of course, died in the following year, but what of Henri IV, his successor? Again the "great saint among our kings whose name Your Majesty bears" refused to appoint incumbents of ecclesiastical livings, and François I repented on his death bed of having done so. Perhaps Louis XIII, listening to the bishop of Luçon, asked himself why his own father had been less conscientious.

Louis might also have reflected that the disorders that Richelieu asked him to end in Béarn because perpetrated by Huguenots against Catholics, would have been more readily amended by the ex-Huguenot *béarnais*, Henri le Grand. Furthermore, as the haranguer points out, enactment of the Tridentine reforms is something to which Henri IV "solemnly committed himself when the church received him in its arms." This was in 1593 and Henri had reigned for seventeen years more without making good on this commitment.[74]

Thus Richelieu exhorts Louis to strike out on a different, more glorious path than that followed by his father. The aim he holds out is exaltation of royal power; almost every argument that he addresses to the young king stresses it. By means of making offices hereditary, he points out, His Majesty has "tied his hands." Without patronage he "would be king for a long time without being able to appear so." The church is the greatest adjunct to royal power: His Majesty will note that all sovereigns are "strictly obliged" to maintain the authority of this "holy spouse" of God—"both out of conscience, which is obvious (*manifeste*) and for reason of state."[75]

The worldliness of the glory that Richelieu stresses becomes less so in the light of this exaltation of royal power. In one paragraph he cites the New Testament (Matthew, xxiv) to support an analogy that equates the survival of the monarchy with world survival:

> Jesus Christ, assigning as an indication of the end of the world the desolation that Daniel predicted would be seen in the temple, we have great reason to fear that that which is seen every day in ours is a sign of the end of this monarchy.

And if, on the other hand, Louis enacts the desired reforms, there is a glorious earthly future ahead: reason and justice will flourish, arts and letters blossom, religion be revived, the church regain its luster, the nobility its honor and privileges, the people will be delivered from oppression; "All of France will be restored to the best condition that . . . we could wish for her." After a striking description of the marvels ahead, he makes this remarkable claim: All of this will be brought about, "it should be noted, with such facility that I may call its reformation as easy as it is just, necessary, and full of glory for Your Majesty."[76] "What then," asks Hanotaux, "was the secret of this eloquent young man who considered 'easy' a task in which others saw nothing but the vast extent and the difficulties?"[77] The biographer does not answer his own question, as he might, by citing the paragraph that follows immediately:

> It is easy, Sire, because in most good things it is with kings as it is with God, for whom to wish it is to do it.[78]

The simile is curious, for although kings were frequently described, in political writings of the time, as partaking of divine authority, no doctrine claimed for them a godlike omnipotence. Richelieu's flight of imagination has reached its apogee in a dream of an almighty earthly monarch. It is a deification of kingly power by one to whom the end of the monarchy seems the same as the end of the world.

The one who has prescribed the cure for the state has painted a dazzling picture of its ruler; if he applies the necessary remedies, "What glory may you not acquire, Sire . . . ?"[79] And, as we have seen, the physician is more than a counselor; in some way he takes on the character of the king himself, "as though their status somehow made their persons royal."

Therefore he hopes from the king "the cure for our ills;" If it can be earned by attachment (*affection*), we deserve it because of the extreme passion we have for his service:

> Passion, Sire, to which all our actions will bear witness, protest-
> ing before God, in the presence of Your Majesty, facing all of
> France, that together with the advancement of the glory of the
> Almighty, the greatest assignment (*soin*) we might wish to have
> is to imprint . . . in the hearts of your subjects . . . the respect
> and the obedience they owe you; to ask of heaven . . . an abun-
> dant effusion of blessings on Your Majesty, to beg Him who is
> its Master to turn His wrath away from this state and, in case
> He might wish to punish it, offer ourselves to endure in this
> world the fire of his lightning-bolts to protect your person from
> them, for which our wishes have such priority (*sont si avanta-
> geux*) that we shall never be touched by any desire that equals
> the one that we have to see the royal status so affirmed in him
> that it is like a strong rock that shatters everything that strikes it.

In terms similar to these had he offered himself, body and soul, to the queen nearly five years before. His *serment de fidélité* had then been deemed inopportune. The queen, "at the mercy of a thousand storms and as many shoals,"[80] had managed, largely without his help, to keep the ship of state afloat during her son's minority. Now, before all of France, Richelieu prom- ises to give all that is in him for the power and glory of Louis XIII. He offers himself as a surrogate for the king.

Eventually, the offer would be accepted.

Sample of Richelieu's handwriting (for transcription, see opposite page). Courtesy of Ministère des Relations Extérieures, Archives et Documentation, Paris.

Appendix A:
Richelieu's Worksheet on Power over the Sea

[Source: AAE, France 792, fol. 183 *vo*. (See Chapter II, Section 3.) Accents and punctuation are supplied. Words and passages within [brackets] are excised by Richelieu; words *emphasized* are inserted by him.]

La mer est de tous les héritages celuy auquel tous les souverains prétendent plus de part. Et cependant c'est celuy sur lequel les droicts d'un chaquun sont le moins esclaircis. L'empire *de cet élément* [n'e] n'a jamais esté bien asseuré à personne. Il a [souvent suivy la nature de cet élément variable et inconstant, si jaloux et si vain qu'il se dépense (?) et qu'il] *esté sujet à divers changements selon l'inconstance de sa nature, si jalouse et si plaine de vanité quelle* s'abandonne tousjours à celuy qui le flatte [d'un (?)] le plus et qui a tant d'amour pour [luy] *elle* qu'il se tient en estat de [l'empescher de faire qu'on (?)] *la posséder par violence contre* tous ceux qui pourraient luy *en* disputer *le droict* par raison.

[Et cependant on peult dire avec vérité [qu'il a] *que son empire a* tousjours suivy, avec les utilités qui l'accompagnent, [tous] ceux qui *en* ont [pris plus] faict plus de cas et qui pour l'acquérir se sont rendus les plus puissants en vaisseaux.]

En un mot les vrays tiltres de cet empire sont la force et non la raison. Il faut estre puissant pour prétendre cet héritage.

Appendix B:
The Original
Compared with
the "Testament Politique"

Richelieu's Editing of his Text

La mer est de tous les heritages celuy auquel tous les souverains pretendent plus de part. Et cependant cest celuy sur lequel les droicts dun chaquun sont le moins esclaircis. Lempire de cet element n a jamais este bien asseure a personne. Il a este sujet a divers changements selon linconstance de sa nature, si jalouse et si plaine de vanite quelle sabandonne tousjours a celuy qui le flatte le plus et qui a tant damour pour elle quil se tient en estat de la posseder par violence contre tous ceux qui pourrayent luy en disputer le droict par raison.

En un mot les vrays tiltres de cet empire sont la force et non la raison. Il faut estre puissant pour pretendre cet heritage.

"Testament" Text [André edition, 400-402.]

"Qui traite de la puissance de la mer."

La mer est celui des héritages sur lequel tous les souverains prétendent plus de part, et cependant c'est celui sur lequel les droits d'un chacun sont moins esclaircis.

L'empire de cet élément ne fut jamais bien assuré à personne. Il a été sujet à divers changements selon l'Inconstance de sa nature, si sujette aux vents qu'il s'abandonne à celui qui le flatte le plus et dont la puissance est si déréglée qu'il se tient en état de le posséder par violence contre tous ceux qui pourroient lui en disputer la domination.

En un mot, les vrais titres de cette domination sont la force et non la raison. Il faut être puissant pour prétendre cet héritage.

216

Notes

Chapter 1

1. Joseph A. Schumpeter, *The Theory of Economic Development*, trans. by R. Opie (Cambridge, Mass., 1934), 82 *n*.
2. Denis-Louis-Martial Avenel, ed., *Lettres, instructions et papiers d'Etat du Cardinal de Richelieu* (8 vols., Paris, 1853–1877), I, *civ*.
3. Quoted by D.-L.-M. Avenel, "L'Evêque de Luçon et le connétable de Luynes," *Revue des Questions Historiques*, IX (1870), 82.
4. Augustin Thierry, *Essai sur l'histoire de la formation et des progrès du tiers état* (Paris, 1868), 203f. The word "innovation," of course, is Thierry's, not Richelieu's. The cardinal did not believe he intended to be a political or religious innovator; he saw himself as sponsoring accepted views. It was an era in which *innover* was still a bad word and Richelieu himself occasionally denied any wish to introduce "novelties."
5. Alphonse Aulard, *Le Patriotisme français de la renaissance à la révolution* (Paris, 1921), 23.
6. Marc Bloch, *Les Rois thaumaturges* (Paris, 1961 reprint ed.), 342–344.
7. *Les Antiquitez et recherches de la majesté des roys de France* (Paris, 1609), Book I;4, 164 *et seq.* On the contrast between the king's status amongst the great nobility before and after Louis XIII's reign, see Georges d'Avenel, *Richelieu et la monarchie absolue*, I (Paris, 1895), 262 *et seq.*
8. On political Gallicanism in this period see Victor Martin, *Le Gallicanisme et le clergé de France* (Paris, 1929), 41–86.
9. An overview of absolutist currents in political thought of the time is Henri Sée, *Les Idées politiques en France au XVIIe siècle* (Paris, 1923), 7–43, though with omissions supplied by Roland Mousnier, *La Plume, la faucille et le marteau* (Paris, 1970), 43–56. Richelieu's youthful position on these issues has been variously interpreted; it is analyzed in Chapter X, below.
10. Henri Hauser, *La Pensée et l'action économiques du cardinal de Richelieu* (Paris, 1944), 191.
11. Louis-André Boiteux, *Richelieu: Grand maître de la navigation et du commerce de France* (Caen, 1955), 347–378.
12. Pierre Viollet, *Le Roi et ses ministres* (Paris, 1912), *vi* f.
13. J. Russell Major, "Henri IV and Guyenne: A Study Concerning Origins of Royal Absolutism," in Ray F. Kierstead, ed., *State and Society in Seventeenth Century France* (New York, 1975), 2–24. In a recent study the same author questions even the attribution to Richelieu of some of the major centralizing tendencies of the regime. See *Representative Government in Early Modern France* (New Haven, 1980), 568–621. On these particular issues, however, the evidence is not yet all in.

14. Lionel Rothkrug, *Opposition to Louis XIV* (Princeton, 1965), 7f.

15. *Lustra Ludovici* (London, 1646), prefatory "Epistle."

16. James B. Perkins, *Richelieu and the Growth of French Power* (Freeport, N.Y., 1971 reprint), 329.

17. Quoted from the *Résumé des cahiers des états généraux de 1789* by Jules Caillet, *L'Administration en France sous le ministère du cardinal de Richelieu* (Paris, 1857), 546.

18. The high motivation to achieve here attributed to Richelieu differs from Achievement, a complex of specifically economic perspectives. See David McClelland, *The Achieving Society* (Princeton, 1961), 302 *et seq*. Closer to the present criterion is simply a "conception of the high-motive person as one who is concentrated on active manipulation of the environment," attributed to R. H. Knapp by Roger Brown, *Social Psychology* (New York, 1965), 443.

19. Quoted, for example, by Avenel in *Lettres*, I, civ, and by Richard Lodge, *Richelieu* (London, 1924), 235.

20. *Mémoires de Monsieur de Montchal*, I (Rotterdam, 1718), 5.

21. Joseph A. Schumpeter, *Capitalism, Socialism and Democracy* (New York, 1942), 132f.

22. *Ibid.*

23. *Richelieu and the Councillors of Louis XIII* (Oxford, 1963), 184.

24. Schumpeter, *Capitalism*, 133.

25. *Richelieu and the Councillors*, 182.

26. Frank H. Knight, *Risk, Uncertainty and Profit* (New York, 1967 Reprint), 270.

27. Pierre Grillon, ed., *Les Papiers de Richelieu: Section politique intérieure* (4 vols., Paris, 1975–1980), I, 558–561. December 2, 1626.

28. *Richelieu and Reason of State* (Princeton, 1972), 173.

29. The lag of France behind England in this respect has been seen as a basic condition for the relatively ineffective resistance in the former to absolutist encroachments. See, for example, John U. Nef, *Industry and Government in France and England, 1540–1640* (Ithaca, N.Y., 1964 reprint ed.), 149–157.

30. Raymond Chalumeau, "Saint Vincent de Paul et les missions en France," *Dix-septième Siècle*, XLI (1959), 317.

31. François de Dainville, *Les Jésuites et l'éducation de la société française* (Paris, 1940), *passim*.

32. Louis Prunel, *La Renaissance catholique en France au XVIIe siècle* (Paris, 1921), 77–79.

33. *The Protestant Ethic and the Spirit of Capitalism*, trans. by Talcott Parsons (Chicago, n.d.), 153f. Application of some of Weber's observations to the France of our period is made in Lucien Febvre, "Aspects méconnus d'un renouveau religieux en France entre 1590 et 1620," *Annales, E. S. C.*, XIII (1958), 639–650.

34. Jean Delumeau, *Naissance et affirmation de la réforme* (Paris, 1965), 364–366. At the beginning of the period, remarks a historian of Jansenism, the appeal of Calvinism over French Catholicism lay in the "evident" superiority of its spirit, which gave it the better claim to be the continuer of the "authentic Christian tradition." In many a divided family the "dynamic proselytism of the Calvinist element gave it moral superiority." Louis Cognet, *La Spiritualité française au 17e siècle* (Paris, 1949), 14f.

35. Saint Vincent de Paul, *Conférences aux Filles de la Charité* (Paris, 1902), 702.

36. Prunel, *La Renaissance catholique*, 28.

37. Henri-Jean Martin, *Livre, pouvoirs et société à Paris au XVIIe siècle* (2 vols., Geneva, 1969), I, 135.

38. *La Renaissance catholique*, 32.

39. For example, in a letter to Cardinal de Marquemont asking approval for foundation of a new chapter in Lyon, Saint François demurs: "Leaving it to the great Orders that are already established in the Church to honor our Lord . . . with striking virtues, I wish that my daughters have no other pretension but to glorify him by their abasement; that the little Institute of the Visitation . . . make itself neither seen nor heard in the world." *Lettres*, ed. by the Religious of the Visitation of Annecy (11 vols., Vols. XI–XXI of *Oeuvres de Saint François de Sales*, Lyon, 1900–1923), I, 17. June, 1615.

40. Ernst Troeltsch, *The Social Teaching of the Christian Churches*, trans. by Olive Wyon (2 vols., London, 1931), I, 48f.

41. Père Gratian, quoted by Henri Bremond, *A Literary History of Religious Sentiment in France in the Seventeenth Century*, trans. by K. L. Montgomery, (3 vols., London, 1930), I, 215.

42. The designation is used by Orest Ranum, *Paris in the Age of Absolutism* (New York, 1968), 109–131.

43. *The Protestant Ethic*, 161f.

44. *Le Tiers état*, 203.

45. J. Russell Major, "The Crown and the Aristocracy in Renaissance France," *American Historical Review*, LXIX (1964), 644. See also, by the same author, "Henri IV and Guyenne," 4f.

46. *Mémoires du cardinal de Richelieu*, ed. by the Société de l'Histoire de France, (10 vols., 1908–1929), IX, 303.

47. "Harangue . . . pour le clergé à la closture des Estats," in *ibid.*, I (Paris, 1927), 358f.

48. Keith Thomas, *Religion and the Decline of Magic* (London, 1971), 431.

49. *The Idea of Progress* (New York, 1932), 76.

50. This analogy, although not unique to Richelieu, was exceptionally frequent in his writings. See, for example, the penultimate paragraph of Chapter XI, below.

51. Grillon, *Papiers*, I, 558. December 2, 1626. Emphasis supplied. Compare, for a somewhat less homocentric idea of royal progress, the address of Claude de Seyssel to François I in 1519, who predicts that, "as to the present . . . monarch of France, there is no doubt that," if he follows policies recommended by the author, "he will do greater things more worthy of memory than any king of France has ever done," *because*, as thus more deserving, God will give him more help than he has given any earlier prince. *The Monarchy of France*, Donald R. Kelley, ed.; Jack H. Hexter, trans. (New Haven, 1981), 161.

52. Jeanne-Baptiste de Bourbon, "Epistre," preface to *La Reigle de l'ordre de Font-evrauld* (Paris, 1642). Emphasis supplied.

53. *Ibid.* It is not only on principle that each gender is mentioned here; for the regulations of this community, which included both men and women, the abbess included two préfaces, the appropriate one to be inserted by the binder, depending on whether *"mes chères soeurs"* or *"mes chers frères"* were to be addressed.

54. Quoted from *L'Année Sainte* in *Lettres de Saint François de Sales*, 360 n.

55. He offers a striking example from one of Descartes's letters: "One is entirely right to take one's time in deliberating before undertaking things of importance; but . . . resolution and promptness are virtues necessary for matters already begun." (Cf. the discussion of Richelieu's similar words on the same subject, below, Chapter III, Section 2, "Anxiety.") Preface to *Le Testament politique de Richelieu*, Louis André, ed., (Paris, 1941), 22f. A modern biographer of Descartes is impatient with that Poitevin pride which attributes the taste for order shown by the cardinal and the mathematician to their common provincial origins. See Maxime Leroy, *Descartes: le philosophe au masque*, (2 vols., Paris, 1929), I, 57.

56. Viz., [1] "Never to accept anything as true that I did not know certainly to be so: that is, carefully to avoid hastiness and prejudice. . . . [2] to divide each difficulty I considered into as many parcels as . . . possible [3] to conduct my thoughts in order . . . [4] to make everywhere enumerations so complete and reviews so comprehensive that I was assured of having omitted nothing." *Discours de la méthode* (Paris, 1947), 18f.

57. Louis Cognet, "La Spiritualité de Richelieu," *Etudes franciscaines*, III (1952), 85f.; 91.

58. Rothkrug, *Opposition to Louis XIV*, 107 n.

59. *Religion and the Decline of Magic*, 431 et seq.

60. AAE (Archives des Affaires Extérieures), *Mémoires et Documents*, France 767, fol. 215; 768, fol. 212 vo; *Correspondance Diplomatique*, Rome 23, fol. 412. June 26, 1610; February 6, 1613; January 17, 1617.

61. Martin, *Livre, pouvoirs et société*, I, 146.

62. Harold D. Lasswell, *Democracy through Public Opinion* (Menasha, Wisc., 1941), 106.

63. Louis Delavaud, "Quelques collaborateurs de Richelieu," *Rapports et notices sur l'édition des Mémoires du cardinal de Richelieu de la Société de l'Histoire de France* (7 vols., Paris, 1905–1922), V, 123f.

64. *Lettres*, I, 129. Emphasis supplied. The date of 1612 for this letter is justified in *ibid.*, VIII, 7 *n.*

65. Armand-Jean Du Plessis de Richelieu, *L'Instruction du chrestien* (Paris, 1621), 5.

66. Paul Ardier, *Mémoires de l'Assemblée des Notables* (Paris, 1652), 132.

67. *Ibid.*

68. Grillon, *Papiers*, I, 561.

69. *Ibid.*

70. Mathieu de Morgues, *Restauration de l'estat* (n.p., 1617), 30. Maximin Deloche's opinion is that Richelieu is the sole author of this work. See his *Autour de la plume du cardinal de Richelieu* (Paris, 1920), 154.

71. Eugène Griselle, ed. *Formulaires de lettres de François I à Louis XIV et Etat de la France dressé en 1642* (N.p., n.d.), 242.

Chapter 2

1. François de La Rochefoucauld, *Les Mémoires du duc de La Rochefoucauld*, Michaud and Poujoulat, eds. (Paris, 1831), 390.

2. *E.g.*, Léon Noël in the Preface to *Testament politique*, 24, and Boiteux, *Richelieu, Grand Maître*, 12.

3. *Lettres* I, civ.

4. Michel Le Masle, quoted by Louis Batiffol, *Richelieu et le roi Louis XIII* (Paris, 1934), 40f.

5. Henri Taine, *Les Origines de la France contemporaine*, I (Paris, 1909), 16–18. See also William F. Church, "France," in Orest Ranum, ed., *National Consciousness, History, and Political Culture in Early-Modern Europe* (Baltimore, 1975), 64f.

6. *Le Patriotisme*, 12–16.

7. *Ibid.*, 14. See also examples given by Roland Mousnier, *Les Institutions de la France sous la monarchie absolue* (2 vols., Paris, 1974), I, 470.

8. Gustave Dupont-Ferrier, "Le Sens des mots 'Patria' et 'patrie' en France au moyen âge et jusqu'au début du XVIIe siècle," *Revue Historique*, CLXXXVIII (1940), 95f.

9. One of the few examples of it that I have noticed in his writings (in addition to the single one in the "Harangue pour le clergé," quoted below, Chapter XI, Section 3, is in his proposal for the "fondation d'une académie pour les gentilshommes pauvres," published in *Mémoires de Mathieu Molé*, Aimé Champollion-Figeac, ed. (4 vols., Paris, 1855–1857), IV, 266. Here Richelieu aims to encourage "l'amour de la patrie," among other civic virtues, in the hearts of these poor but noble students, so like his boyhood self.

10. Aulard, *Le Patriotisme*, 14f. See also Jean Lestocquoy, *Histoire du patriotisme en France* (Paris, 1968), 46f.

11. Without a systematic comparison of samples representative of a wide assortment of texts, such a conclusion is necessarily impressionistic. Nevertheless, inspection of Sully's *Mémoires* fails to disclose any use of the term "France" except in an international context. Henri IV usually uses another word in his letters and harangues, even on the most dramatic, patriotic occasions, such as his public announcement of conversion to Catholicism. See Palma Cayet, *Chronologie novenaire et septenaire*, J.-A.-C. Buchon, ed., (2 vols., Paris, 1836–1875), I, 546–548, or his letter (for wide circulation) to the duc d'Epernon announcing the "victory" of Du Perron over Du Plessis Mornay. See below, Chapter IX, Section 6, "A Forerunner."

By contrast, Richelieu's address on behalf of the clergy, discussed below, may be compared with Denis de Marquemont's harangue for that order at the commencement of the same Estates General convocation and with reports of another remonstrance of the clergy, presented by the bishop of Beauvais in the following year. See the *Mercure françois*, III (1614), 52–54; IV (1615), 198–204.

12. *Lettres*, I, 23; 62; 129. End of April, 1609; 1611. On dating the last letter see *ibid.*, VIII, 7.

13. See below, Chapter X, Section 5.

14. *Lettres*, I, 113f. November 1613.

15. *Mémoires de Richelieu*, I, 340–365.

16. It is not mentioned, for example, in the works on patriotism by Aulard and Lestocquoy already cited, nor in the enlightening essay of Henri Hauser, *Le Principe des nationalités: ses origines historiques* (Paris, 1916). One cause of such omissions may be a misapprehension based on often-quoted passages in the *Testament politique* whose author criticizes the character of *"les français"* in a manner rather uncharacteristic of writings known to be Richelieu's personal work, but has little to say about *"France."* Victor-Lucien Tapié, for example, makes no allusion to Richelieu in his discussion of seventeenth-century French patriotism except in connection with these passages which are, nonetheless, highly doubtfully attributed to the cardinal. See "Comment les français du dix-septième siècle voyaient la patrie," *Le Dix-septième Siècle*, IV (1955), 50f. On the *Testament*, see below, Section 3.

17. *Grandeur and Illusion: French Literature and Society, 1600–1715*, trans. by Herbert Tint (New York, 1972), 155.

18. Joseph A. Schumpeter, *Business Cycles* (2 vols., New York, 1939), I, 341.

19. *Mémoires de Richelieu*, I, 341.

20. Dupont-Ferrier, for example, cites a text, alleged to be of the fourteenth century, in which Paris is said to be the "common *patrie*, like another Rome." It is perhaps significant, however, that he was unable to locate the original, and relies for its antiquity on the authority of Du Cange's seventeenth-century compilation. See "Le Sens des mots 'Patria' et 'patrie,'" 89–91.

21. Louis Batiffol, *Le Louvre sous Louis XIII et Henri IV* (Paris, 1930), 8–14.

22. *Le Patriotisme*, 39f.

23. Jean Héroard, *Journal de l'enfance et de la première jeunesse de Louis XIII*, Eud. Soulié and Edmond de Barthélemy, eds. (2 vols., Paris, 1868), I, 81. August 29, 1604.

24. "Comment les français regardaient la patrie," 47.

25. *La Plume, la faucille*, 229.

26. G. d'Avenel, *Richelieu et la monarchie*, I, 289.

27. Armand de Richelieu, *Traité qui contient la méthode la plus facile et la plus assurée pour convertir ceux qui se sont séparés de l'église* (Paris, 1651), 1f. While this treatise was published posthumously, and probably largely written by others, internal evidence shows that the preface was written in the 1630s, probably by Richelieu himself.

28. *Lettres*, I, 143. May 17, 1615.

29. See Sigismund Peller, "Births and Deaths among Europe's Ruling Families, 1500–1700," in David V. Glass and D. E. C. Eversley, eds., *Population in History* (London, 1965), 87–100; Davis Bitton, *French Nobility in Crisis, 1560–1640* (Stanford, 1969), 6–43; Claude Lévy and Louis Henry, "Ducs et pairs sous l'ancien régime," *Population*, XVI (1960), 807–830.

30. And to women as well. Saint Chantal learned administrative skills on her husband's estate, first during his absence at war and later as a widow; the comtesse de Soissons became skilled in politics as the agent of her warring husband and then as the widowed custodian of her son's interests. She had to be included in the Conference of Loudun.

31. "Responce au libelle intitulé très-humble et très-véritable et très-importante remonstrance au roy" (1631 anonymous pamphlet), in *Recueil de diverses pièces pour servir à l'histoire* (n.p., 1639), 581.

32. Gabriel Du Grès, *Jean Armand Du Plessis, Duke of Richelieu and Peere of France* (London, 1643), 54.

33. *Lustra Ludovici*, 164.

34. Henri d'Orléans, Duc d'Aumale, *Histoire des Princes de Condé* (8 vols., Paris, 1863–1896), III, 49.

35. Cf. G. d'Avenel: "A society that makes such a cult of physical virtues is liable to see excesses. . . . Brute force is imposed and reigns." *Richelieu et la monarchie*, I, 315; 313.

36. Thus the voluntary abstinence of affluent persons from meat was, in that age of chronic scarcity and short life, thought by Richelieu's propagandists to be a virtue in his brother worth mentioning in a political pamphlet. See below, Chapter VII, Section 5.

37. Alain Couprie has discussed efforts of certain clerical writers during Louis XIII's reign to restrain masculine courtly license. See "'Courtisanisme' et christianisme au XVIIe siècle," *Le Dix-septième siècle*, XXXIII (1981), 371–391.

38. On hyper-aggressivity as an effect of segregated all-male societies see John W. M. Whiting and Beatrice B. Whiting, "Aloofness and Intimacy of Husbands and Wives: A Cross-Cultural Study," in Theodore Schwartz, ed., *Socialization as Cultural Communication* (Berkeley, 1976), 91–115.

39. Jeanne de Frémyot, Louise de Marillac, Charlotte de Gondi, and several others of these partners form a group whose social history has not been written. I have discussed some dimensions of their role that such a study might consider in "The *'Honnête Femme'*: French Salons and Women's Changing Role in Seventeenth-Century France," *Comment* (Claremont, CA and Cambridge, Mass.), VII (1973), 1–3.

40. *Lettres*, X, 215f.; 226. Between 1619 and 1622.

41. On this relationship see Gustave Fagniez, *Le Père Joseph et le cardinal de Richelieu* (2 vols., Paris, 1894), I, 58f.; Louis Dedouvres, *Le Père Joseph de Paris* (2 vols., Paris 1931), 101 *et seq.* A striking passage from his *Introduction à la vie spirituelle par une facile méthode d'oraison* (Paris, 1626), 8f., compares his own Capuchin order to Esther and pictures himself as "her son," received in the "chaste bosom" of this "secret queen." Thus has his religion become his mother: "This princess is to my eyes the living image of the religion of Saint Francis."

42. "La Religion du cardinal," in Antoine Adam *et al.*, eds., *Richelieu* (Paris, 1972), 179.

43. *Richelieu*, 235.

44. E. g., "It must be stressed [that] error that might result from an inexact attribution could in no way diminish the *historical value* of the document reproduced." Grillon, *Papiers*, I, 48.

45. "Remarques . . . sur les moeurs," in *Oeuvres de Voltaire*, Beuchot, ed., XLI (1831), 192.

46. This research is summarized in Edmond Esmonin, *Etudes sur la France des XVIIe et XVIIIe siècles* (Paris, 1964), 219–232.

47. Since the analyses of Robert La Vollée and Philippe Lauer, there is no longer room for disputes over identification of the cardinal's handwriting except in very minute specimens. See, by the first, "La Véritable écriture du cardinal de Richelieu et celle de ses principaux secrétaires," and by the second, "L'Ecriture du cardinal de Richelieu révélée par son propre témoignage," *Rapports et notices*, I, *passim*.

48. AAE, France 792, fol. 183 *vo.* The document has been published by Avenel who, however, has read as "*trône*" what seems rather to be "*droict*"—hence transcribing this phrase "dispute her throne." See *Lettres*, II, 187. The original and the *Testament* versions are partially transcribed, with this error, in "Maximes d'état et fragments politiques du cardinal de Richelieu," Gabriel Hanotaux, ed., in *Mélanges historiques* (Paris, 1880), 721 *n.*

49. See Micheline Guiton and J. Aubry, "L'Enfant instable psycho-moteur et la mer," *Revue de Neuropsychiatrie Infantile*, XV (1967), 187.

50. Indeed, the analyst of Richelieu's language notes that he "uses the term *mer océane* much more than *océan*," a more usual contemporary designation of the sea. See Haschke, *Die Sprache Richelieus*, 86.

51. The manuscript is reproduced and transcribed, together with the "*Testament*" version, in the appendix.

52. Armand Baschet, ed., *Mémoire d'Armand Du Plessis de Richelieu, Evêque de Luçon, écrit de sa main, l'année 1607 ou 1610* (Paris, 1880).

53. "Maximes d'état," 716 *n.*

54. *Rapports et Notices*, I, 82–87. Undeterred by evidence, Philippe Erlanger persists in recommending the Baschet version, as Richelieu's work, to his readers. See *Richelieu: L'Ambitieux* (Paris, 1967), 63 *n.*

55. *Risk, Uncertainty and Profit*, 270. Cf. Descartes: "One is obliged to take risks and put oneself in the power of chance." Quoted by Noël, in André, ed., *Testament politique*, 23.

56. Schumpeter, *Theory of Economic Development*, 88.

57. Schumpeter, *Capitalism, Socialism and Democracy*, 132.

58. Knight, *Risk, Uncertainty and Profit*, 270.

59. *Magistrats et sorciers en France au XVIIe siècle* (Paris, 1968), 136.

60. "Un monde mental clos: étude sémantique et historique du vocabulaire religieux d'un noble artésien à l'époque de Philippe II," *Tijdschrift voor Geschiednenis*, LXXXVIII (1975), 182.

61. See, for example, the memoirs of one Bourdonné, the very model of a career soldier of the minor nobility. Raised in the court of Louis XIII, he found himself, as a young man, stationed in Holland, where he was unable to tolerate the "confusion" of religious duality. *Pensées d'un gentilhomme* (Paris, 1658), 192.

62. *La Plume, la faucille*, 56. Elisabeth Labrousse confirms this disposition in eloquent observations on the origins of Bayle's preference for absolutism and his apology for Richelieu. See *Pierre Bayle* (2 vols., The Hague, 1963–1964), II, 488.

63. *Richelieu*, 6; 228.

64. Richelieu himself, of course, was far from being innovative in all spheres of his endeavor. On many—even most—levels, his outlook was that of a man of his time. On some, his views were provincial or archaic. This unevenness, too, should be considered in assessing his appeal to others.

65. *Lustra Ludovici*, Preface.

66. *Mémoires de Montchal*, I, 7.

67. See Ranum, *Richelieu and the Councillors*, especially Chapter III.

68. Michaud, *Biographie universelle*, II (Paris, 1855), 390.

69. See Lewis A. Dexter, "Court Politics: Presidential Staff Relations as a Special Case," *Administration and Society*, IX (1977), 244. Of course, the enthusiasm of his loyal followers was based for each one on a different mix of gratifications from serving the master.

70. *Le Tiers état*, 202f.

Chapter 3

1. Pierre L'Anglois de Bel-Esbat, "Foi aus princes de lis: Sonnet à Monsieur de Richelieu sur l'anagramme de son nom François Du Plessis," quoted by Maximin Deloche, *Les Richelieu: Le Père du cardinal* (Paris, 1923), 182.

2. Gabriel Hanotaux, *Histoire du cardinal de Richelieu*, I (2d ed., Paris, 1911), 56f.

3. Muchembled, "Un Monde mental clos," 186–188.

4. Pierre Goubert, *Beauvais et le Beauvaisis de 1600 à 1730* (2 vols., Paris, 1960) I, 211. A demographic overview is given by the same author's *The Ancien Régime*, trans. by Steve Cox (New York, 1973), 168–179. A similar perspective on England is Peter Laslett, *The World We Have Lost* (London, 1971), Chapter I.

5. Guillaume and Michel Le Riche, *Journal* (Saint-Maixent, 1846), 338; 482. See also Aimé Martineau, *Le Cardinal de Richelieu* (1st ed., Poitiers, 1866), 77.

6. There are, however, signs of such service in the history of Suzanne de La Porte's *mother's* family, which came from Picardy. This is discussed below, Chapter IV, Section 1.

7. According to most accounts, the "stroke of luck" that brought this desirable estate into the family was owed to the fortunate marriage of one of Richelieu's ancestors to the sister of Louis Clérembault, its possessor, who bequeathed it to his nephew, the cardinal's great grandfather. See Hanotaux, *Histoire du cardinal*, I, 22f.; Aimé de Martineau, *Le Cardinal de Richelieu* (2d ed., Paris, 1870), 55f.

8. André Du Chesne, *Histoire généalogique de la maison royale de Dreux et de quelques autres familles* (Paris, 1631), 73–85. Du Chesne's royal favor closely followed Richelieu's own reentry into power in April, 1624. On December 4, 1625, a gift of 1200 *livres* was paid by the king to André Du Chesne in recognition of the "works he has produced concerning the rights of the

crown of France." Bibliothéque Nationale, Département des Manuscrits (hereafter, BN), Fichier Charavay.

9. Pierre Du Puy, "Mémoires . . . pour servir à justifier l'innocence de Messire F.-A. de Thou," in Jacques-Auguste de Thou, *Histoire universelle*, XV (London, 1735), 50.

10. A note on this manuscript reads "communicated by M. Du Bouchet, 1654." BN, Cabinet d'Hozier 271, dossier 7332, fols. 1–2 *vo*. It is followed, in the same collection, by a similar account, also dated 1654, but said to be by "M. de L. C. E. P." (Fol. 3 *vo*.) Jean Du Bouchet (1599–1684), a favored courtier and "extremely laborious" genealogist of high repute, according to Jacques Lelong, was of Poitevin origins and a relative of François de Richelieu's successor as Grand Provost. *Bibliothèque françoise*, II (Paris, 1768), 637. A letter from Du Bouchet to Du Chesne, a sometime collaborator, announces the intention to dedicate to Richelieu a work he is preparing on the first duc de Montpensier "because of several encounters in which one of his predecessors took part." BN, Du Chesne 30, fol. 195. January 14, 1618 (?). The Montpensiers had been patrons of the Richelieus; Du Bouchet could have uncovered some of the information in the Hozier manuscript in the course of his inquiry into that princely family. Du Bouchet's work on the Montpensiers appeared only as his edition of Nicolas de Coustureau, *La Vie de Louis de Bourbon . . . 1er duc de Montpensier* (Rouen, 1642), which makes no mention of the Richelieus except in its dedication to the cardinal.

Yet another unflattering genealogy, containing some of the assertions attributed to Du Bouchet, was implausibly alleged to be the work of André Du Chesne himself. It is discussed in Hanotaux, *Histoire du Cardinal*, I, 19 *n.*, and in Martineau, *Le Cardinal de Richelieu* (2d ed.), Appendix. This may be the "MS original, 22pp. in 4," described as an "interesting document" in BN, Fichier Charavay. These versions, seemingly, can be traced no farther back than the eighteenth century.

11. This summary discussion draws liberally on Roland Mousnier, "Les Survivances médiévales dans la France du XVIIe siècle," *Le Dix-septième Siècle*, CVI-CVII (1975), 59–79.

12. One basis for claiming such a link was the marriage of François Du Plessis, III, Richelieu's great-grandfather, with Anne Leroy, daughter of Guyon Le Roy, allegedly the descendant of Capetian royal forebears, but certainly Vice-admiral of France under King François I and founder of the port of Le Havre. What is not established, seemingly, is that Anne, who was the second wife of François Du Plessis, III, was the mother of his eldest son, Louis Du Plessis, Richelieu's grandfather. See Martineau, *Le Cardinal* (2d ed.), 52f.; Deloche, *Le Père du cardinal*, 2; Hanotaux, *Histoire du cardinal*, I, 22f.

13. BN, Cabinet d'Hozier 271, dossier 7332, fol. 1. One patron, Anne de Polignac, has been identified as Françoise de Rochechouart's benefactress by other sources. See Hanotaux, *Histoire du cardinal*, 32.

14. She did not die until after 1595. *Ibid.*, 59.

15. Pierre L'Estoile, *Journal pour le règne de Henri III*, I (Paris, 1943), 105.

16. Deloche, *Le Père du cardinal*, 12f.

17. BN, Cabinet d'Hozier 271, dossier 7332, fol. 1. Hanotaux summarizes this episode. See *Histoire du cardinal*, I, 33f.

18. The marriage contract is published by Deloche, *Le Père du cardinal*, Appendix I. When teenagers were married at an early age it was customary to postpone cohabitation. See Gustave Fagniez, *La Femme et la société française dans la première moitié du XVIIe siècle* (Paris, 1921), 61f.

19. Antoine Aubéry, generally accurate on such matters, affirms that François made the Polish expedition. See *L'Histoire du cardinal-duc de Richelieu* (2 vols., Cologne, 1666), I, 6. Another authority reports that François was in attendance on Chémerault, a Poitevin ally, on this trip. See Pierre de Guibours (Père Anselme), *Histoire Généalogique . . . de France* (9 vols., Paris 1726–1733), IV, 237f. Confirmation is also lacking that François accompanied Barnabé Brisson to England in 1580 on a royal mission led by Montpensier to secure Elizabeth's hand for the duc d'Alençon, as asserted by the account attributed to Du Bouchet. See BN, Cabinet d'Hozier 271, 7332, fol. 2 *vo*. See also Hanotaux, *Histoire du cardinal*, I, 36 *n*.

20. Deloche, *Le Père du cardinal*, 49f.; 23–25. Alphonse Chéruel, *Dictionnaire historique des institutions de la France* (2 vols., Paris 1874), I, 504f.

21. Eugène Griselle, *Supplément à la maison du roi Louis XIII* (Paris, 1912), 15f.

22. Deloche, *Le Père du cardinal*, 51–66.

23. Hanotaux, *Histoire du cardinal*, I, 36 *n*.

24. Deloche, *Le Père du cardinal*, 204.

25. L'Estoile, *Journal de Henri III*, I, 581.

26. Deloche, *Le Père du cardinal*, 213f., citing *Scaligeriana* (The Hague, 1669), 111.

27. L'Estoile, *Journal de Henri III*, I, 580–582. Jean Héroard, who had been a court physician at the time, later diligently collected information from witnesses of the assassinations. He relates that many of Henri's retinue volunteered for the murder assignments and he identifies those who actually carried them out. Richelieu is not among these. See BN, fr. 16806, fols. 88–89. This account is based only partly on the testimony of François Miron, Henri III's doctor and sometime confidant. It has been published, with some elisions, by Antoine Aubéry who, however, attributes the whole relation to Miron alone. See *L'Histoire des cardinaux françois* (Paris, 1644), 550. The correct attribution has historical significance which will be discussed elsewhere.

28. Deloche, *Le père du cardinal*, 258–263. The reporter was an enemy of the king and therefore possibly interested in showing him to have demanded actions so heinous that even the terrible "Tristan" turned him down. Le Gast, who actually did the job, also had a possible interest in reporting that others had refused the king.

29. BN, fr. 16806, fols. 89–90.

30. Georges Picot, *Histoire des Etats Généraux* (4 vols., Paris, 1872), III, 139f.

31. Deloche, *Le Père du cardinal*, 279.

32. Richelieu's official salary was about 3,000 *écus*, according to *ibid.*, 77. Part of the grant may have been supposed to defray the cost of acquiring the captaincy, and therefore could have been rather theoretical. Normally, a high officer, on leaving one such job for another, would claim succession to the first for a son. As will be seen, however, François completely lacked the funds that would have been needed to secure this right. Henri IV's gift may, on the other hand, have been in settlement for one of the many reckless promissory notes issued by Henri III. A "truly royal" grant of 118,000 *écus* had been made by that king to François in 1585, on the occasion of the baptism of his youngest son, Armand. There is no evidence that such a sum was ever actually put in the hands of the provost. See *ibid.*, 230–240.

33. BN, Fichier Charavay. "From the Camp de Rozay en Brie." (Misdated 1690.)

34. Griselle, *Formulaires de lettres et Etat de la France*, 233–235.

35. L'Estoile, *Journal de Henri III*, I, 595. December 1588.

36. Deloche, *Le Père du cardinal*, 198f.; Griselle, *Formulaires de lettres et Etat de la France*, 235f.

37. Nicolas de Beauvais-Nangis, *Mémoires* (Paris, 1862), 198f.

38. Deloche, *Le Père du cardinal*, 198f.

39. Archives de la Famille Richelieu, XIV, fol. 1. The last paragraph of this letter is published in Louis Lacroix, *Richelieu à Luçon* (2d ed., Paris, 1911), 17 *n*.

40. Quoted from BN, fr. 3407, fol. 73, by Deloche, *Le Père du cardinal*, 256f. September 16, 1588.

41. Quoted by L'Estoile, *Journal de Henri III*, I, 535.

42. Quoted by Deloche, *Le Père du cardinal*, 105.

43. See the preceding section.

44. See Gaston Zeller, "Une Notion de caractère historico-social: la dérogeance," in *Aspects de la politique française sous l'ancien régime* (Paris, 1964), 336–374.

45. Antoine Du Plessis died in 1576; Jacques Du Plessis in 1592.

46. BN, Cabinet d'Hozier 271, dossier 7332, fol. 2 *vo*.

47. François de Paule de Clermont de Montglat, *Mémoires*, Michaud and Poujoulat, eds. (Paris, 1881), 10.

48. Deloche concludes they had vanished by 1578. See *Le Père du cardinal*, 90; 127; 171.

49. *E.g.*, Hanotaux, *Histoire du cardinal*, I, 51.

50. Deloche, *Le Père du cardinal*, 186f.

51. *Ibid.*, 285f.

52. Tallemant Des Réaux, *Les Historiettes*, Monmerqué and Paris, eds. (6 vols., 3d ed., Paris, 1862), I, 371.

53. Jean Le Laboureur, *"Additions"* to Michel de Castelnau, *Mémoires*, II (Paris, 1659), 297.

54. After Henri de Richelieu's death in 1619 a disgruntled family factotum, one Adhumeau, was able to organize a number of François's creditors in a lawsuit against Armand. The final ruling in the latter's favor came on December 18, 1624. The cardinal had become Louis XIII's prime minister the previous April. For details of the lawsuit see Deloche, *Le Père du cardinal*, 300–319. The Adhumeaux had been involved in Richelieu financial affairs at least since the 1570s, according to the "Du Bouchet" account, Cabinet d'Hozier 271, Dossier 7332, fol. 2 *vo*.

55. *Ibid.*

56. *Le Père du cardinal*, 104.

57. *Ibid.*, 274. I have been unable to find the source for this report.

58. An exception is the purchase on credit of the Richelieu Paris house (later either sold or forfeited through foreclosure). See *ibid.*, 110–124, and also Maximin Deloche, *La Maison natale du cardinal de Richelieu* (Poitiers, 1932), 55.

59. *Le Père du cardinal*, 104.

60. BN, Cabinet d'Hozier 271, dossier 7332, fol. 2 *vo*. The word used is *gagné*, which may mean either won or earned. The context suggests the first meaning.

61. Le Laboureur, "Additions à Castelnau," 297.

62. Saint François de Sales, *Introduction à la vie dévote* (Paris, 1934; 1st ed. 1608), 60f.

Chapter 4

1. Hanotaux, *Histoire du cardinal*, I, 45.

2. See above, Chapter II, Section 4, and Chapter V, Section 3, note. Also, *Le Père du cardinal*, 9.

3. Du Chesne, *Histoire de la maison royale*, 73.

4. Hanotaux, *Histoire du cardinal*, I, 44. The simile was suggested by the poem, quoted by Deloche and cited above (at the head of Chapter III), that was apparently written by a retainer of François de Richelieu. See *Le Père du cardinal*, 184.

5. Lacroix, *Richelieu à Luçon*, 17.

6. Jean-F. Du Radier, *Bibliothèque du Poitou*, II (Paris, 1754), 483.

7. The relative unimportance of quarterings in late-Renaissance France is a central theme of George Huppert, *Les Bourgeois gentilshommes* (Chicago, 1977), 14 and *passim*.

8. Hanotaux, *Histoire du cardinal*, I, 41 *n*.

9. *Historiettes*, II, 62.

10. Guillaume and Michel Le Riche, *Journal* (Saint Maixent, 1846), 338; 482.

11. Bibliothèque Municipale de Poitiers, Collection Dom Fontenau, XXXII. "Mémoires historiques dressés par Mr. Bourgeois, Avocat au Siège Présidial de Poitiers," 258.

12. See Catherine Holmès, *L'Eloquence judiciaire de 1620 à 1660* (Paris, 1967), 15f.

13. La Porte's second wife was a first cousin of his first wife, reinforcing the connection with the Bochard family. Deloche, *Le Père du cardinal*, 10; 185.

14. Dreux Du Radier, *Bibliothèque*, II, 483–486.

15. Chéruel, *Dictionnaire historique*, II, 899f.

16. Dreux Du Radier, *Bibliothèque*, II, 485f.

17. BN, Cabinet d'Hozier 271, Dossier 7332, fol. 2 *vo*; 3.

18. One of her nephews eventually became a high legal officer under Louis XIII and Richelieu. See Henry de Calais, *Histoire de la vie du R. P. Honoré Bochart de Champigny* (Paris, 1864), 3.

19. While "Monsieur de La Meilleraye" is listed as a commander of the Order in December, 1584, François de Richelieu was not inducted into it until January 1, 1585. Griselle, *Supplément*, 58; Antoine Aubéry, *Mémoires pour l'histoire du cardinal duc de Richelieu* (5 vols., Cologne, 1667), I, 5.

20. *Lettres missives du roi Henri IV*, Berger de Xivrey and J. Guadet, eds. (8 vols., Paris, 1850–1873), V, 170f. October 6, 1599.

21. Dreux Du Radier, *Bibliothèque*, II, 483f.

22. *Lettres*, I, 181f. N.d. (Suzanne died on November 14, 1616)

23. BN, Fichier Charavay, n.d.

24. Quoted by Fagniez, *La Femme*, 321.

25. Archives de la Famille, XIV, fol. 22.

26. BN, fr. 23200, fol. 98.

27. AAE, France 768, fol. 169. February 14, 1611.

28. See *Lettres*, I, especially 123; 642. This lady's identity is as yet unsettled. Hanotaux supposes her husband to be a member of a family of Paris doctors. See *Histoire du cardinal*, I, 92 *n*. She herself seems to have a legal family background as is indicated by Richelieu's plea to her to intervene in a court process on his behalf. See below, Chapter X, Section 6. A "Marie de Burges (ou Bourges)" was installed in 1637 by Richelieu as Abbess of Val de Grâce to replace a politically unreliable friend of Anne of Austria. See Paul M. Bondois, "Les Documents de la cassette de Richelieu," *Bibliothèque de l'Ecole des Chartes*, LXXXIII (1922), 111–165.

29. BN, Cabinet d'Hozier 271, dossier 7332, fol. 7 and 7 *vo*. December 2, 1602. A version of this letter has been published, omitting the postscript, by Deloche, *Le Père du cardinal*, 293f.

30. Born about 1580, Henri could not have married until after sometime in January, 1610, the month in which Marguerite became a widow. It is not likely that they married before 1611, and impossible that it was as late as 1616, the year suggested by Eugène Griselle, *Louis XIII et Richelieu* (Paris, 1911), 209. Family letters show that they were already man and wife at the incursions of Condé's troops in 1615. See Archives de la Famille, XVIII, and below, Section 3.

31. Archives de la Famille, XIV, fol. 20

32. Quoted from BN, fr. 22398, fols. 15; 16, by Deloche, *Le Père du cardinal*, 348.

33. This remark seems explicable only if Marguerite had been pregnant before. Archives de la Famille, XIV, fol. 20.

34. *Ibid.* I have discussed this generation-independent exchangeability of roles in "Nature versus Nurture: Trends and Patterns in Seventeenth-century French Child Rearing," in *The History of Childhood*, Lloyd Demause, ed. (New York, 1974), 288.

35. Charles de La Porte, her half-brother, was a Calvinist and raised his children as such. See below, Chapter VIII, Section III, note to "Playing."

36. Muchembled, "Un Monde mental clos," 186f.

37. Archives de la Famille, XIV, fol. 15.

38. Quoted by Lacroix, *Richelieu à Luçon*, 155.

39. Archives de la Famille, XIV, fol. 15.

40. *Ibid.*, fol. 21.

41. *Ibid.*

42. See above, Chapter III, Section 3.

43. Archives de la Famille, XIV, fol. 18 *vo*.

44. *Ibid.*, fol. 12.

45. P. Anselme, *Histoire généalogique*, IV, "La Porte."

46. Archives de la Famille, XIV, fol. 15.

47. *Ibid.*, fols. 12; 13.

48. *Ibid.*, fol. 27 *vo*.

49. *Ibid.*

50. *Ibid.*, fol. 23.

51. *Ibid.*, fol. 23 *vo.*

52. *Ibid.*

53. *Ibid.*, fol. 25.

54. *Ibid.*, fol. 23 and 23 *vo.*

55. *Ibid.*, fol. 25.

56. *Ibid.*, fols. 25; 24.

57. *Ibid.*, fol. 27. (End of 1611.)

58. Quoted by Lacroix, *Richelieu à Luçon,* 154.

59. Archives de la Famille, XIV, fols. 14; 12.

60. *Ibid.*, fol. 13.

61. Quoted by Hanotaux, *Histoire du cardinal,* I, 44 *n.*

62. Archives de la Famille, XIV, fol. 12 and 12 *vo.* November 5 (1615). Condé had crossed the Loire on October 30, according to Aumale, *Histoire des princes de Condé,* III, 55.

63. Archives de la Famille, XIV, fol. 18.

64. *Ibid.*

65. On Henri's irritation with the commander, Boisdauphin, who decided not to pursue Condé's men after the crossing, see his letter to Du Perron in *Lettres,* I, 153f. (End of November, 1615[?])

66. Archives de la Famille, XIV, fol. 21. January 23, 1616.

67. *Histoire du cardinal,* I, 44.

68. BN, fr. 23200, fol. 185.

69. Archives de la Famille, XIV, fols. 12; 20.

70. Bibliothèque de Poitiers, Collection Martineau, fols. 120; 121. A copy is in BN, fr. 23201, fol. 200 *vo.* In both versions the last phrase reads, *"qu'elle portoit aux siens."* David Hunt, apparently misreading the last word as *seins,* interpreted the words as evidence that Suzanne personally nursed her children. See *Parents and Children in History* (New York, 1970), 106.

71. Marvick, "Nature versus Nurture," 288f.

72. BN, Fichier Charavay. (Beginning of 1612.) Her response, describing his offer, is in Archives de la Famille, XIV, fol. 28.

73. Poitiers, Collection Martineau, fol. 121.

Chapter 5

1. Sigmund Freud, "From the History of an Infantile Neurosis," *Collected Papers,* Joan Riviére and Alix and John Strachey, trans., (5 vols., London, 1949–1950), III, 603.

2. The most detailed account of these early arrangements is in Hanotaux, *Histoire du cardinal,* I, 67f. The prior of this same abbey was, according to Alfred Bonneau-Avenant, the tutor of Richelieu's favorite niece, the future duchesse d'Aiguillon. This would have been in 1610 or later. If it was still the same incumbent, it would indicate considerable respect of the uncle for his former teacher. See *La Duchesse d'Aiguillon* (Paris, 1879), 25.

3. Le Laboureur, "Additions à Castelnau," 297. Of certain ladies of Poitou related to Magdelaine de Chémerault, a friend and ally of Richelieu also renowned for her learning, a contemporary wrote, "What was admirable was that Catherine Des Roches had no other tutor than her learned mother." Poitiers, Dom Fontenau XXXII, fol. 243.

4. Michel Pure, *Vita Eminentissimi Cardinalis Arm. Joan. Plessei Richelii* (Paris, 1656), 8f.

5. The facts summarized here are recounted in Maximin Deloche, *Un Frère de Richelieu inconnu* (Paris, 1935), 24–26. Following Michel Pure's biographies of both brothers, Deloche draws attention to this original destination of Armand for the career he eventually took up. Hanotaux was unaware of this fact, as have been most other biographers who have followed him.

6. One might expect that, with Alphonse intended for the clergy, Armand, who was well liked by Amador and fascinated by naval affairs, might have succeeded his brother as a prospective chevalier of Malta. Why this did not happen, if indeed it did not, is unexplained.

Such an outcome may, in fact, have been contemplated as a possible outcome of Richelieu's military training. Aubéry, who knew the family well, points out that Armand's title of Marquis Du Chillou, "which he assumed, together with the sword," at the commencement of his academic training, was one descending from Guyon Le Roy, Vice-Admiral of France, and father of his supposed paternal great grandmother. See *L'Histoire du cardinal*, I, 11.

7. Deloche, *Frère inconnu*, 419.

8. Rémy Du Ferron, *Vita Card. Richelii* (Orléans, 1626), 3. This was, however, a work violently inimical to Richelieu, and much of it is manifestly false. Pure's description, discussed below, Chapter VII, Section 5, is far more plausible.

9. *Instruction du chrestien*, 238 n.

10. *Ibid.*, 232 n.

11. *Lettres*, I, 708. April 8, 1622.

12. Antoine Péricaud, *Notes et documents pour servir à l'histoire de Lyon sous le règne de Louis XIII* (Lyons, 1846), 258.

13. Alphonse de Richelieu, "Lettres écrites . . . pendant son ambassade . . . à . . . Rome," *Le Conservateur* (May, 1757), 25f. July 5; May 7, 1635.

14. Lacroix, *Richelieu à Luçon*, 40–45.

15. *Lettres*, VII, 421. April, 1618 (?).

16. The pope granted dispensation from the age requirement, but to a Richelieu who represented himself as twenty-three, two years more than his actual age. Since there were other cases of twenty-one-year old bishops in France, this would seem to have been unnecessary. Apparently Armand's name had simply been substituted for that of Alphonse on the petition—an interesting case of substitutability of roles within a family. For the facts of the case see Lacroix, *Richelieu à Luçon*, 52–62.

17. Pierre Blet, "La Religion du cardinal," in Adam *et al.*, *Richelieu*, 166. See also O. Lanfranc de Panthou, *Richelieu et la direction des âmes* (Evreux, 1896), *passim*.

18. Maximin Deloche, *Autour de la plume de Richelieu*, 35.

19. Adolphe Péricaud, *Le Cardinal de Richelieu: évêque, théologien et protecteur des lettres* (Paris, 1882), 22.

20. Dreux Du Radier, *Bibliothèque*, III, 360.

21. See Ranum, *Richelieu and the Councillors*, 51. On family connections see Suzanne's reference, above, Chapter IV, Section 3, and the familiar letters of L'Aubespine to his former pupil in AAE, France 768, fol. 232, 232 vo, and 212 vo.

22. See Jacques Davy, Cardinal Du Perron, *Les Ambassades et négociations du cardinal Du Perron* (Paris, 1633), 892; Philippe Tamizey de Larroque, ed., *Lettres de Peiresc* (7 vols., 1888–1898), I, 131.

23. Philippe Tamizey de Larroque, ed., *Les Correspondants de Peiresc: Gabriel de L'Aubespine* (Orléans, 1883), 28.

24. AAE France 768, fol. 232. October 28, 1612.

25. *Instruction du chrestien*, 139.

26. Armand de Richelieu, *Traitté qui contient la méthode la plus facile et la plus assurée pour convertir ceux qui se sont séparés de l'église* (Paris, 1651), 409.

27. Jean-Claude Dhotel, *Les Origines du catéchisme moderne* (Aubier, 1967), 193.

28. *Lettres*, I, xcix. 1621 (?).

29. *Richelieu à Luçon*, 169.

30. "Ordonnances synodales," in Jacques de Flavigny, *Briefve et facile instruction pour les confesseurs* (Fontenay, 1613), 30f.

31. *Instruction du chrestien*, 286f.; 419.

32. *Lettres*, I, 94f. November 30 (?), 1612.

33. *Catéchisme du Concile de Trente*, P. Gagey, ed., (2 vols., Paris, 1911), II, 378.

34. *Instruction du chrestien*, 356; 350. Emphasis supplied.

35. Michel de Marolles, *Mémoires* (3 vols., Amsterdam, 1755), I, 236; 238.

36. *Maximes d'état*, 822.

37. Cf. Delavaud: "It is a trait of his character, noticed from his youth and which persisted—this habit of a mutual exchange of services." "Quelques collaborateurs," 163.

38. *Lettres*, I, 123; 28; 89. April, 1614; September, 1609; September 18, 1612.

39. "Testament de son emmentissime Armand-Jean Du Plessis de Richelieu," in *Mémoires du cardinal de Richelieu*, Petitot, ed., 2d series, X (Paris, 1821), 822.

40. *Lettres*, I, 68. July, 1611.

41. Arsenal, MS 4651, Claude Courtin, "Mémoires inédites," fol. 274 *vo*. The tears may indicate a certain amount of satisfaction as well. On reasons for such satisfaction see the discussion below, Chapter V, Section 3, of the *grands*. For the tears, see Chapter VIII, Section 2, "Symptoms." The "sighs," however, as well as Courtin's judgment and the circumstances, suggest a strong conflict, arising out of a felt obligation.

42. *Lettres*, I, 19. (December, 1608?)

43. *Ibid.*, 15. December 21, 1608.

44. He asks the officers of the church for "amnesty," acknowledging that "there are some in the company who were strongly opposed to me, even after the time when it pleased God to make me your leader." *Lettres*, I, 14. December 21, 1608.

45. *Ibid.*, 28; 25. September; April, 1609.

46. Such action by a bishop was not uncommon: Du Perron had done the same for the people of his diocese. See *ibid.*, 20 *n*. Alphonse de Richelieu was later to entreat ministers in his brother's own government for such remissions for the Lyonnais of his diocese. Richelieu then showed sympathy for his elder brother's position, advising his deputy not to try to enlist the Archbishop's cooperation "in the matter of Lyons, for he cannot without great heartache press those whom loves as his flock (*ouailles*)." See Antoine Péricaud, ed., "Deux lettres d'Alphonse de Richelieu," *Bulletin de la Commission Historique de Lyons* (1909), 269–271; *Lettres*, VI, 759. July–August, 1638.

47. *Ibid.* 115f. 1613 (?).

48. Quoted in *Histoire du cardinal*, I, 109.

49. *Le Tiers état*, 204.

50. See above, Chapter III, Section 2.

51. Le Riche, *Journal*, 281 *n*. Entry for January, 1577.

52. *Lettres missives*, III, 118.

53. The best direct evidence for this is Deloche's finding that, in the marriage contract drawn up for François and Suzanne by their parents, no mention is made of François de La Porte's high official status and functions, but only to his *seigneuries* in the region, an omission that suggests contempt for the *robe*. He interprets this as a sign of Françoise's shame at the alliance. *Le Père du cardinal*, 11.

54. Baron de Chappes was Prévôt de Paris, who had "the first rank in Paris after the sovereign" according to Chéruel, *Dictionnaire*, 1016.

55. Institut, Godefroy 268, fol. 282. The letter, misdated 1620, must be from before Suzanne's death in November, 1616.

56. Poitiers, Dom Fontenau XXXII, fol. 258.

57. See above, Chapter IV, Section 3.

58. *Lettres*, I, 127. 1615.

59. *Ibid.*, VII, 319. February, 1616.

60. Institut, Godefroy 269, fol. 205 *vo*. May 26, 1624. Published by Lacroix, *Richelieu à Luçon*, 180f.

61. See below, Chapter X, Section 2.

62. See Bertrand Zeller, *Marie de Médicis et Sully* (Paris, 1892), 224.

63. Quoted by Victor Cousin, *Madame de Chevreuse* (Paris, 1856), 239. February, 1633.

64. His own family had been guilty of this practice where the bishopric of Luçon was concerned. It may be that his reforming zeal in such matters had the additional motive of making amends for this dereliction.

65. *Lettres*, I, 29f. 1609 (?).

66. See below, Chapter X, Section 2.

67. AAE, France 769, fols. 181 *vo*–182 *vo*.

68. Henri Jadart, *Louis XIII et Richelieu à Reims* (Rheims, 1885), 17.

69. One may wonder whether it was not Suzanne's affection for this close relation which led to the choice of a name for her youngest son (and therefore perhaps also to the selection of one of his two godfathers, Armand Gontauld de Biron, Maréchal de France). Armand is, except for one letter, an anagram of Amador. Thus, possibly unconsciously, was the La Porte side of the family represented. Françoise de Rochechouart was the single godmother; Jean d'Aumont, another maréchal, the other godfather. See Auguste Jal, *Dictionnaire critique de biographie et d'histoire* (Paris, 1872), 1060. Richelieu later occasionally took for himself, in his correspondence, the code name of "Amadeau." See *Lettres*, III, 612. March (?), 1630.

70. Letters from Françoise before her marriage to Pont Courlay habitually mention, "my uncle, the commander." See BN, fr. 23201, fols. 143; 149; 150. On October 6, 1599 we find Amador assisting Henri de Richelieu in a legal action against François de Richelieu's successor as Grand Provost. See *Lettres missives*, V, 171.

71. Le Laboureur, *Additions à Castelnau*, II, 297. It is added in the same place that Richelieu was reported by his uncle to have shown little gratitude, an error Tallemant cannot refrain from repeating (see note following), although evidence on this point is entirely to the contrary.

72. It is significant, as will be seen later, that the particular instance of personal virtue cited by Tallemant is one in which the commander renounced an opportunity for professional advancement out of consideration for another's seniority. See Tallemant, *Historiettes*, II, 60; 61 *n*.

73. *Lettres*, I, 682; IV, 15; I, 629; VI, 467. July 1621; November 12, 1639; September 1619; August 10, 1639.

74. This was probably Claude Barbin.

75. AAE, France 771, fols. 35–36. February 15, 1617.

76. Richelieu's relations with his mother's other half brother seem also to have been cordial. See his considerate letter, written during his first ministry, to the Protestant Charles de La Meilleraye. BN, n.a. 5131, fol. 13; 13 *vo*. April 9, 1617.

77. They were characterized in this way by Roland Mousnier at a session of the Colloque sur le Sacre des Rois, Rheims, October, 1975.

78. *E. g.*, "It is permissible for any prelate . . . to remonstrate with him and censure him and . . . the king . . . would not dare . . . harm the men who do this." Seyssel, *The Monarchy of France*, 52f.

79. See below, Chapter XI, Section 3.

80. AAE, France 770, fol. 7. January 22, 1615. He reiterated this claim in a memorandum Grillon believes may date to 1622, shortly after he had himself received the cardinal's bonnet. See *Papiers*, I, 85 *n*.

81. In a fictionalized representation of Richelieu, one of his collaborators depicts him as "envied by all the *grands*." The author may have been aware that Richelieu took satisfaction in this. See Jean Desmarets de Saint Sorlin, *Les Délices de l'esprit* (2d ed., Paris, 1661), 104f.

82. In a remarkable letter to the king Richelieu expresses outrage that "upstart"—literally "*champignons*" or "mushroom"—dukes (including in this Montbazon whose dukedom dated from 1588) should claim parity with the duke of Parma, a royal prince, and suggests that Louis should humiliate them. Were he himself "only a duke, and not cardinal," he writes, he would not be as presumptuous. *Lettres*, VII, 748. February 22, 1636.

Chapter 6

1. Richelieu, "Testament," Petitot ed., 140.

2. "Caput Apologeticum," *Lettres*, VII, 421. April, 1618 (?).

3. Lacroix, *Richelieu à Luçon*, 180. May 26, 1624.

4. "Additions à Castelnau," 297.

5. Archives de la Famille, XIV, fol. 13.

6. British Library (BL), additional MS 22052, fol. 41. August 17, 1616.

7. *Lettres*, VII, 464. July, 1619.

8. AAE, France 771, fols. 35–36. February 15, 1617.

9. He was, however, capable of giving such advice to *others—e.g.*, to the chapter of Luçon. See *Lettres*, VII, 425. February 8, 1619.

10. AAE, France 768, fol. 169; 169 *vo*. February 14, 1611.

11. *Journal de l'enfance de Louis XIII*, I, 391. April 16, 1609.

12. An example of all these is his letter praising Leonora Concini's courageous death, written at a time when expression of such appreciation entailed personal risk. See AAE, France 771, fol. 155. July 12, 1617.

13. BN, fr. 23201, fol. 211 *vo*. December 9, 1618.

14. *Le Palais d'honneur*, 539.

15. See above, Chapter IV, Section 2.

16. Henri himself had an *alter ego*—a lute-playing companion at court, a Poitevin neighbor, and after 1603 the second husband of his sister Françoise—René de Pont Courlay. This man accompanied the two brothers into exile in Avignon. He died on March 16, 1624, just before Richelieu's last prime ministry began. Ultimately, by terms of the cardinal's will, Pont Courlay's grandson became heir to the Richelieu estate and to the cardinal's title of duc de Richelieu. See Bonneau-Avenant, *La Duchesse d'Aiguillon*, 109.

17. This and another lawsuit dating from before Aunt Marconnay's death figure in documents reproduced by Martineau, *Le Cardinal* (1st ed.), 378–385.

18. Letters to Marguerite expressing amity survive from Alphonse, Armand, Suzanne, Nicole, and Françoise, and from Sébastien Bouthillier, the close family friend.

19. See above, Chapter IV, Section 2.

20. AAE, France 768, fol. 169 and 169 *vo*.

21. Martineau, *Le Cardinal* (2d ed.), 658.

22. Archives de Maine et Loire, IIB, vols. 384–385.

23. See above, Chapter IV, Section 3.

24. See below, Chapter X, Sections 1–4.

25. See Hanotaux, *Histoire du cardinal*, II, 263; Griselle, *Louis XIII et Richelieu*, 200–209.

26. BN, fr. 23200, fol. 104 *vo*.

27. Hanotaux, *Histoire du cardinal*, I, 61; Griselle, *Louis XIII et Richelieu*, 209f.

28. *Richelieu et la monarchie*, I, 312.

29. See Suzanne's letters, quoted above, Chapter IV, Section 3.

30. Quoted from Alphonse Thibaudeau, ed., *Catalogue of the Collection of Alfred Morrison* (13 vols., London, 1883–1897), V, 259f., by Griselle, *Louis XIII et Richelieu*, 215f.

31. Quoted from BN, n.a. 223981, fol. 108, by Deloche, *Le Père du cardinal*, 349f. April 20, 1615.

32. Quoted by Martineau, *Le Cardinal de Richelieu* (1st ed.), 157, from the original in the Bibliothèque de Poitiers, Collection Monmerqué, 1085.

33. The event occurred around June, 1619, but its exact date is unknown. The best account of its circumstances is in François Duval de Fontenay-Mareuil, *Mémoires*, Michaud and Poujoulat, eds. (Paris, 1837), 139.

34. *Lettres*, I, 603f.

35. *Maximes d'état*, 773. It was not until after he had published these notes that Hanotaux, the editor, realized that they probably referred to Henri. See *Histoire du cardinal*, II, 299 *n*.

36. *Maximes d'état*, 772. The same simile is further developed as follows: "And, indeed, although the separation of body and mind cannot take place without a great effort of nature, since the tie of an old habit is equal to a natural one, I do not think the effort made in the separation of intimate and faithful friends is less." *Ibid.*, 773.

37. *Lettres*, I, 604. (End of June, 1619.)

38. It was auctioned to satisfy the creditors of François Du Plessis de Richelieu on February 15, 1621. Presumably Armand's purchase price of 75,000 *livres* went to pay off the grand provost's old debts. See Maximin Deloche, *Un Démélé du cardinal de Richelieu avec son suzerain en Poitou* (Poitiers, 1923), 2. (Reprinted from *Bulletin de la Société des Antiquaires de l'Ouest*, 1er trimestre, 1923.)

39. In addition to the lawsuit brought by Adhumeau and others (Chapter III, Section 4, note), Henri had left his wife's property to a religious order's chapter in Avignon (perhaps as an offering for prayers?) in a will which Armand contested successfully. See Deloche, *Le Père du cardinal*, 299; Hanotaux, *Histoire du cardinal*, II, 200.

40. These concerns are discussed below, Chapter IX, Section 2.

41. Ludovic Lalanne, ed., "Un Récit inédit de la mort du cardinal de Richelieu," *Revue Historique*, LV (1894), 5.

42. "Testament," Petitot, ed., 138–140.

43. Maximin Deloche is convinced that it transcribes the cardinal's words directly. See *Autour de la plume du cardinal de Richelieu* (Paris, 1920), 454–456.

44. "Response à un libelle contre les ministres de l'estat," in *Recueil de diverses pieces pour servir à l'histoire* (Paris, 1639), 163.

45. Roland Mousnier, *Les Institutions de la France*, I, 117.

46. See below, Chapter VIII, Section 2, "Anxiety."

47. Maximin Deloche, "Le Cardinal de Richelieu et un de ses voisins en Poitou: un drame à Chauvigny," *Bulletin de la Société des Antiquaires de l'Ouest*, 2e trimestre, 1929.

48. Deloche, "Un Démêlé du cardinal," 1–8.

49. L.-A. Bosseboeuf, *Histoire de Richelieu et de ses environs* (Tours, 1890), 101–132.

50. *Lettres*, VII, 525. April 14, 1623.

51. Deloche, "Un Démêlé du cardinal," 17. June 18, 1623.

52. *Ibid.* May 27, 1623.

53. *Lettres*, VIII, 339f.; VI, 84. August 13; 11, 1638.

54. For an overview of the Bouthilliers' relationship with Richelieu see Ranum, *Richelieu and the Councillors*, 32–36.

55. This was a proceeding against one Dumont whom Richelieu was determined to remove from a church post in his diocese. A far-flung, prolonged campaign was mounted, involving, among others, Richelieu's deputies Bouthillier and Nicolas Orceau, to pursue charges of simony. It can be followed through 1610 and 1611 in AAE, France 767, 173 *vo.*; 211; *ibid.*, 768, fols. 181–184 *vo.*; BL, Additional 22052, fols. 4, 4 *vo.* and 29760, fol. 8. Another case from this period involved a complicated effort to forestall a lawsuit brought by a female plaintiff. AAE, France 768, fol. 175. March 15, 1611.

56. AAE, France 767, fol. 211 and 211 *vo.* June 20, 1610.

57. BN, fr. 23200 fol. 114 *vo.* February 26, 1611.

58. *Lettres*, VII, 458.

59. BN, fr. 23200, fol. 114. February 26, 1611.

60. *Mercure françois*, II (1615), fols. 491 *vo* -493. November 29, 1612.

61. AAE, France 768, fol. 218. September 8, 1612.

62. See Ranum, *Richelieu and the Councillors*, 33 *n.*

63. AAE, France 767, fol. 211 *vo.* June 20, 1610.

64. BN, fr. 23201, fol. 203 *vo.* April 30; June 18, 1618.

65. See below, Chapter X, Section 3.

66. The points of likeness between the two families are noted by Lacroix, as well as the personal parallels between the two sets of brothers: "Père Joseph early lost his father; like him [Richelieu], he saw his family ruined." *Richelieu à Luçon*, 182. It was, however, Père Joseph's father who was the *robin*—from a family of magistrates—and his mother who was the more highly born, with the "temperament and military distinction of the old house of Motier." Gustave Fagniez, *Père Joseph et Richelieu* (2 vols., Paris, 1894), I, 37.

67. Louis Dedouvres, *Le Père Joseph de Paris, Capucin* (2 vols., Paris, 1932), 118–120.

68. *Ibid.*, 124; Fagniez, *Père Joseph et Richelieu*, I, 48; 113f.
69. *Ibid.*, 84f.
70. Michel Houssaye, *Le Père Bérulle et l'Oratoire de Jésus* (611–625) (Paris, 1873), 290.
71. Aldous Huxley, *Grey Eminence* (New York, 1941), 259; Dedouvres, *Le Père Joseph*, I, 364.
72. Auguste Leman, *Richelieu et Olivarès* (Lille, 1938), 20.
73. Fagniez, *Père Joseph et Richelieu*, II. 470f.
74. *Lettres*, VII, 838f. December 21, 1640; January 2, 1641. Alphonse de Richelieu's dislike of Mazarin may reflect an earlier jealousy he felt of the relationship between Armand and Henri. He had for the Italian cardinal the "greatest detestation" (*dernier mépris*), according to his confidant, Pure. See Emile Magne's preface to Michel Pure, *La Pitieuse* (Paris, 1938), *xxiv*.
75. Georges Dethan cites sources for tracing Mazarin's early progress in winning Richelieu's favor in "Mazarin avant le ministère," *Revue Historique* CCXXVII (1962), 33–66.

Chapter 7

1. BN, fr. 24445, fol. 175 *vo*. Funeral remarks of Abra Raconis, Bishop of Vaur.
2. Jacques Lescot, "Preface" to Richelieu, *Traitté pour convertir*. This bishop of Chartres was Richelieu's confessor in his last years.
3. Quoted above, Chapter II, Section 2.
4. Desmarets de Saint-Sorlin *Le Tombeau du grand cardinal de Richelieu* (Paris, 1643), 13.
5. BN, fr. 24445, fols. 187; 176 *vo.*; 192.
6. Desmarets de Saint-Sorlin, *Le Tombeau du cardinal*, 15.
7. Jean de Sirmond, *La Lettre déchiffrée* (Paris, 1627), 32. This compliment gains in significance from the fact that it was probably written under the cardinal's supervision. See Louis Delavaud, *Quelques collaborateurs de Richelieu* (Paris, 1915), 76.
8. P. F. D. G., *Le Miroir royal*, 9f. On this work see below, Chapter X, Section 6, note.
9. Nicolas Coeffeteau, *Réponse au manifeste publié par les perturbateurs du repos de l'estat* (Paris, 1617), cited by Deloche, *Autour de la plume*, 105f.
10. "Ordonnances synodales," especially page 80.
11. "Response à un libelle contre les ministres de l'estat," 165. See above, Chapter VI, Section 2, notes.
12. "Response au libelle intitulé tres-humble, tres-véritable et tres-importante remonstrance au roy," (1632), in *Recueil de diverse pièces*, 583f.
13. See Maximin Deloche, *Le Cardinal de Richelieu et les femmes* (Paris, 1931), 193–198; *Lettres*, I, *xcvii*.
14. Claude Courtin's account is cited fully in Hanotaux, *Histoire du cardinal*, I, 78.
15. Richelieu was baptised at Saint Eustache in Paris on May 5, 1586. The dispute on whether or not he was born in Paris is not of interest here. More significant is the evidence that he considered himself a Parisian (at least when addressing Parisians). This and other facts concerning his birthplace are summarized in Lacroix, *Richelieu à Luçon*, 8f *n.*
16. *Vita A.-J. Richelii*, 4f. Pure's probable informant, Alphonse de Richelieu, died in 1653.
17. Such households were common for the younger sons of warrior-noblemen. A case in point is described by a contemporary of Richelieu, also a cleric, who writes of his parents' thirty-six-year marriage: "If one counted all the time they were together . . . I don't believe it would amount to two whole years; and the longest stay of my father in his house was not more than a month or two. So that from the time I was little up until the age of ten I scarcely knew him except from his portrait. . . . His ambition and his valor did not permit him to stay at home for longer periods and he was not of a disposition, nor rich enough either, to have my mother always along with him." Marolles, *Mémoires*, I, 4f.
18. The Paris house, whose purchase by the grand provost was recorded in 1579, was found in other hands after his death, but the date of its transfer is not known. See Deloche *La Maison natale de Richelieu*, 55.

19. See above, Chapter IV, Section 3. The text quite clearly reads, "Il y a 49 an *[sic]* que je suis en cette maison," although Lacroix transcribes it as "40 ans." *Richelieu à Luçon*, 154.

20. *Histoire du cardinal*, I, 60.

21. Some have supposed that Nicole was born two or three years after Richelieu, but as yet no birthdate has been verified for her. Grillon puts it between 1587 and 1590. See *Papiers*, III, 553. She was married in 1617 and even a birthdate as late as 1590 would have made her a rather old bride, seven years older than her bridegroom, something to which no contemporary refers as far as I have discovered.

22. *Vita A.-J. Richelii*, 8f.

23. "The 'good-enough mother' . . . is one who makes active adaptation to the infant's needs, an active adaptation that gradually lessens, according to the infant's growing ability to account for failure of adaptation and to tolerate the results of frustration. . . . If all goes well the infant can actually come to gain from the experience of frustration, since incomplete adaptation to need makes objects real, that is to say hated as well as loved." Donald W. Winnicott, *Playing and Reality* (New York, 1971), 10f. By suggesting that essential things "went well" with Richelieu, I mean to exclude, in his case, the particular kind of personality and behavior disorders that are the focus of concern, for example, in the work of Heinz Kohut and some of his colleagues. Or, to put it in a more positive, "Kohutian" way, the process of "transmuting internalization" went forward, in Richelieu's case, in an essentially "healthy" manner. (See, by Kohut, "The Psychoanalytic Treatment of Narcissistic Personality Disorders: Outline of a Systematic Approach," *Psychoanalytic Study of the Child*, XXIII (1968), 86–113; and by Kohut and Ernest S. Wolf, "The Disorders of the Self and their Treatment: An Outline," *International Journal of Psychoanalysis*, LIX (1978), 413–425.) The understanding of Richelieu's maturation that is presented here draws on recent studies of child development by such psychoanalytic investigators as Winnicott, René Spitz, Margaret Mahler and her associates, and Selma Fraiberg. For representative inquiries see, by the first, *The Child and the Family* (New York, 1957) and *The Child and the Outside World*; by the second, *The First Year of Life* (New York, 1965); by Mahler, Fred Pine and Anni Bergman, *The Psychological Birth of the Human Infant* (New York, 1975), and by Fraiberg, "Libidinal Object Constancy and Mental Representation," *The Psychoanalytic Study of the Child*, XIV (1968), 9–47.

24. A sensitive discussion of some of the many variables in these early processes is David L. Rubinfine, "Maternal Stimulation, Psychic Structure and Early Object Relations with Special Reference to Aggression and Denial," *Psychoanalytic Study of the Child*, XVII (1962), 265–282.

25. Good wet nurses were supposed to be sexually abstinent. Authorities believed, however, that the mother of the household had overriding obligations to her husband and that the ban on sex while nursing should not apply to her: "It is commanded that man not separate those whom God has joined," writes Laurent Joubert in his widely circulated *Erreurs populaires* (Bordeaux, 1578), 433.

26. Contemporary swaddling practices and their rationales are discussed in my "Nature versus Nurture," 269–271.

27. The possible effect of certain modes of swaddling in reinforcing ocular apprehension and expression has been explored, in a different culture, by John Rickman and Geoffrey Gorer, *The People of Great Russia* (New York, 1950), *passim*.

28. See above, Chapter II, Section 3, and Appendix.

29. *Lettres*, I, 67; 108. July, 1611(?); end of 1612.

30. Quoted from *Traitté pour convertir*, 78f., by Lanfranc de Panthou, *Richelieu et la direction des âmes* 29.

31. The phrase occurs, for example, in *Lettres*, VI, 757; IV, 60. February 1641; December, 1630 (?).

32. For a systematic treatment of these dynamics see Walter Toman, *The Family Constellation* (3d ed., New York, 1976), especially Part I.

33. See Appendix I in Deloche, *Frère inconnu*, 513.

34. Louis Valentin, *Cardinalis Richelieus, Scriptor Ecclesiasticus* (Toulouse, 1900), 198f. Others finding Richelieu lacking in a sense of spirituality are Lanfranc de Panthou, *Richelieu et la direction des âmes*, 29, and Pierre Blet, "La Religion du cardinal," 166. See also below, Chapter IX, Sections 3 and 4.

35. Deloche, *Frère inconnu*, 22.

36. Dreux Du Radier, *Bibliothèque*, III, 358f. *n.*

37. Sirmond, *Lettre déchiffrée*, 28.

38. Part of his pleasure, one may speculate, came from bringing under his own domination one who had been chief household factotum for the great lord who had once employed his father.

39. *Lettres*, I, 23–25. End of April, 1609 (?).

40. *Ibid.*, I, 26f. Mid-1609 (?).

41. *Ibid.*, 55f. June 6, 1610.

42. *Ibid.*, 24. End of April, 1609 (?).

43. "Ordonnances synodales," fols. 81–82 *vo.*

44. *Lettres*, I, 587f. February, 1619 (?).

45. Dreux Du Radier, *Bibliothèque*, III, 358.

46. "The Life of Armand-John de Plessis [*sic*] Cardinal of Richelieu," in *Lustra Ludovici*, 164.

47. His handwriting has been analyzed by Robert Lavollée, "La Véritable écriture du cardinal de Richelieu et celle de ses principaux secrétaires," *Rapports et notices sur les 'Mémoires',* II (1907), 1–14. For an example see the Appendix. It may be noted that the only *i* that is dotted in that sample is the one in *souverain.*

48. Archives de la Famille, XIV, fol. 48. (From Grenoble, misdated February 22, 1619.) Deloche reproduces a holograph of Alphonse in *Frère inconnu*, opposite 58.

49. Letter to Léon Bouthillier, *Le Conservateur* (May, 1757), 26f.

50. A formal, professional study in oils, it is held by the municipal museum of Avignon. Another, less expert, portrait of Alphonse de Richelieu as Cardinal is the frontispiece to Deloche, *Frère inconnu.* It too gives an impression of mournfulness.

51. Institut, Godefroy 395, fol. 151. July 5, 1635.

52. Deloche, *Frère inconnu*, 13.

53. In one of the famous etchings, by Jacques Callot, of the siege of La Rochelle, Richelieu is depicted, on horseback, as a dashing figure.

54. He is described, in an early political interview, as lounging around with some abandon, apparently to intimidate the young abbé de Villeloin, who had been called in by Richelieu to give an accounting of his father's anti-royalist activities. His public gestures are described as "Italianate"—evidently meaning exaggerated—by Howell. Another witness describes how, presumably in order to impress others with his piety, he prostrated himself before the coffin of Père Coton in an extravagant gesture of reverence. Marolles, *Mémoires*, I, cited in *Lettres*, I, 513 *n.*; Howell, *Lustra Ludovici*, 164; Jean-Marie Prat, *Recherches sur la Compagnie de Jésus* (5 vols., Lyons, 1876–1878), IV, 792.

55. *Frère inconnu*, 13.

56. To M. Du Pont Bonnet, cited above, Chapter II, Section 2, note.

57. Péricaud, "Note sur Alphonse de Richelieu," 192f. December, 1629.

58. Michel Pure, *Vita Alphonsi-Ludovici Plessaei Richelii* (Paris, 1653), 3f. On Pure's source see the preface by Emile Magne to Pure, *La Pitieuse*, xxii.

59. *Vita Arm.-Joan Richelii*, 3f.

60. *Lettres*, V, 1008; Péricaud, "Note sur Alphonse de Richelieu," 257. Armand de Richelieu's letter on this matter was written in December 1636, hence, although Péricaud dates Alphonse's reply in early 1638 it should probably be put in early 1637.

61. See Heinz Kohut, *The Restoration of the Self*, (New York, 1977), 105–160.

62. *Vita Alphonsi Richelii*, 17–24.

63. The accusation, insofar as it refers to Armand's conduct as an adult, seems completely unfounded. Not only did he select his brother, apparently with high hopes, for important

state missions and posts, including that of Primate of France, but also none of his surviving letters contain a hint of deprecation of this brother, and, indeed, show an affectionate protectiveness as well as esteem for him. See, for example, *Lettres*, VI, 759. March 20, 1641.

64. *Le Conservateur*, 25–28.

65. Deloche, *Frère inconnu*, 54f.; 433f.

66. *Lettres*, VII, 1034. July 14, 1638. What is apparently Alphonse's reply is reprinted in "Deux lettres d'Alphonse de Richelieu," *Bulletin de la Commission Historique* (1909), 1910. July or August (?) 1638.

Chapter 8

1. *Lettres*, I, 59. 1610 (?).

2. *E.g.* Archives de la Famille, XVI, fol. 60. Letter of 1634 (?).

3. Ranum, *Richelieu and the Councillors*, 182–184.

4. It may be, of course, that male figures, including his father, played a more important role in Alphonse's childhood than in Armand's, especially if he was born as early as 1582.

5. In the twenty-three known letters from Suzanne de La Porte, mostly concerned with family affairs, only one makes mention of either of her two daughters in any but a perfunctory way. The one exception reports, rather apologetically, her grief at Françoise's death. (See above, Chapter IV, Section 3.) Her omission was certainly not due to indifference but to the fact that it was not good form to talk about girl children. The self-effacement and self-deprecation in Nicole's letters to her brothers is instructive on the expectations in which she had been raised. Of a suitor's letter she writes, "he addressed it to me although I had not written him; I tell you this, fearing you might think I was becoming emancipated. . . . I am chagrinned that you don't have a worthier sister." Of the reply that she has been asked to give on the acceptability of a marriage which is being arranged for her: "It seems to me that the one a girl of propriety (*une fille de bien séance*) should make is to submit always to what she is ordered to do." BN, fr. 23200, fol. 120.

6. *Vita A.-J. Richelii*, 6.

7. *Briefve et facile méthode*, 32 vo.

8. *Instruction du chrestien*, 242.

9. *Lettres*, I, lxxxviii; xci. Alphonse's relative immunity from physical sanctions seems less assured than Armand's. Some of the signs that this elder brother enjoyed fantasizing himself abused have already been noted. His reported difficulty in walking, also noted, may be linked to the period in which he acquired that skill, a not unusual time for first applications of physical punishment. His stubbornness also contrasts with his brother's *souplesse*, another, perhaps significant, difference between the two. For example, he steadfastly refused to believe repeated assurances of Monsieur Vincent on a certain matter of fact, thus bewildering that ingenuous cleric. See Pierre Coste, ed., *Correspondance, entretiens, documents de Saint Vincent de Paul* (14 vols., Paris, 1920–1925), IV, 294; VI, 500. The contrast between the two brothers in such matters points up a frequent problem of psychohistorical research: while there is often reason to suppose that a mother did not personally care for all of her infants, there is usually little information on who did, and by what methods.

10. Notably, somewhat later, Jacqueline Pascal, headmistress at Port-Royal. This trend is discussed in Marvick, "Nature versus Nurture," 277–279.

11. Flavigny, *Briefve et facile instruction*, fols. 5 and vo 10 vo 16 and 16 vo and 19 vo.

12. *Les Hommes illustres qui ont paru en France pendant le XVIIe siècle*, I (3d ed., Paris, 1701), 1.

13. BN, fr. 24445, fols. 175 vo.; 176.

14. *Richelieu et les femmes*, 100–104.

15. See below, Section 3, "Using words" and "Playing."

16. Institut, Godefroy 269, fol. 205. Sébastien Bouthillier to Richelieu, May 26, 1624. Published in Lacroix, *Richelieu à Luçon*, 180f.

17. *Vita A.-J. Richelii*, 8.

18. Henri Jadart, "Louis XIII et Richelieu à Reims, 13–26 juillet, 1641," *Travaux de l'Académie de Reims*, LXXV, 17–19.

19. Philippe Fortin de La Hoguette, "Lettres, 1623–1649," Tamizey de Larroque, ed., *Archives Historiques de la Saintonge*, XVI (1888), 95–97.

20. Claude Courtin, Arsenal MS 4651, fol. 276 *vo*.

21. Malherbe, answering Peiresc in a letter of August 7, 1627, reported that the opinion of bishops he had canvassed was all but unanimous that Alphonse's case was ill-taken. *Oeuvres*, III (Paris, 1862), 576.

22. Letter to Bouthillier, *Le Conservateur* (May, 1757), 26f. May 5, 1635. Again, in such hypochondriacal concerns, Alphonse's responses seem to lend themselves (as Armand's rarely do) to "Kohutian" interpretation as dread of loss of the self and "need for the attention of the missing self-objects." See Arnold D. Richards, "Self Theory, Conflict Theory, and the Problem of Hypochondriasis," *Psychoanalytic Study of The Child*, XXXVI (1981), 328.

23. *Le Conservateur* (May, 1757), 28. July 18, 1635.

24. *E.g.*, *Lettres*, I, xcvii.

25. Otto Fenichel, *The Psychoanalytic Theory of the Neuroses* (New York, 1945), 69.

26. *Collected Papers*, III, 572 *n*.

27. As far as I can tell, only an imaginative writer has so far connected Freud's hypothesis with Richelieu's history. See Françoise Mallet-Joris, *The Favorite*, trans. by Herma Briffault (New York, 1962), 130–133.

28. *Theory of Neuroses*, 69.

29. Quoted from BN, n. a. 22398, fol. 108, by Deloche, *Le Père du cardinal*, 349.

30. *Lettres*, I, 164. Beginning of February, 1616.

31. Deloche, *Richelieu et les femmes*, 33; *Autour de la plume*, 77.

32. *E.g.*, *prend l'alarme, fausses alarmes . . . donne l'effroy, épouvante, étonnement* [in the sense of fear] *accidens, disgrâce* [in the sense of bad luck] *. . . arriver mal, arriver faulte, désastre*, and the archaic *mésarriver*. In addition, notes Haschke, *infortune* is, in Richelieu, synonymous (exceptionally for his time) with *malheur* and *misère*. *Die Sprache Richelieus*, 75f.

33. Montchal, *Mémoires*, I, 12. The manuscript origins of this text are cited in Griselle, *Louis XIII et Richelieu*, 51f., *n*.

34. *Lettres*, VI, 404. June 24, 1639.

35. See above, Chapter II, Section 3. As for the sensations of triumph in such an achievement, note Françoise Dolto's report on a ten-year-old enuretic boy who has just conquered his problem and who has dreamed, two days after the end of his enuresis, that he is battling with giants whom he kills: "The following day the dream resumes, and he kills all the giants but one, then he kills him too, and with his sword he cuts off his feet, then his wrists. . . . These dreams, far from being nightmares, were marvellous. He felt so happy, proud and strong that it was from that day that schoolwork seemed to him very easy and enjoyable . . . 'as though a curtain had been lifted.'" This boy, encouraged to draw a picture by his therapist, had sketched a great ocean liner at sea. With his triumphant conquest, he added a tree to the scene, a phallic symbol, as the therapist interpreted it, since the boy explained that the addition was needed because something had been "missing." *Psychanalyse et pédiatrie* (Paris, 1971), 174; 180.

36. *Histoire du cardinal*, II, 135.

37. *Lettres*, VI, 31f. May 1, 1638.

38. *Lettres*, I, 22. February, 1609 (?).

39. AAE, France 769, fol. 4 and 4 *vo*. March 24, 1613.

40. Bibliothèque de Poitiers, Dom Fonteneau II, 14. December 23, 1617.

41. Lacroix, *Richelieu à Luçon*, 105.

42. *Lettres*, IV, 402. November 13, 1632.

43. *Ibid.*, V, 921; 55. June 15; 16, 1635. By *sang*, of course, is meant general physique.

44. *Le Conservateur* (May, 1757), 27. July 18, 1635.

45. Fenichel, *Theory of Neuroses*, 190. Earlier conditions may, of course, give rise to this pattern which can also originate in or be reinforced by anxieties typically experienced at a later time of life. See, for example, Humberto Nagera, "Sleep and its Disturbances Approached Developmentally," *Psychoanalytic Study of the Child*, XXI (1966), 393–447.

46. Sirmond, *Lettre déchifrée*, 60. See also *Lettres*, I, vi.

47. *Catholicon françois*, 39.

48. *Lettres*, IV, 64. December (?) 1630.

49. See Phyllis Greenacre, "Urination and Weeping," *American Journal of Orthopsychiatry*, XV (1945), 81–88; L. Börge Löfgren, "On Weeping," *International Journal of Psychoanalysis*, XLVII (1966), 375–381.

50. So also was Louis XIV's. A valet's account may be recalled describing the childhood quarrel between that king and his little brother which ended in each angrily urinating on the other's bed. Pierre de La Porte, *Mémoires* (Paris, 1792), 280. These boys, too, were raised chiefly by indulgent women. Of the two, only Philippe had noticeable transsexual tendencies as an adult. The ease with which Louis turned on tears was reported with some sarcasm by Louis de Saint-Simon. One such occasion was after the death of Philippe himself in 1701. *Mémoires du duc de Saint-Simon*, V (Paris, 1953), 909f.

51. Letter of Père Suffren, as quoted by Griselle from the *Catalogue of Morrison* in *Louis XIII et Richelieu*, 51. April 15, 1641.

52. *Mémoires*, I, 312. Montchal professed such a single-minded hatred of Richelieu that one wonders if he did not feel an affinity with him which he struggled against. In support of this, consider the archbishop's characterization of his avowed enemy: "His violent nature which drove him constantly, like an *impetuous torrent* to *overturn the dikes* and attack the boundaries which *enclosed his power*." *Ibid.*, 21. (Emphasis supplied.)

53. *Catholicon françois*, 40.

54. *Journal du cardinal de Richelieu . . . pendant le grand orage* (2 vols., Paris, 1665), I, 4.

55. "We have heard him . . . cry to make God more propitious to him when others started to surpass him." The "others," of course, included his younger brother. *Vita Alphonsi*, 12.

56. Greenacre, "On the Development and Function of Tears," in *Emotional Growth*, I, 253.

57. Andrew Peto, "On Laughing and Weeping," *International Journal of Psychoanalysis*, XXVI (1946), 129–138.

58. Suggestive as clues to the sources of this contrast is the notion that Alphonse's ill-chosen exhibitionistic behavior as Archbishop of Aix, like his early self-destructive actions, represented a "mirror-hungry" person's display of himself to counter feelings of worthlessness and his search for admiration that would nourish a "famished self," while Armand's carefully planned self-displays were both instrumental to political aims and served to counter fears of being shamed as well as to ward off tendencies towards depression. See Kohut and Wolf, "The Disorders of the Self," 421f.

59. See Richard Y. Yazmajian, "Pathological Urination and Weeping," *Psychoanalytic Quarterly*, XXXV (1966), 40–46. In considering Alphonse's youthful self-drowning attempt a clinician's observation that in Latin the same word means both "diver" and "urinator" may seem suggestive. Carel van der Heide, "Pollakuiria Nervosa," *ibid.* (1941), 267–283.

60. Letter of Père Nicolas Caussin to Mlle. de La Fayette, cited by Charles Daniel, *Une Vocation et une disgrâce* (Paris, 1861), 63.

61. *Lettres*, IV, 13f. November 12, 1630.

62. As when he described, as a young bishop, the poverty of his resources to a friend: "a stout heart (*bon coeur*)," and, when he suffered from his last, painful malady:"I still hope, with God's help, to recover from my illness (*guérir de mon mal*)." *Ibid.*, I, 56; BN, Fichier Charavay VII, 1054. June 6, 1610; May 10, 1642.

63. He once suggested to Marie de Medici that he "was always dragging around for two or three months every two years or so." *Papiers*, I, 196. July 27, 1625.

64. Avenel is of this opinion. *Lettres*, I, xcviiif.

65. See Greenacre, "Toward an Understanding of the Physical Nucleus of some Defense Reactions," in *Emotional Growth*, I, 142.

66. Karem J. Monsour, "Migraine: Dynamic and Choice of Symptom," *Psychoanalytic Quarterly* XXVI (1957), 484–491.

67. Only 1618 and 1626 are not documented, to my knowledge, by published correspondence. His state in 1618 is mentioned by Henri de Richelieu in BN, fr. 23200, fol. 104 *vo;* and that of 1626 by a letter of May 26 in BL, Additional 24206, fol. 84.

68. I have not found evidence of headaches that Deloche places towards the end of 1634. See *La Maison du cardinal*, 204.

69. See Clark L. Hull and Bertha I. Hull, "Conflict between Overlapping Learning Functions," in Yvonne Brackbill and George Thomson, eds., *Behavior in Infancy and Early Childhood* (New York, 1967), 141–146. Greenacre describes a case in which "ejaculation (also probably signifying urination) is equated with speech and thinking." *Emotional Growth*, I, 142.

70. BN, Fichier Charavay. November 25, 1619.

71. "Tres-humble remonstrance au roi," 23f.

72. *Political Testament*, H. B. Hill, trans. (Madison, 1961), 41. Like many items in the *Testament politique*, this one is most likely a saying collected for or by Richelieu because it captured his attention, or seemed to his aides to suit his inclinations.

73. Cited by Batiffol, *Richelieu et le roi*, 88.

74. *Instruction du chrestien*, 4f.

75. A.-D. de La Fontenelle de Vaudoré, *Histoire du monastère et des évêques de Luçon*, VII (Paris, 1847), 390.

76. *Instruction du chrestien*, 5. On the innovativeness of this presentation in the vulgar tongue see Dhotel, *Origines du cathéchisme*, 192f.

77. *Instruction du chrestien*, 9.

78. *Lettres*, VII, 463f. July (?), 1619.

79. This peculiarity is remarked by Lavollée, "La Véritable écriture," 11.

80. "Responce à la libelle," 167.

81. *Lettres*, VIII, 348. The specimen he cites is AAE, France 831, fol. 421. One change, for example, in this letter to a group of monks is from the promise that miscreants will be *"punis"* (punished) to the warning that they should be *"corrigés."* November 3, 1638.

82. *Ibid.*, I, 117. 1613 (?).

83. *Ibid.*, VII, 413. End of September, 1617.

84. One modern biographer has seen Richelieu's teaching ambition as the key to his character: J.-E. Fidao Justiniani, *Richelieu: Précepteur de la nation française* (Paris, 1936). According to Isadore H. Coriat, an intense desire to teach is a preoccupation frequently associated with urethral erotism. "Character Traits of Urethral Erotism," *Psychoanalytic Review*, II (1924), 432.

85. "Ordonnances synodales," 79f.

86. For example, he specifies each Sunday's program. The priest is to present it in the "vulgar tongue so that everyone may learn . . . what they are supposed to know." *Ibid.*, 88.

87. The first Oratorian chapter, founded earlier in Paris, had been suspended. See Augustin M.-P. Ingold, *L'Oratoire à Luçon* (Luçon, 1884), 1–3.

88. His efforts here, as persistent and urgent as more successful ones, never achieved the results he desired. The innovative project was begun in 1611. Permission from the order to levy a tax to start building was not obtained until 1613. In 1614 the contract between Bérulle, head of the order, and Richelieu, the bishop of Luçon, was signed, specifying, in details that bear the marks of the latter's close attention, what services were to be performed for the diocese he headed. By this time he was no longer resident there, and his chapter took the opportunity afforded by his absence to reject the agreement, when it was to be registered in 1616, because the cost was "extraordinary and too heavy." Richelieu ignored this and apparently advanced money to buy a house for the Oratorians. He continued to try to induce Bérulle to begin administration of the enterprise and to send a superior and priest for that purpose. Bérulle again tried to comply, but was rebuffed by local officials and reported this

to Richelieu who replied asking him to "let me know how he would like the matter to be conducted . . . believing myself to have enough friends to see that it happens as he desires it." Ingold, *L'Oratoire à Luçon*, 1–5; *Lettres*, I, 632f. October, 1619.

89. As quoted from P. J. Jannini, "Il Teatro al Tempo di Luigi XIII," *Quaderni des Seicento francese*, I (1974), in *Dix-septième Siècle*, VIII (1975), 90.

90. BN, fr. 24445, 178 *vo*.

91. *Instruction du chrestien*, 164.

92. Winnicott, *Playing and Reality*, 51.

93. A single sketch on one of his working papers, though attributed to the cardinal (see Lavollée, "La véritable écriture," pl. XII), may actually be the work of Louis XIII.

94. See Delavaud, *Quelques collaborateurs*, 28.

95. For example, see the facetious Latin note from Richelieu to Léon Bouthillier whom he addresses as "Capitaine et Gouverneur du Bois de Vie Saine," a play on the Bois de Vincennes, a royal park whose château confined political prisoners threatening the "healthy life" of the state. Bouthillier had just been made governor of the Bois. See *Lettres*, IV, 713. End of January, 1634. The joke was not original; it dated back at least to Henri IV's day.

96. *Lettres*, VII, 829. October 13, 1640. See also below, Chapter IX, Section 3, where the play on words describes the play of water from fountains.

97. *Les Délices de l'esprit* (2d ed., Paris, 1661), Part 1, 105.

98. Quoted from *ibid*. (1st ed., 1658), by Delavaud, *Quelques collaborateurs*, 38 *n*.

99. Preface to *Traitté pour convertir*.

100. La Fontenelle de Vaudoré, *Histoire des évêques de Luçon*, VII, 386.

101. *Origines du catéchisme*, 193.

102. Jean Orcibal, "Richelieu, homme d'église, homme d'état," *Revue d'Histoire de l'Eglise de France*, XXXIV (1948), 94–101.

103. *Ibid.*, 98–100.

104. AAE, France 768, fol. 212. February 6, 1613. Emphasis supplied. This is misdated in the MS "April 6, 1612." (See below, Chapter X, Section 2.)

105. "Richelieu, homme d'église," 99f. This theme is elaborated by *idem, Jean Duvergier de Hauranne* (2 vols., Louvain, 1947–1948), I, 108–146.

106. Lescot, Preface to *Traitté pour convertir*.

107. *Lettres*, V, 773. May 9, 1637. Emphasis supplied.

108. One may speculate that his family experience also contributed to this view. Doctrinal divisions do not seem to have been very serious. Apparently the Protestantism of Richelieu's uncle, Charles de La Porte La Meilleraye did not estrange him from his nephew. Both La Meilleraye children converted to Catholicism after their father's death, the son, according to a contemporary report, at the request of his sister. See Jean-François Senault, *Oraison funèbre de Madame Magdelaine de La Porte* (Paris, 1671), 4–6.

109. Louis de Grenade, *L'Oraison dominicale* (Clermont-Ferrand, 1889), 52.

110. See Deloche, *Autour de la plume*, 32f. Both François de Sales's *Introduction à la vie dévote* and Grenade's *Guide du pécheur* are reading recommended by Flavigny's *Briefve et facile instruction*, 20f., published under Richelieu's direction.

111. *Instruction du chrestien*, 16; 289. Emphasis supplied.

112. *Traitté pour convertir* (1657 ed.), 574; Preface.

113. For example, the Carmelite, Léon de Saint-Jean. See Jean-Pierre Massaut, "Autour de Richelieu et Mazarin: le Carme Léon de Saint-Jean et la grande politique," *Revue d'Histoire Moderne et Contemporaine*, VII (1960), 11–45.

114. *Instruction du chrestien*, 16f.; 44.

115. *Briefve et facile instruction*, 1 *vo*.

116. Pellisson, *Histoire de l'Académie*, 125.

117. Lacroix, *Richelieu à Luçon*, 65.

118. *Autour de Richelieu* (Paris, 1937), 107.

119. *Richelieu à Luçon*, 65.

120. This was in October, 1616. It was to be a lecturing chair in Catholic-Protestant controversy, held by a secular doctor of theology so that he could be without the diversion of predicatory or pastoral duties. Charles Jourdain, *Histoire de l'Université de Paris au dix-septième siècle* (Paris, 1862), 523f.

121. *Lettres*, I, 557; VII, 424. November, 1617; 1618.

122. Batiffol, *Autour de Richelieu*, 110f.

123. *Ibid.*, 123–125.

124. Actual pets seem to have played little part in the cardinal's life. Doubtless he was surrounded by dogs and horses, like most noblemen of the time. There is a record, aside from the purchase of such birds as swans and egrets for the park, of canaries and warblers being bought for "Monseigneur." Perhaps their gay song and bright color had appeal for him. A bill also survives for boarding "twelve small dogs" at Rueil, his country residence. I have been unable to find a basis for the popular depiction of Richelieu with cats. Could it have been a fondness for tiny dogs? "Documents inédits sur le cardinal de Richelieu," *Revue Héraldique, Historique et Nobiliaire* (1871), 457–463; 536–555. The same material is reprinted by Léon Brièle, ed., in *Collection des documents inédits pour servir à l'histoire des hôpitaux de Paris*, IV (1887), 291–302.

125. On authorship of the religious works see Delavaud, *Quelques collaborateurs*, 17–29 and Deloche, *Autour de la plume*, 25–150. On Richelieu's historical writing, in addition to these, see Robert Lavollée, "Le 'Secrétaire des mémoires' de Richelieu," *Revue des Etudes Historiques* (1904), 449–477.

126. Paper presented to the Society for French Historical Studies, March, 1981.

127. See Josef Engel, "Zur Frage der Echtheit von Richelieus '*Testament politique*,' " in *Aus Mittelalter und Neuzeit: Festschrift Gerhard Kallen*, Josef Engel and Hans M. Klinkenberg, eds. (Bonn, 1957), 185–218.

128. *Testament politique*, André, ed., 90.

129. "Le 'Secrétaire,'" 455.

130. Jean Chapelain, *Lettres* (2 vols., Paris, 1880), I, 90f.; 84. February, 1635; November/ December, 1634.

131. "Ode pour remerciement à Monseigneur le Cardinal de Richelieu," in *Recueil des plus beaux vers des meilleurs poètes français* (Paris, 1627), 521.

132. Arsenal MS 4651, fol. 272; Paul Pellisson-Fontaines, *Relation contenant l'histoire de l'Académie Françoise* (Paris, 1672), 115f. The first was a play on the line *"veni, vidi, vici,"* and the second concerned ducks paddling in the Tuileries pond. Concerning the latter, however, he is said to have proposed a slight revision.

133. Arsenal MS 4651, fol. 275 *vo*.

134. An edict of his first ministry made the royal library depository of all French books. See Isambert, *Anciennes lois françoises*, XVI, 106.

135. *Lettres*, VII, 426. February 8, 1619.

136. *Ibid.*, VIII, 130. This seems to be the project for the plan, dated 1642 in *Mémoires de Molé*, IV, 266 *n*. See above, Chapter II, Section 1, note.

137. *Recueil des harangues prononcées par Messieurs de l'Académie*, I (Paris, 1672), 63f.

138. "Testament," in *Mémoires*, Petitot, ed., 130–132.

139. So was it also in the academy plans described just above. The Sorbonne faculty were to have "perpetual sovereignty over what was best" among "*lumières* of the mind." La Mesnardière, *Recueil des discours*, 67.

140. "Testament," in *Mémoires*, Petitot, ed., 13f.

141. *Ordonnances synodales*, fol. 83 and 83 *vo*.

Chapter 9

1. Montesquieu, *De l'Esprit des lois*, Bk. V, Ch. 10.

2. Archives de la Famille, XIV, fol. 22.

3. A sample from Nicole during Armand's 1617 exile: "Although I know nothing . . . worthy to importune you, you have not in the world . . . a humble servant as attached as I. . . . It is a horrible mortification to me not to be able to show you in person . . . but rather, only to repeat in writing. . . . " BN, fr. 23200, fol. 231. See also fol. 121 vo. Nicole and her husband named their first son, born in 1619, Armand.

4. See Bosseboeuf, *Richelieu*, 24. Roland Mousnier and the vicomte d'Avenel have emphasized the overriding importance of the male-male alliance in marriages of this epoch. Both cite the case of one young man who, according to Tallemant, when denied a first choice of one of Richelieu's cousins in marriage, avers that which one he is assigned is a matter of indifference, since "It is Your Eminence I wed." Quoted in "Les Survivances médiévales," 61; *Richelieu et la monarchie*, I, 371.

5. In this letter, just before his marriage, Brézé also sends Richelieu political news, showing that the two men were already fairly close personal allies. BN, fr. 23201, fols. 168 vo; 169.

6. *Lettres*, I, 681; IV, 476. July, 1621; August, 1633. Mathieu de Morgues suggests that Nicole had to be put under restraint. (*Les Lumières pour l'histoire de France* [n.p., 1636], 20.) Tallemant elaborates on that contention (*Historiettes*, II, 45f.). The correspondence cited here, however, seems more to suggest severe depression, together with agoraphobia and hypochondria.

7. BL, Egerton 1690, fol. 24. September 1, 1631.

8. *Ibid.*, fols. 29; 30.

9. Archives de la Famille, XVI. "De Saulmur ce 8 aoust," (1634 or 1635).

10. "Documents inédits sur le cardinal," 551.

11. BN, fr. 23200, 349 vo. January 6, 1636.

12. AAE, Poitou 1696, fol. 117. July 4, 1635. The correspondent was named Citois, probably the brother of Richelieu's personal physician. See *Papiers*, III, 24. The cardinal availed himself of a variety of services from members of this Poitevin family.

13. See above, Chapter V, Section 1.

14. *Lettres*, VII, 527. April 26, 1623. See also *ibid.*, II, 277. October 22, 1626. The long history of his concern to keep her out of the convent can also be followed in Jean Dagens, ed., *Correspondance de Pierre Bérulle* (3 vols., Louvain, 1939), III, 102–104.

15. Bonneau-Avenant, *La Duchesse d'Aiguillon*, 249.

16. Note also that, in 1629, Richelieu and Marie stood in the meaningful relationship of godfather and godmother to Armand de Vignerod de Pont Courlay, Marie's brother's son and the cardinal's grand-nephew, also to be his heir-designate. *Ibid.*, 184.

17. "Documents inédits," 552; 555. Accounts of 1640, 1641. "Ecarlate d'Hollande," according to Littré, resulted from a dyeing process discovered only after 1630, that treated the wings of a tiny tropical insect with metallic chemicals.

18. Archives de la Famille, XVIII. "Paris, ce 9e novembre."

19. A lenient censor where her uncle was concerned, she seems to have been easily persuaded to his view in this matter. René Rapin, *Mémoires*, in Emmanuel de Domenech, *Histoire du jansénisme* (Paris, 1861), 378f.

20. Sometime around 1616 Nicole wrote Armand, "I shall have the singular favor of serving your nephews, and I persuade myself that their recognition of my attachment will insure that they won't complain of me to you." BN, fr. 23200, fol. 111 and 111 vo.

21. Ludovic Lalanne, ed., "Un Récit inédit de la mort du cardinal de Richelieu," *Revue Historique*, LV (1894), 305–308. This same report claims that Richelieu renewed here his command to Marie to care for her nephews rather than enter a religious order.

22. *Instruction du chrestien*, 244. As has been noted earlier, and will be discussed further below (Chapter XI, Section 2), Richelieu advocated, as a representative of the French Counter-Reform movement, royal endorsement in France of the decrees of the Council of Trent. Clearly, he was familiar with the Latin catechism of the Council which was not, at the time his own catechism appeared, circulated in a French version. While the Council's catechism discussed under this commandment reciprocal obligations of parents and children, those parental duties

stressed concerned the moral education of children. Material considerations were specifically deprecated. See *Catéchisme du Concile de Trente*, II, 259f.

23. *Instruction du chrestien*, 245.

24. Augustin M.-P. Ingold, ed., *Un Sermon inédit de Richelieu* (Luçon, 1889), 9.

25. *Instruction du chrestien*, 52.

26. "*Cum illud omnium hominum corporibus commune sit, ut ex matris sanguine formentur. Quod vero et naturae ordinem, et humanam intelligentiam superat, illud est: . . . statim Sanctissimum Christi corpus formatum, . . . in ipso temporis articulo perfectus Deus, et perfectus homo fuit.*" *Catéchisme du Concile de Trent*, I, 81.

27. BN, fr. 24445, fol. 176.

28. Fire, often associated with such imagery, is less frequently present in Richelieu's works than water. Two metaphors, however, relate to burning in one of his surviving sermons. The subject here is the assumption of the Virgin: "That a body heavy by nature rises on high against its weight is a great miracle indeed; but that a spirit incapable of weight, a spirit all burning with the fire of charity, lowers itself down below, contrary to movement of fire which rises on high—that is another which seems no lesser one."

The king's brother, Richelieu goes on to warn, must honor Louis as his father; otherwise he will have reason to expect "a second descent of the great God upon him . . . in fire and thunder." *Maximes d'état*, 820f. A similar allusion, in which he offers himself as the object of God's lightning-bolt is discussed below, Chapter XI, Section 4.

29. *L'Instruction du chrestien*, 110. This analogy is used by Richelieu in varying contexts. "God's creatures," he writes to a lady correspondent, "are but broken cisterns which cannot contain water. That happiness . . . which ought to quench the thirst of our soul splashes out only from Him who calls himself the fountain of spring water." *Lettres*, I, 1609 (?).

In a letter to Bouthillier water was another valuable substance—money. In this passage Richelieu is playfully facetious but unusually repetitive: "If my waters have become low, the same reason which made them foamy at . . . your house before you had the fountain is the cause: it is that too much has been drawn for the public. Inasmuch as since that event you have found a fountain, if I can find some spring of use to the king's service, it will be a great consolation to me." *Ibid.*, VI, 608. November 2, 1639.

The fascination fountains and cascades of water had for the cardinal is well-known. His partiality for Coussaye as a residence while he was Bishop of Luçon was said to be on account of the pleasant fountains there. After his death an intimate recalls particularly the delights of the "canals and fountains" of Rueil, his regular residence of later years. See François Le Métel, Abbé de Boisrobert, "Epistre à Mr. l'abbé de Richelieu," (1647 or 1648) in *Epistres en vers*, II (Paris, 1927), 59. Another contemporary description of this favorite dwelling of Richelieu describes the "designs and . . . movements of the waters that flowed and then surged upward towards their source; there adam of enormous grandeur vomits a deluge of water with a splash. . . . Spurts . . . issue from its mouth . . . like a torrent and whiten with foam a brass huntsman who seems to offer death from the end of a menacing tube." Quoted in Jules Jacquin and Joseph Duisberg, *Le Château de Richelieu* (Paris, 1845), 32f. There Richelieu had arranged, according to another source, for a high cascade to fall from a great reservoir, supplied with water conducted from more than a half a league away. *Ibid.*, 165. The fountain system that the cardinal helped plan at Richelieu was world-renowned. He mentions the need to complete it in his will. (Petitot, ed., 139.) His favorite pilgrimage is said to have been to the miraculous fountain of Notre Dame d'Ardillers and, in fact, he attributes to this shrine his recovery from the urinary bladder ailment of 1632 for which he endowed the church with a chapel in 1634. Lacroix, *Richelieu à Luçon*, 165f; *Lettres*, I, 110. Note also his curiously explicit and repetitive instructions for the design of a fountain for his new garden at the Palais Cardinal. The figure is to hold the basin on its *head* with both hands. Both statue and basin must be pierced (for the water), and so forth. *Ibid.*, 775–777. In his accounts of the Palais Cardinal for 1626 he pays about two thousand pounds to "the mistress of the pump for the lead pipes and other expenditures which he saw fit" to bring running water into his house in the rue Saint-Honoré—a princely facility for the time. "Documents inédits," 462.

30. *Instruction du chrestien*, 112.

31. Apparently, taking the family name for his church title was Richelieu's own choice. Richelieu was no cathedral town. Indeed, for some time after he was elevated to the cardinalate, clerical colleagues assumed Richelieu would be Cardinal de Luçon.

32. *Vita A.-J. Richelii*, 4. The foundation of this order is actually placed in 1578 rather than in 1585.

33. "Caput Apologeticum," *Lettres*, VII, 421. April, 1618.

34. A perpetuation of this view was demonstrated when Richelieu's skeletal remains were exhumed in the eighteenth century. Autopsists professed to find a brain case spectacularly larger and more complex than the normal one—and a thinner than usual skull! The lobes were perceived to be particularly overdeveloped in the region "serving the operations of understanding." *Journal du Palais*, II (1755), cited by Ernest Jovy in *Trois documents inédits sur Urbain Grandier et un document peu connu sur le cardinal de Richelieu* (Paris, 1906).

35. BN, fr. 24445, fol. 175 vo.

36. François d'Hédelin, Abbé d'Aubignac, *La Pratique du théâtre* (Paris, 1657), 15.

37. Anselme, *Le Palais d'honneur*, 539.

38. Lescot, Preface to Richelieu, *Traitté pour convertir*.

39. "Response au libelle intitulé 'Tres-humble . . . remonstrance au roy,'" in *Recueil de diverses pièces*, 581; BN, fr. 24445, fol. 178 vo.

40. Ernest Jones, "A Psychoanalytic Study of the Holy Ghost Concept," *Essays in Applied Psychoanalysis* (London, 1951), 364f.

41. Quoted in Pierre Champion, *Vie du père Louis Lallemant, Jésuite, 1587–1635* (Paris, 1694), 219; 182.

42. Courtin, Arsenal MS 4651, fol. 359.

43. Philippe Fortin de La Hoguette, *Testament d'un bon père à ses enfans* (Paris, 1690), 164f.

44. Saint-Sorlin, *Le Tombeau du cardinal*, 14.

45. "Response à un libelle contre les ministres. . . ." (1630), in *Recueil de diverses pièces*, 167.

46. See above, Chapter VII, Section 1.

47. *Traitté pour convertir*, 2f.

48. "Ordonnances synodales," 80.

49. BN, fr. 24445, fol. 177.

50. BL, Additional 22052, fol. 4, 4 vo; AAE, France 771, fol. 112. May 10, 1617.

51. *Lettres*, I, 164f. Beginning of February, 1616.

52. BN, fr. 24445, fol. 185.

53. Cf. the discussion of libido sublimation on a parallel occasion—with persistence of curiosity and avoidance of sexual themes—in Sigmund Freud, *Leonardo da Vinci: A Study in Psychosexuality*, A. A. Brill, trans. (New York, 1947), 49f.

54. Cf. a clinical report on the case of a modern man in whom the "drive to know, to understand, to see into things" was related to memories of a "painful and guilt-laden primal scene . . . early enuresis, fantasied phallic competition with the virile father," and "persistent urethral eroticism." Jule Eisenbud, "Behavioral Correspondences to Normally Unpredictable Future Events," *Psychoanalytic Quarterly*, XXIII (1954), 205–218.

55. *Instruction du chrestien*, 4f; 15f.

56. Jones, "The Holy Ghost Concept," 368.

57. *Ibid.*, 362.

58. E. g., Deloche, *Richelieu et les femmes*, 5–50; Marc Pierret, *Richelieu et la déraison d'état* (Paris, 1972), *passim*.

59. Robert J. Stoller, *Perversion: An Erotic Form of Hatred* (New York, 1976), 154–162, and *Sex and Gender*, I (New York, 1968), *passim*.

60. Hanotaux, "Maximes d'état," 771.

61. *Lettres*, I, 41f. 1609 (?).

62. *Ibid.*, IV, 309. June 17, 1632.

63. *Ibid.*, I, 15.

64. Ingold, "Un Sermon de Richelieu," 15; 13.

65. *Ibid.* In the royal court which Richelieu had just left, household disputes were rampant between the king and queen because of Henri IV's failure to contain the "seditious people" of his sexual appetites. These frequent *brouilleries* may have evoked for the young bishop the memory of similar strife between his own parents in which Suzanne, like Marie de Medici, was the victim.

66. AAE, France 774, fol. 261 *vo*.

67. Hanotaux, "Maximes d'état," 811.

68. *Moses and Monotheism*, 11.

69. Note, however, that François de Richelieu had also, according to one account, been destined for the clergy, and only recalled to a military life on account of the violent death of his older brother. See above, Chapter III, Section 2.

70. The terrible "Antoine the Monk," François's uncle, had been induced by his parents to become a monk in the Benedictine Abbey of Saint Florent of Saumur, according to a report to the Holy See of a papal legate who made inquiries in Richelieu's time, but "as soon as he was able . . . he discarded the habit . . . and even took up arms." BN, Dupuy 624, fol. 3.

71. *Lettres*, I, 733. October, 1622.

72. Du Perron may have been a Richelieu family friend from this time, since François de Richelieu, as Grand Provost, presided over the king's household in which the cleric was a familiar.

73. Pierre Feret, *Le Cardinal Du Perron* (Paris, 1877), 128f *n.*

74. *La Réforme et la Ligue: L'Edit de Nantes*, in *Histoire de France*, Ernest Lavisse, ed., VI (Paris, 1904), 380.

75. P. V. Palma Cayet, *Chronologie septenaire*, Michaud and Poujoulat, eds. (Paris, 1838), Part II, 94.

76. *Lettres missives*, V, 230f. May 5, 1600.

77. Aubéry, *Histoire du cardinal*, I, 13.

78. "J. D. Perron," in *Dictionnaire Moreri*.

79. Célestin Hippeau, *Les Ecrivains normands au XVIIe siècle* (Caen, 1858), 33.

80. *Perroniana et Thuana* (Cologne, 1694), 116.

81. Aubéry, *Histoire du cardinal*, I, 13.

82. This certainly authorized version was first published in Sirmond, *La Lettre déchiffrée*, 21. Hanotaux believes, following Sainte-Beuve, that it was at this time that Richelieu studied with the English theologian, Richard Smith, who was later to play an interesting part in the cardinal's life. According to a letter from his good friend Gabriel de L'Aubespine, however, it was in October, 1612 that Richelieu "brought two Englishmen" to help him apply himself to controversy. See Hanotaux, *Histoire du cardinal* I, 77, and AAE, France 768, fol. 232, 232 *vo*. October 28, 1628.

83. *Histoire du cardinal*, I, 13. André Du Chesne, a familiar of Richelieu, repeats the account of *La Lettre déchiffrée* in concluding, "One may say that the loss of his health was the price of this perfection." *Histoire généalogique*, fol. 75.

84. Hanotaux, *Histoire du cardinal*, I, 77, gives the sources on this event.

85. See the nuncio Bufalo's letter recommending Richelieu's confirmation to the papal secretary, Aldobrandini. *Acta Nunciaturae Gallia: Correspondance des nonces en France*, IV (Paris, 1964), 671. February 22, 1604. The belief of Hanotaux that he was not nominated until 1606 may be based on a misdating of the relevant letters of Henri IV. See note below, Section 6, "A forerunner."

86. The nuncio believed Armand de Richelieu was "no more than about twenty years old." *Ibid.* In fact he was only eighteen. The age dispensation granted by Paul V in December, 1606 attributes twenty-three years to him, though he was then only twenty-one. Lacroix, who reports this evidence, believes Richelieu allowed the age listed for Alphonse to remain in the

brief when the petitioner's name was changed to Armand. *Richelieu à Luçon*, 58 *et seq.* This early deception could account for the curious misconception of a later nuncio, Scotti, who believed, in April 1641, that Richelieu was fifty-eight, though the cardinal told him that he was fifty-five. See *Acta Nunciaturae*, V (Paris, 1965), 526.

87. Quoted by Hanotaux, *Histoire du cardinal*, I, 81, whose source is Pure. Pure, however, dates this admission to the *primum cursum* in 1606, while Jourdain finds that records show it was granted on July 27, 1605. *L'Université de Paris*, 40.

88. Family tradition may have played a part in this appeal. François de Richelieu, favored at court by Catherine de Medici, had been involved also in business undertakings with her cousin, Philip Strozzi, underwriting maritime adventures with him and perhaps also with the Florentine mercantile family of Gondi. Deloche, *Le Père du cardinal*, 191–198.

89. The report that he was a special favorite of Henri IV and that the king called him "my bishop," with fond intent, seems to originate with Pure. The king's letters supporting the nomination make purely routine mention of the young man's merits and, instead, specially emphasize his relationship to Henri de Richelieu who was, indeed, a particular favorite of Henri IV, as well as a popular figure whose virtues may even have been known in Rome. *Lettres missives*, VII, 53 *et seq.* These letters, based on copies, are apparently misdated December 1606 and probably should be put in 1603. The king, however, claims that Armand is "already in orders." If the letter is actually from the end of 1603, either Henri attributes Alphonse's status to Armand (as his age seems to have been attributed) or Armand was actually ordained earlier than is believed by, for example, Lacroix, *Richelieu à Luçon*, 61.

90. "La Jeunesse de Richelieu," *Revue des Questions Historiques*, VI (1869), 169.

91. Pure, *Vita A.-J. Richelii*, 24–30.

92. *E.g.*, the otherwise flattering contemporary *Lettre déchiffrée*: "Even His Holiness gave evidence several times of the esteem in which he held him . . . giving him very willingly dispensation for the age he lacked." (P. 22.) This was, in fact, the full extent of the words actually used by the pope, according to Martin Meurisse, *Histoire des évêques de Metz* (Metz, 1633), 660 (cited also by Lacroix, *Richelieu à Luçon*, 60).

93. Lacroix and Hanotaux are of the opinion, based on evidence presented by Avenel and Pure, that the examination taken by Richelieu on October 29, 1607, was for the doctorate. *Ibid.*, 62–64; *Histoire du cardinal*, I, 85, as is Pierre Feret, *La Faculté de théologie de Paris*, IV (Paris, 1906), 28. Jourdain, however, maintains that this *épreuve*, since not presided over by doctors of the Sorbonne, was only for the baccalaureate and cites Richer to confirm that Richelieu never became a doctor of theology. *Histoire de l'Université*, 40–43.

94. Avenel, VII, 317–319. March 1608. Héroard, the dauphin's diarist, mentions that Du Perron administered communion on that Easter but does not identify the preacher. Nor, indeed does he mention Richelieu at all before 1612. See below, Chapter X, Section 3.

95. *E. g.*, the report of the Tuscan ambassador, Giovannini, *Négociations diplomatiques de la France avec la Toscane*, V (Paris, 1875), 527. February 26, 1604.

96. Sully, *Mémoires*, IV, 93f; 226f. 1604; 1605.

97. Du Perron, *Ambassades*, 582f. May 17, 1606.

98. La Fontenelle de Vaudoré, *Histoire des évêques de Luçon*, 340–352.

99. *Lettres*, I, 7–11. December, 1608.

100. AAE, France 769, fol. 182 *vo.*

101. "Harangue pour le clergé," 347f; 353f.

Chapter 10

1. BN, fr. 15644, fol. 505. Attributed to Richelieu, 1633.

2. The company present is identified in *Mercure françois*, I (1619), 427f. Significant absences are discussed by Berthold Zeller, *Marie de Médicis et Sully* (Paris, 1892), 11–13.

3. Pure, *Vita A.-J. Richelii*, 57.

4. Erlanger, *L'Ambitieux* 77.

5. *Lettres*, I, 54. May 20–22, 1610.

6. *Archives Historiques du Poitou*, I (1872), 320–324.

7. AAE, France 767, fol. 211 *vo*. June 20, 1610.

8. *L'Ambitieux*, 77; Lacroix, *Richelieu à Luçon*, 219.

9. AAE 767, fol. 173 *vo*, published in *Mémoires de Richelieu*, I, 431–434. Dated April (actually May) 16, 1610.

10. *Ibid.*, 433.

11. AAE, France 767, fol. 211. June 20, 1610.

12. Aumale, *Histoire des princes de Condé*, II, 575; 345.

13. AAE, France 767, fol. 215. June 26, 1610.

14. *Lettres*, I, 55. June 10, 1610.

15. *Mémoires de Richelieu*, I, 433f.; AAE, France 767, fol. 211 and 211 *vo*; 214. May 16; June 20; 26, 1610.

16. *Ibid.*, fol. 205. May 22, 1610.

17. *Ibid.*

18. Berthold Zeller, *La Minorité de Louis XIII: Marie de Médicis et Villeroy* (Paris, 1897), 152. October 12; 13, 1610.

19. *Lettres*, I, 56f. July, 1610 (?).

20. *Mercure François*, I, 442.

21. Bassompierre, *Mémoires*, I, 442.

22. A member of his chapter who addressed letters to him in Paris on November 12, 1610, addressed him at Richelieu on December 10. BL, Additional 22052, fols. 3–4 *vo*.

23. Chapter II, Section 2.

24. AAE, France 768, fol. 169 *vo*. February 14, 1611. Also cited above, Chapter VI, Section 2.

25. On the "*mauvais bruits*" and "*présages*" of these summer months see L'Estoile, *Journal de Henri IV*, III, 111–187.

26. *De Rege et Regis Institutione* (Toledo, 1599).

27. This declaration (Paris, 1610) is cited in the *Mercure françois*, I, 494 *et seq.*

28. L'Estoile, *Journal de Henri IV*, III, 113.

29. Aerrsens describes the apprehension, in some circles in the capital, of a change in policy at the top: "They want too much at the court of Rome; people fear . . . Spain [and the dismissal of Henri IV's ministers]. . . . Those who take advantage of the queen seem to want to overturn everything." Reprinted in *Documents d'Histoire*, III (1912), 396, from *Catalogue of Morrison*, I. March 4, 1611.

30. Zeller, *Marie de Médicis et Villeroy*, 98.

31. *Ibid.*, 151.

32. Henri Griffet, *Histoire du règne de Louis XIII* (3 vols., Paris, 1756), I, 53.

33. The bishop had addressed a highly deferential letter to this lady soon after arriving in his diocese. *Lettres*, I, 42f.

34. Antoinette d'Orléans resigned on April 10, hence Richelieu's and Père Joseph's visit to court was probably soon after this. See René Richard, *Le Véritable père Joseph* (Hague, 1705), 48f.

35. Information on the Père Joseph project concerning Fontevrault is in Lepré-Balain's "Vie manuscrite du Père Joseph," cited by Lacroix, *Richelieu à Luçon*, 184 *et seq.* Lepré-Balain's account is also the basis for Richard's account.

36. Gustave Fagniez, *Le Père Joseph et Richelieu*, I (Paris, 1894), 109.

37. AAE, France 768, fol. 208. January 20, 1612.

38. *Journal de Henri IV*, III, 157. July 27, 1610.

39. Cited from a dispatch of Matteo Botti in Zeller, *Marie de Médicis et Sully*, 53. June 30, 1610.

40. For details on the Concinis' skills in this respect see Malherbe, *Oeuvres*, III, 413. April 6, 1614. Also, Fernand Hayem, *Le Maréchal d'Ancre et Leonora Galigai*, (Paris, 1910), 192; 165; 208.

41. He had followed "very extended studies" at the University of Pisa and had considered a clerical career. *Ibid.*, 11.

42. The term is Hayem's, who illustrates with the *"maréchaux's"* successful efforts to provide Marie with straw hats trimmed as she desired them. *Ibid.*, 165. Rather interestingly, the term *"maréchale"* for Leonora seems to have been Richelieu's invention. Haschke, *Die Sprache Richelieus*, 92.

43. In addition to his discernment, already noted, in church paraphernalia, costume, and garden adornments, one may note also his younger sister's awareness of his fastidiousness in the execution of a tapestry: "I send you . . . the silks necessary for this work and would have had them made up . . . but . . . I was afraid of messing them up and not doing well." BN, fr. 23100, 121 *vo.* Early 1619 (?). He is remarkably knowledgeable in ordering various "galanteries nouvelles" through Madame Bouthillier: "If there should be found some beautiful emerald of an unusual shape or a comparable turquoise I should . . . be delighted to have them," he writes, in addition to a "box full" of jewelry. *Lettres*, III, 906. September 20, 1630.

44. Père Anselme avers of Richelieu, "The recommendation of the marquise de Guercheville gave him entrée to the court." *Le Palais d'honneur*, 539. Suzanne de Richelieu, as has been noted, had herself been lady-in-waiting to Queen Louise of Lorraine and may still have had contacts at court. Madame de Guercheville herself had a legendary renown for virtue, due to having resisted, as Antoinette de Pons, the pressing attentions of Henri IV, and having earned, on this account, his high respect.

45. Hanotaux, *Histoire du cardinal*, II, 84–87.

46. On Zamet's liaison with Père Joseph's relative see *Lettres*, I, 148 *n.* On the queen's favor for him see Malherbe, *Oeuvres*, III, 274.

47. Malherbe, *Oeuvres*, III, 231. May 22, 1611.

48. *Ibid.*, 226–230. May 13–22, 1611. A relation of Gaufriddi's confession and sentence to death is in the *Mercure françois*, III, fols. 18–26.

49. For a characterization of Père Joseph's affinities for the superstitions of princes see Aldous Huxley, *Grey Eminence*, 218–220.

50. Louis Du Four (Abbé de Longuerue), *La Vie du cardinal de Richelieu* in *Recueil de pièces intéressantes pour servir à l'Histoire de France* (Geneva, 1769), 2f.; Fagniez, *Père Joseph*, I, 75.

51. "Déclaration du roy sur . . . des nouveaux remuements dans son royaume," AAE, France 771, fol. 45. February 18, 1617.

52. That there were limits, as J. Michael Hayden emphasizes, to policy concessions that could be made to Ultramontanist efforts is undeniable. *France and the Estates General of 1614* (Cambridge, 1974), 51f. Contrary to his view, however, is the evidence of Marie's personal concern for the esteem of the pope and of these Italian prelates. Ubaldini was particularly confident with her in attempting to influence state policy, threatening her, for example, with "the wrath of God if . . . despite so many paternal warnings from His Sanctity" she allowed her daughter to be married to an English prince. She was as eager to reassure him that "she would rather see her daughter dead than a heretic." Prat, *Recherches historiques sur la compagnie de Jésus*, V, 318. November 29, 1612.

53. On these negotiations see Léonce Anquez, *Histoire des assemblées politiques des réformés de France, 1573–1622* (Paris, 1859), 227 *et seq.*

54. "The queen, leaving the council . . . came over with a smiling face to Madame de Guise, to whom she said that henceforth she would not get up as early in the morning as she had done for some time, and that the Saumur affair was resolved." *Oeuvres*, III, 238.

55. Bullion reported to his chief Villeroy that the former finance minister's "mind is so agitated he does not know what he is doing." *Documents d'histoire* (1910), 268. June 9, 1611.

56. *Lettres*, I, 82–84. Mid-April, 1612. (The letter is misdated March, 1612, as the text refers to events occurring in Paris in April.)

57. *Lettres*, VIII, 5.

58. Fontenelle de Vaudoré, *Histoire des Evêques de Luçon*, VII, 366f.

59. Auguste Lièvre, *Histoire du protestantisme dans le Poitou*, I (Paris, 1856), 273.

60. Quoted from the Archives de la Famille by Lacroix, *Richelieu à Luçon*, 104. April 21, 1613.

61. The *Lettres Patentes du Roi* are dated August 27, 1611. See Martineau, *Le Cardinal* (1866 ed.), 141–143.

62. AAE, France 768, fol. 184.

63. *Lettres*, I, 70f; 72f. November 25; November 26, 1611. Avenel believes his petition to Sourdis was unsuccessful because Richelieu was not finally listed as present in that assembly. In the event, however, Richelieu seems to have preferred to send Sébastien Bouthillier in his place.

64. A letter to him there, in answer to one of his, is dated January 20. AAE, France 768, fol. 208.

65. (Paris, 1611.)

66. I am indebted to Andrew Lossky for this point. Charles Chesneau points out that Richer flattered the bishops at the expense of the papally sponsored *réguliers*. *Père Yves de Paris et son temps* (2 vols., Paris, 1946), I, 11.

67. As far as I have been able to discover, Richer is the only one to mention Richelieu's presence at this special meeting. It was not a provincial assembly as bishops from several provinces were present, including L'Aubespine of Orléans and Hurault of Aix. The general assembly convened later, on March 12, 1612. Edmond Richer, *Histoire du syndicat d'Edmond Richer* (Avignon, 1753), 89.

68. This was a strategy so blatant on the part of the "Italian," thought Richer, that it "made me marvel in wonder." *Ibid.*, 112.

69. *Ibid.*, 93; 186.

70. *Ibid.*, 91; 103; 107.

71. *L'Enfance de Louis XIII*, II, 100. The manuscript indicates that Marie accompanied the king. BN, fr. 4024, fol. 165 *vo*. Héroard had been absent from Fontainebleau between April 15 and 30, 1611, most probable time of the first visit there of Père Joseph and Richelieu. *L'Enfance de Louis XIII*, II, 60.

72. Sirmond, *La Lettre déchiffrée*, in *Recueil de diverses pièces*, 22.

73. *L'Enfance de Louis XIII*, II, 103.

74. *Lettres*, I, 84. *n*.

75. *Ibid.*

76. *Ibid.*, 86f. Towards the middle of 1612 (?). The terms of this letter are indeed so extravagant as to raise doubt about its authenticity. Since its source is a copy it is possible it was not dispatched in this form.

77. It is Vic's response that survives. AAE, France 768, fo. 216. August 25, 1612.

78. AAE, France 768, fol. 232. October 28, 1612. Only L'Aubespine's side of this correspondence is available.

79. For examples, see foreign diplomats' observations, cited in Zeller, *Marie de Médicis et Sully*, 321–332. January–October, 1611.

80. Quoted by Zeller, *Marie de Médicis et Villeroy*, 144. June 12, 1613.

81. Pontchartrain, *Mémoires*, 323; AAE, France 768, fol. 232 *vo*. October 28, 1612. (Pontchartrain, writing years later, puts the crush in December.)

82. Arnauld d'Andilly, *Journal 1614–1620*, 32; 34; 106; 42. January 10–12, May 8, January 30, 1615.

83. Letter of Jacques-Auguste de Thou in *Histoire universelle de Monsieur de Thou*, XV (London, 1734), 563f. July 13, 1616.

84. Hayem, *Le Maréchal d'Ancre*, 112.

85. Zeller, *Marie de Médicis et Sully*, 22–24.

86. Arnauld d'Andilly, *Journal 1614–1620*, 18; 92f. December, 1614; July 7, 1615. When Mathieu Molé excused himself and his colleagues from following an order, he saw that this "caused anger to rise to the queen's face." *Mémoires*, I, 22. March 30, 1615.

87. Griselle, *Louis XIII et Richelieu*, 119.

88. *Lettres*, I, 169f. April, 1616 (?).

89. *Ibid.*, 48; 94. Early 1610(?); November 30, 1612. 48; 94. Early 1610(?); November 30, 1612.

90. *Ibid.*, 92. September 21, 1612.

91. The characterization is Zeller's. *Marie de Médicis et Villeroy*, 149.

92. Henri's deprecation of such a Spanish alliance and his plans for marrying his children are published from AAE, France 767, fols. 120 *et seq.* in *Mémoires*, I, 421–431.

93. Quoted by Zeller, *Marie de Médicis et Sully*, 253. January 26, 1611.

94. Malherbe, *Oeuvres*, III, 285. January 21, 1613.

95. Quoted by J.-B. H.-R. Capefigue, *Richelieu, Mazarin, et la Fronde* (Paris, 1848), 359f.

96. A summary of the Venetian ambassador's dispatch to his principal during the princes' first uprising is given by Zeller: "What is certain is that the queen . . . sent to the court of Madrid a private account of these events . . . and . . . did not conceal her hope that the Most Catholic King would view with displeasure all these disturbances and that she could hope for aid and succor from him if things went farther." *Marie de Médicis et Villeroy*, 135f.

97. *Ibid.*, 188. March 15, 1614.

98. AAE, France 768, fol. 212 vo. February 6, 1613 (misdated April 6, 1612).

99. It may be surmised that the two also shared a mistrust of the Jesuits. L'Aubespine's hostility was open. (See Griselle, *Louis XIII et Richelieu*, 21.) Richelieu's can only be inferred by his care to exclude them from important positions unless he could scrutinize them closely.

100. Zeller, *Marie de Médicis et Villeroy*, 148. September 2, 1613.

101. AAE, France 768, fol. 232. October 28, 1612.

102. *Ibid.*

103. AAE, France 769, fol. 14. March 24, 1613.

104. On this close colleague of Richelieu see Orcibal, *Duvergier de Hauranne*, I, 170–172.

105. Arnauld d'Andilly, *Journal, 1614–1620*, 3.

106. Jean-Baptiste Legrain, *Décade commençant l'histoire du roy Louis XIII* (Paris, 1619), 312f.

107. Avenel guesses the letter is from the beginning of 1615, but it is unlikely that Richelieu would then have referred to the king's minority (which terminated on October 2, 1614) in the present tense. His words are: "The minority of the latter [Louis] . . . and the assignments with which it has pleased the queen to honor me, *forbid* me to undertake any sort of commerce with you." *Lettres*, I, 139f. (Emphasis supplied.)

108. *Ibid.*, 121f. February 12, 1614.

109. AAE, France 769, fols. 98–143 vo.

110. Hanotaux, *Histoire du cardinal*, I, 145.

111. Hanotaux believes that it was during 1614 that forces involved in the struggle between the princes and the crown overran Madame de Richelieu's territory. (See *ibid.*) However Suzanne's letters describing the route taken by "Monsieur le Prince" (via L'Ile Bouchard) and Richelieu's explicit mention that he was at Coussaye at the time (while most of Condé's 1614 ventures in Poitou took place while the bishop was at court) leave little doubt that the château de Richelieu was overrun in 1615. Further, in a letter from the château de Richelieu complaining of "poor Poitou's" plight in the war, Nicole mentions the recent news of Vitry's murder of Montglat, which took place on December 17, 1615. Archives de La Famille, XVIII (no foliation).

112. *Lettres*, I, 124f. Towards mid-May, 1614.

113. This intention is affirmed in Marie's letters of that month according to Hayden, *Estates General*, 62 n.

114. AAE, France 769, fol. 173. Undated (before the official announcement on June 7, 1614).

115. *Lettres*, I, 123. End of April.

116. In June one of his representatives writes that the seneschal of Fontenay is "highly incensed" against those of Richelieu's officers who have brought suit against himself and that he is waiting for authorization from Paris to subpoena testimony from the bishop in person to determine "whether it is you yourself who are defraying the costs of said lawsuit in which he is cited as defendant." Such forced testimony might have been expected to

jeopardize Richelieu's candidacy in the pending elections. His correspondent knows it would give him *"déplaisir."* AAE, France 769, fol. 171 *vo.* June, 1614.

117. Richelieu's enemy in Fontenay, however, may have had a part in a scheme through which the diocese of Maillezais combined with Fontenay and sent a rival clerical delegation from the latter city. But by the time these clerics actually arrived in Paris in the autumn, Richelieu, his favor at court by now well established, was easily able to obtain an order from the king's council discrediting their claim. Hanotaux, *Histoire du cardinal*, I, 150 *n.* See below, Chapter XI, Section 1.

118. *L'Enfance de Louis XIII*, II, 150f.

119. AAE, France 1696, fols. 22–24. August 9–19, 1614.

120. *Autour de la plume*, 75.

121. AAE, France 769, fol. 215. October 14, 1614. Since a question of a military appointment is involved here one might suspect that it is Henri de Richelieu, then an officer in the army of Piedmont, who is addressed here by Marillac, but the letter is clearly inscribed to "Monsieur l'Evesque de Lussan."

122. He had no house of his own there on September 18, 1612, but had acquired one by the time of this letter. Avenel, unaware of his sojourn in Coussaye in 1614, speculates that it was written in 1615. *Lettres*, I, 90; 146f.; VIII, 8. The satisfaction of Richelieu's longing for his own dwelling, of which Avenel takes note, may have been enhanced by its significance as restoration of property lost by his father.

123. AAE, France 769, fol. 181 and *vo.* See above, Chapter V, Section 1.

124. P. F. D. G., *Le Miroir royal de Saint Louis*, 71; 9 *vo* ; 3. A copy held by the Bibliothèque Nationale (Lb 36. 395) has a contemporary note after the designation "poitevin" on the title page: "Like his grandfather La Porte."

125. *Lettres*, I, 125. Middle of May, 1614.

Chapter 11

1. "Caput Apologeticum," *Lettres*, VII, 417. April, 1618 (?).

2. Héroard, *L'enfance de Louis XIII*, II, 159f.

3. Hanotaux, *Histoire du cardinal*, II, 15.

4. Pierre Blet, *Le Clergé de France et la monarchie*, I (Rome, 1959), 3–39.

5. *Mémoires du comte de Brienne*, Petitot, ed. (Paris, 1824), 298.

6. Arnauld d'Andilly, *Journal, 1614–1620*, 24–26. January 7–8, 1615.

7. Arnauld also noted, with annoyance, that prelates and other clerical deputies managed to be seated in front of the councillors of state at the plenary session opening the meetings. *Ibid.*, 11.

8. Aumale, *Princes de Condé*, III, 35.

9. This is reported by Charles de La Saussaye, an Orléanais cleric and lawyer, and not by Behety, official secretary of the clergy. BN, fr. 4082, fol. 4 *vo.*

10. Pierre Clapisson, "Recueil journalier de ce qui s'est négocié et arrêsté à la chambre du Tiers Etat. . . . " BN, fr. 4085, fols. 58 *vo* -59. November 5, 1614. This has been published in Lalourcé and Duval, *Recueil de pièces originales . . . concernant la tenue des Etats Généraux* (9 vols., Paris 1789), VIII.

11. For a recent analysis of occupational distributions in the various delegations see Hayden, *Estates General*, 81–97.

12. Clapisson, "Recueil journalier," fols. 58 *vo*, 59. November 5, 1614.

13. *Autour de la plume*, 75.

14. Claude Le Doux de Menneville, "Journal," *Recueil des travaux de la Société Libre d'Agriculture, Sciences, Arts et Belles-Lettres de l'Eure*, Series 4, VIII (1889–1890), 561. I have used the form of the witness's name assigned him by Eugène Griselle, who published part of the same account in *Documents d'Histoire*, II (1911), 171–183.

15. Florimond Rapine, *Recueil très exact et curieux de tout ce qui s'est fait et passé de singulier et mémorable en l'assemblée générale des Estats tenus à Paris l'an 1614* (Paris, 1631), 136.

16. Clapisson, "Recueil journalier," fols. 90–91. November 20, 1614.

17. See above, Chapter X, Section 6.

18. Rapine, *Recueil très exact*, 138.

19. Clapisson, "Recueil journalier," fol. 91 *vo*.

20. Quoted by Lacroix from a manuscript copy of Montcassin's *procès-verbal* of the sessions of the nobility in *Richelieu à Luçon*, 229.

21. Zeller, *Marie de Médicis, Chef du Conseil*, 63.

22. Clapisson, "Recueil journalier," fols. 92–94.

23. *Ibid.*, fol. 99 *vo*.

24. *Mercure françois*, III, Pt. 2, 225. February 1, 1615.

25. *Histoire du cardinal*, II, 24.

26. Dugrès, *Armand Du Plessis*, 56.

27. Le Doux, "Journal," 562f.

28. A modern analyst has observed, "There is a certain infectiousness of the 'unconflicted personality constellation' on the 'conflicted one' of the same drive conflict pattern. . . . The influential person must have definitely resolved his own conflict." Fritz Redl, "Group Emotion and Leadership," *Psychiatry*, V (1942), 595.

29. Courtin, Arsenal MS 4651, fol. 302.

30. Arnauld d'Andilly, *Journal, 1614–1615*, 26f. January 8, 1615.

31. See above, Chapter X, Section 2.

32. Hanotaux, *Histoire du cardinal*, II, 28.

33. J.-A. de Thou, *Histoire universelle*, X, 569. Letter of 1616.

34. Quoted by Zeller, *Marie de Médicis, Chef du Conseil*, 70f.

35. Montcassin, "Procès-verbal du 2e Estat," in Lalourcé and Duval, VII, 170f.

36. Quoted by Salvatore Mastellone, *La Reggenza di Maria de' Medici* (Florence, 1962), 207.

37. Words crossed out by Richelieu.

38. AAE, France 769, fols. 316–324.

39. *Histoire du cardinal*, II, 25.

40. *Histoire universelle*, X, 569.

41. Cited by Hayden, *Estates General*, 47 *n*.

42. Arnauld d'Andilly, *Journal, 1614–1620*, 26.

43. *Ibid.*, 29. Curiously, this is the very phrase that Sourdis claims, in a report to the Florentine ambassador, that the king used towards Condé a month later. See Zeller, *Marie de Médicis, Chef du Conseil*, 78. Héroard does not report any conversation of this kind on the later date. (February 6.) On the earlier one (January 8 according to his manuscript, inexplicably January 6 in the published *L'Enfance de Louis XIII*, II, 172), the provocative remarks that evoked Louis's angry rejoinder are attributed by Héroard to Du Perron instead of to Sourdis. BN, fr. 4025, fol. 124 *vo*.

44. Pierre de Behety, *Procès verbal . . . en la chambre ecclésiastique* (2d ed., Paris, 1650), 165.

45. Hanotaux, *Histoire du cardinal*, II, 36.

46. Behety, *Procès verbal*, 250 January 23, 1615.

47. *Autour de la plume*, 77.

48. Behety, *Procès verbal*, 3–90 for the clergy's list; 338–340 for the thirteen points "given" to Richelieu on the morning of his address.

49. For the comparison see Zeller, *Marie de Médicis, Chef du Conseil*, 88.

50. "Harangue . . . pour le clergé," in *Mémoires*, I, 350. Compare this "Machiavellian" reasoning with the axiom, "Because men that think themselves equal, will not enter into conditions of peace but upon equal terms, such equality must be admitted." Thomas Hobbes, *Leviathan* (1651), Chapter XV.

51. "Harangue pour le clergé," 344.

52. *Ibid.*, 345.

53. Arnauld d'Andilly, *Journal, 1614–1620,* 54. February 20, 1615.

54. "Harangue pour le clergé," 356.

55. *Ibid.,* 364.

56. Blet, for example, does not allude to this qualification by Richelieu of the necessity for implementing the Tridentine decrees. See *Le Clergé et la monarchie,* I, 11.

57. "Harangue pour le clergé," 348.

58. Hanotaux, *Histoire du cardinal,* II, 19; *Perroniana et Thuana,* 116.

59. "Harangue pour le clergé," 345–348.

60. *Ibid.,* 346.

61. *Ibid.*

62. *Ibid.,* 342f.

63. *Ibid.,* 356.

64. *Procès verbal,* 350.

65. "Harangue pour le clergé," 360.

66. *Ibid.,* 361.

67. *Ibid.,* 349.

68. *Ibid.,* 363.

69. *Mercure françois,* I (1611), 475.

70. James Howell, *Familiar Letters,* (2 vols., Boston, 1908), I, 48. May 12, 1620.

71. "Harangue pour le clergé," 358.

72. *Ibid.,* 361.

73. *Ibid.,* 346.

74. *Ibid.,* 359f; 364.

75. *Ibid.,* 351; 354.

76. *Ibid.,* 354; 359.

77. *Histoire du cardinal,* II, 41.

78. "Harangue pour le clergé," 359.

79. *Ibid.*

80. *Ibid.*

Selected Bibliography

[Note: Only writings bearing on historical facts are listed here. Not all of those cited in the text are included.]

Manuscripts in France

ARCHIVES DU MINISTERE DES AFFAIRES EXTERIEURES (AAE)

Mémoires et documents, France, 243–246; 248; 373; 767–772; 780; 787; 792; 815; 831; 834; 839; 1696 (Poitou); 2164 [Note: Most of the documents in this volume have been published in the *Catalogue of the Collection of Alfred Morrison,* edited by Thibaudeau. See below.]
Correspondance diplomatique, Rome, 23; 63; 67. Angleterre, 26.

INSTITUT DE FRANCE

Godefroy, 268, 269.
Bibliothèque Condé, Série I:VIII; LXCIV; LXCIV.

ARCHIVES NATIONALES

M74; 129 MI 53–56.
IIB, vols. 384; 385.

ARCHIVES DE LA FAMILLE RICHELIEU

VII; XIV-XIX.

BIBLIOTHEQUE MUNICIPALE DE POITIERS

Collection Martineau.
Collection Dom Fontenau II; IV; XXXII.
Nouvelles acquisitions 3837; 3882; 5340.

BIBLIOTHEQUE NATIONALE (BN)

Français

Ancien fonds, 3145; 3309; 3378; 3407; 3797; 3818; 4022–4025; 4082; 4085; 4680; 6408; 6631; 10876; 15644; 16804; 17333; 18256; 18319; 22398; 22884; 23200–23202; 23340; 24445.
Nouvelles acquisitions, 3145; 3378; 3644; 5131; 7254; 13008; 16803.
Duchesne, 30.
Dupuy, 39; 625; 661; 802.

Selected Bibliography

Cabinet d'Hozier, 271.
Cinq cents Colbert, 2; 221.
Clairambault, 372.
Béthune, 9299.
Baluze, 145.

Italien, 1762–1771.

Arsenal, 187; 3558; 4255; 4651.

Manuscripts Outside France

ARCHIVIO GONZAGA

Francia, Correspondenza Estera (Serie E) 627; 628 *e bis*.

BRITISH LIBRARY (BL)

Egerton, 1169; 1687–1688; 1690–1692.
Additional, 5447; 6873; 10820; 14840; 18741; 22052; 24206; 25446; 29760; 35097; 45142.
Sloane, 2868.

Published Works from Contemporary Sources

MAJOR COLLECTIONS OF DIVERSE DOCUMENTS

Calendar of State Papers. Domestic Series: Reign of James I. Mary Green, editor. Vol. IX (1611–1618). London, 1858.
Catalogue of the Collection of Alfred Morrison. Alphonse Thibaudeau, editor. First Series, Vols. I–VI. London, 1883–1892.
Documents d'histoire. Eugène Griselle, editor. 4 vols. Paris, 1910–1913.
Fichier Charavay (Département des Manuscrits, BN.)
Formulaires de lettres de François I à Louis XIV et Etat de la France Dressé en 1642. Eugène Griselle, editor. N.p.: n.d.
Lettres sur la profession d'avocat. Armand G. Camus and J. Dupin, editors. Vol. II. 4th edition, Paris, 1818.
Mémoires pour l'histoire du cardinal de Richelieu. Antoine Aubéry, editor. 5 vols. Cologne, 1667.
Mémoires du cardinal de Richelieu. Société de l'Histoire de France, editors. 10 vols. Paris, 1908–1929.
Mercure françois. Vols. I–IV. Estienne Richer, editor. Paris, 1611–1614.
Négociations diplomatiques de la France avec la Toscane. Vol. V. Paris, 1875.
Les Papiers de Richelieu: Section politique intérieure. Pierre Grillon, editor. 4 vols. and 1 vol. Index to vols. I–III. Paris, 1975–1980.
Recueil de diverses pièces pour servir à l'histoire. Hay Du Chastellet, editor. N. p., 1639.
Recueil des cahiers généraux des trois ordres aux Etats généraux. Lalourcé and Duval, editors. Vol. IV. 4 vols. Paris, 1789.
Recueil de pièces originales . . . concernant la tenue des Etats généraux. Lalourcé and Duval, editors. Vols. VI-IX. 9 vols. Paris, 1789.
Relazioni degli Stati Europei: Lettere al Senato degli ambasciatori Veneti nel secolo XVIIo. Guglielmo Berchet and Nicolo Barozzi, editors. Second series, vol. I. Venice, 1857.

WRITINGS IDENTIFIED BY INDIVIDUALS

Anselme, Pierre de Guibours, Père. *Histoire généalogique . . . de France*. 9 vols. Paris, 1726–1733.

Selected Bibliography

Ardier, Paul. *Mémoires de l'Assemblée des Notables.* Paris, 1652.

Arnauld d'Andilly, Robert. *Journal, 1614–1620.* Achille Halphen, editor. Paris, 1857.

Aubéry, Antoine. *L'Histoire des cardinaux françois.* Paris, 1644.

———. *L'Histoire du cardinal-duc de Richelieu.* Vol. I. 2 vols., Cologne, 1666.

Guez de Balzac, *Les Premières lettres.* H. Bibas and K. T. Butler, editors. 2 vols. Paris, 1933.

Bassompierre, François de. *Mémoires.* Vol. I. Petitot, editor. 3 vols. Paris, 1822–1823.

Beauvais-Nangis, Nicolas de. *Mémoires.* Paris, 1862.

Behety, Pierre. *Procès verbal . . . en la chambre ecclésiastique.* Second edition. Paris, 1650.

Bentivoglio, Guido. *La Nunziatura di Francia de Cardinale G. Bentivoglio: Lettere a Scipione Borghese.* Luigi de Steffani, editor. Vol. I. Florence, 1863.

Bernard, Charles. *L'Histoire des guerres de Louis XIII.* Paris, 1636.

———. *Histoire de Louis XIII.* Paris, 1646.

Bérulle, Pierre. *Correspondance.* Jean Dagens, editor. Vols. I–III. Paris, 1937–1939.

Birch, Thomas. *An Historical View of the Negotiations between the Courts of England, France and Brussels, from the Year 1592.* London, 1749.

"Lettres addressées, 1585–1625 à Marc-Antoine M. de Boisguérin, Gouverneur de Loudun." G. de Lamarque and Ed. de Barthélemy, editors. *Archives Historiques du Poitou.* XIV (1883), 189–369.

Boisrobert, François le Métel, Abbé de. *Epistres en vers.* 2 vols. Paris, 1647.

Bouche, Honoré. *Histoire de Provence.* Vol. II. Paris, 1664.

Bourbon, Jeanne-Baptiste de. *Reigle de l'ordre de Fontevrauld.* Paris, 1642.

"La Correspondance du maréchal de Brézé, 1632–1649." *Mémoires de la Société Eduenne.* 1895; 1896.

"Les Amis du maréchal de Brézé." Gustave Masson, editor. *Cabinet Historique.* 1869, 32–47; 117–124; 139–158.

Bourdonné, Le Sieur de. *Pensées d'un gentilhomme.* Paris, 1658.

Brienne, Henri Auguste de Loménie, Comte de. *Mémoires du comte de Brienne.* Michaud and Poujoulat, editors. Paris, 1838.

Bufalo, I. del. *Correspondance du Nonce en France, 1601–1605.* B. Barbiche, editor. Vol. IV of *Acta Nunciaturae Gallicae.* Rome, 1964.

Campion, Henri de. *Mémoires.* M. C. Moreau, editor. Paris, 1857.

Carew, George. "A Relation of the State of France (1609)," in Thomas Birch, *An Historical View of the Negotiations.* London, 1749.

Castelnau, Michel de. *Mémoires.* 2 vols. Paris, 1659.

Cayet, Palma. *Chronologie novenaire et septenaire.* J.-A.-C. Buchon, editor. 2 vols. Paris, 1836–1875.

Chanteloube, J. Apchon de. *Lettre du p. Chantelouve au cardinal de Richelieu* [Pamphlet]. Angoulême, 1612.

Chapelain, Jean. *Lettres.* 2 vols. Reprint edition. Paris, 1968.

Chartier, Alain. *Oeuvres.* André Duchesne, editor. Paris, 1617.

Contant, Paul. *Oeuvres de Jacques et Paul Contant, père et fils . . . en cinq traictez.* Poitiers, 1628.

Coton, Pierre. *Lettre dédicatoire des pères Jésuites . . . à la reyne mère suivie de l' Anticoton et Réponse à l'Anticoton.* Paris, 1610.

Déageant, Guichard de, Sieur de Saint-Martin. *Mémoires envoyés à Monsieur le Cardinal de Richelieu.* Vol. III of *Mémoires particuliers pour servir à l'histoire de France.* Paris, 1756.

Desmarets de Saint-Sorlin, Jean. *Les Délices de l'esprit.* Second edition. Paris, 1661.

———. *Le Tombeau du grand cardinal de Richelieu.* Paris, 1643.

Des Réaux, Tallemant. *Les Historiettes.* Monmerqué and Paris, editors. 6 vols. Third edition. Paris, 1862.

"Documents inédits sur le cardinal de Richelieu." *Revue Héraldique, Historique et Nobiliaire,* 1871. 457–463; 536–555.

Duchesne, André. *Les Antiquitez et recherches de la majesté des roys de France.* Paris, 1609.

———. *Histoire généalogique de la maison royale de Dreux et de quelques autres familles.* Paris, 1631.

Selected Bibliography

Duchesne, François. *Histoire des chanceliers.* Paris, 1680.

Du Ferron, Rémi. *Vita Card. Richelii.* Orléans, 1626.

Du Grès, Gabriel. *Jean Armand Du Plessis, Duke of Richelieu and Peere of France.* London, 1634.

Du Laurens, Louis. *Dispute touchant le schisme et la séparation que Luther et Calvin ont faite de l'Eglise Romaine.* Paris, 1655.

Du Perron, Jacques Davy, Cardinal. *Les Ambassades et négociations de l'illustrissime . . . cardinal Du Perron.* 4th Edition. Paris, 1633.

Dupuy, Pierre. *Histoire des plus illustres favoris, anciens et modernes.* Leiden, 1659.

Feuquières, Manassès de Pas de. *Lettres et négociations.* Amsterdam, 1753.

Fontenay-Mareuil, François Duval de. *Mémoires.* Michaud and Poujoulat, editors. Paris, 1837.

Fortin de La Hoguette, Philippe. *Lettres inédites à Pierre Dupuy.* Tamizey de Larroque, editor. La Rochelle, 1888.

Frizon, Pierre. *Galliae Purpuratae.* Paris, 1638.

"Mémoires inédits du père Garasse." Charles Alléaume, editor. *La Correspondance Littéraire,* March 5, 1859, 149–151.

P. F. D. G., poitevin. *Le Miroir royal des Louis.* Paris, 1614.

Girard, Guillaume. *History of the Life of the Duke of Epernon.* London, 1670.

Grenade, Louis de. *Catéchisme ou introduction du Symbole de la Foy.* P. Colin, translator. Paris, 1587.

————. *L'Oraison dominicale.* Clermont-Ferrand, 1889.

Grenaille, Chatonnières de. *Le Mausolée cardinal ou éloge funèbre de feu monseigneur le cardinal.* Paris, 1643.

Griselle, Eugène. *Louis XIII et Richelieu.* Paris, 1911.

————. *Supplément à la maison du roi Louis XIII.* Paris, 1912.

Hanotaux, Gabriel, editor. "Maximes d'état et fragments politiques du cardinal de Richelieu." *Mélanges historiques.* Vol. III. Paris, 1880.

Henri IV. *Lettres missives du roi Henri IV.* Berger de Xivrey and J. Guadet, editors. 8 vols. Paris, 1850–1873.

Herbault, Raymond Phélypeaux de and Ardier, Paul. *Au siège de La Rochelle [Lettres inédites].* Louis Delavaud, editor. Reprint from *Archives Historiques de la Saintonge et de l'Aunis,* XLIII (1912).

Hermant, Godefroy. *Mémoires.* Vol. I. P. Gazier, editor. 10 vols. Paris, 1905–1910.

Héroard, Jean. *Journal de l'enfance et de la première jeunesse de Louis XIII.* Eud. Soulié and Edouard de Barthélemy, editors. 2 vols. Paris, 1868.

Howell, James. *A Brief Admonition of some of the Inconveniences of all the Three Most Famous Governments.* London, 1659.

————. *Familiar Letters.* 2 vols. Boston, 1908.

————. *Lustra Ludovici.* London, 1646.

Joseph, François Leclerc Du Tremblay, [Père]. *Introduction à la vie spirituelle par une facile méthode d'oraison.* Paris, 1626.

Lalanne, Ludovic, editor. "Un Récit inédit de la mort du cardinal de Richelieu." *Revue Historique,* LV (1894), 305–308.

La Mesnardière, Hippolyte-Jule de La. *Recueil des harangues prononcées par Messieurs de l'Académie.* Vol. I. Paris, 1672.

L'Anglois, Pierre, Sieur de Bel-Esbat. *Tableaux hiéroglyphiques.* Paris, 1583.

La Rochefoucauld, François de. *Les Mémoires du duc de La Rochefoucauld.* Michaud and Poujoulat, editors. Paris, 1881.

L'Aubespine, Gabriel de. *Les Correspondants de Peiresc: Gabriel de l'Aubespine.* Philippe Tamizey de Larroque, editor. Orléans, 1883.

Le Doux de Menneville, Claude. "Journal." *Recueil des travaux de la Société Libre d'Agriculture, Sciences, Arts et Belles-Lettres de l'Eure.* Series 4, VIII (1889–1890).

Legrain, Jean-Baptiste. *Décade commençant l'histoire du roy Louis XIII.* Paris, 1619.

Le Riche, Guillaume and Michel. *Journal.* Saint-Maixent, 1846.

L'Estoile, Pierre. *Journal pour les règnes de Henri III, Henri IV , et du début du règne de Louis XIII.* Louis-R. Lefèvre and André Martin, editors. 4 vols. Paris, 1943–1960.

Macé, Jean. [Père Léon de Saint-Jean.] *Epistolae Selectae.* Paris, 1661.

——. *La Très éloquente harangue funèbre . . . à . . . Père Joseph.* Paris, 1638.

Malherbe, François de. *Oeuvres.* Ad. Régnier, editor. Vols. III, IV. Paris, 1862.

Malingre, Claude. *Histoire du règne de Louis XIII.* 2 vols. Paris, 1646.

Marolles, Michel de, Abbé de Villeloin. *Mémoires.* 3 vols., Amsterdam, 1755.

Matthieu, Pierre. *Considerations on the Life and Services of Monsieur Villeroy, together with Certain Political Observations upon the fall of Sejanus.* Thomas Hawkins, translator. London, 1638.

Mersenne, Marin. *Correspondance.* Paul Tannery, editor. 6 vols. Paris, 1932–1960.

La Miliade: Le Gouvernement présent ou éloge de Son Eminence. Antwerp (?), 1633.

Miraulmont, Pierre de. *Mémoires.* Paris, 1584.

Molé, Mathieu. *Mémoires de Mathieu Molé.* Aimé Champollion-Figeac, editor. 4 vols. Paris, 1855–1857.

Montchal, Charles de. *Mémoires de Monsieur de Montchal.* 2 vols. Rotterdam, 1718.

Montglat, François de Paule de Clermont, Marquis de. *Mémoires de Montglat.* Michaud et Poujoulat, editors. Paris, 1881.

Morgues, Mathieu de. *La Restauration de l'estat.* N. p.: 1617.

La Vie de Maître J[ean]-B[aptiste] Morin. Paris, 1660.

Morisot, Claude de Barthélemy. *Peruviana.* Dijon, 1645.

Naudé, Gabriel. *Considerations politiques sur les coups d'estat.* Rome, 1639.

Pasquier, Nicolas. *Lettres.* Paris, 1623.

Peiresc, Fabri de. *Lettres.* Philippe Tamizey de Larroque, editor. 7 vols. Paris, 1888–1898.

Pellisson-Fontaines, Paul. *Relation contenant l'histoire de l'Académie Françoise.* Paris, 1672.

Péricaud, Antoine. *Notes et documents pour servir à l'histoire de Lyon sous le règne de Louis XIII.* Lyons, 1846.

Perrault, Charles. *Les Hommes illustres qui ont paru en France pendant le XVIIIe siècle.* Vol. I. Third edition, Paris, 1701.

Pontchartrain, Paul Phélypeaux de. *Mémoires de Pontchartrain.* Michaud and Poujoulat, editors. Paris, 1837.

Pure, Michel. *La Pitieuse.* Emile Magne, editor. Paris, 1938.

——. *Vita Eminentissimi Cardinalis Arm. Joan. Plessei Richelii.* Paris, 1656.

——. *Vita Alphonsi-Ludovici Plessaei Richelii.* Paris, 1653.

Rapin, René. "Mémoires du père Rapin." *Histoire du jansénisme.* Emmanuel Domenech, editor. Paris, 1861.

Rapine, Florimond de. *Recueil très exact et curieux de tout ce qui s'est fait et passé de singulier en l'assemblée générale des Estats tenus à Paris, l'an 1614.* Paris, 1631.

Richard, L'Abbé. *Le Véritable père Joseph.* Vol. I. Saint-Jean de Maurienne, 1704.

Renaudot, Théophraste. *Stances pour la santé du Roy.* Paris, 1627.

——. *Eloge d'Armand-Jean Du Plessis, Cardinal de Richelieu.* Paris, 1628.

Richelieu, Alphonse de. "Deux lettres." *Bulletin de la Commission Historique de Lyons.* 1909; 1910.

——. "Lettres écrites . . . pendant son ambassade . . . à . . . Rome." *Le Conservateur.* May, 1757.

Richelieu, Armand-Jean Du Plessis de. *L'Instruction du chrestien.* Paris, 1619.

——. *Journal du cardinal de Richelieu . . . pendant le grand orage.* 2 vols. Paris, 1665.

——. *Lettres, instructions et papiers d'Etat du cardinal de Richelieu.* Denis-Louis-Martial Avenel, editor. 8 volumes. Paris, 1853–1877.

—— . "Ordonnances synodales." In Jacques de Flavigny. *Briefve et facile instruction pour les confesseurs.* Fontenay, 1613.

——. *Les Principaux points de la foi chrestienne défendus contre l'escrit addressé au Roy par les quatre ministres de Charenton.* Avignon, 1617.

Selected Bibliography

―――. "Testament de son emmentissime Armand-Jean Du Plessis de Richelieu." In Louis E. Dussieux. *Le Cardinal de Richielieu*. Paris, 1866. 348–376.

―――[attributed to.] *Le Testament politique de Richelieu*. Louis André, editor. Paris, 1941.

―――[attributed to.] *Traité de la perfection du chrestien*. Paris, 1647.

―――[attributed to.] *Traité qui contient la méthode la plus facile et la plus assurée pour convertir ceux qui se sont séparés de l'église*. Paris, 1651.

Richer, Edmond. *Histoire du syndicat d'Edmond Richer*. Avignon, 1753.

Saint Evremond, Charles de Marguetel de Saint-Denis de. *Oeuvres*. Vol. IV. 7 vols. Amsterdam, 1726.

Sales, François de [Saint]. *Lettres*. Vols XI-XXI of *Oeuvres de Saint François de Sales*. Sisters of the Visitation of Annecy, editors. 21 vols. Lyons, 1900–1923.

Scotti, Ranuccio. *Correspondance du Nonce en France (1639–1641)*. Pierre Blet, editor. Vol. V of *Acta Nunciaturae Gallicae*. Rome, 1965.

Senault, Jean-François. *Oraison funèbre de Madame Magdelaine de La Porte*. Paris, 1671.

Seyssel, Claude. *The Monarchy of France*. Donald R. Kelley, editor. Jack H. Hexter, translator. New Haven, 1981.

Siri, Vittorio. *Memorie recondite*. Vol. IV. 8 volumes. Rome, 1677–1679.

Sirmond, Jean de. *La Lettre déchiffrée*. Paris, 1627.

Sully, Maximilien de Béthune, Duc de. *Mémoires du duc de Sully*. 6 vols. Paris, 1822–1827.

Surin, Jean-Joseph. *Correspondance*. Michel de Certeau, editor. Paris, 1966.

Thou, Jacques-Auguste de. *Histoire universelle*. Vol. XV. London, 1735.

Villeroy, Nicolas de Neufville, Seigneur de. *Mémoires servant à l'histoire de notre temps*. Michaud and Poujoulat, editors. Paris, 1822.

Vincent de Paul, [Saint]. *Conférences aux Filles de la Charité*. Paris, 1902.

―――. *Correspondance*. Pierre Coste, editor. 14 volumes. Paris, 1920–1925.

Secondary Works

BOOKS

Aboucaya, Claude. *Les Intendants de la marine sous l'ancien régime: Contribution à l'étude du département, du port et arsenal de la marine de Toulon*. Gap, 1958.

Adam, Antoine. *Grandeur and Illusion: French Literature and Society, 1600–1715*. Herbert Tint, translator. New York, 1972.

―――, et al. *Richelieu*. Paris, 1972.

Albertini, Rudolf von. *Das politische Denken in Frankreich zur Zeit Richelieus*. Marburg, 1951.

Anquez, Léonce. *Histoire des assemblées politiques des réformés de France, 1573–1622*. Paris, 1859.

Aumale, Henri d'Orleans, duc d'. *Histoire des princes de Condé*. Vol. III. 8 vols. Paris, 1863–1896.

Aulard, Alphonse. *Le Patriotisme français de la renaissance à la révolution*. Paris, 1921.

Avenel, Georges d'. *Richelieu et la monarchie absolue*. Vol. I. Paris, 1895.

Barbiche, Bernard. *Sully*. Paris, 1978.

Edouard de Barthélemy. *La Marquise d'Huxelles et ses amis*. Paris, 1881.

Louis Batiffol. *Le Louvre sous Henri IV et Louis XIII*. Paris, 1930.

―――. *Richelieu et le roi Louis XIII*. Paris, 1934.

Baudson, Emile. *Charles de Gonzague, duc de Nevers de Rethel et de Mantoue (1580–1637)*. Paris, 1947.

Bayley, Peter. *French Pulpit Oratory*. Cambridge, England, 1980.

Belvederi, Raffaele. *Guido Bentivoglio e la politica Europea del suo tempo*. Padua, 1962.

Bitton, Davis. *The French Nobility in Crisis, 1560–1640*. Stanford, 1969.

Blet, Henri. *Histoire de la colonisation française*. Vol. I: *Origines à 1789*. Paris, 1946.

Blet, Pierre. *Le Clergé de France et la monarchie*. Vol. I. Rome, 1959.

Bloch, Marc. *Les Rois thaumaturges*. Reprint edition. Paris, 1961.

Selected Bibliography

Boissonade, M. B. *L'Administration royale et les soulèvements populaires en Poitou (1624–1642)*. Poitiers, 1903.

——. *Histoire du Poitou*. Paris, 1926.

Boiteux, L.-André. *Richelieu: Grand maître de la navigation et du commerce de France*. Caen, 1955.

Bonneau-Avenant, Alfred. *La Duchesse d'Aiguillon*. Paris, 1879.

Richard J. Bonney. *The King's Debts: Finance and Politics in France, 1589–1661*. Oxford, 1981.

——. *Political Change in France under Richelieu and Mazarin, 1624–1661*. Oxford, 1978.

Bontems, Claude, Raybaud, Léon-Pierre, and Brancourt, Jean-Pierre. *Le Prince dans la France des XVIe et XVIIe siècles*. Paris, 1965.

Bosseboeuf, L.-A. *Histoire de Richelieu et de ses environs*. Tours, 1890.

Bremond, Henri. *A Literary History of Religious Thought in France from the Wars of Religion Down to our Own Times*. Vol. I. K. L. Montgomery, translator. 3 vols., New York, 1928.

Briçonnet, L'Arche. [Père Henry de Calais.] *Histoire de la vie du R. P. Honoré Bochart de Champigny, capucin*. New edition. Paris, 1864.

Broutin, Paul. *La Réforme pastorale en France au XVIIe siècle: recherches sur la tradition pastorale après le Concile de Trente*. Vol. I. Tournai, 1956.

Caillet, Jules. *L'Administration en France sous le ministère du cardinal de Richelieu*. Paris, 1857.

Capefigue, Jean-B.-H.-R.,. *Richelieu, Mazarin et la Fronde*. Paris, 1848.

Certeau, Michel de. *La Possession de Loudun*. Paris, 1970.

——, et al. *Le Mépris du monde*. Paris, 1965.

Chérot, Henri. *Etudes sur la vie et les oeuvres du père Le Moyne*. Paris, 1887.

——. *Le Père du grand Condé*. Paris, 1892.

Chéruel, Alphonse. *Dictionnaire historique des institutions de la France*. 2 vols., Paris, 1874.

Chesneau, Charles. *Le Père Yves de Paris et son temps*. 2 vols. Paris, 1946.

Chevallier, Pierre. *Louis XIII*. Paris, 1979.

Church, William F. *Richelieu and Reason of State*. Princeton, 1972.

Cognet, Louis. *La Spiritualité française au 17e siècle*. Paris, 1949.

Cousin, Victor. *Madame de Chevreuse*. Paris, 1856.

Dainville, François de. *Les Jésuites et l'éducation de la société française*. Paris, 1940.

Daniel, Charles. *Une Vocation et une disgrâce*. Paris, 1861.

Dedouvres, Louis. *Le Père Joseph de Paris*. 2 vols., Paris, 1931.

Delavaud, Louis. *Quelques collaborateurs de Richelieu*. Paris, 1915.

Deloche, Maximin. *Autour de la plume du cardinal de Richelieu*. Paris, 1920.

——. *Le Cardinal de Richelieu et les femmes*. Paris, 1931.

——. *Un Frère de Richelieu inconnu*. Paris, 1935.

——. *La Maison natale du cardinal de Richelieu*. Poitiers, 1932.

——. *Les Richelieu: le père du cardinal*. Paris, 1923.

Delavignette, Robert, and Julien, Charles-André. *Les Constructeurs de la France d'Outre Mer*. Paris, 1946.

Delumeau, Jean. *Naissance et affirmation de la réforme*. Paris, 1965.

Dewald, Jonathan. *The Formation of a Provincial Nobility: The Magistrates of the Parlement of Rouen, 1499–1610*. Princeton, 1980.

Dhotel, Jean-Claude. *Les Origines du catéchisme moderne*. Aubier, 1967.

Dollot, Louis. *Les Cardinaux-ministres sous la monarchie française*. Paris, 1952.

Dreux Du Radier, Jean-F. *La Bibliothèque du Poitou*. Vol. II, Paris, 1754.

Dubois, Elfrieda. *René Rapin: L'Homme et l'oeuvre*. (Thesis.) Lille, 1970.

Esmonin, Edmond. *Etudes sur la France des XVIIe et XVIIIe siècles*. Paris, 1964.

Fagniez, Gustave. *La Femme et la société française dans la première moitié du XVIIe siècle*. Paris, 1921.

——. *Le Père Joseph et Richelieu*. 2 vols. Paris, 1894.

Flandrin, Jean-Louis. *Familles: Parenté, maison, sexualité dans l'ancienne société*. Paris, 1976.

Fromilhague, René. *La Vie de Malherbe: Apprentissage et luttes (1555–1610)*. Paris, 1964.

Gasté, Armand. *La Querelle du Cid*. Paris, 1898.

261

Selected Bibliography

Godard de Donville, Louise. *La Signification de la mode sous Louis XIII.* Aix-en-Provence, 1978.

Goubert, Pierre. *Beauvais et le Beauvaisis de 1600 à 1730.* 2 vols. Paris, 1960.

Griffet, Henri. *Histoire du règne de Louis XIII.* Vols. I-III. Paris, 1756. (Vols. 13–15 of P. Daniel, editor, *Histoire de France.*)

Griselle, Eugène. *Profils de jésuites du 17e siècle.* Paris, 1911.

Gutton, Jean Pierre. *La Sociabilité villageoise dans l'Ancienne France.* Paris, 1979.

Hanotaux, Gabriel. *Histoire du cardinal de Richelieu.* Vol. I. Second edition, Paris, 1911. Vol. II. Paris, 1896.

Hauser, Henri. *La Pensée et l'action économiques du cardinal de Richelieu.* Paris, 1944.

———. *Le Principe des nationalités: ses origines historiques.* Paris, 1916.

Hayden, J. Michael. *France and the Estates General of 1614.* Cambridge, 1974.

Hayem, Fernand. *Le Maréchal d'Ancre et Leonora Galigai.* Paris, 1910.

Hinrichs, Ernst. *Fürstenlehre und politisches Handeln im Frankreich Heinrichs IV.* Göttingen, 1969.

Houssaye, Michel. *Le Père Bérulle et l'Oratoire de Jésus, 1611–1625.* Paris, 1873.

Hunt, David. *Parents and Children in History.* New York, 1970.

Huppert, George. *Les Bourgeois gentilshommes.* Chicago, 1977.

Ingold, Augustin M.-P. *L'Oratoire à Luçon.* Luçon, 1884.

Jacquin, Jules, and Duesberg, Joseph. *Rueil, le Château de Richelieu.* Paris, 1845.

Jal, Auguste. *Dictionnaire critique de biographie et d'histoire.* Paris, 1872.

Jourdain, Charles. *Histoire de l'Université de Paris au dix-septième siècle.* Paris, 1862.

Kinser, Samuel. *The Works of Jacques-Auguste de Thou.* Hague, 1966.

Labrousse, Elisabeth. *Pierre Bayle.* 2 vols. Hague, 1963–1964.

La Bruyère, René. *La Marine de Richelieu: Richelieu.* Paris, 1958.

———. *Maillé-Brézé: Général des galères, 1619–1646.* Paris, 1945.

Lacroix, Louis. *Richelieu à Luçon.* Second edition, Paris, 1911.

La Fontenelle de Vaudoré, A.-D. de. *Histoire du monastère et des évêques de Luçon.* Vol. VII. Paris, 1847.

———. *Le Maréchal de la Meilleraye.* Paris, 1839.

Lanfranc de Panthou, Octave-F. *Richelieu et la direction des âmes.* Evreux, 1896.

La Roncière, Charles de. *Histoire de la marine française,* Vol. IV. 4 vols. Paris, 1899–1920.

Le Clert, Louis. *Notice généalogique sur les Bouthillier de Chavigny, seigneurs de Ponts sur Seine, de Rancé et de Beaujeu.* Troyes, 1907.

Leiner, Wolfgang. *Der Widmungsbrief in der französischen Literatur (1580–1715).* Heidelberg, 1965.

Leman, Auguste. *Richelieu et Olivarès.* Lille, 1938.

Lestocquoy, Jean. *Histoire du patriotisme en France.* Paris, 1968.

Lièvre, Auguste. *Histoire du protestantisme dans le Poitou.* Vol. I. Paris, 1856.

Lodge, Richard. *Richelieu.* London: 1924.

Lorédan, Jean. *Un Grand procès de sorcellerie au 17e siècle: L'Abbé Gaufridy et Madeleine de Demandolx.* Paris, 1912.

Magne, Emile. *Le Plaisant abbé de Boisrobert.* Paris, 1909.

Major, J. Russell. *Representative Government in Early Modern France.* New Haven: 1980.

Mariéjol, Jean H. *Henri IV et Louis XIII (1598–1643).* Paris, 1911. (Vol. VI of *Histoire de France,* E. Lavisse, editor.)

Martin, Henri-Jean. *Livre, pouvoirs et société à Paris au XVIIe siècle.* 2 vols. Geneva, 1969.

Martin, Victor. *Le Gallicanisme et la réforme catholique: Essai historique sur l'introduction en France des decrets du concile de Trente (1563–1615).* Paris, 1919.

Martineau, Aimé de. *Le Cardinal de Richelieu.* First edition, Poitiers, 1866. Second edition, Paris, 1879.

Mastellone, Salvatore. *La Reggenza di Maria de' Medicie.* Florence, 1962.

Montbas, Hugues de. *Richelieu et l'opposition pendant la guerre de trente ans (1633–1638).* Paris, 1913.

Mortier, Daniel Antonin. *Histoire des maîtres généraux des Frères Prêcheurs.* Vol. VI. 7 vols. Paris, 1903–1914.

Selected Bibliography

Mousnier, Roland. *Les Institutions de la France sous la monarchie absolue.* 2 vols. Paris, 1974–1980.

———. *La Vénalité des offices sous Henri IV et Louis XIII.* Rouen, 1945.

———. *La Famille, l'enfant et l'éducation en France et en Grande-Bretagne du XVIe au XVIIIe siècle.* Paris, 1975.

———. *La Plume, la faucille et le marteau.* Paris, 1970.

Mouton, Léo. *Le Duc et le roi: D'Epernon, Henri IV, Louis XIII.* Paris, 1924.

Muchembled, Robert. *Culture populaire et culture des élites.* Paris, 1978.

Orcibal, Jean. *Jean Duvergier de Hauranne.* 2 vols., Louvain, 1947–1948.

Péraud, Adolphe. *Le Cardinal de Richelieu: Evêque, théologien et protecteur des lettres.* Paris, 1882.

Perkins, James B. *Richelieu and the Growth of French Power.* Reprint edition, Freeport, N.Y., 1971.

Perrens, François T. *Les Libertins en France au XVIIe siècle.* Paris, 1899.

Picot, Georges. *Histoire des Etats Généraux.* Vol. III. 4 vols. Paris, 1872.

Pillorget, René. *La Tige et le rameau: Familles anglaise et française, 16e-18e siècles.* Paris, 1972.

Prat, Jean-Marie. *Recherches sur la Compagnie de Jésus.* Vols. III-V. 5 vols., Lyons, 1876–1878.

Prunel, Louis. *La Renaissance catholique en France au XVIIe siècle.* Paris, 1921.

———. *Sébastien Zamet.* Paris, 1912.

Ranke, Leopold von. *Französische Geschichte im 16ten und 17ten Jahrhundert.* Vol. V. Stuttgart, 1854. (Vol. 12 of *Sämtliche Werke.*)

Ranum, Orest. *Artisans of Glory.* Chapel Hill, 1980.

———. *Paris in the Age of Absolutism.* New York, 1968.

———. *Richelieu and the Councillors of Louis XIII.* Oxford, 1963.

———, editor. *National Consciousness, History, and Political Culture in Early Modern Europe.* Baltimore, 1975.

Rothkrug, Lionel. *Opposition to Louis XIV.* Princeton, 1965.

Rowen, Herbert H. *The King's State: Proprietary Dynasticism in Early Modern France.* New Brunswick, N.J., 1980.

Sée, Henri. *Les Idées politiques en France au XVIIe siècle.* Paris, 1923.

Sippel, Cornelius III. *The "Noblesse de la robe" in Early Seventeenth Century France: A Study in Social Mobility.* [Ph.D. Dissertation, University of Michigan.] Ann Arbor, 1963.

Sutcliffe, Frank. *Guez de Balzac et son temps: littérature et politique.* Paris, 1959.

———. *Le réalisme de Charles Sorel.* Paris, 1965.

Thierry, Augustin. *Essai sur l'histoire de la formation et des progrès du tiers état.* Paris, 1868.

Eugène Thoison. *Madame de Guercheville, esquisse historique.* Fontainebleau, 1891.

Vaillé, Eugène. *Histoire générale des postes français.* Vols. II, III. Paris, 1949–1950.

Valentin, Louis. *Cardinalis Richelieus, Scriptor Ecclesiasticus.* Toulouse, 1900.

Vaumas, Guillaume. *L'Eveil missionaire de France.* Vol. I. Paris 1959.

Vermeylen, Alphonse. *Sainte Thérèse en France au XVIIe siècle, 1600–1660.* Louvain, 1958.

Vidal, Jean-Marie. *Henri de Sponde, 1568–1643.* Castillon, 1929.

Viollet, Pierre. *Le Roi et ses ministres.* Paris, 1912.

Wollenberg, Jörg. *Richelieu: Staatsräson und Kircheninteressen.* Bielefeld, 1977.

Wood, James B. *Nobility of the Election of Bayeux, 1463–1666.* Princeton, 1980.

Zeller, Berthold. *Marie de Médicis, Chef du Conseil.* Paris, 1898.

———. *Marie de Médicis et Sully.* Paris, 1892.

———. *Marie de Médicis et Villeroy.* Paris, 1897.

Zeller, Gaston. *Aspects de la politique française sous l'ancien régime.* Paris, 1964.

ARTICLES

Avenel, Denis-Martial. "L'Evêque de Luçon et le connétable de Luynes." *Revue des Questions Historiques,* IX (1870), 77–113.

———. "La Jeunesse de Richelieu." *Revue des Questions Historiques,* VI (1869), 146–224.

Selected Bibliography

Bailey, Donald A. "Anti-Richelieu Propaganda and the *Dévôts:* A Reinterpretation of Mathieu de Morgues." *Proceedings of the Second Meeting of the Western Society for French History* (1975), 94–103.

Bataillon, Marcel. "L'Académie de Richelieu. Indre et Loire." *Pédagogues et juristes. De Pétrarque à Descartes,* IV (1963), 255–270.

Beaucaire, Horric. "Les Machines de Du Plessis Besançon au siège de La Rochelle." *Archives Historiques de la Saintonge et de l'Aunis,* XVIII (1887), 368–388.

Blet, Pierre. "Richelieu et les débuts de Mazarin. *Revue d'Histoire Moderne et Contemporaine,* VI (1959), 241–268.

——. "Le Plan de Richelieu pour la réunion des Protestants," *Gregorianum,* XLVIII (1967), 100–129.

——. "Libertés gallicaines et Jésuites en 1611." *Archivum Historicum Societatis Iesu,* XXIV (1955), 165–188.

Bondois, Paul M. "Les Documents de la cassette de Richelieu." *Bibliothèque de l'Ecole des Chartes,* LXXXIII (1922), 111–165.

Cappelletti, Licurgo. "La Sorella di latte di Maria de Medici." *Rassegna Nazionale,* CLXXIII-CLXXIV (1910), 544–560; 3–20.

Certeau, Michel de. "Politique et mystique: René d'Argenson (1596–1651)." *Revue d'Ascétique et de Mystique,* XXXIX (1963), 45–82.

Chalumeau, Raymond. "Saint Vincent de Paul et les missions en France." *Dix-septième siècle,* XLII (1959), 317–327.

Cognet, Louis. "La Spiritualité de Richelieu." *Etudes franciscaines,* III (1952), 85–91.

Couprie, Alain. "'Courtisanisme' et christianisme au XVIIe siècle." *Dix-septième siècle,* XXXIII (1981), 371–391.

Cousin, Victor. "La Fronde à Paris." *Revue des Deux Mondes,* March 15, 1859, 250–271.

Deloche, Maximin. "Le Cardinal de Richelieu et un de ses voisins en Poitou: Un drame à Chauvigny." *Bulletin de la Société des Antiquaires de l'Ouest,* 2e trimestre, 1929.

——. "Un Démêlé du cardinal de Richelieu avec son suzerain en Poitou." *Bulletin de la Société des Antiquaires de l'Ouest.* 1er trimestre, 1923.

Dethan, Georges. "Mazarin avant le ministère." *Revue Historique,* CXXVII (1962), 33–66.

Dupont-Ferrier, Gustave. "Le Sens des mots 'Patria' et 'patrie' en France au moyen âge et jusqu'au début du XVIIe siècle." *Revue Historique,* CLXXXVIII (1940),

Engel, Josef. "Zur Frage der Echtheit von Richelieus 'Testament Politique.'" In Josef Engel and Hans M. Klinkenberg, editors. *Aus Mittelalter und Neuzeit: Festschrift Gerhard Kallen.* Bonn, 1957.

Esmonin, Edmond. "Le Testament politique de Richelieu." *Bulletin mensuel de la Société d'Histoire Moderne,* (December 1951; January, 1952), 42–47; 7–21.

Fagniez, Gustave. "L'Opinion publique au temps de Richelieu." *Revue des Questions Historiques,* LX (1896), 442–484.

——. "Mathieu de Morgues et le procès de Richelieu. *Revue de Deux Mondes,* CLXII (1900), 550–586.

Febvre, Lucien. "Aspects méconnus d'un renouveau religieux en France entre 1590 et 1620." *Annales, E. S. C.,* XIII (1958), 639–650.

Florand, F. "Le Père Chardon et son milieu." *La Vie Spirituelle* (supplement to April 1, 1935), 15–58.

Golden, Richard M. "Religious Extremism in the Mid-Seventeenth Century: The Parisian *Illuminés.*" *European Studies Review,* IX (1979), 195–210.

Jadart, Henri. "Louis XIII et Richelieu à Reims, 13–26 juillet, 1641." *Travaux de l'Académie de Reims,* LXXV. (Reprint.)

Labatut, Jean-Pierre. "Louis XIV et les chevaliers de l'Ordre du Saint-Esprit." *Dix-septième Siècle,* XXXII (1980), 267–278.

Lachmann, Hans-Georg. "Antoine Aubéry (1616–1695): Chercheur ou publiciste ou agent de propagande?" *Actes du 6ème Colloque de Marseille,* (1976), 145–152.

264

Selected Bibliography

Lavollée, Robert. "Le 'Secrétaire des mémoires' de Richelieu." *Revue des Etudes Historiques* (1904), 449–477.

Le Blant, Robert. "La Compagnie de la Nouvelle-France et la restitution de l'Acadie (1627–1636). *Revue d'Histoire des Colonies*, XLII (1955), 69–93.

Lévy, Claude and Henry, Louis. "Ducs et pairs sous l'ancien régime." *Population*, XVI (1960), 807–830.

Lossky, Andrew. Review of Lublinskaya, A. D., [*France at the Beginning of the Seventeenth Century: 1610–1620*. Leningrad, 1959.] *American Historical Review*, LXVII (1962), 399f.

Major, J. Russell. "The Crown and the Aristocracy in Renaissance France." *American Historical Review*, LXIX (1964).

———. "Henri IV and Guyenne: A Study Concerning Origins of Royal Absolutism." In Ray F. Kierstead, editor. *State and Society in Seventeenth Century France*. New York: 1975.

Marvick, Elizabeth W. "Nature versus Nurture: Trends and Patterns in Seventeenth Century French Childrearing." In Lloyd Demause, editor. *The History of Childhood*. New York, 1974, 259–301.

Massaut, Jean-Pierre. "Autour de Richelieu et de Mazarin: Le Carme Léon de Saint-Jean et la grande politique." *Revue d'Histoire Moderne et Contemporaine*, VII (1960), 11–45.

Mousnier, Roland. "Les Survivances médiévales dans la France du XVIIe siècle." *Dix-septième Siècle*, CVI-CVII (1975), 59–79.

Muchembled, Robert. "Un Monde mental clos: étude sémantique et historique du vocabulaire religieux d'un noble artésien à l'époque de Philippe II." *Tijdschrift voor Geschiednenis*, LXXXVIII (1975), 169–189.

Orcibal, Jean. "Richelieu, homme d'église, homme d'etat." *Revue d'histoire de l'église de France*, XXXIV (1948), 94–101.

Pagès, Georges. "Autour du Grand Orage: Richelieu et Marillac: Deux politiques." *Revue Historique*, CLXXIX (1937), 63–97.

Préclin, Edmond. "Edmond Richer." *Revue d'Histoire Moderne et Contemporaine*, V (1930), 242–269; 321–336.

Ranum, Orest. "Léon Bouthillier, Comte de Chavigny, créature de Richelieu et secrétaire d'état aux Affaires Etrangères." *Revue d'Histoire Diplomatique*, LXXIV (1960), 323–334.

———. "Richelieu and the Great Nobility: Some Aspects of Early Modern Political Motives." *French Historical Studies*, III (1963), 184–204.

———. "Courtesy, Absolutism and the Rise of the French State, 1630–1660." *Journal of Modern History*, LII (1980), 426–451.

Rothrock, George A. "The French Crown and the Estates General of 1614." *French Historical Studies*, I (1961), 295–381.

Salmon, J. H. M. "Storm over the Noblesse." *Journal of Modern History*, LIII (1981), 242–257.

Secret, F., "Un Episode oublié de la vie de Peiresc: le sabre magique de Gustave Adolphe." *Dix-septième siècle*, CXVII (1977), 49–52.

Société de l'Histoire de France. *Rapports et notices sur l'édition des Mémoires du cardinal de Richelieu*. 7 vols., Paris, 1905–1922.

Tapié, Victor-Lucien. "Comment les français du dix-septième siècle voyaient la patrie." *Dix-septième siècle*, IV (1955), 37–58.

Teall, Elizabeth. "The *Seigneur* of Renaissance France." *Journal of Modern History*, XXXVII (1965), 131–150.

Wirtz-Daviau, B., "Accord passé entre le cardinal de Richelieu et Saint Vincent de Paul pour la fondation d'une mission à Luçon." *Revue du Bas-Poitou*, LVI (1953), 44–48.

Index

Index

Bochard, Claude. *See* La Porte, Claude Bochard de

Boisdauphin, maréchal de, 228 n. 65

Boisrobert, François Le Métel, abbé de, 137, 244 n. 29

Bonneau-Avenant, Alfred, 145

Bons français (*see also* Gallicanism), 184, 202

Bonzi, Cardinal, 175, 177, 184, 192, 202

Bonzi, Dominique de, 184

Bordeaux, 121–22

Bordeaux, cardinal of. *See* Sourdis, François d'Escoubleau de

Botti, Matteo, 173

Bouillon, Henri de La Tour d'Auvergne, duc de, 170–71, 175, 180, 185

Bourbon, Eléanore de, coadjutrix abbess of Fontevrault, 171

Bourbon, Jeanne-Baptiste de, abbess of Fontevrault, 9–10

Bourbon-Montpensier. *See* Montpensier family

Bourdonné, le sieur de, 223 n. 61

Bourges, Madame de (friend of Richelieu), 50, 71, 108, 168, 187, 188, 227 n. 28

Bourges, Magdelaine de, 71

Bournazel, le sieur de (Antoine de Buisson), 39

Bouthillier, Claude, comte de Chavigny, 94, 95, 244 n. 29

Bouthillier, Denis I, 93, 94, 173

Bouthillier, Denis II, 95

Bouthillier, Léon, 95, 241 n. 95

Bouthillier, Madame (Catherine de Machéco, wife of Denis I), 50

Bouthillier, Madame (Marie de Bragelongne, wife of Claude), 50

Bouthillier, Sébastien, abbé de La Cochère, bishop of Aire, 76, 82, 93–94, 116, 166–68, 186, 233 n. 55

Bouthillier, Victor, 94

Bouthillier family, 28; and the Richelieus, 84, 93, 95

Brézé, Urbain de Maillé, marquis de (Richelieu's brother-in-law), 89, 92–93, 142–44, 243 n. 3

Briefve et facile instruction pour les confesseurs (*see also* Richelieu, Armand-Jean Du Plessis de—writings: *Ordonnances synodales*), 115–16, 135

Brisson, Barnabé, 47, 224 n. 19

Brown, Roger, 218 n. 18

Bufalo, Monsignor del, papal nuncio in France, 246 n. 85

Buisson, Antoine de (le sieur de Bournazel), 39

Bureau d'Adresse, 130

Bury, J. B., 9

Callot, Jacques, 236 n. 53

Calvarians, 7

Calvinism (*see also* Protestants), 6, 52

Capuchins (*see also* Joseph, Père), 7, 121

Caragnan, Le (Richelieu property), 49

Carmel, Order of, 7, 241 n. 113

Carthusian Order (Chartreux) (*see also* Richelieu, Alphonse-Louis de—career), 65

Catalonia, 138

Catherine de Medici, 32, 167, 183, 247 n. 88

Catholic League, 31, 183, 184

Catholicism. *See* Council of Trent; Counter Reform movement

Chalumeau, Raymond, 7

Champagne (province), 180

Champaigne, Philippe de, 21

Chantal, Saint (Jeanne de Frémyot), 8, 22, 221 n. 30, 222 n. 39

Chapelain, Jean, 137

Chappes, baronne de, 75

Charlemagne, 195, 211

Charles, duc de Lorraine, 153

Charles II (king of England), 3, 28

Charles IX, 167

Charmeaux. *See* Richelieu, Marguerite de Charmeaux

Charpentier, Denys (secretary of Richelieu), 150

Chatellerault, 171, 175, 187

Chémerault, le sieur de, 224 n. 19

Chémerault, Magdelaine de, 228 n. 3

Chevreuse, Marie de Rohan-Montbazon, duchesse de, 153

Chinon, 55

Christian's Teaching, The. See Richelieu, Armand-Jean Du Plessis de—writings: *Instruction du chrestien*

Church, William F., 6

Citois, Antoine, 144, 243 n. 12

Citois, François (Richelieu's physician), 243 n. 12

Clapisson (Third Estate secretary), 197

Clement VIII, 157

Clérembault, Louis, 223 n. 7

Clerical assemblies, 1611–12 (*see also* Protestants—under regency: conferences of), 176, 250 nn. 63 and 67

Cognet, Louis, 10, 218 n. 34

Index

Index

Enuresis, 118–19, 121–22, 126–27, 238 n. 35, 245 n. 54

Epernon, Henri de Nogaret, duc d', 170, 183, 192

Erlanger, Philippe, 166, 222 n. 54

Estates General Assembly
—of 1588, 37, 39, 211
—of 1614–15 (see also Richelieu, Armand-Jean Du Plessis de—career: at Estates General Assembly): First Estate at, 192, 204, 252 n. 7; Huguenots at, 192, 106; representation dispute at, 194; Second Estate at, 191–92; Third Estate at, 191, 198–200, 202

Estrées, Gabrielle d', 95

Fenichel, Otto, 118–20

Feudal survivals (see also Noblesse), 91–92

"First Article." See Estates General Assembly—of 1614–15: Third Estate at

Flavigny, Jacques de (see also Richelieu, Armand-Jean Du Plessis de—writings: Ordonnances synodales), 135, 136

Fontainebleau, 171–72, 174, 250 n. 71

Fontenay-le-comte, 121, 194, 251 n. 117

Fontevrault, 9–10, 171–72

Fraiberg, Selma, 235 n. 23

François I, 17, 211

François II, 31

François de Sales, Saint, 7, 10, 21, 44, 218 n. 39, 241 n. 110

Frémyot, Jeanne de. See Chantal

Freud, Sigmund, 63, 118, 120, 155, 245 n. 53

Galigai, Leonora. See Ancre, maréchale d'

Gallicanism (see also Richelieu, Armand-Jean Du Plessis de—policies: Gallicanism), 170, 176, 198–203

Gambling, 43–44

Gaston d'Orléans, 17, 153, 155, 209

Gaufriddi affair, 174

Gazette, La, 130

Germigny, Monsieur de (neighbor at Richelieu), 55

Gil, Maître (Richelieu family legal advisor), 56

Gondi, Charlotte de, 222 n. 39

Gondi, Henri de, bishop of Paris, later Cardinal de Retz, 136, 174, 175, 177

Gonesse, 102

Gorer, Geoffrey, 235 n. 27

Goubert, Pierre, 32

Goulaine, Madame de (neighbor at Richelieu), 55

Grand Almoner. See Bonzi, Cardinal; Du Perron

Grandier, Urbain, 174

Grand Maître de France. See Guise, third duc de

Grand Prévôt de France. See Provostship

Grand Prieur. See La Porte, Amador de; Order of Malta

Grands, Les, 18, 217 n. 7; regency policy toward, 189, 192, 194

Grands Augustins, 192

Greenacre, Phyllis, 240 n. 69

Grenade, Père Louis de, 133, 241 n. 110

Grillon, Pierre, 23

Guercheville, Antoinette de Pons, marquise de, 173, 174, 249 n. 44

Guide du pécheur. See Grenade, Père Louis de

Guillon, Père Hardy, prior of Saint-Florent, 64, 102, 156

Guise, Cardinal de, 18, 36–37

Guise, Catherine de Clèves, dowager duchesse de, 183, 249 n. 54

Guise, le chevalier de, 183

Charles, "le balafré," Grand Maître de France, third duc de, 35, 40, 183

Guise, Charles de Lorraine, fourth duc de, 170

Guise, Henriette de Joyeuse, duchesse de, 183

Guise, Mademoiselle de. See Conti

Halincourt, Charles de Neufville, marquis d', 160

Hanotaux, Gabriel, 25, 45, 73, 120, 197, 202

Haschke, Friedrich, 222 n. 50, 238 n. 32

Hayden, J. Michael, 249 n. 52

Hayem, Fernand, 180

Henri III: assassinated, 32, 43; character and tastes of, 36, 37; Code of, 47; and Epernon, 183; and François de Richelieu, 35–37, 41, 74, 101, 167, 225 n. 32; funeral of, 93; and Richelieu family, 54, 161; Richelieu on, 211

Henri IV
—abjures Protestantism, 32, 151
—assassinated, 165, 169–70
—character and tastes of, 21, 37, 42, 246 n. 65, 249 n. 44
—funeral and mourning of, 93, 210

270

Index

Index

Index

Milly, 142, 143
Mirame, 70
Mirebeau, 187
Miron, Charles, bishop of Angers, 180, 192, 199, 202
Miron, François (physician of Henri III), 225 n. 27
Molé, Mathieu, 250 n. 86
Montbazon, duc de, 231 n. 82
Montchal, Cardinal Charles de, archbishop of Toulouse, 28, 123, 239 n. 52
Montesquieu, quoted on Richelieu, 140
Montglat, Baron de, 251 n. 111
Montglat, François, marquis de, 41
Montmorency, Henri I, duc and connétable de, 167
Montmorency, Henri II, duc de, 71–72
Montpensier, Louis I de Bourbon, duc de, 37, 108, 224 nn. 10 and 19
Montpensier, Louis II de Bourbon, prince de Dombes and duc de, 74
Montpensier family, 34, 74, 224 n. 10, 236 n. 38
Morgues, Mathieu de, abbé de Saint-Germain, 13, 100, 116, 122–23, 127
Motier, House of. *See* Joseph, Père
Mousnier, Roland, 18, 45, 224 n. 11
Muchembled, Robert, 26, 32, 53

Nagera, Humberto, 238–39 n. 45
Narbonne, 138
Navarre, Henri de. *See* Henri IV
Nef, John U., 218 n. 29
Nevers, Charles de Gonzague, duc de, 170, 180, 185
Niort, 194
Noblesse (*see also* Counter Reform movement; *Grands, Les; Poitou; Robins*): family relations in, 34, 45–46, 51–53, 63; norms of, 18, 20, 33–34, 41, 45, 194, 196–97, 227 n. 34, 234 n. 17, 243 n. 4; and women, 49–50, 64, 221 n. 30, 237 n. 5
Noël, Léon, 10
Notre-Dame d'Ardillers, shrine of, 52, 244 n. 29
Nueil-sous-Faye, 91–92

Oratorians (*see also* Bérulle, Pierre de), 7, 130, 138, 240 nn. 87 and 88
Orçeau, Nicolas, 233 n. 55
Orcibal, Jean, 132–33
Order of Malta, 48, 64, 78, 83, 228 n. 6
Ordonnance de Moulins, 47

Ordonnance d'Orléans, 47
Ordre du Saint Esprit. See Holy Spirit, Order of the
Orléans (*see also* L'Aubespine, Gabriel de; Marquemont, Denis de), 187
Orléans, Antoinette d', coadjutrix abbess of Fontevrault, 171–72

Palais Cardinal, 138
Papacy, 203, 206
Paris: as center, 17; mood in, summer 1610, 169–70, 248 n. 25; and Richelieu, 16, 18–19, 157, 160–61, 168, 188, 234 n. 15
Parlement de Paris, 165, 177, 187, 190, 199–200, 202, 203
Parthenay, 35
Pascal, Jacqueline, 237 n. 10
Paul V, 159–60, 229 n. 16, 246 n. 86
Paul, Saint, 201
Paulette, 191, 194
Peiresc, Fabri de, 68
Perrault, Charles, 116
Philip III, 182–83, 251 n. 96
Phélypeaux, Paul, marquis de Pontchartrain, 178–79
Philippe d'Orléans, 239 n. 50
Picardy, 223 n. 6
Pidoux family, 32
Pidoux, François, 32, 46
Pidoux, Jean, 46–47
Pidoux, Monsieur (sieur de Malaguet), 47
Pidoux, Pierre, 46
Pillaging, 59, 76
Pine, Fred, 235 n. 23
Pithou, François, 157–58
Plato, 12
Poitiers, 33, 186, 188, 194
Poitou: in civil wars, 75, 227 n. 30, 228 nn. 62 and 65, 251 n. 111; clergy of, 186–88, 195; cultural pride of, 219 n. 55; Protestants in, 76, 178–79; social structure of, 32, 46, 74, 76; women in, 228 n. 3
Pont Courlay, Armand de Vignerod de (Richelieu's grand-nephrew), 145–46, 232 n. 16, 243 n. 16
Pont Courlay, François de Vignerod, marquis de (Richelieu's nephew), 89
Pont Courlay, Marie de Vignerod de. *See* Aiguillon, duchesse d'
Pont Courlay, René de Vignerod, marquis de (Richelieu's brother-in-law), 57, 157, 232 n. 16
Poyane (governor of Navarre), 76

Index

Praslin, Charles de Choiseul, marquis de, 188

Prévôt de l'Hôtel du Roi. See Provostship; Richelieu, François de

Progress (norm of), 9, 219 n. 51

Protestants
—at beginning of seventeenth century, 157–58, 218 n. 34
—under regency: conferences of, 171, 175, 184, 249 n. 54; unease of, 170–71, 175, 178, 184, 205
—in the Estates-General Assembly, 1614–15, 188, 206

Provence, 168, 200

Provisorship. *See* Sorbonne

Provostship (*see also* Richelieu, François de), 35–40, 43

Prunel, Louis, 7

Psychoanalysis, as historical method, 22–25, 237 n. 9

Pure, Michel, 65, 101, 102, 104, 110–11, 116, 124, 228 n. 5, 247 n. 87

Raconis, Abra, bishop of Vaur, 99–100, 116, 130, 148, 150

Ranum, Orest, 4, 219 n. 42

Ravaillac, François, 165, 169

Redl, Fritz, 253 n. 28

Regicide, doctrine on, 198, 199–200, 205, 206

Religious wars in France, 31–32, 36–37

Retz, Cardinal de. *See* Gondi

Rheims: archbishop of, 18; city of, 77, 116–17, 169

Richelieu (château, territory, town and duchy), 79–80, 90, 144, 232 n. 38, 244 n. 29, 251 n. 111

Richelieu (family) (*see also* Brézé; La Porte; Marconnay; Rochechouart), 18, 33–34, 65, 84, 196–97

Richelieu, Alphonse-Louis Du Plessis de, Cardinal-archbishop of Lyons (brother)
—career: plans and changes, 64, 66, 107, 111, 152, 228 n. 6, 246 n. 86, 247 n. 89; as archbishop of Aix, 239 n. 58; as archbishop of Lyons, 66, 107, 112, 230 n. 46
—childhood of, 237 nn. 4 and 9, 239 nn. 55 and 58
—personality and tastes of, 64–66, 107, 109–13, 117–18, 123–24, 140, 222 n. 36, 234 n. 74, 238 n. 22

—and Richelieu: attitudes toward, 65–66, 101, 122; Richelieu's views of Alphonse-Louis, 230 n. 46, 236 n. 63

Richelieu, Antoine Du Plessis de ("the monk"; great-uncle), 34–35, 246 n. 70

Richelieu, Armand-Jean Du Plessis, Marquis Du Chillou, Bishop of Luçon, Cardinal-duc de
—birth and baptism, 234 n. 15
—career: plans, 64, 66, 158–59, 186, 228 nn. 5 and 6; becomes bishop, 159–61, 229 n. 16, 247 n. 89; as bishop, 72–73, 76–77, 121, 130, 154–55, 160–62, 175–76, 194, 230 n. 64; enters secular politics, 178–79, 185; at Estates-General Assembly of 1614–15, 15–17, 67, 80, 162, 187–88, 194–96, 205
—contemporaries' views of, 3, 20–21, 27–28, 99–101, 148–49, 188–89, 196–97, 223 n. 64, 236 nn. 53 and 54
—and duels, 87–89, 90–92
—education of, 19, 64, 68, 115–16, 133, 135, 147, 156, 158–60, 228 n. 2, 246 n. 82, 247 n. 93, 247 n. 87
—as family member, 64–66, 81–82, 89–92, 115, 142–48, 232 n. 36, 245 n. 31
—illnesses, 60, 101–5, 121–22, 125–26, 138–40, 151, 159, 162, 169, 181, 240 nn. 67 and 68
—lawsuits and legalism of, 71–73, 226 n. 54, 233 nn. 39 and 55, 251 n. 116
—personality: conflict resolution in, 117–20, 122–25, 134; and early experience, 19–21, 101–5, 114–15, 151, 166–67, 181–82, 189; Montesquieu on, 140; and sexuality, 100–101, 141–42, 151–53
—policies: characterized, 2–3; Gallicanism, 176–77, 183–84, 201–2, 206; modernism of, 12, 217 n. 4, 223 n. 64; nationalism, 14–16, 178, 220 nn. 9 and 11, 234 n. 15; on patronage, 76–77, 195, 204; royalism, 207, 212–13
—and Protestants, 134, 149, 166, 175–76, 178–79, 184–85, 241 n. 108
—as religious thinker, 67–70, 132–35, 151, 235 n. 34
—strategy and tactics, 10–13, 105, 121, 129–30, 178–79, 184–85, 189, 200, 219 n. 55
—style and tastes, 107–10, 130–39, 145, 160, 173–74, 222 n. 47, 234 n. 134, 236 nn. 47 and 54, 241 n. 95, 242 nn. 124 and 132, 244 n. 29, 248–49 nn. 42 and 43
—testaments: of 1619, 138; last, 81, 90, 138–39

274

Index

Index